Renewing Social and Economic Progress in Africa

The United Nations Research Institute for Social Development (UNRISD) is an autonomous agency engaging in multidisciplinary research on the social dimensions of contemporary problems affecting development. Its work is guided by the conviction that, for effective development policies to be formulated, an understanding of the social and political context is crucial. The Institute attempts to provide governments, development agencies, grassroots organizations and scholars with a better understanding of how development policies and processes of economic, social and environmental change affect different social groups. Working through an extensive network of national research centres, UNRISD aims to promote original research and strengthen research capacity in developing countries.

Current research programmes include: Business Responsibility for Sustainable Development; Emerging Mass Tourism in the South; Gender, Poverty and Well-Being; Globalization and Citizenship; Grassroots Initiatives and Knowledge Networks for Land Reform in Developing Countries; New Information and Communication Technologies; Public Sector Reform and Crisis-Ridden States; Technical Co-operation and Women's Lives: Integrating Gender into Development Policy; and Volunteer Action and Local Democracy: a Partnership for a Better Urban Future. Recent research programmes have included: Crisis, Adjustment and Social Change; Culture and Development; Environment, Sustainable Development and Social Change; Ethnic Conflict and Development; Participation and Changes in Property Relations in Communist and Post-Communist Societies; Political Violence and Social Movements; Social Policy, Institutional Reform and Globalization; Socio-Economic and Political Consequences of the International Trade in Illicit Drugs; and the War-Torn Societies Project. UNRISD research projects focused on the 1995 World Summit for Social Development included: Economic Restructuring and Social Policy; Ethnic Diversity and Public Policies; Rethinking Social Development in the 1990s; and Social Integration at the Grassroots: the Urban Dimension.

A list of the Institute's free and priced publications can be obtained by contacting the Reference Centre, United Nations Research Institute for Social Development, Palais des Nations, 1211 Geneva 10, Switzerland; Tel (41 22) 917 3020; Fax (41 22) 917 0650; Telex 41.29.62 UNO CH; e-mail: info@unrisd.org; World Wide Web Site: http://www.unrisd.org

Philip Ndegwa (courtesy of Maridadi Oix Ltd)

Renewing Social and Economic Progress in Africa

Essays in Memory of Philip Ndegwa

Edited by

Dharam Ghai
Director
United Nations Research Institute for Social Development (UNRISD)
Geneva
Switzerland

in association with

UNRISD

First published in Great Britain 2000 by
MACMILLAN PRESS LTD
Houndmills, Basingstoke, Hampshire RG21 6XS and London
Companies and representatives throughout the world

A catalogue record for this book is available from the British Library.

ISBN 0–333–73412–2 hardcover
ISBN 0–333–77911–8 paperback

First published in the United States of America 2000 by
ST. MARTIN'S PRESS, INC.,
Scholarly and Reference Division,
175 Fifth Avenue, New York, N.Y. 10010

ISBN 0–312–22623–3

HC
800
, R 457
2000

Library of Congress Cataloging-in-Publication Data
Renewing social and economic progress in Africa : essays in memory of
Philip Ndegwa / edited by Dharam Ghai.
p.   cm.
Includes bibliographical references and index.
ISBN 0–312–22623–3 (cloth)
1. Ndegwa, Philip.   2. Africa—Economic conditions.   3. Africa–
–Social conditions.   4. Africa—Politics and government.   I. Ghai,
Dharam P.
HC800.R457   1999
338.96—dc21
99–32870
CIP

This book is printed on paper suitable for recycling and made from fully managed and sustained
forest sources.

10   9   8   7   6   5   4   3   2   1
09   08   07   06   05   04   03   02   01   00

Printed and bound in Great Britain by
Antony Rowe Ltd, Chippenham, Wiltshire

Contents

Preface

I was on home leave with my wife in Mombasa in February 1996 when I received a telephone call from Alison Ndegwa concerning the possibility of bringing out a volume in Philip Ndegwa's memory. Later we met in Nairobi to discuss the nature of the book and possible themes and contributors. Subsequently, the Ndegwa family asked me to take responsibility for the preparation of the book. For me this assignment has been a labour of love. Philip Ndegwa was an intimate friend and a cherished associate.

I first came to know Philip when I joined Makerere University College in August 1961 as a lecturer in Economics. Philip was then in his last year doing an honours degree in economics. I had thus the honour to be his 'teacher' during my first year at Makerere. Teacher is a wrong word to describe my relationship with him, for in truth I learnt much more from him than he ever did from me. And this for a very good reason: I had been away from East Africa for seven years studying at Oxford and Yale. When I started teaching at Makerere, I knew practically nothing about the East African economies. My first teaching assignments were Economic Theory and Public Finance. In order to make these subjects interesting and relevant for our students, I had to relate the theory to the structure and working of the East African economies. Philip, on the other hand, possessed a solid knowledge and understanding of these economies from four years of study. He had already built up a reputation as a star student among the faculty and his colleagues. I, therefore, often turned to him to learn about the East African economies in my desperate attempts to keep one step ahead of students in my lectures! In effect I never ceased to learn from Philip.

During my thirteen years of teaching and research at Makerere and the University of Nairobi, I came to know and taught many talented students from all over East and Central Africa. A high proportion of them went on to pursue distinguished careers as ministers, top civil servants, governors of central banks, ambassadors, prominent businessmen and researchers and lecturers. But I cannot recall any who attained such stature and excelled in so many fields as Philip Ndegwa. It was thus for me always a badge of honour to claim that I had once been his teacher, even though this was true only in a formal sense.

We stayed in close personal and professional touch in the subsequent years though our careers took us to different places and concerns. After graduating brilliantly at Makerere, Philip spent a year doing graduate studies at Harvard. He returned to Makerere to take up a Research Fellowship at the East African Institute of Social Research. We interacted constantly as he prepared his first book on the East African Common Market and I struggled with my doctoral dissertation for Yale on the income elasticity of the tax system in Uganda! He introduced me to squash and we played tennis on a regular basis.

He left Makerere to join the Kenya civil service where he had a meteoric career which carried him to all the top posts in economic planning and management. Our friendship and professional relationship grew during my years at the University of Nairobi. Our paths continued to cross when I moved to Geneva to take up the post of head of research under ILO's World Employment Programme and he notched one success after another as a senior official of UNEP, Presidential Advisor, Governor of the Central Bank of Kenya, and as a leading businessman and a rising political star. As we were of the same generation and lived through many common experiences, we shared many interests. The strongest link that bound us together was our passionate preoccupation with problems of development in Africa and the Third World.

Philip Ndegwa was a perfectionist who worked hard and excelled in many fields. Although he did not pursue an academic career, he was an outstanding thinker and analyst of African development problems. In an extremely busy life, he found time to author or co-edit seven books and write numerous technical papers. As a development economist, he was remarkable for his breadth of vision, grasp of technical economics, pragmatic approach to analysis of concrete problems and mature judgement of policy options. He always arose above arcane ideological disputes. His approach to development problems was refreshingly informed by deep reflection and practical experience. He put his economic expertise at the service of the country as a top planner and manager of economic policy. His years as the highest policy maker in the ministries of finance and planning were a golden period of economic performance in post-independent Kenya. After a spell as an international civil servant, he returned to national service first as Presidential Advisor and later as Governor of the Central Bank of Kenya. In both these capacities, he successfully addressed a number of critical financial and economic problems.

Indeed, Philip Ndegwa gained reputation as the leading trouble shooter in the country. The top political leadership turned to him repeatedly to sort out impossible problems, as when the President of Kenya asked him to take over the management of Kenya Airways when the national airline was the on the verge of collapse. He also set the policy direction on strategic issues on several occasions when he chaired a series of presidential commissions on the working of the parastatal bodies, on public expenditure and on employment. He also served as Chairman of the Kenya Revenue Authority. He performed these difficult tasks with great distinction and success.

His services were not confined to Kenya alone. He was greatly distressed by the profound political and economic crisis that has convulsed Sub-Saharan Africa over the past two decades and made a series of efforts to chart a path to recovery and progress. He played a critical role in UNEP under Maurice Strong's leadership to convince developing countries of the link between development and environment and helped develop policy guidelines and operational programmes. He advised the World Bank and the IMF on their African policies, took part in a number of UN appointed committees and task forces, wrote articles and books on political and economic reform in Africa, and organized high-level conferences to promote his ideas. He served on the governing boards of several prestigious research centres such as the Institute of Development Studies, University of Sussex, the International Food Policy Research Institute, European Centre for Development Policy Management and the World Institute of Development Economics Research of the United Nations University.

Most of us would have been content with achievements in any one of the domains of development thinking, management of the economy and international service. But not Philip Ndegwa, who went on to become one of the most successful businessmen in the country, with extensive investments in real estate, hotels, banking and insurance. As in all his other activities, he succeeded through dint of hard work, careful planning and sound management. In the last years of his life, he was persuaded by some influential persons to devote his enormous talents and energy to politics. His own convictions about the key role of politics in social and economic development also propelled him to introduce the ethic of service in the realm of politics. Indeed he had already developed and was beginning to implement some innovative ideas on securing the participation of economic, professional and political elites in broad-based development programmes in the countryside. There is little doubt that but for his untimely death, Philip would have excelled in politics as he did in everything else he tried his hand on, and would have given it a social and moral dimension.

I think, of all the causes that he worked for, the goal of eliminating poverty and deprivation and promoting human development and welfare in Africa was the closest to his heart. It is, therefore, appropriate that his friends should have come together to honour his memory with this collection of essays on political, economic and social reforms designed to bring about sustained improvement in the living standards of the people of Africa. At a time of deep and widespread pessimism about the prospects for development in Africa, there are rays of hope that Philip's tireless efforts will bear fruit in greater prosperity and larger freedom for African people.

DHARAM GHAI

Acknowledgements

Several individuals and institutions have helped me put together this volume. First of all, I thank the Ndegwa family – Alison, Maina, Mwangi and Wakeni – for asking me to take responsibility for preparing a book of essays in Philip's memory and for their contribution of the biographical profile. Throughout this period, I have benefited from their advice and suggestions. I am grateful to the contributors to this volume for readily agreeing to write the essays. Ed Edwards, Reg Green, Gerry Helleiner and Sir Hans Singer made valuable suggestions on the initial proposals for the book. Dunstan Wai and Jim Adams helped secure the necessary funds. Jessica Vivian, Uzma Hashmi and Jenifer Freedman assisted me with the final editing of the book and Rosemary Max with publication arrangements. Rhonda Gibbes, Véronique Martinez, Kizito Nsarhaza, Wendy Salvo and Christine Vuilleumier helped with research materials, administration and formatting of the manuscript. I thank Neela Korde for her ideas and support.

Most of the work on this book was done while I was Director of the United Nations Research Institute for Social Development, and I am deeply indebted for its institutional and administrative support. My thanks also go to the World Bank for providing the financial assistance to cover some of the costs.

DHARAM GHAI

Notes on the Contributors

Yusuf Bangura is a Project Coordinator at the United Nations Research Institute for Social Development (UNRISD). He was formerly a lecturer in Political Science at Ahmadu Bello University. He was educated at the London School of Economics and Political Science, and has published widely on the socio-political contexts of the African crisis and structural adjustment. His current research interest is in the field of public sector reform and democratization. He is the co-editor of *Authoritarianism, Democracy and Adjustment: The Politics of Economic Reform in Africa*.

Giovanni Andrea Cornia is Director of the World Institute for Development Economics Research (UNU/WIDER). He has also held research positions with UNICEF, UNCTAD, UNECE and FIAT, lectured on development economics in universities and published widely on economic and social issues in developing and transitional countries. His recently co-authored and co-edited books include *From Adjustment to Development in Sub-Saharan Africa* (with G. K. Helleiner) and *Child Poverty in Industrialized Countries, 1945–1995* (with S. Danziger).

Edgar O. Edwards has recently been Senior Policy Research Consultant with the Africa Office of the International Center for Economic Growth. He has served as adviser on planning, finance and economic policy in Kenya (for many years between 1963 and 1984) and in Botswana (1989–95) and on shorter consultancies in Lebanon, Swaziland and the Palestinian Authority. He served on the faculty of Princeton (1950–59) and Rice (1959–70, 1975–84) Universities, and was economic adviser to the Ford Foundation's Asia and Pacific Program from 1969 to 1975.

Dharam Ghai was Director of UNRISD from 1987 to 1997. Previously, he was Head of Research of the ILO World Employment Programme and Director of the Institute for Development Studies at the University of Nairobi. He is the author/ editor of several books and numerous articles on a wide range of development issues, particularly poverty, employment, rural development and social dimensions of structural adjustment and environment. His recent publications include *The IMF and the South: The Social Impact of Crisis and Adjustment, Grassroots Environmental Action: People's Participation in Sustainable Development* (co-edited with Jessica Vivian), and *Development and Environment: Sustaining People and Nature*.

Reginald Herbold Green has been a student of the Political Economy of Africa since 1959 in the course of which he has researched, advised and/or taught in 37 African countries as a civil servant, university staff member and consultant. Since 1974 he has been based at the Institute of Development Studies (Sussex). He first met Philip Ndegwa in 1964 and worked with him closely in several contexts including co-editing three volumes, the last entitled *Africa to 2000 and Beyond: Imperative Political and Economic Agenda*.

Gerald K. Helleiner is Professor of Economics at the University of Toronto. He is also Research Coordinator of the Group of Twenty-four at the IMF/World Bank and Director of a research project on non-traditional exports and African growth for the World Institute for Development Economics Research (UNU/WIDER). Among his many published books is *The New Global Economy and the Developing Countries*.

Richard Jolly is Editor-in-Chief of the *Human Development Report* and Special Adviser to the Administrator of the United Nations Development Programme (UNDP). He was Deputy Executive Director of the United Nations Children's Fund (UNICEF) from 1982 to 1995, and Director of the Institute of Development Studies at the University of Sussex from 1972 to 1981. He first worked with Philip Ndegwa at Makerere University in Uganda in 1963–4. In 1971–2, with Hans W. Singer, he was co-leader of the ILO Employment Mission Report to Kenya entitled 'Employment, Incomes and Inequality', when Philip Ndegwa was Permanent Secretary of the Ministry of Finance and Economic Planning.

Wilson Kinyua is General Manager of the African Mercantile Banking Company Ltd. He was Group Planning Manager of the First Chartered Securities Ltd. from 1989 to 1994. He served the Central Bank of Kenya between 1981 and 1989 in various capacities, including Personal Assistant to the Governor and Assistant Director of Research. From 1975 to 1981 he worked in the Ministry of Economic Planning and National Development as Economist/Statistician. He is a member of the Society for International Development and Chairman of its Kenya Chapter.

Germano Mwabu is Associate Professor of Economics, Kenyatta University and was, until recently, Senior Research Fellow at the World Institute for Development Economics Research (UNU/WIDER). His areas of specialization include health economics, development economics, labour economics and applied econometrics. He has worked as a consultant to a number of bodies, including the World Health Organization (WHO), the Ministries of Health of Zambia and Kenya, and the World Bank. He is Associate Editor of *Environment and Development Economics*, Editorial Adviser to *Health Policy and Planning*, and author of a number of articles.

Sir Hans W. Singer is Emeritus Professor at the University of Sussex and Professorial Fellow at the Institute of Development Studies. He served for 22 years in the United Nations, last as Director of the Economic Division of UNIDO. In association with Richard Jolly, he led the ILO Employment Mission Report to Kenya in 1971–2, entitled 'Employment, Incomes and Inequality'. He is the author of numerous articles, reports and books, the latest of which is *The Foreign Aid Business* (jointly with K. Raffer).

Frances Stewart is Director of the International Development Centre, Queen Elizabeth House, University of Oxford and Fellow of Somerville College. She has worked as a consultant to many organizations, including the ILO, UNCTAD, UNIDO, the OECD and UNDP, as well as IDRC, the Ford Foundation, Appropriate Technology International and the government of the Netherlands. Her major areas of work include appropriate technology, basic needs, adjustment and poverty, and development during conflict. Her latest book is *Adjustment and Poverty: Options and Choices*.

Maurice Strong currently serves as Executive Coordinator for United Nations Reform. He is Chairman of the Earth Council, and previously served as the Secretary-General of the United Nations Conference on Environment and Development, the 'Earth Summit', which took place in Rio de Janeiro, Brazil in 1992. He was also the first Executive Director of the United Nations Environment Programme located in Nairobi, Kenya.

Michael P. Todaro is Professor of Economics at New York University and Senior Consulting Associate at the Population Council, New York. He is the author of eight books, including his best-selling text *Economic Development*, and over 40 articles. He has been selected for inclusion in *Who's Who in Economics: A Biographical Dictionary of Major Economists, 1700–1980* and *Who's Who in the World*. His most well-known essays have recently been collected and published in the prestigious series Economists of the Twentieth Century. He lived in Africa for five years and has travelled and lectured extensively throughout Asia and Latin America.

Dunstan M. Wai was born in Southern Region, Sudan, and was educated at Oxford and Harvard. He was for many years Senior Advisor to the Vice President for Africa at the World Bank, where he is currently Acting Sector Manager of the Capacity Building Technical Group in the Africa Region. His various publications include *The African-Arab Conflict in the Sudan, Interdependence in a World of Unequals, The African Capacity Building Initiative: Toward Improved Policy Analysis and Development Management*, and *The Essence of Capacity Building*. His research interests include governance and capacity building, and politics, power and money.

List of Abbreviations

AAFSAP	African Alternative Framework for Structural Adjustment Programmes, 1987
ADB	African Development Bank
ANC	African National Congress
APPER	African Priority Programme for Economic Rehabilitation
CAMPFIRE	Communal Areas Management Programme for Indigenous Resources
CEAC	Central African Economic Community
CELA	Economic Commission for Latin America
CFA	Communauté Financière Africaine
CIDA	Canadian International Development Agency
CITES	1973 Convention on International Trade in Endangered Species of Wild Fauna and Flora
CMEA	Council for Mutual Economic Assistance
COMESA	Economic Community of Eastern and Southern Africa
EAC	East African Community
EADB	East African Development Bank
ECOMOG	ECOWAS' Monitoring Group
ECOWAS	Economic Community of West African States
EEC	European Economic Community
EU	European Union
FAO	Food and Agriculture Organization
FDI	foreign direct investment
FLS	Front Line States
FPTP	first-past-the-post system
HDI	Human Development Index
IBRD	International Bank for Reconstruction and Development
IFAD	International Development Fund for Agricultural Development
IGAD	Intergovernmental Group Against Desertification
IGADD	Intergovernmental Group Against Drought and Development
ILO	International Labour Organization
IMF	International Monetary Fund
IMR	infant mortality rate
MMR	maternal mortality rate
MPLA	Popular Movement for the liberation of Angola
NGOs	non-governmental organizations
OAU	Organization of African Unity
ODA	Overseas Development Assistance
OECD	Organization for Economic Co-operation and Development
OED	World Bank Operations and Evaluation Department
ORAP	Organization of Rural Associations for Progress

PCY	per capita household income
PHC	population health coverage indicators
PTA	Preferential Trade Area of Eastern and Southern Africa
RWG	Redistribution with Growth
SADC	Southern African Development Community
SADCC	Southern African Development Coordination Conference
SAPs	Structural Adjustment Programmes
SIPRI	Swedish International Peace Research Institute
UDEAC	Economic and Customs Union of Central Africa
UMOA	L'Union Monetaire de l'ouest de l'afrique
U5MR	under-five mortality rate
UNCTAD	UN Conference on Trade and Development
UNDP	UN Development Programme
UNECA	UN Economic Commission for Africa
UNEP	United Nations Environment Programme
UNESCO	UN Educational, Scientific and Cultural Organization
UNHCR	UN High Commissioner for Refugees
UNICEF	United Nations Children's Fund
UNITA	National Union for the Total Independence of Angola
UNPAERD	United Nation's Programme for African Economic Recovery and Development
WHO	World Health Organization
WIDER	World Institute for Development Economics Research
WRI	World Resources Institute
WTO	World Trade Organization

1
African Development in Retrospect and Prospect

Dharam Ghai

In the eyes of the world and to many of its own citizens, Africa has become a synonym for failure. Thanks in part to the world media, Africa is associated in the popular imagination with economic crisis, political disorder, civil wars, military regimes and endemic corruption. For nearly two decades, the continent has evoked images of widespread starvation, mass impoverishment, environmental disaster, bloody conflicts, ever-growing numbers of refugees and internally displaced persons, and endless suffering of its people, especially of women and children (Harden, 1991; Kaplan, 1994).

The above portrayal of Africa undoubtedly captures many elements of the harsh reality of the region in recent years. But like all images that dominate mass media and popular perception, it tends to exaggerate, distort and simplify. Not all parts of Africa have shared the dismal fate depicted in much of the writing and reporting on the region. Notable progress registered in some domains is rarely dwelt upon. Above all, the dominant view fails to take into account the changes underway that may in the coming years render obsolete the analyses and predictions based on past trends. Certainly, recent history provides abundant illustrations of robust predictions going awry. It is instructive to recall that some prominent analysts in the 1950s had assigned South Korea to the category of hopelessly desperate economies. India in the 1960s was predicted to continue suffering from ever-rising numbers of starving people threatening to swallow the world's dwindling surpluses of grain. And Bangladesh in the 1970s was branded as a permanent basket case. In the 1980s and 1990s, Africa has come close to being labelled by many commentators as beyond repair and destined to sink ever deeper into the infernal cycle of impoverishment, chaos and violence.

It is thus important to take a balanced and realistic view of the prospects of Africa in the coming years and decades. Such a view must be informed by a sober assessment of past experience, of the changing global environment and regional context and of the changes currently underway. Proposals for reform grounded in such analysis are more likely to be relevant and helpful than are blueprints inspired by alarmist prognostication of gloom and doom. The essays in this volume seek to contribute to an effort to develop an agenda for social and economic revival and progress. As a background to the essays, this chapter attempts to

1

identify circumstances and policies behind the crisis in Africa, considers the implications of recent changes in the global and regional environment and assesses the significance of reforms currently underway.

1. The great African crisis

Starting in the late 1970s, an increasing number of African countries began to experience economic stagnation or decline. The crisis acquired increasing momentum in the 1980s as even countries which had performed well in the two preceding decades started to show signs of stress and strain. As the 1980s drew to a close, there were less than half a dozen countries which were able to escape deepening social and economic distress. The poor performance has continued into the 1990s, though the last two years have seen revival of growth in an increasing number of countries.[1] These declines for most countries represented a sharp reversal of the social and economic achievements of the post-war period.

The crisis was manifested at all levels and in all spheres. Industrial and agricultural production per capita at best stagnated or more frequently entered a period of sustained decline. Export earnings declined as did the volume of imports. There was a big drop in average consumption of goods and services. Public and private investment fell precipitously. Real wages and salaries declined sharply for most categories of workers. Wage employment in the formal sector fell or stagnated. The rates of urban unemployment rose to record heights. The per capita volume and quality of vital social services such as health, education, housing and water deteriorated in most countries. The physical infrastructure of roads, electricity, communications and buildings suffered from lack of repair and maintenance.

The great majority of the population suffered severe declines in their living standards. The worst affected were the unemployed and low-income wage earners in urban areas. Even if the latter succeeded in retaining their employment, the levels of remuneration fell below minimum subsistence needs. The middle and upper echelons in the salary scale often suffered even sharper declines in their real incomes but few were driven into destitution. The peasants were less severely affected and some commercial farmers profited from rising prices for food and export crops brought about by market liberalization and currency devaluation. Some traders engaged in export and import trade also benefited from trade liberalization, though in view of the relative shrinkage of the external trade sector in most countries, the average incomes must have declined. Even many of the industrialists producing for the protected domestic markets suffered losses occasioned by greater competition from abroad brought about by policies of trade liberalization (Jamal and Weeks, 1993).

People have resorted to a wide variety of strategies to counter the effects of economic crisis. The commonest form of survival strategy in urban areas is engagement in informal sector activities. New entrants to the labour force, those who lost jobs in the formal sector as well as members of households with jobs, have all been forced to turn to this sector to eke out a living and to supplement their meagre incomes from other sources. Since the informal sector itself is partly dependent upon incomes and demand in the formal sector, and overall incomes have been stagnant or declining in most African countries, this sector is unlikely to have been a dynamic source of employment and incomes for its members. The outcome in most countries appears to have been declining average earnings in the informal sector with much greater numbers participating in slowly expanding activities (Meagher and Yunusa, 1996; see also Chapters 3 and 4, this volume).

A typical response to the crisis has been pursuit of multiple activities by most households in rural and urban areas. Families from low-, middle- and high-income groups across a wide spectrum of sectors and occupations have sought to protect their living standards through diversification of their activities. This multiple livelihood strategy has reduced risks, opened up new channels for supplementing income from other sources and occasionally led to innovations in products and methods of production. But in most cases it has been a case of redistribution of employment and incomes with declining average family incomes. Its adverse effects include loss of specialization and decline in productivity in existing posts as public employees especially begin to treat their jobs as sinecures and launching pads for other gainful activities (Mustapha, 1991; Bangura, 1996).

Other responses to the crisis have been less savoury. These include the use of public facilities and equipment for private gains; increase in corruption and bribery; recourse to parallel markets, smuggling and contrabands; rise in organized crime, thefts and robberies; and intensification of begging, prostitution and child labour. There have also been more positive social responses. The traditional mechanisms of income redistribution and provision of social security and welfare through extended families and ethnic associations have been used more intensively. New institutions, such as self-help groups and organizations at the level of villages or urban localities, have come into being to cope with economic and social distress created by the crisis. Indeed, the rapid expansion of private initiatives to promote social and economic development has been a marked feature of recent years throughout the African continent (Ghai and Hewitt de Alcantara, 1991; Engberg-Pedersen *et al.*, 1996).

The crisis has not been confined only to the economic and social spheres. It has also spilled into the environmental domain. All available evidence points to widespread deterioration of natural resources and urban infrastructure. The former is reflected in rapid deforestation, growing population pressure on land, major losses in soil and biodiversity, depletion in stocks of wildlife, and reduction in soil fertility and agricultural productivity. The latter is manifested above all in serious deterioration in sanitary conditions, especially in rapidly expanding slums, intensification of air and water pollution and growing traffic density and bottlenecks. The reduction in the quality and quantity of natural resources is equivalent to decumulation of machinery and physical infrastructure in industrial economies. Its economic consequences are especially serious in Africa where the quality of life and standard of living of a significant proportion of the population is directly dependent on the abundance, diversity and fertility of natural resources (Harrison, 1987; Chapters 6 and 7, this volume).

National policies and economic crisis

What have been the underlying forces behind the great crisis since the late 1970s? This topic has been much debated in the growing literature on the subject and discussed at national, regional and international levels. Unlike earlier discussions, which sought simple or single explanations of the crisis, there is now an increasing recognition of its complexity and multi-faceted nature. There is wider acceptance of the view that a full analysis of the crisis must probe the politics as well as the economics of African countries and dig into national policies as well as developments in the international economy. There is growing recognition that a variety of factors – economic policy errors, an adverse external environment, political disorder and conflicts, climatic disturbances – have contributed to economic and environmental crisis. Nevertheless, there continue to be differences about the core processes and the relative importance of different factors in the generation of the crisis.[2]

Led by earlier World Bank analysis, a number of influential commentators have blamed the crisis in Africa on inappropriate economic policies and excessive state intervention in the economy.[3] It was argued that certain policies such as heavy taxation of the agricultural sector, protection of industry, import and export controls, state regulation of marketing, prices and licences for foreign exchange and state ownership of productive enterprises distorted resource allocation and blunted incentives to work, save, invest and take risks. Regulation of the economy through market forces and reduction in state intervention were proposed as central elements of a strategy to restore and sustain growth.

While recognizing the importance of national policies in determining economic performance, it is necessary to make some qualifying remarks. State planning and regulation of the economy and industrialization through import substitution were not unique to African countries. Indeed, these policies were part of the conventional wisdom on development and were advocated and supported by a wide range of economists, advisers, policy-makers and aid administrators in multilateral and bilateral agencies. Furthermore, it is useful to recall that historically, contrary to the currently fashionable views, most countries achieved industrialization through protection and that the state played an important role in stimulating and managing economic growth. Even in the case of East and South-east Asian countries, with the exception of Hong Kong, the state played an important role in guiding and managing their economies.

Thus there was nothing wrong in principle with state planning and management of the economy and promotion of industrialization in African and other Third World countries. The key mistakes made related rather to the methods and instruments used to achieve these objectives. In particular, most of the distortions and inefficiencies flowed from the growing use of direct controls and administrative methods in allocating resources. Direct allocation of key inputs such as imports, credit and raw materials, and administrative decisions on prices and protection of industry, inevitably led to inefficient resource use, shortages, parallel markets and corruption. However, these problems are not intrinsic to planning;

industrialization can be achieved efficiently through reliance on market forces with the state promoting strategic changes in investment, technological progress, trade, human skills and physical infrastructure.

The literature on the African crisis has not given adequate attention to the negative impact of corruption on efficiency and growth. Regulation of the economy through administrative means greatly facilitates the extraction of rent by the authorities at all levels of the economy. The cancer of corruption and bribery has spread deep into the African body politic. Its inevitable consequences have been growing distortion of the economy, with decisions taken without regard to considerations of cost, efficiency, growth or equity. Corruption directs scarce human resources to unproductive channels, imposes massive burdens on the productive sections of the society, violates principles of equity and justice, breeds alienation and eventually justifies rebellions and coups d'état.

Corruption is not of course a phenomenon peculiar to Africa alone. Other developing regions and several industrialized countries have also been afflicted by corruption, it has not prevented growth in all regions. It may, however, be argued that these countries' growth might have been even higher and more sustainable in the absence of significant corruption. The crisis of Latin America in the 1980s and of East and South-east Asia in the late 1990s and mediocre performance in South Asia and the Middle East certainly cannot be completely divorced from the nature and extent of prevalent corruption. Evidently, the economic impact of corruption depends on its scale and pervasiveness, the utilization of its proceeds, its incidence and the severity of sanctions and punishments, and the environment in which it is generated. It can be argued that in Africa corruption has been disproportionately greater, its proceeds used more in conspicuous consumption, it has been less frequently and severely punished and has been generated through processes which have been especially conducive to market distortions and other inefficiencies in allocation of investment and public expenditure.

International dimensions of the crisis

While neo-classical economists tend to stress national policies, radical analysts put the blame for the crisis on developments in the international economy. Few dispute the importance of the international environment for African economies, which are heavily dependent on external trade and finance. This dependence exposes African countries to greater risks because of the concentration of exports on a narrow range of primary products.

Five developments in the international economy since the mid 1970s have had adverse effects on economic performance in African countries. First, there has been a remarkable reduction in the growth rate of industrialized countries, with an adverse effect on the demand for most primary product exports from developing countries. Second, in part because of this factor, the terms of trade have moved sharply against non-oil exporting countries, exceeding in some recent years the low levels reached in the 1930s during the Great Depression. Even for oil exporters, the period since the early 1980s has been marked in most years by declining terms of trade. Third, the sharp increase in real interest rates in the world market since the early 1980s has greatly added to the debt burdens of African countries. Fourth, flows of private capital have fallen sharply in most African countries. Finally, the period has been marked by a massive flight of capital to Europe and the US. These factors go a long way in explaining the deteriorating economic performance in African countries over the past decade and a half. Some of them, such as movements in private capital, stem in part from the political and economic crisis that has engulfed many African countries, but they have also exacerbated the crisis.

The fact that, unlike in earlier periods, practically all African, Latin American and West Asian countries faced economic difficulties simultaneously in the 1980s, gives further support to the thesis that a deteriorating international environment played a significant role in the African crisis. It is of course not possible to quantify this role. Most analysts would perhaps agree with the proposition that both weaknesses in national policies and deterioration in global economic conditions contributed jointly to the generation and intensification of the crisis, though differing on the relative weight to be attached to the two factors.[4] The position taken here is that an adverse external environment was critical in determining the timing and the severity of the crisis but that weaknesses in economic policies, especially the replacement of markets by administrative decisions on resource allocation, both worsened the economic problems and delayed the necessary adjustments.

Political conditions and economic crisis

It is inappropriate to look at the economic and political aspects of the crisis in a separate and isolated manner. The two interact in varied and complex ways. The characteristics of political regimes are determined in an important manner by such features of economic systems as patterns of resource ownership, distribution of income and modes of production and accumulation. At the same time, the nature of the political system has a major impact on patterns of accumulation, growth and distribution of wealth. Even more than in most other countries, the political dynamics in African countries have played a crucial role in their economic performance.

On the eve of independence, most African countries were endowed by the colonial authorities with all the trappings of western democratic systems. These were, however, destined for a short life. Within years of independence, democratic regimes were replaced in most African countries by military rule, one-party systems or personal dictatorships. Opposition parties were outlawed or harassed, the press was muzzled, freedom of association quashed, the rule of law endangered, the freedom of the judiciary compromised and critics of the regime jailed, tortured or killed. There were a few exceptions to this dismal record of destruction of democracy and violation of fundamental human rights. And even in one party states, there was a great deal of variation in the extent of freedom of expression, protest and association. Nevertheless, the general trend was towards restriction of basic human rights and concentration of power in the hands of the president, the party, the military and the state (Jackson and Rosberg, 1982; Anyang'Nyong'o, 1987).

This is not the place for an analysis of the breakdown of the nascent democratic systems in African countries. It may, however, be useful to mention some relevant factors. Colonial rule was characterized for most of the period by authoritarian structures. Opposition activities, when they were allowed, consisted naturally of attempts to secure independence from colonial rule. The civil society institutions such as free press, independent media, established intelligentsia, unions, co-operatives and other associations of interest groups, were limited in number and strength. Most educated persons were drawn into the struggle for independence. Once independence was attained, the head of the state and the ruling party naturally sought to consolidate and perpetuate their power through suppression of whatever limited opposition existed in the early post-colonial period. These moves were justified as being necessary to accelerate social and economic development. The fragility of the new nation states and the endemic ethnic tensions were also cited in defence of personal rule and military and one-party regimes. Domestic resistance was suppressed and there was little opposition from abroad. The international politics revolved around the Cold War (Rothchild and Chazan, 1988; Gibbon, Bangura and Ofstad, 1992).

The political dynamics have aggravated the economic problems of the African countries in at least three principal ways. First, the civil wars and prolonged violence engendered by political strife have devastated the economies of several countries in the past two decades: Angola, Chad, Ethiopia, Liberia, Mozambique, Namibia, Rwanda, Sierra Leone, Somalia, Sudan, Western Sahara, Uganda, Zaire and Zimbabwe are among the countries the most seriously affected. But there are also others which have suffered from limited rebellions and wars, periodic coups, political instability and sustained tensions: Burundi, Ghana and Nigeria are among the important countries falling in this category. The economic performance of these countries has been adversely affected not only by the diversion of resources to military expenditure, but also by the destruction of social and economic infrastructure. In addition, the climate of insecurity and lawlessness has reduced foreign and domestic investment and encouraged flight of capital and skills to other countries (Collier, 1997; Chapter 5, this volume).

Political instability and violence are not the sole prerogative of African countries. Indeed in the 1970s and well into the 1980s, several Latin American countries experienced periods of guerrilla uprisings and ideological conflicts. Likewise, several Asian and Middle Eastern countries – Vietnam, Cambodia, Laos, Sri Lanka, India, Pakistan, Afghanistan, Lebanon, Israel, Palestine, Iraq, Iran, Kuwait, Algeria – have been convulsed by regional, ideological or ethnic conflicts of varying intensity over the past two decades. It can, however, be argued that conflicts in African countries have often been more prolonged and more destructive of human life and physical and social infrastructure, in some cases such as Somalia, Liberia, Sierra Leone and Zaire, resulting in virtual collapse of state structures. Furthermore, while some conflicts have been resolved – as in Zimbabwe, Namibia, Mozambique, South Africa, Uganda and Ethiopia – others have continued and new ones have erupted in the 1990s (UNHCR, 1995 and 1997).

More conflicts in Africa than elsewhere have been struggles for liberation from colonial or local settler domination. Africa has also had its share of ideological conflicts fanned by the Cold War, though these often concealed ethnic and regional dimensions. Fundamentally, however, African conflicts, more than elsewhere, are a reflection of the fragility of political institutions, the comparatively recent creation of 'nation states' out of a motley of tribes and clans, the persistence of the colonial patterns of unequal development of different parts of the country and the widespread use of state power and resources for personal enrichment, ethnic favouritism and political patronage. The lack of legitimacy and popular support for many political regimes added further to their vulnerability to coups and rebellions (Amin, 1994; Diouf, 1994; Lemarchand, 1994; Nnoli, 1995; Stavenhagen, 1996).

There is another dimension to the political process that has had deleterious economic consequences. Politics in Africa, even more than elsewhere, have been seen primarily as a route to acquisition of wealth. In turn, personal wealth and control over state resources have been important means of gaining and retaining political power. The distribution of resources by the president, the political elite and the ruling party is considered necessary to legitimize the regime, reward supporters and broaden its popular base. Whatever the motivation, the effect has generally been to channel resources to projects and activities which bear little relation to the criteria of efficiency in resource allocation and stimulation of long-term growth. The mechanisms used to acquire wealth and control over resources, such as reliance on licenses and other administrative rules, have further undermined economic efficiency and growth and have had deleterious social and political effects, as argued earlier.

The repressive character of the political regimes in many African countries over much of the period has also contributed to economic failure. The suppression of freedom of expression and rights to organize, demonstrate and protest, has effectively killed off all serious debate about alternative development strategies and policies. More importantly, it has prevented the exposure of misappropriation and misuse of resources, mismanagement of economic policy and state enterprises and other forms of theft and abuse of public property and resources.

2. Changing international and national environment

The past few years have been marked by some important changes in the political and economic environment affecting African and other developing countries. These changes have resulted from some developments in world politics and economics. They are likely to have far-reaching effects on the development patterns and prospects of African countries (Mair, 1996).

In the economic domain, the most significant changes relate to reorientation of policies in favour of markets and private enterprise and against state regulation and public ownership of productive activities. At the political level, there has been a trend in favour of democracy and against totalitarian and authoritarian regimes. These changes in turn have been reflected in the national political and economic regimes in African countries. A growing number of countries have adopted stabilization and structural adjustment policies and have moved or are in the process of moving from military, one party and personal dictatorships to some sort of pluralist, multi-party democratic systems (Ake, 1996; Chapter 8, this volume).

Global economic integration and market liberalization

The new economic policies originated in the industrialized countries and were then exported to the developing world. They were triggered off by the crisis faced by the developed countries after 1973, but there were also some deeper, structural factors which played a role in the shift towards greater reliance on market forces and reduced role of the state in the economy. The progressive integration of the world economy in the post-war period and accelerated technological progress were among the more important factors. The new policies comprised deregulation of utilities and financial and other services; removal of restrictions on capital mobility; restraint or curtailment of public expenditure, especially on social welfare and social security; curbs on trade unions and the creation of more flexible labour markets; and privatization of state enterprises.

There were some exceptions to this trend towards market liberalization. The progress towards trade liberalization was halted and even reversed, especially with respect to some products of special export interest to developing countries such as textiles, clothing, leather products, toys and electronic goods. Agricultural protection in most industrialized countries was further intensified. Finally, increasing restrictions were placed on the immigration of unskilled workers in the rich countries. The Uruguay Round and other international agreements to liberalize trade in goods and services have sought to roll back some of these impediments to trade. But these multilateral agreements will also in some cases result in the erosion of trade preferences hitherto enjoyed by African countries.

Despite these setbacks to liberalization of product and factor markets, the world is moving rapidly towards a single market for goods, services, technology, capital and skills. The 1980s witnessed a strong movement towards global economic integration manifested in rapid growth in trade in goods and services, foreign exchange transactions, foreign direct investment, technology transfers, telecommunications and foreign travel. The accelerating global integration and continuing technological progress are likely to have far-reaching effects on patterns and location of production and distribution of resources within and across countries.

The rate and pattern of growth of individual countries will be increasingly influenced by their ability to attract foreign capital, skills and technology and to sell products and services in the global market. This in turn will be affected not only by economic considerations such as the availability of natural resources and physical infrastructure, the cost and efficiency of the labour force, the fiscal and other incentives to foreign investment but also by the prevailing political and social climate such as maintenance of law and order, absence of social strife and existence of basic human rights and freedom.

The global trend towards a greater reliance on markets and a reduced role for the state has also been reflected in the economic policies pursued by African countries. In the 1980s and '90s, a growing number of African countries have been adopting measures of economic reform aimed at liberalization of markets and limitation of state intervention in the economy. These measures have comprised reduction or restraint of public expenditure, especially on physical infrastructure and social welfare and services; removal of subsidies on inputs and goods of mass consumption; price and trade liberalization; reduction in the progressivity of the tax structure; increase in real interest rates and credit liberalization; devaluation of the domestic currency; enhanced incentives to foreign investment; deregulation and privatization (Collier, 1997; Cornia and Helleiner, 1994; Chapters 9 and 10, this volume).

The new policies have been introduced as essential components of stabilization and structural adjustment packages negotiated with the IMF and the World Bank. The recourse to the IMF was necessitated by the growing deficits in the balance of payments of most African countries generated by a deterioration in the external economic environment, errors in domestic economic policies and mismanagement and misappropriation of resources, as indicated above. The new policies represented a sharp break with those pursued in the preceding three decades with their emphasis on planning, promotion of industrialization through import substitution and increasing the role of the state in enterprise ownership and management of the economy through administrative means.

These policies were initially adopted in response to pressure exerted by the international financial organizations, donor countries and foreign enterprises. The relief of debt and the granting of new credits and assistance were made conditional on the adoption of these policies. In most African countries, in contrast, for example, to the situation in Latin America, there was little domestic pressure in favour of new policies. The industrialists, the political and bureaucratic elite and the urban working class benefited from many of the policies associated with the model of state-directed development. The commercial farmers, peasants growing export crops and private mining interests that stood to gain from policies of trade liberalization and currency devaluation did not constitute a strong enough political force in most countries to persuade or compel the state to alter those policies. Nor did the few technocrats who did not derive income from licences wield sufficient political clout to challenge the old orthodoxy, which after all had received the blessing of most development economists and the international development community.

In part because of these factors, the reform process was slower and has been less consistent and thoroughgoing in Africa than in Latin America. The emphasis has been on price liberalization, reduction or removal of subsidies, control of state expenditure and currency devaluation. In general, the progress in removing quantitative restrictions on foreign trade and payments has been more patchy and relatively few countries have made significant headway with privatization and reform of financial and parastatal sectors and of public services. Nevertheless, the economic environment in many African countries has changed considerably and most countries have made commitments to initiate or widen economic reforms (Faruqee and Husain, 1994; Collier, 1997; World Bank, 1994; Bennell, 1997).

Global democratic upsurge

The world political context has also changed radically in recent years. The late 1970s and the 1980s have been marked by an upsurge in democracy worldwide. The process started with the transition from military to democratic regimes in Latin American countries. The continent has gone a full circle from a situation in 1973 when only two countries were governed by pluralist regimes to 1997 when only one island state retained one-party rule. There was a similar though less spectacular movement towards democracy in Asia. Military or one-party regimes in South Korea, Taiwan, Province of China, Bangladesh, Pakistan, Cambodia, Philippines and Thailand gradually gave way to civilian governments elected in multi-party elections.

Momentous changes took place in the late 1980s and the early 1990s in East and Central Europe and the Soviet Union with the collapse of the communist regimes and their replacement by governments elected in multi-party elections. These developments further reinforced the global trend in favour of liberal democratic regimes. The remaining regions still dominated by non-democratic regimes, such as the Middle East and Africa, came under increasing pressure from several quarters for liberalization of their political systems. The pressure exerted by the western powers encouraged the domestic opposition to organize active resistance to the military, one-party or one-person regimes. The besieged countries found it difficult to turn to other major powers for moral and material support, as was possible at the height of the Cold War. Increasingly the donor countries and international financial organizations began to tie development assistance to the recipient country's record in human rights and progress towards establishing liberal democratic systems.

The political situation in African countries has become quite fluid under these multiple sources of pressure. In the early 1980s only Botswana, Mauritius, Senegal and Zimbabwe practised multi-party democracy. In the last few years, a large number of countries have organized free elections contested by several political parties. The conversion to multi-party politics has affected a wide spectrum of regimes ranging from former Marxist–Leninist states such as Ethiopia, Mozambique and Angola to one-man dictatorships and civilian one-party regimes such as in Ghana, Malawi, Kenya, Tanzania, Côte d'Ivoire and Cameroon. One of the epochal events in African history was the end of apartheid in South Africa and its replacement by majority rule. On the other hand, there have also been setbacks and reversals of democratic transitions such as in Sierra Leone, Nigeria and Congo (Brazzaville).

The forces behind the global trend towards democracy in the last decade and a half are complex and diverse and vary from one region to another and indeed from one country to another. In many cases, sustained economic crisis was a major contributory factor. This appears to have been the case in much of Latin America. Even in the communist countries in Eastern and Central Europe, the slowdown in growth and consumption in the 1970s and the growing gap in material prosperity between the East and West appear to have played an important role in the increasing disenchantment with the communist system. But in other countries such as South Korea and Taiwan, the Province of China, it was on the contrary the rapid economic growth, higher living standards, big increase in the working class and rising aspirations of an increasingly educated and professional middle class that triggered off the popular demands for a liberal democratic system. Everywhere the image of the market industrialized countries as islands of prosperity and freedom, powerfully projected through the media and official propaganda, acted as an irresistible magnet for other parts of the world and reinforced the yearning for the end of tyranny and repression and the struggle for basic human rights of freedom of expression, organization and pursuit of one's faith.

Most of these factors were also present in the African quest for democracy. The economic crisis suffered by most countries in Africa in the 1970s and 1980s was more severe than elsewhere. The failure of the political regimes to resolve problems of ethnic and religious conflicts and to establish popular legitimacy due in part to lack of accountability, harsh repression and gross violation of human rights, also generated strong resistance to the existing regimes among a growing section of the population from different social, ethnic and regional groups. Finally, the economic and political pressure from western countries following the end of the Cold War was an important factor in the move towards plural political systems (Mkandawire, 1994).

Despite the rapid progress made in several African countries with political liberalization, there is a great deal of uncertainty about the nature and durability of new regimes. Fears have been raised in many quarters about the danger to political stability posed by multi-party politics, especially about its tendency to fan ethnic tensions and conflicts. It has also been argued that democracies can only be sustained by the existence of a large middle class, a sizeable and independent intelligentsia, widespread civil society institutions and a considerable industrial and commercial bourgeoisie. Judged by these standards, relatively few African countries would pass the test for durability of incipient democracies. These observations have, however, been contradicted by the experience of several countries. In any case in a rapidly changing national and international situation, some conclusions based on past experience may not hold in the future. One thing however is undeniable: African countries are entering their democratic phases in most inhospitable economic circumstances.

3.   Development prospects and challenges

The new environment of globalization and democratization opens up both windows of opportunity and threats of stagnation and disorder. The outcome will depend, as before, on the interaction between domestic forces and external circumstances. Paradoxically, however, national and regional efforts and policies will be increasingly influential in determining the impact of the powerful changes unleashed by the processes of globalization and democratization. There may thus be increasing divergence in the social and economic progress achieved by different countries and regions in Sub-Saharan Africa.

The conventional barriers to economic growth – limited size of the domestic market, low savings and investment rates, scarcity of managerial and professional skills, dominance of technologies of low productivity – have been even more of a constraining factor in Africa than in other developing regions. The globalization of economies should in principle help in easing these constraints. Indeed, the complete removal of obstacles to trade and payments and to flows of capital, technology and know-how should result in the creation of an integrated global economic space. In such a world, except for controlling movement of labour, national boundaries lose all economic relevance.

Although there has been gradual liberalization of trade and payments and greater mobility of capital, technology and skills in most parts of the world, including Sub-Saharan Africa, the ideal of a completely integrated world economy is far from being realized. Nevertheless the movement in that direction opens up possibilities of unprecedented rates of economic expansion in some countries and regions. The quality of the national environment will play a decisive role in determining the relative attractiveness of different regions to domestic and foreign investors and enterprises. The efficiency of physical infrastructure – transport, power, communications – and the quality of the labour force will increasingly influence the behaviour of domestic economic agents and inflows of capital, technology and skills. A stable macro-economic setting reinforces the confidence of investors. Countries which also succeed in creating a hospitable climate for capital and in fostering social harmony and political stability will enjoy additional advantages in the competition for domestic and foreign skills, technology and capital. In the long term, a democratic culture, widespread participation, equality of opportunity and equitable sharing of benefits of growth offer the best prospects for sustained political stability and social cohesion.

The impressive potential benefits offered by advancing globalization must be set against the obstacles faced by African countries (Cantwell, 1997; Chapter 12, this volume). Indeed many observers have argued convincingly that globalization may accentuate the marginalization of African countries from the dynamics of the world economy. The stimulus to global economic expansion has flowed from booming investment in manufacturing and modern services and it is the rapid increase in exports from these sectors that has underpinned unprecedented rates of economic growth in many countries, especially in Asia, in recent years. Poor infrastructure and scarcity of managerial, technological and entrepreneurial skills in most African countries are likely to constitute major obstacles to their emergence as significant centres of world production and exports for manufacturing and modern services in the foreseeable future. Indeed, globalization may accentuate the crisis in countries suffering from political instability and economic misman- agement through facilitating flight of capital and skills. However, countries which already have a headstart in development, and which maintain political stability and pursue appropriate economic policies, may be able to reinforce their advantage and grow into important regional, sub-regional and even global centres of production with respect to some products. Nigeria, Côte d'Ivoire and Cameroon in West Africa, Kenya in East Africa and Zimbabwe and South Africa in Southern Africa, have certainly the potential to derive major gains from economic liberalization and integration.

Most African countries will need to rely on other sectors to provide dynamism to their economies. While the short- and medium-term prospects do not look too bright for traditional primary products, several African countries are exceptionally endowed with a range of minerals which face good prospects for growing world demand. With appropriate policies, it should be possible for these countries to establish or reinforce their position as significant centres of world production and exports. Non-traditional agricultural products such as fruits, vegetables and flowers may provide some countries with a dynamic source of employment and foreign exchange earnings. Tourism based upon extensive beaches, unrivalled nature parks and unique wildlife constitutes another pillar of economic expansion and source of foreign exchange earnings. Further processing of agricultural and mineral products and a manufacturing sector based on them can also impart a strong impulse to growth in many African countries. There are no doubt many other niches which can be successfully exploited for penetration of the world markets.

Even where the global environment provides exceptional opportunities for trade and inflows of investment, technology and skills, it cannot provide the sole route out of poverty and under-development. The core of the effort to achieve equitable and sustainable development must be anchored in a framework of sound domestic policies and resource mobilization. Even the possibilities offered by advancing globalization are conditional upon economic reform and maintenance of political stability.[5] At the national level, the trends towards market liberalization and democratization hold out the possibility of improved economic performance and wider political participation. But a great deal will depend on the strength and durability of these changes. Most African countries have not yet benefited much from the significant economic reforms carried out in recent years. This is at least in part because of the investor perception of the fragility of these reforms and doubts about their durability.[6] The issue of contagion is important here. Just as countries in East and South-east Asia benefited until recently from the rapid growth of their neighbours and the benign perception of investors about profitability, growth and stability in the region, individual reforming African countries have been dragged down by decline and stagnation of the neighbouring economies and by negative perception of investors – domestic and foreign – generated by images of a continent in the throes of mismanagement, disorder and bloodshed.

Economic reforms launched in most African countries in recent years will thus need to be widened and deepened. Unlike the more advanced developing countries, the greatest priority for African countries is to create an efficient infrastructure of roads, transport, power and telecommunications. Many countries also face the problem of creating conditions for the functioning of markets. There is continuing need to improve managerial, technical and entrepreneurial skills. But perhaps the greatest challenge is to build up capacity and a reputation for honest, impartial and competent administration. All these tasks require leadership by the state and its organs. Thus an efficient and transparent public sector is key to the recovery and sustained growth of African economies. Improvements in markets and in infrastructure can best be undertaken within a regional framework. Hence the great importance of initiatives to achieve greater political and economic co-operation through regional agreements. Their greatest contribution to improved economic performance may consist not in removing trade and payment barriers in a preferential area but in enhancing the quality of physical and social infra-structure and strengthening security and political ties (Chapter 11, this volume).

Thus at the political level, three prerequisites for sustained and equitable growth are a strong and efficient state, a functioning political democracy, and national consensus and social cohesion. A strong and efficient state is needed to give direction and leadership to the development effort, to generate resources for investment in human resources and physical infrastructure, and to provide an economic environment conducive to savings, productive investment and techno-logical progress. Political democracy is essential for accountability and legitimacy, for popular participation and control, for debate and dialogue on development goals and methods and eventually for replacement of incompetent or corrupt governments.

National consensus and social cohesion are necessary to mobilize resources and promote national unity. Social solidarity is built around a widely shared vision of national objectives, due recognition of the legitimate interests of different social groups, a fair distribution of both the fruits of growth and the burdens of austerity, and equality of opportunities in access to social and economic services, employ-ment and productive resources. Thus the pattern of growth is as important as its pace. While in poor countries rapid growth is a prerequisite for poverty eradication and social development, past experience has shown that growth in itself will not be sufficient to improve the living standards of the majority of the population. Indeed, it is easier to achieve rapid growth than equitable distribution of its fruits. This tendency is reinforced by several elements in the globalization processes (Ghai, 1997a).

Broad-based growth requires rapid expansion of employment opportunities, as in Mauritius, and expansion of production and incomes of small farmers, as in the first decade of independence in Kenya and Zimbabwe (Dommen and Dommen, 1997; Loewenson and Chisvo, 1997). In countries where mineral wealth is the basis of rapid growth, it is essential that the mining revenues be used prudently to expand health and education services and economic infrastructure. This has been the key to success in Botswana (Duncan, Jefferis and Molutsi, 1997). In contrast Zaire is a notorious example of squandering of vast mineral resources. The South African experiment to bring about major improvements in access to social services and living standards of the impoverished groups under conditions of moderate growth and of political constraints to significant asset and income redistribution should thus be of great interest both in itself and in its lessons for other African countries.

The imperatives of strong and efficient states, political democracy and social solidarity point to the enormity of the challenge facing the regimes emerging from the political bankruptcy and economic collapse of the previous decades. But there are already some hopeful signs that the process of political regeneration and economic and social recovery has started and may gather pace in the coming decade. African political systems have become more open and critical voices are being heard again. The freedom of press and association has expanded in countries which until recently were run along authoritarian lines. The growing professional and middle classes and multiplication of private development initiatives and civil society institutions are forces which are compelling greater accountability and responsibility on the part of political parties and public institutions. There is increasing convergence on the imperative and content of economic reform among key interest groups.

These favourable trends are reflected in the emergence of new styles of leadership with a greater commitment to efficiency and integrity in public administration and greater realism in economic policy (Apter and Rosberg, 1997). They are also foreshadowed in the improved economic performance of a growing number of countries, although it is too early to say whether this trend will be generalized and sustained. They need to be accompanied by sustained improvement in living standards of the people – in reduction in malnutrition, infant and maternal mortality, adult illiteracy and gender disparities, and widening access to basic education, primary health, water supply and decent shelter. African countries made impressive progress in the decade of the 1960s and the '70s in extending education and literacy, improving access to health services, reducing infant mortality and malnutrition and increasing life expectancy. But there was a distinct slowdown in the improvement of such indicators of development in the 1980s and indeed retrogression occurred in a number of countries (Chapter 2, this volume).[7]

Sub-Saharan Africa has the lowest human development index of any region – the lowest educational enrolment rates and life expectancy and the highest infant, child and maternal mortality and total fertility rates. But it has higher adult literacy rates, lower child malnutrition and lesser gender disparities on most social indicators than the South Asian region. The persistence of high total fertility rates for most African countries over the past 25 years sets their experience apart from other developing regions. The resulting high rates of population growth in the coming decades and their implications for economic growth, human development and environmental preservation are among the most difficult challenges facing the African countries (Adepoju, 1996; Caldwell, 1991; Chapters 9 and 10, this volume).

Human development is an area which perhaps offers the best prospects of rapidly closing the gap between African countries and other regions of the world. Experience has shown that it is possible to achieve high indicators of human development even at relatively low income levels and rates of economic growth. Political commitment to provide basic social services to the entire population is the first essential step. Lack of finance and skills is not such an obstacle as in some other areas of economic advance. However, adequate state capacity to reach major segments of the population with basic services is indispensable, as is the concentration of resources on programmes such as adult literacy, universal basic education and primary health, infant and maternal nutrition, and health education and family planning (Ghai, 1997b; UNICEF, UNFPA, WHO, UNESCO, various years). The prospects for improved social performance look better now than they have over the past fifteen years. The gradual strengthening of democratic processes, the multiplication of civil society institutions and the worldwide consensus on achievement of minimum goals of human development over a specified period, provide a favourable environment for the launching and implementation of policies and programmes designed to promote rapid social progress.

This essay has sought to emphasize the interdependencies and complementarities between political, economic, social and environmental domains. For nearly two decades political malaise, economic crisis and social distress have jointly fed the downward spiral in most African countries. Similarly, the mutually reinforcing reforms currently being undertaken in many African countries in these domains can be expected to power the upward spiral towards political stability, economic growth and social equity.

Notes

1 The average weighted growth rate in Sub-Saharan Africa plummeted from 3.9 per cent in the 1960s and 3.8 in the 1970s to 1.7 in the 1980s and 0.9 over the period 1990–94. In 1995–7, it is estimated to have risen to around 4.0 per cent per annum (World Bank, World Development Report, various years).

2 It is not possible to do justice to this vast and diverse literature in a short space. The early discussions, led by international agencies and economists, tended to focus on economic factors, whether internal policies or external factors (World Bank, 1981; Organization of African Unity, 1980, 1985; Organization for Economic Co-operation and Development, 1985; Mkandawire, 1991; Ndegwa, 1986, Ravenhill, 1986). Subsequently political scientists and sociologists joined the ranks of scholars studying African development problems and the analyses done by international agencies have become more multidisciplinary and less technocratic, e.g., Bates (1981, 1983); Hyden (1983); Sandbrook (1985); World Bank (1989); Economic Commission for Africa (1986).

3 The analysis of the African crisis by the World Bank has been especially influential but it has evolved over time with a more balanced view of the role played by national and international factors and by economic and political forces (World Bank, 1981, 1989, 1994). See also Helleiner (1992); Ndegwa (1989); Havnevik (1987).

4 A number of studies have attempted to make quantitative estimates of the importance of different factors. These include Collier (1997); Elbadawi and Ndulu (1996); Fosu (1992); Ghura (1995); Hadjimichael and Ghura (1996); Morrisson *et al.* (1994); and Oshikoya, (1994). Fosu has estimated that political instability reduced economic growth by 1.1 percent points for a sample of 31 Sub-Saharan countries over the 1960–85 period. This represents 33 per cent of the sample mean annual GDP growth. Oshikoya found a positive relationship between economic growth and private investment, the latter being influenced positively by real exchange rates, lower inflation, credit availability, public sector investment and low debt service ratio. Ghura highlights the negative effect of the world real interest rate on growth in Sub-Saharan Africa. The terms of trade were also found to be strongly correlated with growth. His results also confirm the important roles of physical and human capital, inflation, government consumption ratio, export

volume growth, macro instability, and political and civil instability. Similarly, Elbadawi and Ndulu find that growth was affected negatively in Africa by 'exogenous' shocks associated with terms of trade, real world interest rates, weather and political instability. Their results also show the significance of financial depth, real exchange rate misalignment and high government consumption. In his review of the literature, Collier found the following factors to be of major importance: market distortions, especially of products and finance, a lack of social capital (social institutions, trust, information flows), high risk and poor public services. On the other hand, the lack of formal finance was found to be a minor factor and education surprisingly did not have clear effects.

5   A number of important documents produced or adopted by inter-governmental organizations have sketched out the nature and content of political and economic reform that is needed for sustained and equitable growth. These include Economic Commission for Africa (1986, 1990); World Bank (1989); Africa Leadership Forum (1992); United Nations (1995, 1996); Global Coalition for Africa (1992). Among numerous works by academic specialists, see Hyden and Bratton (1992); Ndegwa and Green (1994); Ihonvbere (1996); Green (1996); Griffin (1996); Stewart, Lall and Wangwe (1992).

6   Several commentators have stressed the importance of earning and retaining investor confidence in the durability of political and economic reforms and have made proposals for reducing risk and uncertainty through insurance, mediation and internal and external 'agencies of restraint' – institutional reforms designed to demonstrate the willingness to lock in reforms through surrender or sharing of sovereignty in key areas of economic policy. See in particular Collier (1997).

7   For instance, average yearly decline in under-5 mortality decreased slightly from 3.69 in 1960–70 to 3.62 in 1970–80, but more sharply to 2.94 in 1980–90 and 2.03 in 1990–95 (see Chapter 2, this volume).

References

Adepoju, Aderanti (1996) *Population, Poverty, Structural Adjustment Programmes and Quality of Life in Sub-Saharan Africa*, PHRDA Research Paper No. 1. Dakar: IDEP.

Africa Leadership Forum (1992) *The Kampala Document: Towards a Conference on Security, Stability, Development and Co-operation in Africa*. Kampala: ALF

Ake, Claude (1996) *Democracy and Development in Africa*. Washington, DC: Brookings Institute.

Amin, Samir (1994) *L'ethnie à l'assault des Nations: Yougoslavie, Ethiopie*. Paris: UNRISD and Editions L'Harmattan.

Anyang'Nyong'o, Peter (ed.) (1987) *Popular Struggles for Democracy in Africa*. London: Zed Press.

Apter, David and Carl G. Rosberg (eds) (1997) *Political Development and the New Realism in Sub-Saharan Africa*. Charlottesville: University of Virginia.

Bangura, Yusuf (1996) 'Economic restructuring, coping strategies and social change: implications for institutional development in Africa', in Mats Lundhal and Benno J. Ndulu (eds), *New Directions in Development Economics*. London: Routledge.

Bates, R. H. (1981) *Markets and States in Tropical Africa*. Berkeley, CA: University of California Press.

Bates, R. H. (1983) *Essays in the Political Economy of Africa*. Cambridge: Cambridge University Press.

Bennell, P. (1997) 'Privatisation in Sub-Saharan Africa: progress and prospects during the 1990s', *World Development*, 25(11).

Caldwell, J. (1991) *Population Trends and Determinants: Is Africa Different?* mimeo. Paris.

Cantwell, John (1997) 'Globalization and development in Africa', in John H. Dunning and Khalil A. Hamdani (eds), *The New Globalism and Developing Countries*. Tokyo: United Nations University Press.

Collier, Paul (1997) *The Marginalization of Africa in the World Economy* (manuscript). Geneva: ILO.

Cornia, Giovanni Andrea and Gerald Helleiner (eds) (1994) *From Adjustment to Development in Africa.* London: Macmillan.

Diouf, Makhtar (1994) *Sénégal: Les ethnies et la nation.* Geneva and Paris: UNRISD/Editions L'Harmattan.

Dommen, Bridget and Edward Dommen (1997) 'Mauritius: the roots of success', in Santosh Mehrota and Richard Jolly (eds), *Development with a Human Face: Experiences in Social Achievement and Economic Growth.* New York: UNICEF.

Duncan, Tyrrell, Keith Jefferis and Patrick Molutsi (1997) 'Social development in Botswana', in S. Mehrota and R. Jolly (1997).

Economic Commission for Africa (1986) *African Alternative Framework to Structural Adjustment Programmes for Socio-Economic Recovery and Transformation.* Addis Ababa: ECA.

Economic Commission for Africa (1990) *African Charter for Popular Participation in Development and Transformation,* Addis Ababa: ECA.

Elbadawi, Ibrahim and Bennu Ndulu (1996) 'Long-tern development and sustainable growth in Sub-Saharan Africa', in Mats Lundhal and Benno J. Ndulu (eds), *New Directions in Development Economics.* London: Routledge.

Engberg-Pedersen, Poul, Peter Gibbon, Phil Raikes and Lars Udsholt (eds) (1996) *Limits of Adjustment in Africa: The Effects of Economic Liberalisation, 1986–94,* London and Copenhagen: James Currey Centre for Development Research.

Faruquee, Rashid and Ishrat Husain (eds) (1994) *Adjustment in Africa: Lessons from Country Case Studies.* Washington, DC: World Bank.

Fosu, Augustin Kwasu (1992) 'Political instability and economic growth: evidence from Sub-Saharan Africa', *Economic Development and Cultural Change,* 40(4).

Ghai, Dharam and Cynthia Hewitt de Alcántara (1991) 'The Crisis of the 1980s in Africa, Latin America and the Caribbean: An overview', in Dharam Ghai (ed.), *The IMF and the South: The Social Impact of Crisis and Adjustment.* London, Geneva and Kingston: Zed Books/ UNRISD/University of the West Indies.

Ghai, Dharam (1997a) *Economic Globalization, Institutional Change and Human Security,* Discussion Paper No. 91. Geneva: UNRISD.

Ghai, Dharam (1997b) *Social Development and Public Policy: Lessons from Some Successful Experiences,* Discussion Paper No. 89. Geneva: UNRISD.

Ghura, Dhaneshwar (1995) Macro policies, external forces, and economic growth in Sub-Saharan Africa, *Economic Development and Cultural Change,* 43(4).

Gibbon, Peter, Yusuf Bangura and Arve Ofstad (eds) (1992) *Authoritarianism, Democracy and Adjustment: The Politics of Economic Reform in Africa.* Uppsala and Geneva: Scandinavian Institute of African Studies and UNRISD.

Global Coalition for Africa (1992) *Africa's Challenge: Taking Charge and Moving Ahead.* Washington, DC: GCA.

Green, Reginald Herbold (1996) 'Not farewell but fare forward voyagers: Africa in the 21st century', in Bade Onimode and Richard Synge (eds), *Issues in African Development.* Lagos: Heinemann Educational Books.

Griffin, Keith (1996) *Macroeconomic Reform and Employment: An Investment-led Strategy of Structural Adjustment in Sub-Saharan Africa.* Geneva: ILO.

Hadjimichael, Michael and Dhaneshwar Ghura (1996) 'Cross-country analysis', in Michael Hadjimichael *et al., Adjustment for Growth: The African Experience.* Washington, DC: IMF.

Harden, Blaine (1991) *Africa: Dispatches from a Fragile Continent.* London: HarperCollins.

Harrison, Paul (1987) *The Greening of Africa.* Harmondsworth: Penguin Books.

Havnevik, Kjell (ed.) (1987) *The IMF and the World Bank in Africa: Conditionality, Impact and Alternatives.* Uppsala: Scandinavian Institute of African Studies.

Helleiner, Gerald (1992) 'The IMF, the World Bank and Africa's adjustment and external debt problem: An unofficial view', *World Development,* 20(6).

Hyden, Goran (1983) *No Shortcuts to Progress: African Development Management in Perspective,* London: Heinemann.

Hyden, Goran and Michael Bratton (eds) (1992) *Governance and Politics in Africa*. Boulder, CO: Lynne Rienner.

Ihonvbere, Julius (1996) 'Africa in the 1990s and beyond: alternative prescriptions and projections', *Futures*, 28(1).

Jamal, Vali and John Weeks (1993) *Africa Misunderstood: or Whatever Happened to the Rural Urban Gap*. London: Macmillan.

Jackson, Robert and Carl Rosberg (1982) *Personal Rule in Africa: Prince, Autocrat, Prophet, Tyrant*. Berkeley, CA: University of California Press.

Kaplan, Robert (1994) 'The coming anarchy', *Atlantic Monthly*, February.

Lemarchand, René (1994) *Burundi: Ethnocide as Discourse and Practice*. Geneva, Washington and Cambridge: UNRISD/Woodrow Wilson Center Press/Cambridge University Press.

Loewenson, Rene and Munhamo Chisvo (1997) 'Social development in Zimbabwe', in S. Mehrota and R. Jolly (1997).

Mair, Stefan (1996) 'Africa between structural adjustment, democratisation and state disintegration', *Aussen Politik*, 47(2).

Meagher, Kate and Mohammed-Bello Yunusa (1996) *Passing the Buck: Structural Adjustment and the Nigerian Urban Informal Sector*, Discussion Paper No. 75. Geneva: UNRISD.

Mehrota, Santosh and Richard Jolly (eds) (1997) *Development with a Human Face: Experiences in Social Achievement and Economic Growth*. New York: UNICEF.

Mkandawire, Thandika (1991) 'Crisis and adjustment in Sub-Saharan Africa', in Dharam Ghai (ed.), *The IMF and the South: The Social Impact of Crisis and Adjustment*. London, Geneva and Kingston: Zed Books/UNRISD/University of the West Indies.

Mkandawire, Thandika (1994) 'Adjustment, political conditionality and democratisation in Africa', in Cornia and Helleiner (eds) (1994).

Morrisson, Christian *et al.* (1994) 'Adjustment programmes and politico-economic interactions in developing countries: lessons from an empirical analysis of Africa in the 1980s', in Cornia and Helleiner (eds) (1994).

Mustapha, Abdul Raufo (1991) *Structural Adjustment and Multiple Modes of Social Livelihood in Nigeria*, Discussion Paper No. 26. Geneva: UNRISD.

Ndegwa, Philip (1986) *The African Challenge: In Search of Appropriate Development Strategies*. Nairobi: Heinemann.

Ndegwa, Philip (1989) *The Catalytic Role of the World Bank in the Development Process*, mimeo. Nairobi.

Ndgewa, Philip and Reginald Green (1994) *Africa to 2000 and Beyond: Imperative Political and Economic Agenda*. Nairobi: East African Educational Publishers.

Nnoli, Okwudiba (1995) *Ethnicity and Development in Nigeria*. Geneva, Warwick and London: UNRISD/Centre for Research in Ethnic Relations, University of Warwick/Avebury.

Organization for Economic Co-operation and Development (1985) *Crisis and Recovery in Sub-Saharan Africa*. Paris: OECD Development Centre.

Organization of African Unity (1980) *The Lagos Plan of Action for the Economic Development of Africa: 1980–2000*. Addis Ababa: OAU.

Organization of African Unity (1985) *Africa's Priority Programme for Economic Recovery, 1986–90*. Addis Ababa: OAU.

Oshikoya, Temitope (1994) 'Macroeconomic determinants of domestic private investment in Africa: an empirical analysis', *Economic Development and Cultural Change*, 42(3).

Ravenhill, J. (ed.) (1986) *Africa in Economic Crisis*. London: Macmillan.

Rothchild, D. and N. Chazan (eds) (1988) *The Precarious Balance: State and Society in Africa*. Boulder, CO: Westview Press.

Sandbrook, Richard (1985) *The Politics of Africa's Economic Stagnation*. Cambridge: Cambridge University Press.

Stavenhagen, Rodolfo (1996) *Ethnic Conflict and the Nation State*. Geneva and London: UNRISD/Macmillan.

Stewart, F., S. Lall and S. Wangwe (eds) (1992) *Alternative Development Strategies in Sub-Saharan Africa*. London: Macmillan.

UNESCO (various years) *World Education Report*. Paris: UNESCO.

UNFPA (various years) *State of the World Population.* New York: UNFPA.

UNICEF (various years) *State of the World's Children.* New York: Oxford University Press.

UNHCR (1995) *The State of the World's Refugees: In Search of Solutions.* Oxford: Oxford University Press.

UNHCR (1997) *The State of the World's Refugees: A Humanitarian Agenda.* Oxford: Oxford University Press.

United Nations (1995) *Priority Africa: Summary of the work of the panel of high-level personalities on African development.* New York: UN.

United Nations (1996) *The United Nations System-wide Special Initiative on Africa.* New York: UN.

WHO (various years) *World Health Report.* Geneva: World Health Organization.

World Bank (various years) *World Development Report.* New York: Oxford University Press.

World Bank (1981) *Accelerated Development in Sub-Saharan Africa.* Washington, DC: World Bank.

World Bank (1989) *Sub-Saharan Africa: From Crisis to Sustainable Growth – A Long-term Perspective Study.* Washington, DC: World Bank.

World Bank (1994) *Adjustment in Africa: Reforms, Results, and Road Ahead.* New York: Oxford University Press.

Part I

Human Development, Social Progress and Environmental Sustainability

2

Health Status and Policy in Sub-Saharan Africa: A Long-term Perspective

Giovanni Andrea Cornia and Germano Mwabu[1]

Abstract

This paper discusses the main changes in infant, child and maternal mortality that have occurred over 1960–95 in Sub-Saharan Africa and analyses the main factors responsible for the observed shifts in these health trends. To do so, the paper surveys the major mortality models discussed in the literature and appraises their applicability to the Sub-Saharan African situation. Pooled cross-section and time series data from 40 African countries, each with a population of over one million people, are then used to estimate explanatory models of infant, under-five and maternal mortality, and of female life expectancy at birth.

After controlling for the time trend, we find that the main determinants of child health status in Africa are real average per capita household income, female literacy rate, nutritional status, safe water supply, immunization coverage and broad accessibility to health services. All these factors are statistically significant, though their importance varies according to the population group considered. For instance, while significant, income per capita does not appear to be – as is often argued – the most important determinant of health status. Similarly, and somewhat in contradiction with the received theory, female literacy appears to have an impact on infant and child mortality comparable to that of income per capita and access to health care. As expected, immunization has a greater impact on child and maternal mortality than on infant mortality. Calorie supply has a particularly strong impact on under-five mortality but not on infant mortality. Also, maternal mortality falls significantly with the availability of safe water and with increases in vaccinations against neonatal tetanus.

The paper also provides evidence that over the period 1960–95 the trend in the health status of the African child and female population was not stable, and that a negative break in the trend occurred over the period 1980–95. Specifically, there was a significant upward shift in all mortality trends analysed over this period, while the trend for female life expectancy shifted downward. We interpret this finding as the effect of the adverse changes (falling incomes per capita, declining health coverage and spread of conflicts and new diseases) which affected most of Africa in the 1980s and early 1990s. Further, we find that there was a change in the structural relationship between per capita income and health status indicators during the period 1980–95. Over that period, a given increase in per capita income was associated with a greater decline in infant, child and maternal mortality than in the previous two decades. We interpret this result as a manifestation of better use of resources in spite of or, rather, because of the increased economic hardships of that period.

Our findings reveal the complexity of the evolution of health status since independence. The average health outcome for the entire study period (1960–95) is the result of the shifts and breaks in the mortality trend over that time span. It is important therefore to understand the factors responsible for such shifts and breaks in order to effectively use public policy to influence the future course of health status in Africa. Previous economic investigations of mortality trends (see, for example, Musgrove, 1987; Anand and Chen, 1996) have associated a fall in mortality during periods of economic crisis with the delayed effects of past investments in health care infrastructure. While this might be true also for Africa, it appears that a more efficient use of public health resources (for instance for child immunization) can lead to a fall in mortality even during a recession. Finally, by providing empirical evidence regarding the relative importance of different policy interventions such as general health coverage, immunization, provision of water supply, female education and poverty alleviation, the paper can help national and international policy-makers in the selection of the most efficient mix of policy interventions.

Apart from providing a framework for analysing the linkages between the evolution of health status and public policy, the paper takes a broader view of mortality determinants. We consider, for instance, the effects of ethnic conflicts on mortality. As one would expect, mortality in Africa is positively correlated with ethnic conflicts; we have however been unable to find statistical significance for the association. The finding is nonetheless interesting from a policy perspective.

The paper ends by providing tentative suggestions on how policy making can help improve health status in Sub-Saharan Africa in the years ahead. The main focus here is on health sector policies, particularly expenditure and pricing policies. The paper argues that policies should enhance access to publicly guaranteed basic health services to all of the population by a multiplicity of providers regulated by public authorities. In addition, the paper emphasizes the importance of acting on factors outside the health sector: as conflict prevention and anti-poverty programmes have been found to influence mortality in an important way, policy makers in health ministries need to consider them in formulating overall health care strategies.

1. Introduction

Over the past two decades, growing evidence has emerged on the growth and distributive effects of health care, nutrition and fresh water supply, and on the rationality of investing in human resources to promote development in low-income economies, and in Sub-Saharan Africa in particular. By now, it is well demonstrated that appropriate health and nutritional interventions have a large impact on the productivity of low-income workers. More important, it is now clear that the provision of simple health care at an early age sharply reduces child and overall mortality and overall health outlays over the life cycle. Despite this mounting evidence, over the last two decades investment in human development in most Sub-Saharan African countries has been modest or has declined. The first half of the 1980s was characterized by an acute recession followed by a decade of stagnation, spreading civil unrest and ethnic conflict, giving rise to a sharp increase in the number of refugees and internally displaced people living in extremely difficult situations, and the diffusion of AIDS and other non-curable viral diseases such as ebola.

The 1980s also witnessed considerable changes concerning the financing and provision of public health services. The advent of structural adjustment entailed in most cases a reduction in public spending. With sharp falls in tax revenues, it was argued, African governments could no longer afford to provide health care free of charge. Governments were thus to encourage the private sector and make households bear a greater share of the cost of publicly provided social services. At the same time, the 1980s witnessed substantial efforts to expand selective health interventions (such as child immunization and oral rehydration therapy) which – despite their modest cost – can have a potentially large life-saving effect.

In a situation dominated by a severe fiscal crisis, little thought was given to protecting the provision of basic health care for all; neither was sufficient attention paid to the rationalization and better use of existing resources, or to the mobilization of additional revenue through traditional and/or presumptive taxation (Taube and Tadesse, 1996). During this period, public policy abandoned the key public finance principles concerning 'market failures' (typical of cases where externalities, natural monopolies, merit goods and asymmetric information dominate) which had inspired the public provision of health services until then. While no doubt some 'government failures' were such as to demand a redefinition of health care provision, this was certainly not the general case.

The relative health impact of these different trends – falling household incomes per capita and public health and education expenditures; increasing recourse to user fees and private provision; greater emphasis on low-cost, high-efficiency health interventions; erosion of female literacy; increasing ethnic instability and spread of new diseases – has not been assessed so far in a model attempting to account simultaneously for all these factors.

While there is a general recognition of the large potential impact of each of the sets of factors mentioned above, precise changes in health status for most of Sub-Saharan Africa are poorly documented; the establishment of precise causal linkages between these factors and changes in health status remains controversial; interpretation of the relative importance of the conditioning factors is not clearly established; and the policy approaches proposed to improve the present situation vary considerably.

The paper is organized into five sections following this introduction. In section 2, we present and discuss trends in health status in Sub-Saharan Africa over the period 1960–95. Section 3 critically reviews the literature on mortality models, and is followed by an exposition in section 4 of an eclectic model of mortality suitable for Sub-Saharan Africa. In section 5, we present and discuss analytical results obtained from the estimation of the model via a generalized least squares technique for panel data. These results concern effects of socio-economic and public health variables on mortality and life expectancy at birth; the effects of the time trend discussed early in section 2. Finally, we conclude in section 6 with tentative recommendations for better health in Africa.

2.   Trends in health status in Africa

Long-term changes in infant and under-five mortality rates: a sustained 1960–80 improvement, followed by a long stagnation

At independence, most Sub-Saharan countries inherited weak and dualistic health care structures – which were almost perfect mirror images of the domestic economies, with the traditional and modern sectors coexisting side by side. Modern health services were understaffed, distorted and located mainly in urban areas; in consequence, the bulk of the population, which resided in rural areas, relied on traditional medicine to meet basic health needs. Apart from some vertical disease eradication programmes, broad-based public health efforts were insignificant. Curative care was equally underdeveloped. Except for four or five countries, the average number of people per doctor varied between 12,000 and 100,000 (Burkina Faso), compared to a South Asian average of 6,000 (World Bank, 1989). As a result, mortality rates – which were particularly high among children under five – were comparatively higher than those of countries with similar levels of income per capita, and were mainly caused by communicable and waterborne diseases such as respiratory infections, diarrhoea, tuberculosis and measles.

By any standard, between the early 1960s and the early 1980s, most Sub-Saharan countries realized substantial advances in extending health care coverage. Large-scale campaigns were implemented to reduce the incidence of infectious diseases and training for health workers was upgraded in many countries. In contrast, progress in expanding access to potable water in rural areas was more limited, and by 1980 only 33 per cent of the population was covered. Vertical campaigns against infectious diseases were probably the main cause for the fall in IMR (infant mortality rate) and U5MR (under-five mortality rate) in Africa over the period 1960–80 (Table 2.1 and Figures 2.1–2.3). With an average linear decline of 2.9 points per thousand per year, progress in reducing infant mortality rate was faster than that achieved in South Asia (2.2 points a year), but slower than that realized in East Asia and China and the Arab countries (3.8 and 3.4 points a year), despite the lower initial rates of these two regions (Cornia, 1990).

These average region-wide improvements in mortality rates conceal important variations in both levels and rates of improvements over time across the main subregions of Sub-Saharan Africa (Tables 2.1 and 2.2 and Figures 2.1 and 2.2). For instance, infant, under-five and maternal mortality rates have consistently

Table 2.1 Average yearly rate of decline in under-five mortality and infant mortality for Sub-Saharan Africa, 1960–95

	Average yearly decline in U5MR				Average yearly decline in IMR			
	1960–70	1970–80	1980–90	1990–95	1960–70	1970–80	1980–90	1990–95
Angola	-4.4	-4.0	3.6	-1.0	-2.9	-2.4	-1.8	-0.6
Benin	-5.8	-7.6	-2.6	-1.6	-3.6	-4.4	-1.5	-0.8
Botswana	-3.1	-4.5	-3.2	-2.0	-1.9	-2.9	-2.2	-1.2
Burkina Faso	-4.3	-2.9	-5.2	-6.0	-2.1	-2.7	-3.0	-3.8
Burundi	-2.7	-3.5	-1.3	-0.8	-1.6	-1.9	-0.7	-0.6
Cameroon	-5.0	-4.1	-4.8	-3.8	-2.9	-2.2	-2.6	-2.6
Central African Rep.	-10.5	-5.8	-1.2	-0.6	-5.2	-2.6	-0.5	-1.6
Chad	-7.3	-4.6	-3.8	-3.2	-4.6	-2.7	-2.0	-1.6
Congo	-6.0	-3.5	-1.5	-0.4	-4.3	-1.2	-0.5	-0.4
Côte d'Ivoire	-6.0	-7.0	-2.0	-0.0	-3.5	-5.0	-1.8	-0.4
Eritrea	-2.4	-1.0	-4.4	-4.2	-1.6	-0.5	-2.7	-2.6
Ethiopia	-2.4	-1.0	-4.4	-4.2	-1.6	-0.5	-2.7	-2.6
Gabon	-5.5	-3.8	-3.0	-3.2	-3.1	-2.3	-1.8	-2.0
Gambia	-5.3	-7.2	-11.0	-6.0	-2.7	-3.3	-5.8	-3.0
Ghana	-2.6	-3.2	-2.0	-1.0	-1.4	-2.0	-1.2	-0.6
Guinea	-2.8	-3.3	-3.8	-3.8	-2.1	-2.0	-2.2	-2.4
Guinea-Bissau	-2.0	-2.6	-4.4	-3.8	-1.4	-1.6	-2.4	-2.4
Kenya	-4.5	-4.5	-2.2	-0.0	-2.3	-2.5	-1.0	-0.2
Lesotho	-1.3	-2.2	-2.0	-1.6	-1.2	-1.0	-1.3	-1.0
Liberia	-2.5	-2.8	-1.6	-0.6	-1.6	-1.9	-1.0	-0.6
Madagascar	-7.9	-6.9	-5.2	-0.0	-3.5	-4.4	-4.0	-0.0
Malawi	-2.2	-5.3	-6.0	-2.2	-1.2	-2.4	-2.4	-1.6
Mali	-10.0	-10.0	-5.0	-5.0	-6.0	-5.2	-2.3	-2.6
Mauritania	-2.9	-4.3	-3.6	-3.6	-2.4	-2.4	-2.1	-2.0
Mauritius	-0.2	-4.0	-1.6	-0.6	-0.1	-2.7	-1.2	-0.6
Mozambique	-0.1	-0.1	-3.0	-6.0	-0.0	-0.0	-1.3	-2.8
Namibia	-5.1	-4.1	-3.0	-1.2	-2.5	-2.0	-1.9	-0.8

Table 2.1 (Contd.)

	Average yearly decline in U5MR				Average yearly decline in IMR			
	1960–70	1970–80	1980–90	1990–95	1960–70	1970–80	1980–90	1990–95
Niger	-0.0	-0.0	-0.0	-0.0	-0.0	-0.0	-0.0	-0.0
Nigeria	-0.4	-0.4	-0.5	-0.0	-0.2	-0.3	-0.3	-0.0
Rwanda	-1.9	-1.2	-7.2	-2.2	-1.0	-0.6	-4.6	-1.0
Senegal	-2.1	-6.1	-7.1	-3.4	-1.0	-3.5	-3.8	-1.6
Sierra Leone	-4.0	-4.4	-1.7	-0.0	-2.1	-2.5	-0.9	-0.0
Somalia	-2.6	-2.2	-3.1	-0.8	-1.6	-1.3	-1.9	-0.4
South Africa	-1.8	-1.7	-1.8	-1.2	-0.9	-1.2	-1.3	-0.8
Tanzania	-2.6	-4.3	-2.0	-0.0	-1.4	-2.3	-1.0	-0.0
Togo	-4.9	-4.0	-3.2	-3.0	-2.7	-2.2	-1.8	-1.6
Uganda	-3.9	-0.5	-1.5	-4.0	-2.3	-0.2	-0.8	-2.0
Zaire	-5.7	-3.5	-0.3	-0.0	-2.8	-1.7	-0.2	-0.0
Zambia	-4.0	-2.0	-3.7	-1.2	-2.7	-1.7	-1.9	-0.8
Zimbabwe	-2.7	-2.9	-4.5	-1.2	-1.2	-1.6	-2.8	-0.6
Sub-Saharan average	-3.69	-3.62	-2.94	-2.03	-2.13	-2.07	-1.7	-1.22

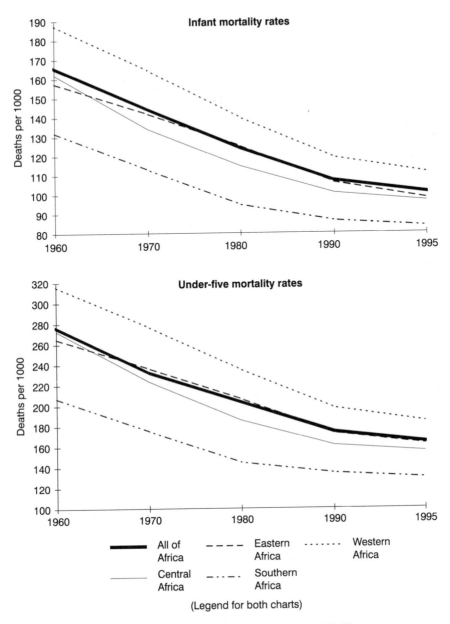

Figure 2.1 Trends in infant and under-five mortality in Africa, 1960–95

remained the lowest in Southern Africa (South Africa, Botswana, Zimbabwe, Zambia, Angola, etc.). This region has also maintained the highest life expectancy at birth in Africa (Figure 2.3). In contrast, all three mortality rates have remained the highest in West Africa (Nigeria, Sierra Leone, Liberia, Ghana, Mali, Burkina Faso,

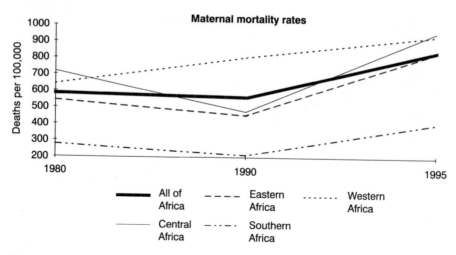

Figure 2.2   Trends in maternal mortality in Africa, 1980–95

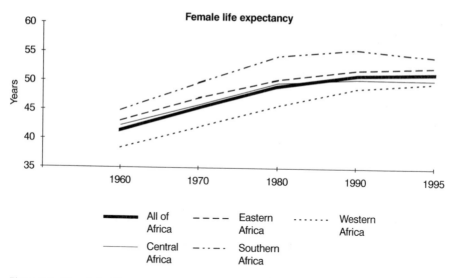

Figure 2.3   Trends in life expectancy in Africa, 1960–95

Senegal, Gambia, etc.), and this region has also the lowest female life expectancy (Figure 2.3).

The above observations are confirmed by the regression results presented in Tables 2.2 and 2.3. The results come from estimation of an *eclectic* model of health status determination that is particularly applicable to Sub-Saharan Africa during the period 1960–95. The model, the estimation methodology and data are described in section 4. The analytical results in Table 2.2 focus on the effects of

Table 2.2 The regression of health status on time trend controlling for regional-specific factors, 1960–95

Explanatory variables	Health Status Indicators			
	Log of infant mortality	Log of under-five mortality	Log of maternal mortality	Log of female life expectancy
Constant term	5.257	5.793	5.092	3.661
	(65.76)	(62.04)	(11.45)	(129.72)
Log of the time trend	−.346	−.372	.972	.141
	(20.16)	(19.15)	(3.07)	(19.32)
Eastern Africa dummy	−.184	−.218	−.349	.082
	(1.46)	(1.48)	(1.37)	(1.86)
Central Africa dummy	−.155	−.178	−.072	.061
	(1.09)	(1.07)	(.26)	(1.23)
Southern Africa dummy	−.382	−.487	−.883	.141
	(2.69)	(2.94)	(2.83)	(2.84)
Overall R-squared	.357	.347	.215	.403
Sample size	200	200	86	200

Notes: West Africa is excluded to avoid linear dependence. Absolute T-values are in parentheses below the coefficients. The estimation procedure used is the Generalized Least Squares with Random Effects.

Table 2.3 Tests for structural breaks in time trends of the health status indicators

Variables	Heath status indicators			
	Log of infant mortality	Log of under-five mortality	Log of maternal mortality	Log of female life expectancy
Constant term	6.029	6.721	6.906	3.609
	(30.52)	(30.00)	(10.89)	(30.37)
Log of the time trend	−.401	−.424	1.387	.015
	(6.39)	(6.29)	(4.33)	(.35)
Log of per capita income	−.117	−.144	−.256	.005
	(2.99)	(3.01)	(2.83)	(.24)
Log of adult female literacy rate	−.058	−.069	−.315	.065
	(2.37)	(2.61)	(2.45)	(5.72)
Period dummy (= 1 for the period 1980–95 and zero for 1960–70s)	.514	.579		−.203
	(1.97)	(1.94)		(2.00)
Log of per capita income times the period dummy	−.079	−.088		.037
	(1.76)	(1.72)		(2.02)
Chi-square test-statistic	231.1	216.5	31.6	246.3
	[p-value = .000]	[p-value = .000]	[p-value = .000]	[p-value = .000]
Sample size	133	133	81	133

Note: Absolute T-values in parentheses under the coefficients.
Source: Authors' calculations.

the time trend on health status indicators (infant/under-five mortality, maternal mortality and female life expectancy) accounting also for regional-specific effects. Table 2.3 shows the structural changes in these indicators over the period analysed.

The improvement in African health over the period 1960–95 (Table 2.1) is confirmed by the values and significance of the coefficients in Table 2.2 which underscore the negative association between the time trend over 1960–95 and infant and under-five mortality, as well as the positive trend in female life expectancy. These data also stress, however, the positive correlation between the time trend and maternal mortality (both relationships are illustrated graphically in Figures 2.1 through 2.3).

Moreover, in line with the regional variations in health status already noted, the estimation results in Table 2.2 show that the regional dummy variables (which alter the subregion specific intercept) for infant, under-five and maternal mortality rates have the highest negative values for Southern Africa in relation to Western Africa (the comparison subregion that we have omitted from the regression to avoid the well known dummy variable trap). It can be seen from the results that life expectancy is consistently higher in Southern Africa as indicated by the higher positive value and statistically significant coefficient of the Southern Africa dummy.

The rapid descent in the mortality rates of most age groups recorded over 1960–80 was followed by a major slow-down over the 1980–95 period. During this time span, the average yearly rate of decline in infant and under-five mortality rates for many countries fell below one point a year (Table 2.1), a rate that was substantially lower than the rate recorded over the previous two decades, and which was much smaller than that normally observed in developing countries with infant and under-five death rates of around 100 and 180 per thousand. The slow-down was particularly acute during the first half of the 1990s, a period during which in many Sub-Saharan countries infant mortality rates stopped declining (Zaire, Sierra Leone, Niger, Nigeria, Madagascar and Tanzania) or marked an increase (Angola and Zambia). The slow-down in the improvement of African health over the period 1980–95 is also clearly borne out in Figures 2.1 through 2.3. While the rate of the decline in infant and child mortality flattened around this period, maternal mortality actually rose in Central and Eastern Africa.

With few exceptions, during the last fifteen years the health situation has become increasingly complicated by the re-emergence of diseases which were thought to have been eradicated (smallpox), the spread of old ones (cholera and yellow fever) to new areas, the development of drug-resistant varieties (pneumonia, malaria and gonorrhoea) and the spread of new health risks such as AIDS. The uniqueness of the recent African health crisis is underscored by the much more favourable health developments which have occurred in developing regions facing similar economic and political difficulties. For instance, in the 1980s, most of Latin America experienced a significant decline in incomes and health expenditure per capita. In addition, it presented a lower incidence of infectious and respiratory diseases (which can be prevented at relatively low cost) than Africa and a higher incidence of costly-to-treat diseases such as cancer and heart ailments (UNICEF–ICDC, 1994). Yet, the main indicators of maternal and child health continued to improve during this period. Possible explanations for the divergence between the Latin American and African health trends would centre around the initial fragility and poor coverage of the health care systems in Africa (in part due to the greater share of the rural population there); the faster expansion of cost-effective child-survival interventions in Latin America; the lesser political instability; and the more limited effect of AIDS in this region. Furthermore, in the 1980s, Latin America's strong network of non-governmental organizations was able to replace, if only in part, a weakened public health sector, a fact less evident in Sub-Saharan Africa (ibid.).

Information about the socio-economic profile of the African population groups affected by the stagnation in health status over the last fifteen years is extremely scant. Hereafter we note the very limited material available to us. Past studies on Africa and elsewhere have documented the negative relation between child and maternal mortality risk and level of maternal education, controlling for income and other relevant variables (Caldwell, 1979). The recent stagnation or increase in mortality is therefore likely to have affected more than proportionately the infants and the children of the poor and the less educated strata of the population. Some direct evidence confirms this hypothesis (Gertler and van der Gaag, 1990), especially in rural areas – which, in addition, have been disproportionately affected by the cutbacks in the public provision of health services observed over the 1980s and early 1990s – and among the people living in incomplete families. In much of Sub-Saharan Africa, as in most other parts of the world (Becker, 1991), marriage is an important social event requiring considerable expenditures for the ceremony, gifts to the parents of the groom or the bride, to the extended family members etc. The abrupt impoverishment in the 1980s of many families in Sub-Saharan Africa must have contributed to the postponement in marriages and possibly to an increase in incomplete families – with adverse effects on health.

It is also likely that migrant and refugee populations have suffered a greater proportional decline in health status than have other populations, at least since the mid-1980s. Past analyses confirm that migrants face greater mortality risks than people who remain in their community. The last ten years have witnessed in Sub-Saharan Africa a sharp increase in the number of distress migrants, international refugees, internally displaced people, people repatriating to the country of ethnic origin and asylum seekers (see sections 3 and 4). For most of these groups, distress migration or displacement have entailed considerable hardship, a difficult redefinition of survival strategies, and – as the result of all this – impoverishment, hunger, greater stress and heightened susceptibility to infection and disease. In an increasing number of countries of Sub-Saharan Africa, mortality has been pushed upwards (though no one knows by exactly how much) by the spread of war and civil unrest.

While the slow-down and stagnation in health status due to 'traditional causes of death' seem to have affected 'the traditional vulnerable groups' (children, delivering mothers, the elderly, people in remote rural areas, the poor, etc.), there is scattered evidence that the mortality due to the 'new causes of death' (such as AIDS and ethnic or political conflicts) have affected also the better educated, the urban middle class in the reproductive age group, males in the combat age, children born to parents affected by HIV, and people with considerable spatial mobility.

Testing for structural break in the long-term mortality trend

Hereafter we test formally whether the infant and the under-five mortality trends observed over the 1960–80 period could predict accurately the changes recorded over the subsequent fifteen years. To test this hypothesis, and to estimate the causal models in section 5, we use data from 40 African countries with a population of over one million people. For all of them we compiled data on infant and under-five mortality rates, maternal mortality, female life expectancy, per capita income, female literacy rates, and other relevant variables such as immunization coverage and health service access indicators. The time series are for the years 1960, 1970, 1980, 1990 and 1995. All data come from UNICEF (1995 and 1997), UNDP (1995 and 1997), World Bank (1983, 1993 and 1997) and IMF (1990).

The aim of the test presented below is to ascertain whether negative events (of whatever nature, but particularly the economic recessions and shocks such as ethnic conflicts) have caused a break-in-trends during the 1980s and 1990s. The information as to whether or not there was a structural break in mortality and longevity over 1980–95 is crucial for credible predictions of future health status and for the identification of the causes of the premature slow-down in mortality rates.

The test of the break in the time trend is carried out by including in a long-term causal model of infant, child and maternal mortality, and in that of female life expectancy, dummy variables for the years 1980–95. A positive and statistically significant value for the dummy variable in the first three cases – and a negative one for the fourth – would signal a clear deterioration in the rate of health improvement over the recent period. The model thus includes as explanatory variables income per capita, female literacy, the time trend (which captures information on all other past causal variables) and the 1980–95 dummy variable. The estimation is carried out in a log-log form using the estimation technique of the generalized least squares (with random effects) for panel data (Greene, 1993).

The results of the test (Table 2.3) show that the coefficients of the 1980–95 dummy across all specifications are positive and significant at about the 5 per cent level. The results lead us to reject the hypothesis of a *stable* mortality trend over the period 1960–95, and to accept the hypothesis that there was an upward shift in all mortality curves during the period 1980–95. Correspondingly, there was a downward shift in female life expectancy, as is evident from the negative sign of the coefficient for the 1980–95 dummy. The chief suspects for these unfavourable shifts are the adoption of inappropriate domestic policies or wrong implementation of correct ones (especially in the field of health expenditure and financing), emergence of new diseases such as AIDS, and intensification of ethnic conflicts due to frailty of domestic economies.

The regression results in Table 2.3 show also that there were changes in the slopes of these indicators. The coefficient on the interaction term (the 1980–95 time dummy multiplied by income per capita) is negative for the infant and child mortality equations and – consistent with this – it is positive for the life expectation equation. This finding indicates that for a given increase in per capita income over the period 1980–95, the decline in child mortality was greater than the decline brought about by the same increase in income during the 1960s and 1970s. That is, the available family resources were being used more efficiently during the period 1980–95 than in the period spanning the preceding two decades. These results provide important lessons for the design of health policies in Africa over the next several decades.

3. Mortality models: applicability to Sub-Saharan Africa

In this section, we discuss first the main mortality models in the literature and their applicability to the Sub-Saharan case. We would like to emphasize that we focus on *long-term theories of mortality*, as well as on *theories of short-term mortality crises*.

Mortality models focusing on famine, conflicts, and displacements

Large and sudden increases in mortality – or major deviations from its trend – have often been caused by wars, famines, major epidemics, and large-scale civil unrest. For example, three million people were wiped out during the Great Bengal Famine of 1943–7, while considerable mortality rises were observed in the 1980s in the Wollo province, other famine-stricken parts of Ethiopia (Sen, 1981), and in the Sudan. During the Bangladesh war of 1971 and severe famine of 1974–5, death rates in Matlab Thana increased 35 per cent. The increase was particularly pronounced for infants and children, and was mainly caused by a surge in deaths due to nutrition-related and infectious diseases (Murray and Chen, 1993). On the occasion of the collapse of food production and forced peasant migrations following the collectivization of land in Russia and Ukraine in 1930–3, the crude death rate rose by 49 and 260 per cent respectively. Similarly, during the Dutch Famine of 1944–5, life expectancy at birth dropped by 8 years for men, and by 4.6 for women. Mortality due to hunger was most common among the very young and the very old (Lumey and Van Poppel, 1994).

Over the last decade, Sub-Saharan Africa has also witnessed a sharp increase in wars, domestic conflicts and ethnic struggles, all factors that have led to an increase in deaths due to violent causes, starvation and infectious diseases (see Nafziger, 1996; and Tables 2.4–2.5). However, while in typical famine–war models the sudden peaking of death rates was consistently followed by its return to pre-crisis levels in just 1–2 years, it is unclear whether this has been the case in Sub-Saharan Africa – where severe food shortages have recurred, conflicts have become endemic, and social problems due to displacement of refugees and distress migration have taken a long time to resolve.

Thus, short-term mortality models focusing on famines and wars offer interesting insights for the interpretation of the mortality changes observed in Sub-Saharan

Africa during the last fifteen years. In a few cases, the recent increases in mortality in Africa refer to contextual situations (large social dislocations), categories of population groups affected (the old, the very young and the biologically vulnerable) similar to those mentioned in the famine literature; and as noted in this literature, the rise in death rates has been commonly caused by starvation, undernutrition, exhaustion, endemic diseases and epidemics. It is unclear, however, if the pattern of quick 'large increase/large decrease' in mortality rates can be observed in Sub-Saharan Africa, where many of these phenomena have often become endemic.

Epidemics and pandemics models

In this class of mortality models (such as those used to explain the impact of the plague in Europe of the Middle Ages), very large mortality increases occurring in just a few years (depending on the mechanisms of diffusion of the contagion) are followed, a few decades later, by a gradual and endogenous recovery in the population level and structure. Only in a few cases – as on the occasion of the black plague in Central Europe during the fifteenth century – did such epidemics lead to a lasting and significant decline in population size.

Except for a few acute, but circumscribed, viral infections that quickly impose their deadly toll on the populations, during the last fifteen years or so Sub-Saharan Africa seems to have avoided major epidemics (typhus, cholera, smallpox, etc.) which tend to cause large peaks in mortality rates. However, since the mid-1980s (and possibly before), the African countries have been affected by the gradual spread of Acquired Immune Deficiency Syndrome (AIDS), a deadly pandemic. While other new infectious diseases (hepatitis C and D, ebola and other haemorrhage fevers) have emerged, their mortality impact seems, so far, to be modest. Because of the long period of incubation and slow speed of contagion, AIDS has probably produced an important but gradual upward effect on mortality rates. In a sense, AIDS is taking on the characteristics of a pandemic – rather than an epidemic – which is, *ceteris paribus*, likely to produce a clear but gradual and permanent uplift of the mortality curve.

Recession and growth models

This class of models explains short- and medium-term changes in health status on the basis of economic growth or recession and adjustment policies. Studies in this class of models utilize ideas derived from the Mosley–Chen model (1984), which synthesizes demographic, epidemiological and economic variables into a coherent framework, and which reflects the epidemiological and mortality patterns prevailing in low-income countries. This model is thus particularly appropriate for the conditions prevailing in Sub-Saharan Africa. In the model, health status is proxied by infant/child mortality (a key element of the overall mortality in poor nations), and the main *immediate* causes of death are infectious, parasitic, nutritional and environment-related diseases. The main *underlying* determinants of mortality are maternal factors (including maternal education and health), food intake, environmental conditions (pollution, but also values), personal behaviour, and household disease control measures.

Many of the mortality determinants in this model are *slow-moving stock variables* (female education, physical infrastructure, environmental conditions), though most analyses focus on *fast-changing flow variables* (household incomes, public health expenditure and price of health care). For instance, Cornia *et al.* (1987) analyse the linkages between adjustment policies and child health through changes in food prices and subsidies, family incomes, availability of health services, changes in the relative prices of the goods consumed by the poor, and time use and literacy rates of mothers. This family of models underscores the fact that health status can be influenced by economic factors and not only by changes in health sector variables; that *stock effects* can shelter people's health even in the presence of sudden and large economic changes; and that there are strong non-linearities and threshold effects in the relationship between economic growth or decline and health status of the population (Benefo and Schultz, 1996; Mwabu, 1996; Pritchett and Summers, 1996). With their emphasis on economic factors – which have shown adverse variations over the last fifteen years – these models are relevant to the analysis of long-term mortality changes in Sub-Saharan Africa.

Models emphasizing changes in access to health care

Even in periods of severe recession and fiscal crisis, the mortality impact of falling incomes and health expenditures and rising stress can be strongly mitigated by the adoption of new health technologies, as shown by the introduction of antibiotics in the USA in the early 1930s, or the diffusion of vaccinations and other basic health measures in the 1980s in many developing countries. Access to health care can be also influenced by health sector policy reforms which have been adopted widely in Sub-Saharan Africa during the last fifteen years, though with uncertain effects. These reforms have pivoted around measures aimed at increasing the efficiency of health expenditure (as, for example, through the introduction of the essential drugs programme), the introduction of user fees, the decentralization of service provision and the reliance on non-governmental organizations for health service delivery. Controversy remains, however, regarding the effects of these reforms on health care quality and access (Mwabu *et al.*, 1995).

Many argue that community organizations (which are well established in several parts of Sub-Saharan Africa) can effectively replace eroding state bureaucracies in the provision of basic health services. This does not always occur, however (Robinson and White, 1997). While in Latin America in the 1980s the non-governmental organizations were able to replace, if only in part, a weakened public health sector, in the Eastern European countries in transition, the frailty of civil society and a tradition of dependency on the state resulted in a worsening of health status when the public health system contracted (Cornia, 1996).

Another important factor affecting access to health care is the type of political regime in power. Recent social and economic reforms have stressed good governance, usually defined in terms of democratic regimes and multiparty politics (World Bank, 1995, 1997). Yet it has often been argued that widespread access to health care and broadly shared health gains can be achieved in countries with different regimes. However, in the African context, a simple analysis suggests otherwise. For instance, despite its considerably more slender natural resource base, democratic Tanzania did much better than military-ruled and oil-rich Nigeria in improving the health of the population over the period 1960–95. In 1960, under-five mortality rates in Nigeria and Tanzania were 204 and 249 respectively; by 1995, these rates were 191 and 160 for Nigeria and Tanzania respectively (UNICEF, 1995).

Health behaviour models

Models in this class emphasize the role of health knowledge and practices and personal behaviour in health improvements. In the Sub-Saharan context, these models emphasize empowering parents, particularly mothers, in their functions as health agents at the household level. They stress, for instance, the desirable behaviours to be adopted (e.g., washing hands before preparing food and observing other aspects of personal hygiene); knowledge about home-based oral rehydration therapy to treat children affected by diarrhoea (the second cause of death among African infants); and – in the case of sexually transmitted diseases – responsible behaviour and safer sex. In this approach, promotion of health information and changes in personal hygiene are more important long-term determinants of health status than are income, food intake and health expenditure. One could reasonably assume, however, that the availability of health information in Sub-Saharan Africa is strongly correlated with that of outreach health services and female literacy.

Smoking, drinking, lack of physical activity and unbalanced diet (or, in short, 'lifestyles') are also often mentioned as a main cause of ill-health and high mortality in studies falling under this category. For instance, smoking and excessive alcohol consumption are the underlying factors in premature deaths due to various types of cancers and cardiovascular problems. However, the relevance of this last set of considerations to Sub-Saharan Africa appears to be limited. These health behaviour models focus on causes of death and population groups different from those seen in Sub-Saharan Africa. They refer to consumption patterns (e.g., of fats, cigarettes, alcohol, etc.) which are found primarily in parts of urban areas. If anything, dietary intake in Africa has probably been negatively affected by the belt-tightening imposed on most households by the stagnation-recession of the last fifteen years; the decline in food consumption has aggravated nutritional problems due to insufficient – rather than inappropriate – calorie and protein intake for a sizeable share of the population.

Unemployment-stigma models

Mortality studies in industrialized economies do not emphasize as much the causal variables in the models discussed so far but rather stress the effects of rising unemployment and of changes in social roles of people. Loss of employment is not analysed so much in terms of its income effect, but in terms of the loss of the intrinsic value of work, the termination of the social role associated with having a job, and the social stigma associated with joblessness. Most of these analyses conclude that people with unemployment experience, particularly the long-term unemployed, suffer far worse mental conditions and mortality rates than the employed. While, during the last decade and a half, underemployment has risen everywhere in Sub-Saharan Africa, the relevance of stigma models appears limited in a continent where a large part of the population is made up of small farmers, and where urban underemployment has traditionally been high and unstigmatizing. The mortality pattern among adult males due for example to cardiovascular and mental problems (typically associated with the factors just mentioned) is not frequently observed in Africa.

Marginalization and psycho-social stress models

Stress is being increasingly recognized as a key factor in sudden deaths, i.e., deaths due to heart problems, psychosis, violence, ulcers and so on (Cornia, 1996). Mental and physical stress may arise when individuals are forced to face new and unexpected situations for which coping behaviours are unknown, and for which traditional survival strategies are no longer effective. The health effects of such adverse situations are likely to be particularly severe when they are unanticipated, and thus have to be faced without preparedness. Among the unsettling situations emerging recently on a grand scale, particularly in countries in transition, are unemployment, distress migration, civil conflicts, personal insecurity, sudden changes in social hierarchies, and unstable family circumstances. The immediate causes of death associated with stress are cardiovascular, psychosomatic illnesses and stress-induced irrational behaviour leading to accidents, homicide and suicide.

Undoubtedly, many of the drastic social changes just mentioned cropped up in Sub-Saharan Africa in the 1980s, together with a severe recession and harsh economic reforms. The health effects of these adverse social changes were likely compounded by the massive increase in conflicts and ethnic unrest of the same period, and by the weakening – or outright collapse – of health care systems and of national institutions responsible for law and order. While it is likely that a considerable number of violent deaths have been caused by the greater number of conflicts themselves, the extent to which increased stress has contributed to greater mortality in Africa remains unclear.

Summing up: elements for a relevant model for interpreting health changes in Sub-Saharan Africa

The above review allows us to exclude, a priori, a number of potential explanations of the recent stagnation in health conditions in Sub-Saharan Africa. For instance, 'lifestyles' and 'unemployment-stigma' models offer only limited insights to the health situation in Sub-Saharan Africa, as they refer to different contextual situations (reflecting different income levels and social organizations), affect different population groups (the middle aged and the elderly), and reflect different immediate and underlying causal patterns. Also, the 'psycho-social stress' models are only partially applicable to the African case, though there are scattered indications of higher risks of mental problems and stress-related deaths due to suicide and other violent causes in populations facing unexpected crisis situations (involuntary displacement, surging insecurity, acute food scarcity and so on).

An ex-ante interpretation of the changes in health status in Sub-Saharan Africa is thus probably best carried out on the basis of the long-term mortality frameworks (such as the 'recession', 'access to health care' and 'pandemics' models), which emphasize variables such as income per capita, population coverage of basic health services, maternal education (proxied by female literacy) and incidence of deadly viral diseases. The short-term mortality models, such as the 'famine and war models', which emphasize the impacts of quasi-exogenous factors, are also possibly relevant in explaining a few recent peaks in mortality in Sub-Saharan Africa. We combine the key elements from these approaches to construct an eclectic model of health status determination and estimate its parameters using panel data from 40 Sub-Saharan countries. We use the estimation results and a synthesis of the various strands of the literature we have reviewed to recommend policies for improving health status in Africa.

4. An eclectic mortality model for Sub-Saharan Africa

Specification issues

The literature reviewed above and other studies (see e.g., Musgrove, 1987; Pritchett and Summers, 1996; Fogel, 1997; Schultz, 1997) suggest the following eclectic model of child mortality for a low-income region which has been subject to shocks of the kind experienced in Sub-Saharan Africa during the last fifteen years:

$$\text{IMR/U5MR/MMR} = f(\text{PCY, PHC, LIT, SHOCKS, RETI, U})$$

where

IMR/U5MR/MMR	Infant, under-five and maternal mortality rate
PCY	Per capita household income
PHC	Population health coverage indicators
LIT	Literacy rate, especially for females
SHOCKS	Exogenous shocks such as famines, wars, epidemics
RETI	Region- or time-specific factors
U	Disturbance term

The above equation attempts to capture both the short- and the long-term effects on mortality – the effects of famine for example, are short-lived, while those of literacy rates are long-lasting. Four aspects of the model specified above need to be noted. First, since mortality measurement is at the national level, the model is aggregate in nature (see Benefo and Schultz, 1996, for the microeconomic foundations of such a model). Second, infant and under-five mortality rates are assumed to be random events, uncorrelated with the fertility behaviour of parents (Schultz, 1976, 1997; see Eckstein, Schultz and Wolpin, 1985, for an alternative specification assumption). Third, as Pritchett and Summers (1996) note, infant and under-five mortality rates are better measures of health status than is life expectancy because they are less prone to measurement errors and are exogenous to income (children are not part of the labour force), a fact that mitigates the endogeneity problem in the estimation of long-term mortality model. We have nonetheless also estimated an equation for female life expectancy for comparison purposes. The fourth and final issue is that the error term, U, has a component that is country-specific and that could vary or remain constant over time.

The above model was estimated with panel data for the period 1960–95 (see p. 36 for data sources and estimation technique). Before turning to model estimation, we comment in detail on the key explanatory variables.

Famines, war and displacement

Major food shortages, often reaching famine proportions, have been frequently recorded in Sub-Saharan Africa since 1970, particularly over the 1983–5 period and in the early 1990s. At the same time, the ability of national governments and the international community to avert the worst impact of famines has improved substantially, though in some cases this has resulted in increased dependence on foreign support.

The most devastating famines in Africa are those that have affected the Horn of Africa over 1982–5 and again in the early 1990s. Important famines were also recorded in the Sudan and Southern Eastern Africa in 1990–92. Deaths to famines and hunger are not necessarily the result of climate changes or entitlement failures, but are now increasingly being aggravated by civil unrest, which prevents the delivery of humanitarian aid. Hunger has thus been particularly severe in war zones, such as Rwanda, Southern Sudan and Somalia. This explains why improvements in predicting famines have not resulted in parallel improvements in their prevention.

Since the mid-1980s, the number of full-fledged wars in Sub-Saharan Africa has steadily escalated. According to Wallensteen and Sollenberg (1995 and 1996), by 1994 there were no less than thirteen full-fledged wars in the region. The number, however, declined to nine in 1995. The main conflicts affected Angola, Ethiopia (Eritrea and Tigray), Liberia, Mozambique, Rwanda, Somalia, South Africa, Sudan, and Uganda, to which one should add Burundi, Sierra Leone and former Zaire. If a less restrictive definition is adopted, the number of internal or external armed conflicts underway during this period rises by about a third. Most of these conflicts are increasingly due to internal problems (struggle for power, secession, or autonomy) and only few have been fought between states or have witnessed external interventions. Military conflicts increasingly involve non-state actors, such as armed clans and ethnic movements. This exposes civilian populations to greater suffering as battles are fought in their midst. As a result, conflicts have become more of a social and public health problem than an instrument of state politics. However, the measurement of the mortality impact of civil wars is an extremely difficult task. Whatever the problems involved in their measurement, the numbers are considerable (Table 2.4).

The deteriorating health status of the Sub-Saharan African population has also been due to an increase in the number of external and internal displacements which leave growing scores of refugees without adequate access to food, fresh

Table 2.4   Number of war casualties in Sub-Saharan Africa, 1992–4

	Number	The worst year
Rwanda	200–500,000	1994
Angola	100,000	1994
Burundi	100,000	1993
Mozambique	100,000	1992
Liberia	20–50,000	1993
Sudan	6,000	1993
South Africa	3–4,500	1993

Source: IFRCS (1994: 111, Table 16).

Table 2.5   Refugees and internally displaced people (IDPs) in 1995

	Refugees	IDPs	Total	Share
Sudan	448,000	1,700,000	2,148,000	7.6
Rwanda	1,545,000	500,000	2,045,000	25.7
Angola	313,000	1,500,000	1,813,000	16.4
Liberia	725,000	1,000,000	1,725,000	56.7
Sierra Leone	363,000	1,000,000	1,363,000	30.2
Somalia	480,000	300,000	780,000	8.4
Ethiopia	500,000	111,000	611,000	1.1
Mozambique	97,000	500,000	597,000	3.7
Eritrea	325,000	200,000	525,000	14.9
South Africa	10,000	500,000	510,000	1.2

Sources: *World Refugee Survey 1996* (Tables 3 and 4). These data have been supplemented by information from IFRCS (1994: Tables 12 and 14) and UNHRC (1996). The population figures for 1995 have been obtained from WHO (1996, Table A1), cited in Väyrynen (1996).

water and health care – and which deprives them of their coping strategies. Since the late 1970s, the number of external and internal refugees has increased constantly (Väyrynen, 1996). In 1995, there were 5.2 million refugees in Sub-Saharan Africa as a whole, with the biggest group being in Zaire (1.3 million), followed by Tanzania (0.7 million), and Guinea (0.6 million) (World Refugee Survey, 1996:4–5). The number of internally displaced people was even greater (Table 2.5).

The AIDS pandemic

The precise mortality impact of the human immunodeficiency virus (HIV), the virus that causes Acquired Immune Deficiency Syndrome (AIDS) is difficult to ascertain. AIDS killed 0.7 million people in 1993 and the death toll is expected to rise to 1.8 million by the end of the decade (Ainsworth and Over, 1994). Some 60 per cent of the 24 million HIV-infected people live in Sub-Saharan Africa, and an even higher share of the total deaths is estimated to have occurred there (other estimates give comparable but somewhat lower figures; ibid.). While the disease has been shown to be always fatal, its mortality impact over time depends on the lag between HIV infection and development of AIDS. While in the industrialized countries such lag is estimated at about ten years, preliminary evidence would suggest it is somewhat shorter (five to seven years) in Sub-Saharan Africa, because of the lower nutritional standards of the populations affected and the lack of drugs to delay the onset of AIDS. Already now, baseline mortality rates for the population groups affected have doubled or tripled (ibid.).

Unprotected sex between high-income males and low-income single females is the most common vehicle of contagion. HIV then spreads subsequently to spouses, and through pregnancy, to the newborn children. For the moment, HIV and AIDS seem to affect the Sub-Saharan population in a highly differentiated manner. Its incidence is generally higher among the following social groups: in males rather than females of reproductive age, in urban rather than rural populations; in the better-off and better educated, and in special population groups (prostitutes and people with high spatial mobility), in the reproductive-age population rather than among children and the elderly (the phenomenon has however already spread to the child population). The incidence is also generally higher in Eastern than Western Africa. Around 1993, urban HIV prevalence rates among adults in Eastern Africa ranged from 12 per cent in Tanzania to 35 per cent in Rwanda. In West Africa it ranged between 1 per cent in Cameroon and a maximum of 15 per cent in Côte d'Ivoire. Rural prevalence rates were estimated at 20–30 per cent of urban rates, with the exception of Zambia (where mortality rates, including for under-fives, rose drastically in the 1990s), Zimbabwe, Tanzania and Central African Republic – which all exhibit rural rates equal to two thirds of urban rates.

HIV prevalence is highest among the urban well-educated classes. WHO-sponsored surveys for the late 1980s show a positive association between male schooling and number of sexual partners in Central Africa Republic, Côte d'Ivoire, Kenya and Togo. In Rwanda, the rate of infection among women attending prenatal clinics was found to be related to the level of education and income of their partners. Seropositive prevalence among women was twice as high among those who had partners with eight or more years of education as compared with those whose partners had four or fewer years of education. Infection rates correlated also with the level of income and (even more pronouncedly) with the sector of employment. While 9 per cent of the women with a partner working as a farmer were infected, the proportion rose to 38 per cent among those with their husband/partner working in the civil service (Allen *et al.*, 1991, cited in Ainsworth and Over, 1994). Similar results were found in studies conducted in Uganda, Zaire and Zambia.

The health impact of economic stagnation

Over 1980–95, Sub-Saharan Africa has successively experienced a strong recession (1981–4), followed by a moderate recovery, and a long period of weak growth (about 1.5 per cent a year over 1986–95). If population growth is factored in, incomes per capita become – in most cases – slightly to moderately negative,

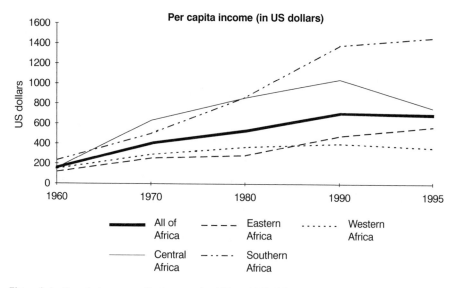

Figure 2.4   Trends in per capita income in Africa, 1960–95

although acceptable growth rates of GDP were achieved in a number of countries, including Mauritius, Ghana, Burkina Faso, Botswana, and Uganda. On average the fall in per capita GDP was more pronounced in Western and Central Africa (Figure 2.4).

With few exceptions, poverty and underemployment have escalated in Sub-Saharan Africa, at times sharply. The limited information available about changes in the distribution of income seems to suggest that the rural–urban income gap has shrunk, while inequality surged within both sectors. Though information about poverty rates and food consumption is scarce, it is plausible to surmise that low income urban dwellers, members of incomplete families and landless farmers have experienced a fall in food intake which has rendered them less resistant to disease. While for the population above, say, the 30th percentile of the distribution of income, a cumulative drop in incomes can be weathered by rationalizing consumption and by adopting other survival mechanisms, these options are not necessarily available to the poorest groups, which may already be well below a minimum subsistence threshold. *Ceteris paribus*, it might thus be expected that the income fall observed during these years has provoked an increase in mortality due to an escalation in the incidence of the 'diseases of poverty'. The negative trends in income per capita and in public expenditure on education and adult literacy have also affected female literacy rates (Figure 2.5). In Southern and Eastern Africa, female literacy rates dropped in the 1980s and recovered only mildly in the 1990s.

Changes in access to health services and population coverage

The last fifteen years have witnessed a number of health policy dilemmas in many Sub-Saharan countries. In response to the fiscal crisis affecting the region in the

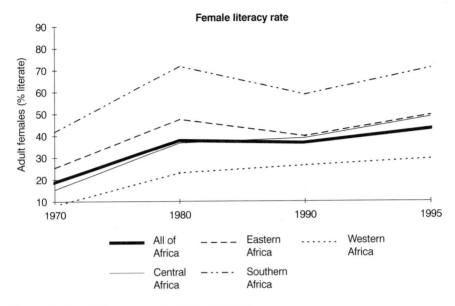

Female literacy rate

Figure 2.5 Female literacy rates in Africa, 1960–95

early 1980s, most governments introduced a series of measures with the intention of achieving one or more of the following objectives: increasing the overall efficiency of the health care system; increasing the volume or the quality of the services rendered; and increasing monetary contributions from service users.

The specific measures implemented to achieve these objectives could be listed in the following order: reallocation of expenditure among different levels of the health care system; introduction of new high-cost and high-efficiency basic health technologies; large cuts in public health expenditure; introduction of user fees and other community-based financing mechanisms; and privatization of government hospitals or parts of these facilities. The focus of previous analyses in this area in Africa has been on the effect of the above measures on service provision, quality and utilization (see e.g., Mwabu *et al.*, 1995; Reddy and Vandemoortele, 1996; Appleton, 1997). Only a few studies have looked at the impact of these measures on health status (Mwabu, 1996). The effects of these measures on health outcomes however are unclear because of the delayed favourable effects of previous policies or because of the offsetting effects of events in other sectors of the economy, or because of the effect of the sharp increase in immunization rates in the 1980s (Figure 2.5). Vaccination coverage against all immunizable diseases rose from 20 to about 50 per cent between 1980 and 1990 for Sub-Saharan Africa as a whole, and concerned all immunizable diseases (Figure 2.6, bottom panel). However, in the 1990s the increase in vaccination rates levelled off and was reversed in Central Africa (Figure 2.6, top panel).

It should be noted, finally, that the negative changes in health status observed in some Sub-Saharan African countries may not have only been due to the

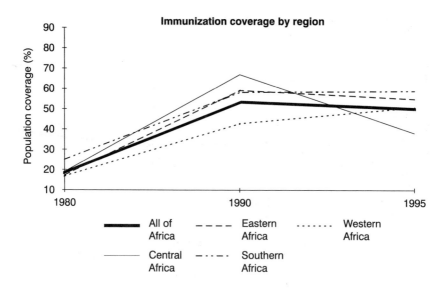

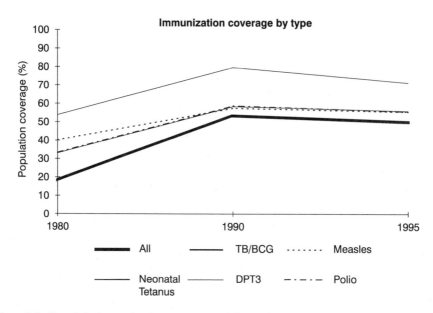

Figure 2.6   Trends in immunization coverage in Africa, 1960–95

shortage of public and private resources, or to negative environmental changes. Indeed, even in the presence of adequate resources, the collapse of the state and political repression – which have often led to the breakdown of public order, graft, concentration of privileges for the few and marginalization of many, and erosion of social cohesion – generally led to worse health outcomes than otherwise achievable under conditions of good or even adequate governance. The depth of the health crises in Nigeria and the former Zaire, for instance, cannot be comprehended fully without considering the misuse and misallocation of public resources in these collapsed states.

5. Further estimation results and discussion

Results

In this section we provide results of various estimations of the eclectic model illustrated in section 4, in addition to those already reported and discussed in section 2. As prelude, we start by presenting a correlation matrix of the variables for which adequate information could be collected. The correlations were calculated with variables expressed in logarithmic form, so as to capture any non-linearities in the models considered (Table 2.6). The correlation matrix indicates that all coefficients have the expected signs and are – with some exceptions – sufficiently large.

We now turn to regressions of infant, under-five and maternal mortality rates on the set of explanatory variables included in the correlation matrix for the period

Table 2.6 Regression of infant, under-five and maternal mortality rates on various socio-economic factors

Explanatory variables	Estimated equations		
	Log of infant mortality	Log of under-five mortality	Log of maternal mortality
Constant term	6.670	7.380	7.550
	(17.25)	(16.84)	(6.78)
Log of per capita income	−.130	−.159	
	(2.72)	(2.95)	
Log of adult female literacy rate	−.126	−.127	
	(1.99)	(1.82)	
Log of proportion of population with access to health services	−.115	−.075	−.165
	(1.61)	(1.05)	(.81)
Log of proportion with access to safe water	−.066	−.116	−.648
	(.99)	(1.49)	(2.93)
Log of proportion immunized (all vaccinations)	−.038	−.042	
	(1.99)	(2.06)	
Log of proportion immunized against neonatal tetanus			−.307
			(2.54)
Log of time trend			2.124
			(3.87)
Overall R-squared	.502	.500	.508
Chi-square statistic	38.0	37.3	34.3
	[p-value = .000]	[p-value = .000]	[p-value = .000]
Sample size	72	72	44

Note: Absolute T-values in parentheses under the coefficients.
Source: Authors' calculations.

Table 2.7 Regression of infant, under-five and maternal mortality rates on various socioeconomic factors (alternative specification)

Explanatory variables	Estimated equations		
	Log of infant mortality	Log of under-five mortality	Log of maternal mortality
Constant term	6.058	10.378	6.749
	(21.25)	(6.91)	(4.69)
Log of per capita income	−.123	−.178	
	(2.65)	(3.10)	
Log of adult female literacy rate	−.147	−.207	
	(2.65)	(5.25)	
Log of daily per capita calorie supply (as a % of requirement)		−.767	
		(2.14)	
Log of proportion with access to safe water			−.649
			(3.22)
Log of proportion immunized (all vaccinations)	−.052		
	(3.18)		
Log of proportion immunized against neonatal tetanus			−.307
			(2.54)
Log of time trend			2.177
			(4.69)
Overall R-squared	.472	.537	.489
Chi-square statistic	35.4	84.6	34.0
	[p-value = .000]	[p-value = .000]	[p-value = .000]
Sample size	133	66	51

Note: Absolute T-values in parentheses under the coefficients.
Source: Authors' calculations.

1980–95, as it was not possible to reconstruct the entire dataset for the years 1960 and 1970. To avoid multicollinearity, we use two similar specifications in which all variables are expressed in logarithmic form. The first specification (the results of which are presented in Table 2.6) includes as an explanatory variable the share of the population with access to health services, while the second specification (the results of which are reported in Table 2.7) omits this variable but includes the per capita calorie supply. All other variables appear in both estimations. The estimations have been carried out using the generalized least square procedure for panel data.

The regression results can be considered satisfactory and confirm a number of relationships that are well established in the literature (see e.g., Schultz, 1976; Lee and Schultz, 1982). All variables have the expected signs and, with one exception (access to health services in the first specification) are significant at, at least, the 5 per cent level. Consistent with a priori expectations, the factors which appear to have the strongest impact on mortality vary considerably across the three population groups considered, thus lending some credibility to our results. In the case of infant mortality, income per capita, female literacy and access to health services have a broadly comparable impact, while immunization coverage and access to safe water have a considerably smaller, though positive, impact. In contrast, the under-five mortality rates appear much more sensitive to calorie supply and immunization coverage, while maternal mortality seems to be most sensitive to the availability of fresh water and immunization against neonatal tetanus.

Finally, we attempt to capture the health impact of civil and ethnic conflicts. While it is clear that the 'silent emergencies' due to poor health care, low maternal education and insufficient income and food intake have a continuous pernicious effect on child and maternal mortality, this paper has argued that the spread of civil conflict and ethnic strife has had an additional effect on the health status of the African population over the last ten years.

The models estimated in Tables 2.6 and 2.7 have thus been modified by introducing a dummy variable for ethnic conflicts and by eliminating variables such as immunization coverage, access to safe water and health care and calorie supply, the inclusion of which would have entailed large losses of degrees of freedom because of a consequent deletion of observations due to missing data. The results reported may also be biased by the unavoidable arbitrariness entailed by the assigning to the dummy variable of the values of 1 (ethnic strife or war) or 0 (peace) during the entire period considered. This problem is compounded by the fact that for all other variables the data refer only to the years 1980, 1990 and 1995 while conflicts have often intervened in between and for shorter duration. Despite these and other measurement problems, the results in Table 2.8 indicate that countries beset by civil wars and ethnic struggles seem to have experienced higher mortality rates than countries without internal conflicts. Even though the coefficients of the ethnic conflict are low and statistically non-significant, these findings nonetheless point to the need for further work in this area, and emphasize the importance of internal peace and conflict prevention as key policies for the overall improvement of mortality over time.

Discussion

The empirical findings presented above show large effects of policy and non-policy factors on mortality and health status in Africa. The non-policy variables include time and unobservable regional-specific factors. The policy variables include real per capita income, immunization, access to health care, safe water supplies, female education and calorie intake. These variables can be modified by public policy to improve health status. The paper also provides weak evidence of the mortality impact of political strife and ethnic conflicts.

The time variable has the commonly observed negative effect on child mortality; however, its effect on maternal mortality is surprisingly and unplausibly positive, suggesting that some important factor has been omitted in our analysis. In our analysis, time generally represents progress in medical and public health technology, a phenomenon which is favourable to health. It also captures the temporal pattern of allocation of resources in the health sector and within

Table 2.8 Regression of infant, under-five and maternal mortality rates on ethnic conflicts controlling for other covariates

Explanatory variables	Estimated equations		
	Log of infant mortality	*Log of under-five mortality*	*Log of female life expectancy*
Constant term	6.356	7.074	3.430
	(21–65)	(20.63)	(41.04)
Log of time trend	−.368	−.384	.026
	(6.65)	(6.54)	(.83)
Log of per capita income	−.191	−.226	.038
	(3.98)	(3.46)	(2.52)
Log of female literacy rate	−.027	−.033	.066
	(1.11)	(1.28)	(5.75)
Ethnic conflict	.007	.006	−.025
(=1 in case of ethnic strife and zero otherwise)	(.06)	(.08)	(.69)
Chi-square statistic	167	179	111
	[p-value = .000]	[p-value = .000]	[p-value = .000]
Sample size	133	133	133

Note: Absolute T-values in parentheses under the coefficients.
Source: Authors' calculations.

households, a pattern that might be favourable or unfavourable to health (see Schultz, 1984 and 1993).

The overall results of the analysis summarized in Figure 2.7 provide evidence that public policy is an important determinant of the health status of the population. They also offer a tentative guidance to the policy maker about the optimal mix of various public policies in the health and non-health sector. That is, public policy can be used in a deliberate and systematic manner to reduce child and maternal mortality rates and thus improve the health of the population.

Specifically, we find that, after controlling for the time trend, the main determinants of child and maternal health are the six variables included in Tables 2.6 and 2.7. Their relative importance is not always the one commonly mentioned in the literature, and varies considerably according to the population group examined. For instance, income per capita does not appear to be the most important determinant of the health status of the three population groups considered. Similarly, and in contradiction with received theory, female literacy appears to have an effect on infant and under-five mortality broadly equal to that of income per capita and health care. As expected, immunization has a greater impact on under-five and maternal mortality than on infant mortality. Calorie supply has a strong impact on under-five mortality but was not found to be significant (and was thus dropped) in the infant mortality equation, possibly because of the high prevalence of breastfeeding until one year of age in most of Africa. In addition, maternal mortality declines sharply with the availability of safe water and with increases in vaccinations against neonatal tetanus. The decline in maternal

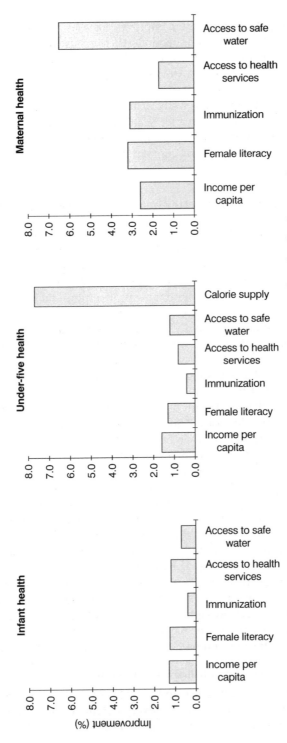

Figure 2.7 Summary of the percentage health impact of a 10 per cent improvement in selected policy interventions
Source: Based on authors' calculations. These charts are based on the figures given in Tables 2.7 and 2.8.

mortality as the supply of safe water improves suggests a positive correlation between generalized access to safe water and other factors that contribute to the lowering of maternal deaths such as better nutrition, sanitation at maternity clinics and restraint from excessive workload during pregnancy – work such as fetching water from long distances.

From a policy standpoint, the novelty of these findings is not that improvements in the factors listed above enhance health; its significance is in showing the relative health benefits from such improvements – information that is important for allocating scarce resources among competing health care, education and anti-poverty programmes.

6.   What to do? Policies for better health in Sub-Saharan Africa

The prior discussion has shown that some of the causes of the slow-down in health improvement in most of Sub-Saharan Africa, as in other countries, originate from outside of the health sector, e.g., the economic decline, complex humanitarian emergencies, famines and to a certain extent AIDS. Thus, without a shift to a new model of economic development, to a more stable political conditions, and to less tense ethnic and social relations, it will be difficult to improve permanently, substantially and rapidly the health status in many Africa countries.

Yet much can be achieved, even within the health sector itself, particularly if existing resources are utilized more efficiently, and if additional funds are mobilized for this sector. In all cases, including those of famine and conflict prevention as well as the control of the spread of AIDS, the success of public interventions depends on a more efficient, decentralized and flexible government. Neither the traditional state, nor the 'downsized' liberal state would be able to put through the measures discussed hereafter. In several cases, the government's role should shift from direct provision to that of a funder-regulator-provider, making more room for community, non-governmental and private providers. With the clear mortality impact of health coverage, fresh water supply, vaccination coverage and female education, it is necessary therefore to stop the 'retreat' of the state underway in most of Sub-Saharan Africa for several years and to promote its thorough reform.

In this section, we provide only a brief mention of the global measures (be they economic or political) necessary to improve health status. Nor do we discuss in any detail policies to mitigate the worst forms of poverty so as to allow a truly universal access to health care. For these we make reference to the relevant literature. In contrast, we discuss in somewhat more detail desirable changes concerning the level, targeting, composition and funding of health expenditure. All in all, we think that six sets of measures discussed hereafter are required to provide an answer to the continuing health crisis of Sub-Saharan Africa.

An improved economic and political environment

Strong macro-economic performance and a stable political environment are prerequisites for an effective health service delivery system. Sound economic growth provides the basic resources necessary to improve health, while predictable political institutions provide the structure necessary to design and implement sustainable social policies. Thus, effective macro-economic management and good governance are important elements of a framework for improving health status in Sub-Saharan Africa. While growth *per se* is important for health, we would like to underscore that the growth with the most beneficial impact is that which is of a broad-based nature and which entails, *inter alia*, widespread access to production assets (land and credit in particular), adequate pricing policies for the goods produced by the poor, sustained investment in human development and promotion of labour-intensive exports.

Anti-poverty measures

Poverty is a major problem in Sub-Saharan Africa; in many countries poverty rates are as high as 50 to 60 per cent. Policies for improving health status should thus include strategies for dealing with this problem. Targeting expenditure on a broad range of social services to particular groups, using, for example, a regional characteristic such as area of residence of the poor, is one strategy for improving health status through poverty reduction. Other measures which have been shown to be successful in poverty alleviation include micro-credit schemes for small producers, public works programmes (in urban areas), training programmes focusing on new skills and the development of collective infrastructure which enhances the functioning of markets in rural areas.

Raising efficiency by reducing costs

In some cases, health status can be improved by reducing the unit costs of health services, and thus, other things being equal, achieving greater coverage with a given set of resources. The introduction of product standards and better 'production techniques' more in line with local factor endowments, as in the case of the substitution of local materials for imported ones in the construction of clinics and other health facilities, can substantially lower unit costs and facilitate the expansion of health service coverage. Savings are often possible, too, in the area of wages and current inputs. For instance, large savings are possible in the procurement, management, distribution and prescription of pharmaceuticals. And there is a need for more carefully articulated manpower policies, with recognition of the cost implications of alternative skill mixes. In this regard, there is scope for the application of nominal fees as a tool to guide demand for simple health care services away from hospitals. However, great care should be exercised both in the design and implementation of such fees, as they can result in unwarranted reduction in health service utilization.

Improving the targeting and decentralization of health expenditure

The evidence provided by the regression analysis regarding the strong impact of access to basic health services, water supply and vaccination coverage suggests that substantial improvements can be achieved by a better allocation and management of public expenditure. While resources are needed at all levels, the overall impact of health expenditure would rise if a greater share of resources were allocated to training for village health workers, adequate supervision, mobilization of communities and the strengthening of family planning services in the first tier of the primary health-care pyramid. Most of all, the introduction of key programmes such as child immunization, oral rehydration therapy, promotion of breastfeeding, essential drugs and so on, needs to receive priority in low income Sub-Saharan countries. Correcting existing misallocations, however, is not simple, as labour and – particularly – capital are only partially mobile; such a strategy has a greater chance to succeed in periods of expanding budgets.

Greater decentralization is also likely to improve the targeting of services and overall efficiency. Poor communications and transport systems, population dispersion and the fact that the supervision of personnel, resource distribution and operations is easier at lower levels of administration are all arguments in favour of such decentralization. Nonetheless, where it means loss of control over the implementation of national policies (as in manpower training, drug procurement and so forth), or where a large increase in the financial burden is placed on households and communities, decentralization is potentially damaging.

Increasing the flow of resources to basic social services

Despite the considerable scope for protecting the delivery of high-impact health services during crisis periods, there are limits to what can be achieved through the measures discussed above, particularly when health expenditure is already low. Indeed, in most Sub-Saharan countries, greater access to health care will require that the flow of resources to the health sectors must be increased substantially. The options available to achieve this include the following:

Increasing the share of efficient social services in government expenditure

Top priority should be given to restructuring government expenditures, involving the shifting of resources towards health, rural water supply and maternal education, and away from defence, production subsidies and interest payments on the foreign debt.

Increasing the revenue of the central or local government

Between the late 1970s and the middle-late 1980s the average tax to GDP ratio in Sub-Saharan Africa fell from 18 per cent to 16–17 per cent. Recently there are signs of recovery, but these are limited to only a few countries. This fall in tax effort resulted from the neglect of revenue collection in the 'first generation' stabilization programmes, where fiscal deficit reduction was achieved mainly by cutting expenditure. As they took effect rapidly, expenditure cuts probably led to excessive drops in public expenditure on 'quasi-public' goods and might have had a regressive impact. It is now widely recognized that a more active tax policy is needed. Such a policy should aim at improving revenue generation, enhancing the efficiency of the tax system, and permitting a modest rise in 'efficient' public expenditures.

A non-distortionary and equitable increase in the tax ratio of 1–2 points of GDP appears technically feasible in a good number of African countries, and would by itself make it possible to add to the flow of resources to health care, even assuming no growth and no shift in priorities towards the health sector. In some countries (including Burkina Faso, Kenya, Malawi and Zimbabwe), efforts along these lines have been initiated since the mid-1980s. Resource allocation to health could be augmented more readily if the new revenue generated, or at least part of it, were directly earmarked for specific health activities, or if these taxes were raised directly for by district and provincial authorities.

Mobilizing additional resources from household and communities

In Sub-Saharan Africa, households have long been bearing a substantial share of the national expenditure on health care, water supply and so on by contributing resources (in kind, cash and time) for the construction of facilities, covering direct and indirect costs (transportation, fees, drugs, etc.) associated with attendance to clinics and making payments to private providers. Despite these already considerable contributions, user charges have often been introduced in recent years to alleviate the budgetary crisis.

While the small but significant contribution of user charges to health budgets should be acknowledged, their negative impact needs also to be emphasized: first, the introduction of substantial fees leads to a contraction in the demand for health services. Second, it discourages the utilization of preventive services for which potential patients may not see an immediate relevance. Third, it may adversely affect a household's ability to meet other basic needs, such as the purchase of food. In addition, there is little evidence that the revenue from user charges is actually reinvested to improve the quality or expand the coverage of local services. Moreover, user charges usually generate a relatively small proportion of the total operating cost of health care sector, with net yields at around 5 per cent or less. While user charges are not well suited to disease control programmes, basic curative services and communal water supply, the same cannot be said of 'high-income' services.

While direct user fees (levied on patients at the moment of their treatment) are problematic, there are other ways to mobilize resources from communities, such as prepayment schemes, health insurance, lotteries, mutual funds and the sale of produce from community fields. These schemes have two attractive features: they shift the moment of payment, so that individuals are not burdened with significant expenditures at the time of illness, and they spread the burden of costs over a larger group.

Increasing the volume of international aid

Since the early 1980s, there has been a considerable increase in the share of official development assistance (ODA) allocated to Sub-Saharan Africa (its share rose from 19.4 per cent in 1975–6 to 34.2 per cent in 1988–9). However, the share assigned to human development dropped, while debt-service obligations compressed indirectly all discretionary expenditures. In addition, the trend in the 1990s has been towards an absolute decline in aid flows. The simplest and the most cost-effective way to effect new aid transfers would be through debt relief. Improvement in the quality of aid, including greater participation in the financing of recurrent costs and more focus on primary health care and rural water supply, is also required.

Move towards a multiplicity of service providers

Much of the market-oriented literature tends to be over-optimistic about the scope for expanding private services in order to replace those provided by the government. First, private sector services in Africa are typically concentrated in urban areas and cater to upper-income groups. Non-governmental providers (especially missions) are often located in rural areas, and often provide valuable services, but are seldom able to furnish extensive coverage and may duplicate government services. Second, private providers often receive state subsidies and typically offer higher salaries and better working conditions. This draws manpower away from the public sector, thus causing – especially in countries with limited numbers of health workers – a costly and inequitable 'human capital flight' from the public sector. Third, the view that private health institutions in Sub-Saharan Africa are more efficient tends to be based largely on analyses in developed countries.

Yet a multiplicity of providers is desirable, and probably unavoidable; there are several reasons why such an approach should be fostered. While this approach is not without limitations, it allows the harnessing of the social service motivations of NGOs as well as the self-interested motivations of private agents. To be sure, the growing pressure for pluralism in social service provision requires that governments be able to provide central co-ordination and regulation through well designed incentive structures. Indeed, the proper functioning of a health care system based on a multiplicity of providers depends on the existence of a strong state able to regulate, co-ordinate and ensure that basic health services of acceptable quality are delivered to all citizens of a nation.

Note

1   The authors wish to thank Gareth Jones and Eva Jespersen for their support in compiling the dataset used in the paper, Paivi Mattila-Wiro for her excellent research assistance, and Liisa Roponen for the processing of the text. They also wish to thank the participants to the UNICEF West African Regional Seminar on Economic and Social Policy held in Accra, 21–23 April 1997, for the comments provided on an initial draft on this paper. Obviously, all remaining errors are only ours.

References

Ainsworth, Martha and Mead Over (1994) 'AIDS and African development', *World Bank Research Observer*, 9(2):203–40.
Albanez, Teresa, Eduardo Bustelo, Giovanni Andrea Cornia and Eva Jespersen (1989) 'Economic decline and child survival: the plight of Latin America in the 1980s', Innocenti Occasional Papers, No. 1. Florence: ICDC–UNICEF.
Anand, Sudhir and Lincoln Chen (1996) 'Health implications of economic policies: a framework of analysis', Discussion Paper Series. New York: UNDP.
Appleton, Simon (1997) 'User fees, expenditure restructuring and voucher systems in education', *WIDER Working Papers*, No. 134. Helsinki: WIDER.

Becker, Gary (1991) *A Treatise on the Family*. Cambridge, Massachusetts: Harvard University Press.

Benefo, Kofi and Schultz, T. Paul (1996) 'Fertility and child mortality in Côte d'Ivoire and Ghana', *World Bank Economic Review* 10(1):123–58.

Brenner, Harvey (1987) 'Economic instability, unemployment rates, behavioural risk and mortality rates in Scotland', *International Journal of Health Services*, 17(3).

Caldwell, J. C. (1979) 'Education as a factor in mortality decline: an investigation of Nigerian data', *Population Studies*, 33(3):395–413.

Cornia, G. A. (1990) 'Global socio-economic changes and child welfare: what will the 21st century bring us?' in B. Chang Po-King (ed.), *Early Childhood Toward the 21st Century*. Hong Kong: Yew Chung Education.

Cornia, G. A. (1996) *Labour Market Shock, Psychosocial Stress and the Transition Mortality Crisis*, Research in Progress, No. 4. Helsinki, Finland: UNU/WIDER.

Cornia, Giovanni Andrea, Richard Jolly and Frances Stewart (1987) *Adjustment with a Human Face*, Vol. I. Oxford: Clarendon Press.

Eckstein, Zvi, T. Paul Schultz and Kenneth I. Wolpin (1985) 'Short-run fluctuations in fertility and mortality in pre-industrial Sweden', *European Economic Review*, 26:295–317.

Fogel, Robert William (1997) 'New findings on secular trends in nutrition and mortality: some implications for population theory', in Mark R. Rosenzweig and Oded Stark (eds), *Handbook of Population and Family Economics*, Vol. 1A. Amsterdam: North-Holland/Elsevier Science.

Gertler, Paul and J. van der Gaag (1990) *The Willingness to Pay for Medical Care: Evidence from Two Developing Countries*. Baltimore: Johns Hopkins University Press.

Greene, William H. (1993) *Econometric Analysis*. Englewood Cliffs, New Jersey: Prentice-Hall.

Lee, B. S. and T. Paul Schultz (1982) 'Implications of child mortality reductions for fertility and population growth in Korea', *Journal of Economic Development*, 7(1):21–44.

Lumey, L. H. and W. A. Van Poppel (1994) 'The Dutch famine of 1944–45: mortality and morbidity in past and present generations', *Society for the Social History of Medicine*, No. 07/02.

McKweon, T. (1976) *The Modern Rise of Population*. London: Academic Press.

Mosley, K. and Lincoln Chen (1984) 'An analytical framework for the study of child survival in developing countries', *Population and Development Review*, 10(suppl.):25–45.

Murray, Christopher and Lincoln Chen (1993) 'In search of contemporary theory for understanding mortality change', *Social Science and Medicine*, 36(2).

Musgrove, Philip (1987) 'The economic crisis and its impact on health and health care in Latin America and the Caribbean', *International Journal of Health Services*, 7(3):411–41.

Mwabu, Germano (1996) 'Health effects of market-based reforms in developing countries', Working Paper No. 120. Helsinki: UNU/WIDER.

Mwabu, G., J. Mwanzia and W. Liambila (1995) 'User charges in government health facilities in Kenya: effect on attendance and revenue', *Health Policy and Planning*, 10(2):164–70.

Nafziger, Wayne E. (1996) *The Economics of Complex Humanitarian Emergencies: Preliminary Approaches and Findings*, Working Paper No. 119. Helsinki: UNU/WIDER.

Pritchett, Lant and Lawrence H. Summers (1996) 'Wealthier is healthier', *Journal of Human Resources*, 30(4):841–68.

Reddy, Sanjay and Jan Vandemoortele (1996) *User Financing of Basic Social Services: A Review of Theoretical Arguments and Empirical Evidence*, UNICEF, EPP Working Paper, mimeo. New York.

Robinson, Mark and Gordon White (1997) *The Role of Civic Organizations in Provision of Social Services: Towards Synergy*, Research for Action, No. 37. Helsinki: UNU/WIDER.

Schultz, T. Paul (1976) Interrelationships between mortality and fertility', in Ronald G. Ridker (ed.), *Population and Development: The Search for Selective Interventions*. Baltimore: Johns Hopkins University Press.

Schultz, T. Paul (1981) *Economics of Population*. Reading, Massachusetts: Addison-Wesley.

Schultz, T. Paul (1984) 'Studying the impact of household, economic and community variables on child mortality', *Population and Development Review*, 10(suppl.):215–35.

Schultz, T. Paul (1993) 'Mortality decline in the low income world: causes and consequences', *American Economic Review*, 82:337–42.

Schultz, T. Paul (1997) 'Demand for children in low-income countries', in Mark Rosenzweig and Oded Stark (eds), *Handbook of Population and Family Economics*. Amsterdam: North-Holland Publishers.

Sen, Amartya (1981) *Poverty and Famines: An Essay on Entitlements and Deprivation*. Oxford: Clarendon Press.

Väyrynen, Raimo (1996) *The Age of Humanitarian Emergencies*, Research for Action No. 25. Helsinki: UNU/WIDER.

Taube, G. and H. Tadesse (1996) *Presumptive Taxation in Sub-Saharan Africa: Experiences and Prospects*, IMF Working Paper Series, No. 96/5. Washington, DC: IMF.

UNDP (1992, 1993, 1994, 1997) *Human Development Report*. Oxford: Oxford University Press.

UNICEF (1989, 1995) *The State of the World's Children*. Oxford: Oxford University Press.

UNICEF–ICDC (1994) *Crisis in Mortality, Health and Nutrition,* Central and Eastern Countries in Transition: Regional Monitoring Report No. 2. Florence: UNICEF–ICDC.

Wallensteen, Peter and Margaret Sollenberg (1995) 'After the cold war: emerging patterns of armed conflict 1989–94', *Journal of Peace Research*, 32(3):345–60.

Wallensteen, Peter and Margaret Sollenberg (1996) 'The end of international war? armed conflict 1989–95', *Journal of Peace Research*, 33(2):353–70.

Wolpin, Kenneth I. (1997) 'Determinants and consequences of the mortality and health of infants and children', in Mark R. Rosenzweig and Oded Stark (eds), *Handbook of Population and Family Economics*. Amsterdam: North-Holland/Elsevier Science.

World Bank (1983) *World Development Report*. Oxford: Oxford University Press.

World Bank (1994) *Social Indicators of Development*. Washington, DC: World Bank.

World Bank (1997) *The World Development Indicators*. Washington, DC: World Bank.

3
Urbanization, Unemployment, and Migration in Africa: Theory and Policy[1]

Michael P. Todaro

> In the early 1990s, approximately half the governments of the world, mostly those of developing countries, considered the patterns of population distribution to be unsatisfactory. A key issue was the rapid growth of urban areas.
>
> *Program of Action*, 1994 International Conference on Population and Development, Cairo

> Rural and urban development are interdependent...we must work to extend employment opportunities to rural areas in order to minimize rural-to-urban migration.
>
> *Istanbul Declaration on Human Settlements* (HABITAT II), 1996

During the past three decades, the cities of the developing world in general, and of Africa in particular, have witnessed a remarkable and in many ways unprecedented demographic growth spurt. Despite some slow-down in rates of increase in the past few years as a result of falling wages and contracting social services, contemporary Third World urban areas remain the growth poles of economic progress and the lightning rods of political and social unrest. Nowhere is this dilemma more visible nor the problems more intractable than in the crowded cities of Sub-Saharan Africa, where projections of urban population growth remain the highest in the world.

This essay focuses on the conceptual, empirical, and policy-relevant linkages between urbanization, rural–urban migration, and economic development. It first reviews recent trends and future scenarios for urban population growth, with special emphasis on African urbanization, then examines the growth and significance of the urban informal economy and the role of women in informal economic activities. We then discuss rural–urban migration in both a descriptive and an analytical framework, and we consider the economic crisis in Africa and its relationship to urbanization and migration, concluding with an analysis of policy options designed to ameliorate the deteriorating economic, social, and environmental dilemmas posed by Africa's rapid urban growth.

1. Urbanization: trends and projections

One of the most significant of all post-war demographic phenomena and the one that promises to loom even larger in the future is the rapid growth of cities in developing countries. In 1950, some 275 million people were living in Third World cities, 38 per cent of the 724 million total urban population. According to United Nations estimates, the world's urban population had reached 2.3 billion by 1990, with 61 per cent (1.4 billion) living in metropolitan areas of developing countries. The UN projects that in 2025, over four billion, or 77 per cent of the urban dwellers of the world, will reside in less developed regions. This will represent an overall increase of 186 per cent, or 2.61 billion new urbanites in Africa, Asia, and Latin America since 1990. Depending on the nature of development strategies pursued, the final total could be substantially higher or lower than the 4 billion estimate. Figure 3.1 provides a three-stage portrayal of the projected growth of urban populations in four Third World regions and China between 1950 and 2000; Table 3.1 presents a more detailed statistical breakdown with projections to 2025.

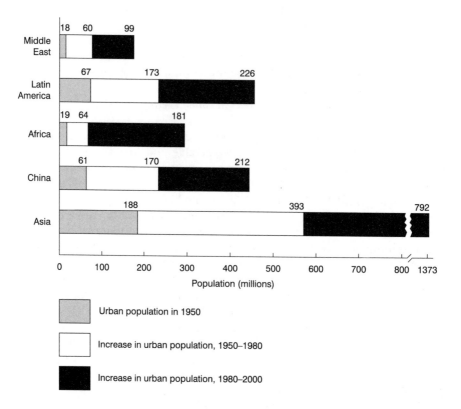

Figure 3.1   Urban population, 1950–2000

Table 3.1 Urban population in major world regions, 1950–2025 (millions)

Region	1950	1960	1970	1980	1990	2000*	2025*
World	724	1,012	1,352	1,807	2,282	3,208	5,187
More developed regions	449	573	698	834	881	965	1,177
Less developed regions	275	439	654	972	1,401	2,101	4,011
Africa	32	50	83	133	206	331	857
Latin America	68	107	162	241	315	413	592
Asia	218	342	407	596	879	1,291	2,556

* Estimate.
Sources: United Nations, *Patterns of Urban and Rural Population Growth* (New York: United Nations, 1980); Pii Elina Berghäll, *Habitat II and the Urban Economy: A Review of Recent Developments and Literature* (Helsinki: United Nations University World Institute for Development Economics Research, 1995), Tables 2 and 4.

With regard to particular cities, current rates of population growth range from under 1 per cent per annum in two of the world's largest cities, Tokyo and New York, to over 6 per cent per annum in many African cities, including Nairobi, Lagos and Lusaka. In Asia and Latin America, many cities are growing at rates in excess of 5 per cent. Table 3.2 provides data on the world's fifteen largest cities in 1950 and 1995 along with UN projections to 2015. Note that in 1950 only four of the fifteen were in the developing world. Their combined population was 19 million. In 1995, twelve out of the fifteen largest cities were in the Third World, with a total population of 141 million. By 2015, it is anticipated that

Table 3.2 Fifteen largest cities, 1950, 1995, and 2015 (millions)

City	1950 population (millions)	City	1995 population (millions)	City	2015 population (millions)
1. New York	12.3	Tokyo	26.8	Tokyo	28.7
2. London	8.7	São Paulo	16.4	Bombay	27.4
3. Tokyo	6.9	New York	16.3	Lagos	24.4
4. Paris	5.4	Mexico City	15.6	Shanghai	23.4
5. Moscow	5.4	Bombay	15.1	Jakarta	21.2
6. Shanghai	5.3	Shanghai	15.1	São Paulo	20.8
7. Essen	5.3	Los Angeles	12.4	Karachi	20.6
8. Buenos Aires	5.0	Beijing	12.4	Beijing	19.4
9. Chicago	4.9	Calcutta	11.7	Dhaka	19.0
10. Calcutta	4.4	Seoul	11.6	Mexico City	18.8
11. Osaka	4.1	Jakarta	11.5	New York	17.6
12. Los Angeles	4.0	Buenos Aires	11.0	Calcutta	17.6
13. Beijing	3.9	Tianjin	10.7	Delhi	17.6
14. Milan	3.6	Osaka	10.6	Tianjin	17.0
15. Berlin	3.3	Lagos	10.3	Manila	14.7

Sources: United Nations, *World Urbanization Prospects: The 1994 Revision* (New York: United Nations, 1995), Table 1; World Resources Institute, *World Resources 1996–97: The Urban Environment* (New York: Oxford University Press, 1996), Table. 1.1.

Table 3.3 African urban growth rates, 1990–1995, and per cent urban, 1975, 1995 and 2025

	Urban growth rate 1990–95 (per cent)	Per cent urban		
Country		*1975*	*1995*	*2025*
Botswana	7.0	12	28	56
Burkina Faso	11.2	6	27	66
Burundi	6.6	3	8	21
Ghana	4.3	30	36	58
Kenya	6.8	13	28	51
Lesotho	6.2	11	23	47
Malawi	6.2	8	14	32
Mozambique	7.4	9	34	61
Nigeria	5.2	23	39	62
Tanzania	6.1	10	24	48
Uganda	5.8	8	13	29
Zimbabwe	5.0	20	32	55
Region				
Africa	4.4	25	34	55
South America	2.5	64	78	88
Asia	3.3	25	35	55
Europe	0.6	67	74	83

Source: World Resource Institute, *World Resources 1996–97* (New York: Oxford University Press, 1996), data Table. A.1.

less-developed countries' (LDC) cities will comprise thirteen out of the fifteen largest, with a combined population in excess of 261 million. Note in particular how Lagos, Nigeria, which does not even appear on the list until occupying the fifteenth position in 1995, jumps to the number three spot in 2015, as its population grows by over 135 per cent during the twenty-year period. In fact, if we focus solely on African urban areas (as in Table 3.3), we find that the phenomenal growth of Lagos is the rule rather than the exception. While their absolute numbers are lower than many Asian and Latin American cities, African cities have uniformly higher growth rates and more rapidly expanding numbers.

A central question related to the unprecedented size of these urban agglomerations is how African cities will cope – economically, environmentally, and politically – with such acute concentrations of people. While it is true that cities offer the cost-reducing advantages of agglomeration economies and economies of scale and proximity as well as numerous economic and social externalities (e.g., skilled workers, cheap transport, social and cultural amenities), the social costs of a progressive overloading of housing and social services, not to mention increased crime, pollution, and congestion, tend gradually to outweigh these historical urban advantages. Former World Bank president Robert McNamara expressed his scepticism that huge urban agglomerations could be made to work at all:

These sizes are such that any economies of location are dwarfed by costs of congestion. The rapid population growth that has produced them will have far outpaced the growth of human and physical infrastructure needed for even moderately efficient economic life and orderly political and social relationships, let alone amenity for their residents.[2]

(McNamara, 1984)

Along with the rapid spread of urbanization and the urban bias in development strategies has come the prolific growth of huge slums and shantytowns. From the *favelas* of Rio de Janeiro and the *pueblos jovenes* of Lima to the *bustees* of Calcutta and the *bidonvilles* of Dakar, such makeshift communities have been doubling in size every five to ten years. Today slum settlements represent over one-third of the urban population in all developing countries; in many cases they account for more than 60 per cent of the urban total (see Table 3.4). During the late 1980s, fully 72 out of every 100 new households established in urban areas of developing countries were located in shanties and slums. In Africa, the number was 92 out of every 100. Most of the settlements are without clean water, sewage systems or electricity. For example, metropolitan Cairo is attempting to cope with a population of ten million people with a water and sanitation system built to serve two million. Abidjan, Côte d'Ivoire has 30 per cent of its population without piped water and 70 per cent without sewers. Much the same can be found in Nairobi, Lusaka, Kinshasa, Dakar, and Lagos, where economic decline over the past decade has led not only to falling incomes and rising unemployment but also to a breakdown in urban services and rising social tensions.

Table 3.4 Slums and squatter settlements as a percentage of urban population

City	Slums as percentage of city population
Latin America	
Bogotá, Colombia	60
Mexico City, Mexico	46
Caracas, Venezuela	42
Middle East and Africa	
Addis Ababa, Ethiopia	79
Casablanca, Morocco	70
Ankara, Turkey	60
Cairo, Egypt	60
Kinshasa, Zaire	60
Asia	
Calcutta, India	67
Manila, Philippines	35
Seoul, South Korea	29
Jakarta, Indonesia	26

Source: Population Crisis Committee, *World Population Growth and Global Security*, Report No. 13 (Washington, DC: Population Crisis Committee, 1983), p. 2.

Although population growth and accelerated rural-to-urban migration are chiefly responsible for the explosion in urban shantytowns, part of the blame rests with LDC governments. Their misguided policies regarding urban planning and outmoded building codes often mean that 80 to 90 per cent of new urban housing is 'illegal'. For example, colonial-era building codes in Nairobi, Kenya make it impossible to build an 'official' house for less than US $3,500. The law also requires every dwelling to be accessible by car. As a result, two-thirds of Nairobi's land is occupied by 10 per cent of the population, while 100,000 slum dwellings cannot legally be improved. Similarly in Manila, Philippines, 88 per cent of the population is too poor to be able to buy or rent an officially 'legal' house (UNFPA, 1991:61).

The extent of Third World government concern and even alarm at the trends in urban population growth was vividly revealed in a 1988 UN report on population policies in the world (UN Population Division, 1988).[3] It showed that out of a total of 158 countries, 73, all but five of which were developing nations, considered the geographic distribution of their population 'highly unacceptable'. Another 66 countries, 42 of them developing, considered their urban population size 'unacceptable to a degree'. Only six developing countries considered their distribution acceptable. Almost all countries dissatisfied with the size and growth of their urban population believed that internal rural–urban migration was the most prominent factor contributing to city growth. Statistics show that rural migrants constitute anywhere from 35 to 60 per cent of recorded urban population growth (see Table 3.5). Accordingly, 90 out of 116 developing countries responding to the UN survey indicated that they had initiated policies to slow or reverse their accelerating trends in rural–urban migration.

Given this widespread dissatisfaction with rapid urban growth in Africa and other developing countries, the critical issue that needs to be addressed is the extent to which national governments can formulate development policies that can have a definite impact on trends in urban growth. It is clear that the

Table 3.5 Importance of rural–urban migration as a source of urban population growth in selected developing countries

Country	Annual urban growth (per cent)	Share of growth due to migration (per cent)
Argentina	2.0	35
Brazil	4.5	36
Colombia	4.9	43
India	3.8	45
Indonesia	4.7	49
Nigeria	7.0	64
Philippines	4.8	42
Sri Lanka	4.3	61
Tanzania	7.5	64
Thailand	5.3	45

Source: K. Newland, *City Limits: Emerging Constraints on Urban Growth*,
Worldwatch Paper 38 (Washington, DC: Worldwatch, 1980), p. 10.

Table 3.6 Urban versus rural demographics and health in Kenya, 1993

	Urban residents (per cent)	Rural residents (per cent)
Household population with no education		
Female (6 years and above)	13.5	29.1
Male (6 years and above)	7.0	18.2
Household possessions and amenities		
Radio	67.7	48.1
Television	22.0	2.4
Electricity	42.5	3.4
Drinking water piped to residence	55.8	10.7
Flush toilet	44.9	1.6
Health of children		
Mortality rate of children under age 5[a]	75.4	95.6
Infant mortality rate[a]	45.5	64.9
Per cent of children between 12 and 23 months with all vaccinations	80.9	78.3
Underweight[b]	12.8	23.5
Maternal health		
Women receiving tetanus toxoid during pregnancy	92.9	88.8
Women receiving prenatal care from a health provider[c]	97.6	94.5
Women receiving delivery care from a health provider[c]	77.6	39.2
Total fertility rate	3.4	5.8

[a] Deaths per 1,000 live births. Mortality rates by characteristics such as place of residence are based on the last 10 years prior to the survey in order to ensure sufficient sample size. Mortality rates are based on a minimum of 500 live births.
[b] Underweight is defined as the percentage of children whose height-for-age, weight-for-age, weight-for-height z-score is below −2 standard deviations from the median of the International Reference Population (WHO/CDC/NCHS).
[c] Doctor, nurse, or trained midwife.
Source: Institute for Resource Development, Demographic and Health Survey Archive, Columbia, MD.

unquestioning pursuit of the orthodox development strategies of the past few decades, with their emphasis on industrial modernization, technological sophistication and metropolitan growth created a substantial geographic imbalance in economic and non-economic opportunities and contributed significantly to the steadily accelerating influx of rural migrants into urban areas. (Some non-economic components of this urban–rural imbalance are vividly portrayed for Kenya in 1993 in Table 3.6.) Is it possible or even desirable now to attempt to reverse these trends by pursuing a different set of population and development policies? With birth rates beginning to decline in some African countries, the problem of rapid urban growth and accelerated rural–urban migration will undoubtedly be one of the most important development and demographic issues of the early twenty-first century. And within urban areas, the growth and development of the informal sector as well as its role and limitations for labour absorption and economic progress will assume increasing importance. A brief look at this component of African and other Third World cities is therefore in order.

2. The urban informal sector

A major focus of development theory has been on the dualistic nature of developing countries' national economies – the existence of a modern, urban, capitalist sector geared toward capital-intensive, large-scale production and a traditional, rural, subsistence sector geared toward labour-intensive, small-scale production. In recent years, this dualistic analysis has also been applied specifically to the urban economy, which has been decomposed into a formal and an informal sector.

The existence of an unorganized, unregulated, and mostly legal but unregistered informal sector was recognized in the early 1970s, following observations in several African countries that massive additions to the urban labour force failed to show up in formal modern-sector unemployment statistics. The bulk of new entrants to the urban labour force seemed to create their own employment or to work for small-scale, family-owned enterprises. The self-employed were engaged in a remarkable array of activities, ranging from hawking, street vending, letter writing, knife sharpening, and junk collecting to selling fireworks, prostitution, drug peddling, and snake charming. Others found jobs as mechanics, carpenters, small artisans, barbers, and personal servants. Still others were highly successful small-scale entrepreneurs with several employees (mostly relatives) and high incomes. Some could eventually graduate to the formal sector, where they become legally registered, licensed, and subject to government regulations. Studies reveal that the share of the urban labour force engaged in informal sector activities ranges from 20 to 70 per cent, the average being around 50 per cent (see Table 3.7). With the unprecedented rate of growth of the urban population in developing countries expected to continue, and with the increasing failure of the rural and urban formal sectors to absorb additions to the labour force, more attention is being devoted to the role of the informal sector in serving as a panacea for the growing unemployment problem.

The informal sector is characterized by a large number of small-scale production and service activities that are individually or family owned and use labour-intensive and simple technology. They tend to operate like monopolistically competitive firms with ease of entry, excess capacity, and competition driving profits (incomes) down to the average supply price of labour of potential new entrants. The usually self-employed workers in this sector have little formal education, are generally unskilled, and lack access to financial capital. As a result, worker productivity and income tend to be lower in the informal sector than in the formal sector. Moreover, workers in the informal sector do not enjoy the measure of protection afforded by the formal modern sector in terms of job security, decent working conditions, and old-age pensions. Most workers entering this sector are

Table 3.7 Estimated share of the urban labour force in the informal sector in selected developing countries

Area	Share (per cent)
Africa	
Abidjan, Côte d'Ivoire	31
Lagos, Nigeria	50
Kumasi, Ghana	60–70
Nairobi, Kenya	44
Urban areas, Senegal	50
Urban areas, Tunisia	34
Asia	
Calcutta, India	40–50
Ahmedabad, India	47
Jakarta, Indonesia	45
Colombo, Sri Lanka	19
Urban areas, western Malaysia	35
Singapore	23
Urban areas, Thailand	26
Urban areas, Pakistan	69
Latin America	
Córdoba, Argentina	38
São Paulo, Brazil	43
Urban areas, Brazil	30
Rio de Janeiro, Brazil	24
Belo Horizonte, Brazil	31
Urban areas, Chile	39
Bogotá, Colombia	43
Santo Domingo, Dominican Republic	50
Guayaquil, Ecuador	48
Quito, Ecuador	48
San Salvador, El Salvador	41
Federal District and State of Mexico	27
Mexico, D.F., Guadalajara, and Monterey	42
Asunción, Paraguay	57
Urban areas, Peru	60
Urban areas, Venezuela	44
Caracas, Venezuela	40
Kingston, Jamaica	33

Source: S. U. Sethuraman, *The Urban Informal Sector in Developing Countries* (Geneva: International Labour Organization, 1981).

recent migrants from rural areas unable to find employment in the formal sector. Their motivation is usually to obtain sufficient income for survival, relying on their own resources to create work. As many members of the household as possible are involved in income-generating activities, including women and children, and they often work very long hours. Most inhabit shacks that they themselves have built in slums and squatter settlements, which generally lack minimal public services such as electricity, water, drainage, transportation, and educational and health services. Others are less fortunate. Many millions are homeless, living on the pavements of Calcutta, Manila, Dakar, Nairobi, Rio de Janeiro, and Bogotá – to mention just a few Third World cities. They find sporadic, temporary employment in the informal sector as day labourers and hawkers, but their incomes are insufficient to provide even the most rudimentary shelter.

In terms of its relationship with other sectors, the informal sector is linked with the rural sector in that it allows excess labour to escape from rural poverty and underemployment, although under living and working conditions and for incomes that are not much better. It is closely connected with the formal urban sector: the formal sector depends on the informal sector for cheap inputs and wage goods for its workers, and the informal sector in turn depends on the growth of the formal sector for a good portion of its income and clientele. The informal sector also often subsidizes the formal sector by providing raw materials and basic commodities for its workers at artificially low prices maintained through the formal sector's economic power and legitimacy granted by the government.

The important role that the informal sector plays in providing income opportunities for the poor is no longer open to debate. There is some question, however, as to whether the informal sector is merely a holding ground for people awaiting entry into the formal sector and, as such, is a transitional phase that must be made as comfortable as possible without perpetuating its existence until it is absorbed by the formal sector, or whether it is here to stay and should in fact be promoted as a major source of employment and income for the urban labour force.[4]

There seems to be a good argument in support of the latter view. The formal sector in developing countries has a small base in terms of output and employment. In order to absorb future additions to the urban labour force, the formal sector must be able to generate employment at a very high rate of at least 10 per cent per annum, according to estimates made by the International Labour Organization (ILO). This means that output must grow at an even faster rate, since employment in this sector increases less than proportionately in relation to output. This sort of growth seems highly unlikely in view of current trends. Thus the burden on the informal sector to absorb more labour will continue to grow unless other solutions to the urban unemployment problem are provided. Moreover, the informal sector has demonstrated its ability to generate employment and income for the urban labour force. As pointed out earlier, it is already absorbing an average of 50 per cent of the urban labour force. Some studies have shown the informal sector generating almost one-third of urban income.

Seven other arguments can be made in favour of promoting the informal sector. First, scattered evidence indicates that the informal sector generates surplus even under the currently hostile policy environment, which denies it access to the advantages offered to the formal sector such as the availability of credit, foreign exchange, and tax concessions. Thus the informal sector's surplus could provide an impetus to growth in the urban economy. Second, as a result of its low capital intensity, only a fraction of the capital needed in the formal sector is required to employ a worker in the informal sector, offering considerable savings to developing countries so often plagued with capital shortages. Third, by providing access to training and apprenticeships at substantially lower costs than that provided by formal institutions and the formal sector, the informal sector can play an important role in the formation of human capital. Fourth, the informal sector generates demand for semi-skilled and unskilled labour whose supply is increasing in both relative and absolute terms and is unlikely to be absorbed by the formal sector with its increasing demands for a skilled labour force. Fifth, the informal sector is more likely to adopt appropriate technologies and make use of local resources, allowing for a more efficient allocation of resources. Sixth, the informal sector plays an important role in recycling waste materials, engaging in the collection of goods ranging from scrap metals to cigarette butts, many of which find their way to the industrial sector or provide basic commodities for the poor. Finally, promotion of the informal sector would ensure an increased distribution of the benefits of development to the poor, many of whom are concentrated in the informal sector.

Promotion of the informal sector is not, however, without its disadvantages. One of the major disadvantages in promoting the informal sector lies in the strong relationship between rural–urban migration and labour absorption in the informal sector. Migrants from the rural sector have both a lower unemployment rate and a shorter waiting period before obtaining a job in the informal sector. Promoting income and employment opportunities in the informal sector could therefore aggravate the urban unemployment problem by attracting more labour than either the informal or the formal sector could absorb. Furthermore, there is concern over the environmental consequences of a highly concentrated informal sector in the urban areas. Many informal sector activities cause pollution and congestion (e.g., pedicabs) or inconvenience to pedestrians (e.g., hawkers and vendors). Moreover, increased densities in slums and low-income neighbourhoods, coupled with poor urban services, could cause enormous health and environmental problems for urban areas. Any policy measures designed to promote the informal sector must be able to cope with these various issues.

There has been limited discussion in the literature as to what sorts of measures might be adopted to promote the informal sector. The ILO has made some general suggestions. To begin with, governments will have to dispense with the currently hostile attitude toward the informal sector and maintain a more positive and sympathetic posture. For example, in Latin America, bureaucratic red tape and an inordinate number of administrative procedures needed to register a new business typically result in delays up to 240 days in Ecuador, 310 days in Venezuela, and 525 days in Guatemala. Brazil, Mexico, and Chile all require more than 20 applications before a company can be approved for business. These procedures not only cause excessive delays but can also inflate the costs of doing business by up to 70 per cent annually. So informal sector businesses simply skirt the law.

Because access to skills plays an important role in determining the structure of the informal sector, governments should facilitate training in the areas that are most beneficial to the urban economy. In this way, the government can play a role in shaping the informal sector so that it contains production and service activities that provide the most value to society. Specifically, such measures might promote legal activities, and discourage illegal ones, by providing proper skills and other incentives. It could also generate taxes that now go unpaid.

The lack of capital is a major constraint on activities in the informal sector. The provision of credit would therefore permit these enterprises to expand, produce more profit, and hence generate more income and employment. Access to improved technology would have similar effects. Providing infrastructure and suitable locations for work (e.g., designating specific areas for stalls) could help alleviate some of the environmental consequences of an expanded informal sector. Most important, better living conditions must be provided, if not directly, then by promoting growth of the sector on the fringes of urban areas or in smaller towns where the population will settle close to its new area of work, away from the urban density. Promotion of the informal sector outside the urban areas may also help redirect the flow of rural–urban migration, especially if carried out in conjunction with the policies discussed at the end of this paper.

3. Women in the informal sector

In some regions of the world, women predominate among rural–urban migrants and may even comprise the majority of the urban population. Though historically many of these women were simply accompanying their spouses, a growing number of unattached African women migrate to seek economic opportunity. Few of these migrants are able to find employment in the formal sector, which is generally dominated by men. As a consequence, women often represent the bulk of the informal-sector labour supply, working for low wages at unstable jobs with no employee or social security benefits. The increase in the number of single female migrants has also contributed to the rising proportion of urban households headed by women, which tend to be poorer, experience tighter resource constraints, and retain high fertility rates. The changing composition of migration flows has important economic and demographic implications for many urban areas of the Third World.

Because members of female-headed households are generally restricted to low-productivity, informal sector employment and experience higher dependency burdens, they are more likely to be poor and malnourished and less likely to obtain formal education, health care, or clean water and sanitation. Among the Brazilian poor, for example, male-headed households are four times as likely as female-headed households to have access to government-sponsored health services. Dropout rates among children from households headed by women are much higher because they are more likely to be working so as to contribute to household income.

Many women run small business ventures, called microenterprises, which require little or no start-up capital and usually involve the marketing of home-made foodstuffs and handicrafts. Though women's restricted access to capital leads to high rates of return on their tiny investments, the extremely low capital–labour ratios confine women to low-productivity undertakings. Studies in Latin America and Asia have found that where credit is available to women with informal-sector microenterprises, repayment rates have been as high as or higher than those for men. And because women are able to make more productive use of capital, their rates of return on investments often exceed those for men.

Despite the impressive record of these credit programmes, there are very few in Africa. The vast majority of institutional credit is channelled through formal sector agencies, and as a result, African women generally find themselves ineligible for small loans. Government programmes to enhance income in poor households will inevitably neglect the neediest households so long as African governments continue to focus on formal sector employment of men and allocation of resources through formal sector institutions. To solve the plight of poor urban women and their children, it is imperative that efforts be made to integrate women into the economic mainstream. Ensuring that women benefit from development programmes will require that women's special circumstances be considered in policy design.

The legalization and economic promotion of informal sector activities, where the majority of the urban female labour force is employed, could greatly improve women's financial flexibility and the productivity of their ventures. However, to enable women to reap these benefits, African governments must repeal laws that restrict women's rights to own property, conduct financial transactions, or limit their fertility. Likewise, barriers to women's direct involvement in technical training programmes and extension services must be eradicated. And finally, the provision of affordable childcare and family-planning services would lighten the burden of African women's reproductive roles and permit them a greater degree of economic participation.

4. Urban unemployment in Africa

As we have seen, one of the major consequences of the rapid urbanization process has been the burgeoning supply of job-seekers into both the modern (formal) and traditional (informal) sectors of the urban economy. In most African countries, the supply of workers far exceeds the demand, the result being extremely high rates of unemployment and underemployment in urban areas. Table 3.8 provides some detailed data on urban unemployment for twelve African countries. Note that the table focuses solely on rates of open unemployment. It thus excludes the very many more people who are chronically underemployed in the informal sector. The problem is therefore much more serious than even these data suggest. Also, as these statistics are from the 1960s (unfortunately, more recent detailed data for these countries are mostly non-existent), they are likely to show unemployment rates considerably below current levels (but see Table 3.9 for some 1980s data), since the sharp economic decline of the 1980s substantially increased urban unemployment and underemployment.[5] Nevertheless, Table 3.8 indicates that even in the 1960s, before the labour-force explosion and economic free-fall of the 1980s, African cities had very high rates of open urban unemployment. If we had included scattered information on the very substantial numbers of the urban

Table 3.8   Rates of urban and rural unemployment as a percentage of the active population in Africa

Country	Year	Area	Urban	Rural
Algeria	1966	Urban areas	26.6	–
Benin	1968	Urban areas	13.0*	–
Burundi	1963	Capital city	18.7*	–
Cameroon	1962	Largest city	13.0*	–
	1964	Capital city	17.0	–
Côte d'Ivoire	1963	Capital city	15.0	–
Ghana	1960	Large towns	12.0	–
	1970	Two large cities	9.0	–
Kenya	1968–9	Capital city	10.0*	–
	1968–9	Second largest city	14.0*	–
Morocco	1960	Urban areas	20.5	5.4
Nigeria	1963	Urban areas	12.6	–
Sierra Leone	1967	Capital city	15.0	–
Tanzania	1965	Urban areas	7.0	3.9
	1971	Seven towns	5.0*	–
Zaire	1967	Capital city	12.9	–

*Men only

Source: Paul Bairoch, *Urban Unemployment in Developing Countries* (Geneva: International Labour Organization, 1973), p. 49; Josef Gugler, *Internal Migration: The New World and the Third World*, ed. A. Richmond and D. Kubat (Beverly Hills, CA: Sage, 1976), p. 185.

Table 3.9   Open urban unemployment in four African countries, 1980s

Country	Year	Average percentage unemployed
Botswana	1985	31
Kenya	1986	16
Liberia	1984	13
Tanzania	1984	22

Source: International Labour Organization, *World Labour Report, 1989* (Geneva: International Labour Organization, 1989), Tables 1.7 and 1.12.

labour force who were underemployed in part-time, informal sector service activities, the overall figures for urban surplus labour (both openly unemployed and underemployed) would well exceed 30 per cent in most countries. Moreover, had we focused on residents in the 15–24 age bracket (the majority of whom are recent migrants), the rate would typically exceed 50 per cent. Because a major contributing factor to both high rates of urban growth and high rates of unemployment is rural–urban migration, it is essential to investigate this critical issue in some detail.

5. Migration and development in Africa

For many years, rural–urban migration was viewed favourably in the economic development literature. Internal migration was thought to be a natural process in which surplus labour was gradually withdrawn from the rural sector to provide needed manpower for urban industrial growth. The process was deemed socially beneficial because human resources were being shifted from locations where their social marginal product was often assumed to be zero to places where this marginal product was not only positive but also rapidly growing as a result of capital accumulation and technological progress. This process was formalized in the Lewis theory of development. However, as Richard Jolly noted in 1970:

> Far from being concerned with measures to stem the flow, the major interest of these economists (i.e., those who stressed the importance of labor transfer) was with policies that would *release* labor to *increase* the flow. Indeed, one of the reasons given for trying to increase productivity in the agricultural sector was to release *sufficient* labor for urban industrialization. How irrelevant most of this concern looks today.
>
> (Jolly, 1970: 4)

In contrast to the pro-migration viewpoint, it is now clear from three decades of African experience that rates of rural–urban migration have greatly exceeded rates of urban job creation and swamped the absorptive capacity of both formal sector industry and urban social services. Migration can no longer be casually viewed by economists as a beneficent process necessary to solve problems of growing urban labour demand. On the contrary, migration today remains a major factor contributing to the phenomenon of urban surplus labour; a force that continues to exacerbate already serious urban unemployment problems caused by the growing economic and structural imbalances between African urban and rural areas.

Migration exacerbates these rural–urban structural imbalances in two direct ways. First, on the supply side, internal migration disproportionately increases the growth rate of urban job-seekers relative to urban population growth, which itself is at historically unprecedented levels, because of the high proportion of well-educated young people in the migrant system. Their presence tends to swell the urban labour supply while depleting the rural countryside of valuable human capital. Second, on the demand side, urban job creation is generally more difficult to accomplish than rural job creation because of the need for substantial complementary resource inputs for most jobs in the industrial sector. Moreover, the pressures of rising urban wages and compulsory employee fringe benefits in combination with the unavailability of appropriate, more labour-intensive production technologies means that a rising share of modern-sector output growth is accounted for by increases in labour productivity. Together this rapid supply increase and lagging demand (what many now refer to as 'jobless growth') tend to convert a short-run problem of resource imbalances into a long-run situation of chronic and rising urban surplus labour.

But the impact of migration on the African development process is much more pervasive than its obvious exacerbation of urban unemployment and underemployment. In fact, the significance of the migration phenomenon throughout much of Africa is not necessarily in the process itself or even in its impact on the sectoral allocation of human resources. Rather, its significance lies in its implications for economic growth in general and for the character of that growth, particularly in its distributional manifestations.

Migration in excess of job opportunities is both a symptom of and a contributor to African underdevelopment. Understanding the causes, determinants, and consequences of internal rural–urban labour migration is thus central to understanding the nature and character of the development process and to formulating policies to influence this process in socially desirable ways. A simple yet crucial step in underlining the centrality of the migration phenomenon is to recognize that any economic and social policy that affects rural and urban real incomes will directly or indirectly influence the migration process. This process will in turn itself tend to alter the pattern of sectoral and geographic economic activity, income distribution, and even population growth. Because all economic policies have direct and indirect effects on the level and growth of either urban or rural incomes or of both, they will all have a tendency to influence the nature and magnitude of the migration stream. Although some policies may have a more direct and immediate impact (e.g., wages and employment-promotion programmes), there are many others that, though less obvious, may in the long run be no less important. Included among these policies, for example, would be land-tenure arrangements; commodity pricing; credit allocation; taxation; export promotion; import substitution; commercial and exchange-rate policies; the geographic distribution of social services; the nature of public-investment programmes; attitudes toward private foreign investors; the organization of population and family-planning programmes; the structure, content, and orientation of the educational system; the functioning of labour markets; and the nature of public policies toward international technology transfer and the location of new industries.

There is thus a clear need to recognize the central importance of rural–urban migration and to integrate the two-way relationship between migration and population distribution on the one hand and economic variables on the other into a more comprehensive framework designed to improve development-policy formulation.

In addition, we need to understand better not only why people move and what factors are most important in their decision-making process but also what the consequences of migration are for rural and urban economic and social development. If all development policies affect migration and are affected by it, which are the most significant, and why? What are the policy options and trade-offs among different and sometimes competing objectives (e.g., curtailing internal migration and expanding educational opportunities in rural areas)? Part of our task in the following sections will be to seek answers to these and other questions relating to migration, unemployment, and development.

6. Internal migration in Africa: some general observations

An understanding of the causes and determinants of rural–urban migration and the relationship between migration and relative economic opportunities in urban and rural areas is central to any analysis of African employment problems. Because migrants comprise a significant proportion of the urban labour force in most African nations, the magnitude of rural–urban migration has been and will continue to be a principal determinant of the supply of new job-seekers. And if migration is a key determinant of the urban labour supply, the migration process must be understood before the nature and causes of urban unemployment can be properly understood. Government policies to ameliorate the urban unemployment problem must be based, in the first instance, on knowledge of who comes to town and why.

7. The migration process

The factors influencing the decision to migrate are varied and complex. Because migration is a selective process affecting individuals with certain economic, social, educational, and demographic characteristics, the relative influence of economic and non-economic factors may vary not only between nations and regions but also within defined geographic areas and populations. Much of the early research on migration tended to be focused on social, cultural, and psychological factors while recognizing, but not carefully evaluating, the importance of economic variables. Emphasis has variously been placed in five broad areas:

1 Social factors, including the desire of migrants to break away from traditional constraints of social and/or tribal organizations;
2 Physical factors, including climate and meteorological disasters like floods and droughts;
3 Demographic factors, including the reduction in mortality rates and the concomitant high rates of rural population growth;
4 Cultural factors, including the security of African urban extended-family relationships and the allure of the 'bright city lights';
5 Communication factors, including improved transportation, urban-oriented educational systems, and the modernizing impact of the introduction of radio, television, and the cinema.

All these non-economic factors are, of course, relevant. However, there now seems to be widespread agreement among economists and non-economists alike that rural–urban migration can be explained primarily by the influence of economic factors. These include not only the standard push from subsistence agriculture and the pull of relatively high urban wages but also the potential push back toward rural areas as a result of high urban unemployment.

8. Migrant characteristics

It is convenient to divide the main characteristics of migrants into three broad categories: demographic, educational, and economic.

Demographic characteristics

Urban migrants in Third World countries tend to be young men and women between the ages of 15 and 24. Various studies in Africa and Asia have provided quantitative evidence of this phenomenon in countries such as Kenya, Tanzania, Ghana, Nigeria, India, Thailand, South Korea, and the Philippines. In recent years, the proportion of migrating women has increased as their educational opportunities have expanded. This increase, substantial in many countries, has been particularly evident in Latin America, Southeast Asia, and West Africa. In fact, women now constitute the majority of the migration stream in Latin America, largely as a result of its relatively advanced state of urbanization compared with other developing regions (Brigg, 1971). Basically, there are two types of female migration: the 'associational' migration of wives and daughters accompanying the 'primary' male migrant and the migration of unattached females. It is the latter type of migration that is increasing most rapidly in Africa.

Educational characteristics

One of the most consistent findings of rural–urban migration studies is the positive correlation between educational attainment and migration. There seems to be a clear association between the level of completed education and the propensity to migrate – people with more years of schooling, everything else being equal, are more likely to migrate than those with fewer. In a comprehensive study of migration in Tanzania by Barnum and Sabot, for example, the relationship between education and migration was clearly documented, especially in terms of the impact of declining urban employment opportunities on the educational characteristics of migrants (Barnum and Sabot, 1975). Secondary school dropouts were found to constitute a rising proportion of the migration stream. The explanation that Barnum and Sabot offered was that limited urban employment opportunities were being rationed by educational levels, and only workers with at least some secondary education had a chance of finding a job. Those with only a primary-school education were finding it very difficult to secure employment, and hence their proportionate numbers in the migrant stream began to decline.

Economic characteristics

For many years, the largest percentage of urban migrants were poor, landless, and unskilled individuals whose rural opportunities were for the most part non-existent. In colonial Africa, seasonal migration was predominant, with migrants from various income levels seeking short-term urban jobs. Recently, however, with the emergence of a stabilized, modern industrial sector in most African urban areas, the situation has changed. Migrants, both male and female, seem to come from all socioeconomic strata, with the majority of them being very poor only because most rural inhabitants are poor.

9. An economic theory of African rural–urban migration

Historically, the economic development of Western Europe and the United States was closely associated with, and in fact defined in terms of, the movement of labour from rural to urban areas. For the most part, with a rural sector dominated by agricultural activities and an uban sector focusing on industrialization, overall economic development in these countries was characterized by the gradual reallocation of labour out of agriculture and into industry through rural–urban migration, both internal and international. Urbanization and industrialization were in essence synonymous. This historical model served as a blueprint for the development of Third World nations, as evidenced, for example, by the original Lewis theory of labour transfer.

But the overwhelming evidence of the past few decades, when Third World nations in general and African countries in particular witnessed a massive migration of their rural populations into urban areas despite rising levels of urban unemployment and underemployment, lessens the validity of the Lewis two-sector model of development.[6] An explanation of the phenomenon, as well as policies to address the resulting problems, must be sought elsewhere. In a series of articles over the past two decades I have attempted to develop a theory of rural–urban migration to explain the apparently paradoxical relationship (at least to economists) of accelerated rural–urban migration in the context of rising urban unemployment (see e.g., Todaro, 1969; Harris and Todaro, 1970). This theory has come to be identified in the literature as the Todaro Migration Model.

10. A verbal description of the Todaro model

Starting from the assumption that migration is primarily an economic phenomenon, which for the individual migrant can be a quite rational decision despite the existence of urban unemployment, the Todaro model postulates that migration proceeds in response to urban–rural differences in expected income rather than actual earnings. The fundamental premise is that migrants and their families consider the various labour-market opportunities available to them in the rural and urban sectors and choose the one that maximizes their expected gains from migration. Expected gains are measured by the difference in real incomes between rural and urban work and the probability of a new migrant's obtaining an urban job. A schematic framework showing how the varying factors affecting the migration decision in Africa interact is given in Figure 3.2.

In essence, the theory assumes that members of the labour force, both actual and potential, compare their expected incomes for a given time horizon in the urban sector (the difference between returns and costs of migration) with prevailing average rural incomes, and migrate if the former exceeds the latter.

Consider the following illustration. Suppose that the average unskilled or semi-skilled rural worker has a choice between being a farm labourer (or working his own land) for an annual average real income of, say, 50 units, or migrating to the city, where a worker with his skill or educational background can obtain wage

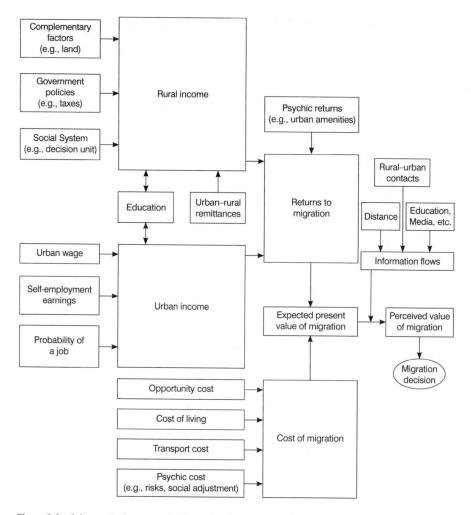

Figure 3.2   Schematic framework for analysing the migration decision
Source: Derek Byerlee, 'Rural–urban migration in Africa: Theory, policy and research implications', *International Migration Review*, 3 (Winter 1974): 553.

employment yielding an annual real income of 100 units. The more commonly used economic models of migration, which place exclusive emphasis on the income-differential factor as the determinant of the decision to migrate, would indicate a clear choice in this situation. The worker should seek the higher-paying urban job. It is important to recognize, however, that these migration models were developed largely in the context of advanced industrial economies and hence implicitly assume the existence of full or near-full employment. In a full-employment environment, the decision to migrate can be based solely on the desire to secure the highest-paid job wherever it becomes available. Simple economic theory would then indicate that such migration should lead to a reduction in wage differentials through the interaction of the forces of supply and demand, in areas of both emigration and immigration.

Unfortunately, such an analysis is not realistic in the context of the institutional and economic framework of most African nations. First, these countries are beset by a chronic unemployment problem so that a typical migrant cannot expect to secure a high-paying urban job immediately. In fact, it is much more likely that on entering the urban labour market, many uneducated, unskilled migrants will either become totally unemployed or will seek casual and part-time employment as vendors, hawkers, repairmen, and itinerant day labourers in the urban traditional or informal sector, where ease of entry, small scale of operation, and relatively competitive price and wage determination prevail. In the case of migrants with considerable human capital in the form of a secondary or university certificate, opportunities are much better, and many will find formal sector jobs relatively quickly. But they constitute only a small proportion of the total migration stream. Consequently, in deciding to migrate, the individual must balance the probabilities and risks of being unemployed or underemployed for a considerable period of time against the positive urban–rural real income differential. The fact that a typical African migrant can expect to earn twice the annual real income in an urban area than in a rural environment may be of little consequence if the actual probability of his securing the higher-paying job within, say, a one-year period is one chance in five. Thus the actual probability of his being successful in securing the higher-paying urban job is 20 per cent, and therefore his expected urban income for the one-year period is in fact 20 units and not the 100 units that an urban worker in a full-employment environment would expect to receive. So with a one-period time horizon and a probability of success of 20 per cent, it would be irrational for this migrant to seek an urban job, even though the differential between urban and rural earnings capacity is 100 per cent. However, if the probability of success were 60 per cent and the expected urban income therefore 60 units, it would be entirely rational for our migrant with his one-period time horizon to try his luck in the urban area, even though urban unemployment may be extremely high.

If we now approach the situation by assuming a considerably longer time horizon – a more realistic assumption, especially in view of the fact that the vast majority of migrants are between the ages of 15 and 24 – the decision to migrate should be represented on the basis of a longer-term, more permanent income calculation. If the migrant anticipates a relatively low probability of finding regular-wage employment in the initial period but expects this probability to increase over time as he is able to broaden his urban contacts, it would still be rational for him to migrate, even though expected urban income during the initial period or periods might be lower than expected rural income. As long as the present value of the net stream of expected urban income over the migrant's planning horizon exceeds that of the expected rural income, the decision to migrate is justifiable. This, in essence, is the process portrayed in Figure 3.2.

Rather than equalizing urban and rural wage rates, as would be the case in a competitive model, we see that rural–urban migration in our model acts as an equilibrating force that equates rural and urban expected incomes. For example, if average rural income is 60 and urban income is 120, a 50 per cent urban unemployment rate would be necessary before further migration would no longer be profitable. Because expected incomes are defined in terms of both wages and employment probabilities, it is possible to have continued migration despite the existence of sizeable rates of urban unemployment. In our example, migration would continue even if the urban unemployment rate were 30 to 40 per cent. Conversely, if the urban–rural wage gap declines, migration could continue to accelerate if the urban unemployment rate also declines.

11. A diagrammatic presentation

This process of achieving an unemployment equilibrium between urban expected wages and average rural income rather than an equalized rural–urban wage as in the traditional neo-classical free-market model can also be explained by a diagrammatic portrayal of the basic Todaro model. This is done in Figure 3.3.[7] Assume only two sectors, rural agriculture and manufacturing. The demand for labour (the

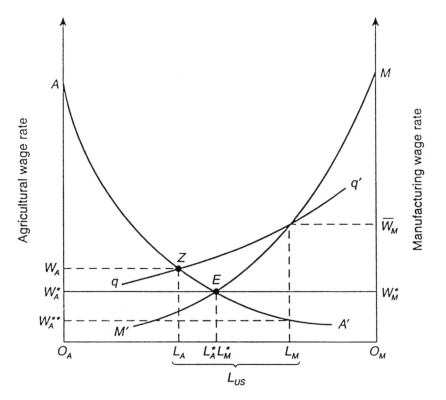

Figure 3.3 The Todaro migration model

marginal product of labour curve) in agriculture is given by the negatively sloped line AA'. Labour demand in manufacturing is given by MM' (reading from right to left). The total labour force is given by line O_AO_M. In a neo-classical, flexible-wage, full-employment market economy, the equilibrium wage would be established at $W_A^* = W_M^*$, with $O_AL_A^*$ workers in agriculture and $O_ML_M^*$ workers employed in urban manufacturing. All available workers are therefore employed.

But what if urban wages are institutionally determined at a level $\bar{W}_M$, which is at a considerable distance above W_A^*?[8] The validity of this assumption was recently confirmed in a careful econometric study of urban formal sector wage determination in Ghana.[9] If for the moment we continue to assume that there is no unemployment, O_AL_M workers would get urban jobs, and the rest, O_AL_M, would have to settle for rural employment at $O_AW_A^{**}$ wages (below the free-market level of $O_AW_A^*$). So now we have an urban–rural real wage gap of $\bar{W}_M - W_A^{**}$, with $\bar{W}_M$ institutionally fixed. If rural workers were free to migrate (as they are almost everywhere except in parts of China), then despite the availability of only O_AL_M jobs, they are willing to take their chances in the urban job lottery. If their chance (probability) of securing one of these favoured jobs is expressed by the ratio of employment in manufacturing, L_M, to the total urban labour pool, L_{US}, then the expression

$$W_A = \frac{L_M}{L_{US}}(\bar{W}_M)$$

shows the probability of urban job success necessary to equate agricultural income W_A with urban expected income $(L_M/L_{US})(\bar{W}_M)$ thus causing a potential migrant to be indifferent between job locations. The locus of such points of indifference is given by the qq' curve in Figure 3.3.[10] The new unemployment equilibrium now occurs at point Z, where the urban–rural actual wage gap is $\bar{W}_M - W_A$, O_AL_A workers are still in the agricultural sector, and O_ML_M of these workers have modern (formal) sector jobs paying $\bar{W}_M$ wages. The rest, $L_{US} = O_ML_A - O_ML_M$, are either unemployed or engaged in low-income informal sector activities. This explains the existence of urban unemployment and private economic rationality of continued rural-to-urban migration despite this high unemployment. However, although it may be privately rational from a cost-benefit perspective for an individual to migrate to the city despite high unemployment, it can, as we shall soon discover, be socially very costly. Finally, note that if instead of assuming that all urban migrants are the same, we incorporate the reality of different levels of human capital (education), we can understand why a higher proportion of the rural educated migrate than the uneducated – because they have a better chance (a higher probability) of earning even higher urban wages than unskilled migrants.

To sum up, the Todaro migration model has four basic characteristics:

1 Migration is stimulated primarily by rational economic considerations of relative benefits and costs, mostly financial but also psychological.
2 The decision to migrate depends on expected rather than actual urban–rural real wage differentials where the expected differential is determined by the

interaction of two variables, the actual urban–rural wage differential and the probability of successfully obtaining employment in the urban sector.

3   The probability of obtaining an urban job is directly related to the urban employment rate and thus inversely related to the urban unemployment rate.

4   Migration rates in excess of job opportunity growth rates are not only possible but also rational and even likely in the face of wide urban–rural expected-income differentials. High rates of urban unemployment are therefore inevitable outcomes of the serious imbalance of economic opportunities between urban and rural areas in most African countries.

12. Five policy implications

Although this theory might at first seem to devalue the critical importance of rural–urban migration by portraying it as an adjustment mechanism by which workers allocate themselves between rural and urban labour markets, it does have important policy implications for African development strategy with regard to wages and incomes, rural development, and industrialization.

First, imbalances in urban–rural employment opportunities caused by the urban bias of many African development strategies must be reduced. Because migrants are assumed to respond to differentials in expected incomes, it is vitally important that imbalances between economic opportunities in rural and urban sectors be minimalized. Permitting real urban wage rates to rise at a greater pace than average rural incomes (or, indeed, to fall, as in the 1980s, at a slower pace) will stimulate further rural–urban migration in spite of rising levels of urban unemployment. This heavy influx of people into urban areas not only gives rise to socioeconomic problems in the cities but may also eventually create problems of labour shortages in rural areas, especially during the busy seasons. These social costs may exceed the private benefits of migration.

Second, urban job creation is an insufficient solution for the urban unemployment problem. The traditional (Keynesian) economic solution to urban unemployment (the creation of more urban modern-sector jobs without simultaneous attempts to improve rural incomes and employment opportunities) can result in the paradoxical situation where more urban employment leads to higher levels of urban unemployment! Once again, the imbalance in expected income-earning opportunities is the crucial concept. Because migration rates are assumed to respond positively to *both* higher urban wages *and* higher urban employment opportunities (or probabilities), it follows that for any given positive urban–rural wage differential (in most of Africa, urban wages are three to four times as large as rural wages), higher urban employment rates will widen the expected differential and induce even higher rates of rural–urban migration. For every new job created, two or three migrants who were productively occupied in rural areas may come to the city. Thus if 100 new jobs are created, there may be as many as 300 new migrants and therefore 200 more urban unemployed. Hence a policy designed to reduce urban unemployment may lead not only to higher levels of urban unemployment but also to lower levels of agricultural output, due to induced migration.

Third, indiscriminate educational expansion will lead to further migration and unemployment. The Todaro model thus has important (and unconventional) policy implications for curtailing investment in excessive educational expansion, especially at the higher levels. The heavy influx of rural migrants into urban areas at rates much in excess of new employment opportunities has necessitated a rationing device in the selection of new employees. Although within each educational group such selection may be largely random, many observers have noted that employers tend to use educational attainment of number of years of completed schooling as the typical rationing device. For the same wage, they will hire people with more education in preference to those with less, even though extra education may not contribute to better job performance. Jobs that could formerly be filled by those with a primary education (sweepers, messengers, filing clerks, etc.) now require secondary training; those formerly requiring a secondary certificate (clerks, typists, bookkeepers, etc.) must now have a university degree. It follows that for any given urban wage, if the probability of success in securing a modern-sector job is higher for people with more education, their expected income differential will also be higher, and they will be more likely to migrate to the cities. The basic Todaro model therefore provides an economic rationale for the observed fact in most LDCs that rural inhabitants with more education are more likely to migrate than those with less.

From the viewpoint of educational policy, it is safe to predict that as job opportunities become scarce in relation to the number of applicants, students will experience increasing pressure to proceed further up the educational ladder. The private demand for education, which in many ways is a derived demand for urban jobs, will continue to exert tremendous pressure on African governments to invest in post-primary school facilities. But for many of these students, the spectre of joining the ranks of the 'educated unemployed' becomes more of a reality with each passing year. Government overinvestment in post-primary educational facilities thus often turns out to be an investment in idle human resources.

Fourth, wage subsidies and traditional scarcity-factor pricing can be counterproductive. A standard economic policy prescription for generating urban employment opportunities is to eliminate factor-price distortions by using 'correct' prices, perhaps implemented by wage subsidies (fixed government subsidies to employers for each worker employed) or direct government hiring. Because actual urban wages generally exceed the market or 'correct' wage as a result of a variety of institutional factors, it is often argued that the elimination of wage distortions through market price adjustments or a subsidy system will encourage more labour-intensive modes of production. Although such policies can generate more labour-intensive modes of production, they can also lead to higher levels of unemployment in accordance with our argument about induced migration. The overall welfare impact of a wage-subsidy policy when both the rural and urban sectors are taken into account is not immediately clear. Much will depend on the level of urban unemployment, the size of the urban-rural expected-income differential, and the employment elasticity of induced migration as more urban jobs are created.[11]

Finally, programmes of integrated rural development should be encouraged. Policies that operate only on the demand side of the urban employment picture, such as wage subsidies, direct government hiring, elimination of factor-pricing distortions, and employer tax incentives, are probably far less effective in the long run in alleviating the unemployment problem than policies designed directly to regulate the supply of labour to urban areas. Clearly, however, some combination of both kinds of policies is most desirable.

Policies of rural development are crucial to this aim. Many informed observers agree on the central importance of African rural and agricultural development if the urban unemployment problem is to be solved. Most proposals call for the restoration of a proper balance between rural and urban incomes and for changes in government policies that currently give development programmes a strong bias toward the urban industrial sector (e.g., policies in the provision of health, education, and social services).

Given the prevailing urban bias and thus the political difficulties of reducing urban–rural real wage differentials, the need continuously to expand urban employment opportunities through judicious investments in small- and medium-scale labour-extensive industries, and the inevitable growth of the urban industrial sector, every effort must be made to broaden the economic base of the rural economy. The present unnecessary economic incentives for rural–urban migration must be minimized through creative and well-designed programmes of integrated rural development. These should focus on both farm and nonfarm income generation, employment growth, health-care delivery, educational improvement, infrastructure development (electricity, water, roads, etc.), and the provision of other rural amenities. Successful rural development programmes adapted to the socioeconomic and environmental needs of diverse African countries seem to offer the only viable long-run solution to the problem of excessive rural–urban migration.

To assert, however, that there is an urgent need for policies designed to curb the excessive influx of rural migrants is not to imply an attempt to reverse what some observers have called inevitable historical trends. Rather, the implication of the Todaro migration model is that there is a growing need for a policy package that does not *exacerbate* these historical trends toward urbanization by artificially creating serious imbalances in economic opportunities between urban and rural areas.

13. Summary and conclusions: the shape of a comprehensive migration and employment strategy

In this essay, we have looked at possible policy approaches designed to improve the very serious migration and employment situation in African countries. We conclude with a summary of what appears to be the growing consensus of most economists on the shape of a comprehensive migration and employment strategy.[12] This would appear to have six key elements:

1 *Creating an appropriate rural–urban economic balance.* A more appropriate balance between rural and urban economic and noneconomic opportunities appears to be indispensable for amelorating both urban and rural unemployment problems and for slowing the pace of rural–urban migration. The main thrust of this activity should be in the integrated development of the rural sector, the spread of small-scale industries throughout the countryside, and the reorientation of economic activity and social investments toward the rural areas.

2 *Expansion of small-scale, labour-intensive industries.* The composition or 'product mix' of output has obvious effects on the magnitude (and, in many cases, the location) of employment opportunities because some products (often basic consumer goods) require more labour per unit of output and per unit of capital than others. Expansion of these mostly small-scale and labour-intensive industries in both urban and rural areas can be accomplished in two ways: directly, through government investment and incentives, particularly for activities in the urban informal sector, and indirectly, through income redistribution (either directly or from future growth) to the rural poor, whose structure of consumer demand is both less import-intensive and more labour-intensive than that of the rich.

3 *Elimination of factor-price distortions.* There is ample evidence to demonstrate that correcting factor-price distortions, primarily by eliminating various capital subsidies and curtailing the growth of urban wages through market-based pricing, would increase employment opportunities and make better use of scarce capital resources. But by how much or how quickly these policies would work is not clear. Moreover, their migration implications would have to be ascertained. Correct pricing policies by themselves are insufficient to alter significantly the present employment situation.

4 *Choosing appropriate labour-intensive technologies of production.* One of the principal factors inhibiting the success of any long-run programme of employment creation both in urban industry and rural agriculture is the almost complete technological dependence of African nations on imported (typically labour-saving) machinery and equipment from the developed countries. Both domestic and international efforts must be made to reduce this dependence by developing technological research and adaptation capacities in the countries themselves – ideally as a co-operative and co-ordinated regional endeavour. Such efforts might first be linked to the development of small-scale, labour-intensive methods of meeting rural infrastructure needs, including roads, irrigation and drainage systems, and essential health and educational services. This is an area where scientific and technological assistance from developed countries and their non-governmental organizations could prove extremely helpful.

5 *Modifying the direct linkage between education and employment.* The emergence of the phenomenon of the educated unemployed is calling into question the appropriateness of the massive quantitative expansion of African educational systems, especially at the higher levels. Formal education has become the

rationing tunnel through which all prospective jobholders must pass. As modern-sector jobs multiply more slowly than the numbers of persons leaving the educational tunnel, it becomes necessary to extend the length of the tunnel and narrow its exit. Although a full discussion of educational problems and policies is beyond the scope of this essay, one way to moderate the excessive demand for additional years of schooling (which in reality is a demand for modern-sector jobs) would be for African governments, often the largest employers, to base their hiring practices and their wage structures on other criteria. Moreover, the creation of attractive economic opportunities in rural areas would make it easier to redirect educational systems toward the needs of rural development. At present, many African educational systems, being transplants of colonial systems, are oriented toward preparing students to function in a small modern sector employing at the most 20 to 30 per cent of the labour force. Many of the necessary skills for development thus remain largely neglected.

6   *Reducing population growth* through reductions in absolute poverty and inequality, particularly for women, along with the expanded provision of family planning and rural health services. Clearly, any long-run solution to African employment and urbanization problems must involve a lowering of current high rates of population growth. Even though the labour force size for the next two decades is already determined by today's birthrates, the hidden momentum of population growth applies equally as well to labour-force growth. Together with the demand policies identified in points 1 through 5, reducing rural population growth with its delayed impact on urban labour supply provides an essential ingredient in any strategy to combat the severe employment problems that African countries face now and in future years.

Notes

1   This paper draws on material that appears in Chapter 8 of my book, *Economic Development*, sixth edition (New York and London: Addison-Wesley Longman, 1997). Support from the Compton Foundation is gratefully acknowledged.
2   For additional information on the problems of rapid urban population growth, see Renaud (1981). A less concerned viewpoint is expressed in Williamson (1988).
3   These results were reiterated in the *Program of Action* of the 1994 International Conference on Population and Development, para. 91.
4   For a concise review of this debate, see Rakowski (1994).
5   For evidence of the deteriorating urban employment situation in Sub-Saharan Africa during the 1980s, see ILO (1988, 1989); Ghai (1987); and especially Becker *et al.* (1994).
6   Although the *rate* of rural–urban migration slowed during the 1980s, especially in Latin America and Sub-Saharan Africa, as a result of declining urban real wages and fewer formal-sector employment opportunities, the actual number of migrants continued to expand.
7   This graph was first introduced in Corden and Findlay (1975), and reproduced and described in Williamson, (1988:443–5).
8   While the Todaro model focuses on the institutional determinants of urban wage rates above the equilibrium wage, several other authors have sought to explain this phenomenon by focusing on the high costs of labour turnover in urban areas and the notion of an

efficiency wage – an above-equilibrium urban wage that enables employers to secure a higher-quality workforce and greater productivity on the job. For a review of these various models, see Stiglitz (1974) and Yellen (1984).

9   Francis Teal, 'The size and sources of economic rents in a developing country manufacturing labour market', *Economic Journal* 106 (July 1996):963–76.

10 Note that qq' is a rectangular hyperbola, a unitary-elasticity curve showing a constant urban wage bill; that is, $L_M \times W_M$ is fixed.

11 For a formal treatment of the determinants of induced migration, see Todaro (1976).

12 See, for example, Fields (1987); Becker *et al.* (1994, Chapters 4–7); Turnham (1993:245–53); and Streeten (1994:50–64).

References

Barnum, Henry N. and Richard H. Sabot (1975) *Migration, Education and Urban Surplus Labour*, OECD Development Center Employment Series Monograph. Paris: OECD.

Becker, Charles M., Andrew M. Hammer and Andrew R. Morrison (1994) *Beyond Urban Bias in Africa: Urbanization in an Era of Structural Adjustment*. Portsmouth, NH: Heinemann.

Brigg, Pamela (1971) *Migration to Urban Areas: A Survey*, World Bank Staff Working Paper, No. 107. Washington, DC: World Bank.

Corden, W. Max and Ronald Findlay (1975) 'Urban unemployment, intersectoral capital mobility, and development policy', *Economica*, 42:59–78

Fields, Gary S. (1987) 'Public policy and the labor market in less developed countries', in David P. Newberry and Nicholas Stern (eds), *The Theory of Taxation for Developing Countries*. New York: Oxford University Press.

Ghai, Dharam (1987) *Economic Growth, Structural Change and Labour Absorption in Africa, 1960–85*, UNRISD Discussion Paper No. 1. Geneva: United Nations Research Institute for Social Development.

Harris, John R. and Michael P. Todaro (1970) 'Migration, unemployment, and development: a two-sector analysis', *American Economic Review*, 60 (March):126–42.

International Labour Organization (1988 and 1989) *World Labour Report*. Geneva: ILO.

Jolly, Richard (1970) 'Rural–urban migration: Dimensions, causes, issues and policies', in *Prospects for Employment Opportunities in the Nineteen Seventies*. Cambridge: Cambridge University Press.

McNamara, Robert S. (1984) 'The population problem: Time bomb or myth?' *Foreign Affairs*, 62:1107–131.

Rakowski, Cathy A. (1994) 'Convergence and divergence in the informal sector debate: A focus on Latin America, 1984–92', *World Development*, 22:501–16.

Renaud, Bertrand (1981) *National Urbanization Policy in Developing Countries*. New York: Oxford University Press.

Stiglitz, Joseph (1974) 'Alternative theories of wage determination and unemployment in LDCs: the labor turnover model', *Quarterly Journal of Economics*, 88 (May).

Streeten, Paul P. (1994) *Strategies for Human Development: Global Poverty and Unemployment*. Copenhagen: Handelshøjskolens.

Teal, Francis (1996) 'The size and sources of economic rents in a developing country manufacturing labour market', *Economic Journal*, 106 (July):963–76.

Todaro, Michael P. (1969) 'A model of labor migration and urban unemployment in less developed countries', *American Economic Review*, 59 (March):138–48.

Todaro, Michael P. (1976) 'Urban job expansion, induced migration and rising unemployment: a formulation and simplified empirical test for LDCs', *Journal of Development Economics*, 3 (September):211–25.

Turnham, David (1993) *Employment and Development: A New Review of Evidence*. Paris: Organization for Economic Coordination and Development.

United Nations Population Division (1988) *World Population Monitoring, 1987*. New York: United Nations.

UNFPA (United Nations Population Fund) (1991) *Population, Resources, and the Environment.* New York: United Nations.

United Nations (1988) *The Prospects of World Urbanization.* New York: United Nations.

Williamson, Jeffrey G. (1988) 'Migration and urbanization', in Hollis B. Chenery and T.N. Srinivasan (eds), *Handbook of Development Economics*, Vol. 1. Amsterdam: North Holland, pp. 426–65.

Yellen, Janet L. (1984) 'Efficiency wage models of unemployment', *American Economic Review*, 74 (May).

4

Poverty, Employment and the Informal Sector: Some Reflections on the ILO Mission to Kenya

Hans W. Singer and Richard Jolly[1]

As Permanent Secretary of Finance and Planning, Philip Ndegwa played a major role in guiding and supporting the ILO (International Labour Organization) Employment Mission to Kenya in 1972. The report of this Mission made pioneering contributions to development thinking in the 1970s, most notably by developing the innovative strategy of redistribution from growth, by introducing for the first time internationally the concept of the informal sector and by pursuing a structural analysis to employment, which put major emphasis on problems of poverty, income distribution and the working poor. Philip ensured that the Kenya Government responded to the report's recommendations by issuing a Sessional Paper on the Mission.

With hindsight, one can see that the Mission's proposals came at the end of the Golden Age of the Keynesian Consensus. Fixed exchange rates had already been abandoned in 1971, and within months of the Mission's report oil prices had risen more than three times. The possibility of maintaining rapid growth rapidly faded, the terms of trade sharply declined and Kenya's debt mounted. These problems continued over the 1980s, compounded by growing political difficulties. Notwithstanding these impediments, some elements of progress were maintained in basic health and education, which represented, at least partially, implementation of some of the recommendations of the report and a modest degree of redistribution of human capital in favour of the poorer sectors of Kenya.

Ironically, the informal sector has grown even more than the Kenya Mission envisaged, though much less as a positive force for poverty reduction and more as an employment sector of last resort. Internationally the informal sector has received enormous attention, in both analysis, policy and action. With the preoccupation with adjustment, concepts of redistribution with growth have been relatively neglected in the literature, though they have recently found a revival, especially in interpreting the dramatically successful experience of the Asian economies. Philip, in his writings of the 1980s, frequently emphasized the need for much greater international action to tackle debt, commodity prices and the other severe pressures bearing down on the economies of Sub-Saharan Africa. When these international pressures are eased and the prospects for rapid economic growth return, redistribution with growth and the other messages of the Kenya report may still find their place.

Philip Ndegwa's name is closely linked with the ILO Employment Mission to Kenya of 1972 (ILO, 1972). He does not figure as one of the authors of the Mission's report, since he was of course technically a recipient. However, the Mission was a good example of the participatory approach, in effect a joint effort of the Kenyan side and the international experts. On the Kenyan side, Philip was a member of a highly competent trio – certainly every bit as competent as the international 'experts'. The trio consisted of Mwai Kibaki (then Minister of Finance and Planning), Philip Ndegwa (then Permanent Secretary of the Ministry), and Harris Mule (then Deputy Permanent Secretary). These three were a source of inspiration to the members of Mission; their advice and guidance were essential. Among the three, Philip Ndegwa was unquestionably considered to be the chief Kenyan counterpart of the Mission. So, when this contribution opens with a discussion of the ILO Mission, it should be on the understanding that much of Philip's thinking and influence was already involved at this early stage.

Philip Ndegwa's influence on the ILO Mission raises the general issue of 'mission integration with host governments' (see ILO, 1973). Quoting Jolly, Seers and Singer ('The Pilot Missions under the World Employment Programme'), the ILO evaluation points out that one of the main virtues of such an international mission is that it possesses the freedom from daily involvements – so rarely made available to government servants – which is necessary for a fundamental review of a strategic problem. On the other hand, the greater the degree of integration between the mission and the government, the greater the mission's access to information, the more likely it will be that the mission's proposals will be sensitive to local thinking and will concentrate on the practicable, and the greater the chances of implementation (ibid.:128). Retrospectively, and largely thanks to Philip, the ILO Kenya Mission seems to have struck the right compromise – in fact, getting the best of both worlds. Philip Ndegwa, although a busy civil servant, could distance himself sufficiently from daily involvements to help the Mission take a broad strategic view. Also, as a result of his contribution, the Mission Report did in fact deal with the topical and urgent actual problems of the Kenyan economy, and hence proved to be in line for a considerable degree of implementation.

Some other features of the Mission are worth recording. A particular effort was made to ensure that Mission members had first-hand knowledge of the Kenya economy: over half were Kenyans or had lived or worked two years or longer in Kenya. Friendship with Philip dating back to Makerere University was also important. It made for confidence and informal trust, both in working relationships and in achieving a shared economic and political perspective within which to tackle the problems presented.

In these respects, the Mission's approach contrasted strongly with some of the sceptical views of the time, illustrated in the article by Dudley Seers: 'Why visiting economists fail' and another by David Wall 'The new missionaries'. The experience of the Kenya Mission showed that such doubts over many missions which often failed reflected a weakness of approach and organization – not the inevitability of failure. Indeed, at an early stage, the Kenya Mission considered inviting a journalist research worker to participate in the meetings of the Mission, in order to document the strengths and weaknesses of the Kenya Mission approach. Philip himself was willing to do this, but ultimately overruled it when told the name of the person we were proposing, whom Philip judged unsuitable for this task. In some ways, this was a pity. With the enormous attention obtained by the Mission's report, and its record-breaking distribution, over 20,000 copies, it would have provided an interesting record of the strengths and weaknesses of the Kenya Mission process.

1. Employment and informal sector

The neglect of unemployment issues in the early 1960s is well illustrated by the following comment from the World Bank Report on Kenya of 1963: 'Unemployment is less of a social burden in Kenya than in industrial countries, in that in Kenya most people still have ties with the land which provide some minimum means of subsistence outside paid employment. The unemployment problem could be in large measure a transitory problem. It should not be a major determinant of the composition of the next development program' (IBRD, 1963:49).

The emphasis on full employment as perhaps the main objective of economic policy had only in the late 1960s been extended to developing countries. Earlier it was thought that unemployment was a characteristic only of industrial countries. Under the influence of Arthur Lewis and his concept of surplus labour, and combining it with the concept of 'disguised unemployment' developed by Joan Robinson, the mainstream of development economics had come round to the idea that the objective of full and productive employment was as essential to the reduction of poverty in developing countries as it was in industrial countries. Arthur Lewis had thought of surplus labour as confined to the agricultural and rural sector and hence of urbanization as a way of absorbing surplus labour into productive employment.

Though nine-tenths of Kenya's population was still rural, it was rapidly urbanizing, at nearly 8 per cent per year, a rate which placed its urban growth among the highest in the world. But a new element added to mainstream thinking was the Harris–Todaro model. Under this model, which in fact was developed with Kenya in mind, urbanization would not solve the problem of surplus labour but simply transfer it from the rural sector to the urban sector. This was attributed to the urban–rural income differential, which would cause rural–urban migration to be excessive in relation to urban jobs and thus lead to unemployment and surplus labour in the urban sector as well.

The new emphasis on employment as a development objective had other sources, in addition to Arthur Lewis, Joan Robinson, and Harris–Todaro. While the earlier emphasis had been on investment as the source of economic growth, embodied in the Harrod–Domar formula, it was soon felt and empirically established that human capital was as important or more important than physical capital. In the Harrod–Domar formula, this insight was tucked away in the denominator of the capital–output ratio. But clearly this did not do justice to the importance of skills, training, education and work experience as a major element in growth. To this was added a growing doubt as to whether growth was the proper ultimate objective rather than reduction of poverty or satisfaction of basic needs. This also led to the emphasis on employment: labour power is one of the chief assets of poorer people, and productive employment, for the great majority of the poor, is the most obvious way of obtaining a livelihood.

All these were modifications of, or variations from, thinking in the early years of the Keynesian Consensus. But the spirit of the time and of the ILO Mission was still very much part of the Keynesian Consensus. Keynes had been the forerunner of the idea of dual economies: the economic relations and policies in a state of unemployment equilibrium were not the same as the policies appropriate to a shift towards fuller employment or the maintenance of full employment equilibrium. In the same way, the situation in developing countries such as we found in Kenya was also dualistic. The conditions and relations governing what we called the formal sector were different from those governing the informal sector. Thus we came to look at the informal sector as part of a dualistic economic structure and not just as disguised unemployment or surplus labour.

Much of the creative passion with which the Mission argued the case for a positive view of the informal sector came from the pen of John Weeks. John had been a participant with ourselves in the seminar on the informal sector held at IDS Sussex in 1971. This seminar had taken the pioneering article by Keith Hart on the informal sector in Ghana as a key starting point (Hart, 1973). Keith had argued for a productive view of the informal sector but had focused on its illegal aspects as much as on its creativity. John Weeks stressed even more the productive aspects of the informal sector and emphasized its unenumerated activities as its essence. Thus the Mission came with this new insight, a new frame of analysis, and with a determination to explore its relevance to Kenya. The analysis of the informal sector became one of the significant points of innovation in the Mission's work, a point later taken up and developed in many other ways and countries by the ILO.

In re-evaluating the informal sector, the Kenya Mission acted very much in line with the approach of Dudley Seers, who at that time was leading an attack on GNP as the essence of development. Dudley Seers was a driving force behind the ILO Employment Missions and had spoken strongly for a need to 'dethrone GNP'. A unit of income accruing to a poor person has little weight in conventional calculations of growth of a country's GNP, but it is of major significance in assessing changes in the incomes and welfare of the poor. Under these influences the Kenya Mission emphasized that the income created in the informal sector accrued to poor producers and benefited poor consumers – hence the social value of the informal sector was not adequately measured by the national income statistics. This was in addition to other ways in which the national income was underestimated – such as ignoring transactions in kind – which might affect the informal sector more than others.

The Kenya Mission took place in the twilight of the Keynesian Consensus, with the Washington Consensus dawning over the horizon. The nemesis of the Keynesian Consensus was the inflationary pressure resulting from long-maintained full employment and the abolition of the fear of unemployment. This climaxed in the explosion of oil prices, which hit Kenya very hard and altered the macro-economic projections on which the Kenya Report was based. Today we find ourselves in the twilight of the Washington Consensus. Its nemesis was the new rise in unemployment. This gives the analysis of the Kenya Report and the other Employment Missions a new significance today. Philip Ndegwa was among the first to see the implications of this new shift – see the report of the Presidential Commission on Employment in Kenya, which he chaired and shaped.

Ironically, the organization of the formal industrial sector has itself moved in the direction of greater informality. The post-Fordist model of mass production has been superseded by a model of 'flexible specialization', based on lessons from Japanese and East Asian experience. Some of the things which the Kenya Report cites in describing informal sector activities could be written today in describing this shift within the formal sector. It provides ex-post justification not just for the re-evaluation of the informal sector in the Kenya Report, but also for such early approaches as Schumacher's 'small is beautiful' concept and the activities of the Intermediate Technology Development Group (ITDG). Both these were among the contemporary influences on the Report.

In addition to this structural shift in the nature of the formal industrial sector there has been the effect of 'downsizing' and deregulations. This has resulted in the much discussed (certainly in the UK) 'casualization' of work and greater job insecurity. There is now talk of an 'intermediate labour market'. All this moves the formal sector – now often qualified as the 'conventional formal sector' – in the direction of the informal sector and enhances its discussion in the ILO report. So we have two separate phenomena: the growth of the informal sector as a result of downsizing and dismissals in the formal sector, and the informalization of the formal sector itself. Both these phenomena have been described as applying in Latin America (ECLAC/CEPAL, 1996). Insofar as the downsized labour force moves into either unemployment (with nil productivity) or into low productivity informal sector activity, the overall or social gain in the productivity of private firms (a hallmark of adjustment) is lost or dissipated in the overall or social sense.

In addition to the shift in the organization of the formal industrial sector, there is also the pronounced shift from the industrial sector or manufacturing towards services. Services lend themselves particularly well to small-scale and flexible methods of production and the Kenya Mission Report put considerable emphasis on the value of the service activities of the informal sector. Services rendered by poor producers to poor customers are a self-targeting contribution to the reduction of poverty.

All this creates the danger of an idealization of the informal sector. Some of the critics of the Report believe that it did not escape that danger. However, there is plenty of emphasis in the Report on the low efficiency of informal sector activities, the poor environmental impacts of these activities, the danger that the informal sector might serve as an exploitative annex of large formal sector producers, the poor and often dangerous working conditions in the informal sector, etc. Indeed, the need for upgrading the informal sector is one of the main points of emphasis in the Report. Its main distinguishing feature was that we thought such upgrading not only to be necessary but also to be possible, and several ways of doing this were outlined. In the previous model of the informal sector as disguised unemployment such upgrading was considered not in terms of improvements within the informal sector but as a reduction of the informal sector and its progressive absorption by the formal sector.

The emphasis on the informal sector had some other important implications. It drew attention to the agricultural and rural sector in employment creation. If migration to the urban areas was so much in excess of formal sector employment opportunities, it would follow that greater efforts should be made to retain people in the rural areas and deal with the problem of surplus population at its source. Hence the Kenya Report suggested a rural public works programme, as well as many measures to raise small-farmer productivity and reduce rural poverty. Greater incentives to small farmers were suggested.

Given the important role of women in agricultural production in Kenya, and also the high proportion of woman-led rural households (with husbands in the urban areas), the Report also anticipated much of the later concentration of development thinking on gender issues. The strategic importance of women became a significant theme of the Kenya Report. The important roles of women in agriculture and rural development were emphasized, along with the need for training to raise their productivity and leadership skills. In urban areas, the need for self-help groups was recognized, along with more opportunities for employment and greater involvement of women in planning committees. To prepare for the future, a special emphasis was laid on achieving more equal access by girls to education and training and the establishment of a national women's bureau and a national commission to review the status of women.

2. Redistribution with growth

At the core of the Kenya Report was the proposal for a strategy of Redistribution with Growth (RWG). In part, this arose from the Report's emphasis on the 'working poor', rather than of unemployment in the strict sense or even of disguised unemployment. The Kenya Report proposed 'temporarily stabilising the real incomes of the receivers of the top 10 per cent of total incomes' (ILO, 1972:13). The resources gained would be *invested* in the programmes required to attain minimum income targets for the poorest rural and urban households, especially in labour-intensive employment-oriented projects benefiting the unemployed and the working poor. By this strategy, it was suggested that the incomes of the poorest 40 per cent of the rural population and the poorest 25 per cent of the urban population could be increased by 50 per cent within five years and doubled within twelve years at most. In terms of the real politik of this strategy, it was pointed out that those who would benefit would number almost two-fifths of the country's population, all Kenyans. Those who would pay the price would be the top 1 per cent of income receivers, all of course the power elite, but not all Kenyans, some being expatriate and non-citizens.

It is important to stress that this was an investment strategy, channelling the redistributed resources into productive investment in permanent opportunities for earning reasonable incomes, not into income transfers for consumption.

The RWG strategy proposed in the Kenya Report led directly to subsequent international work on this theme. There were close links, both between the leading members of the Missions and the Kenyan 'recipients' on the one hand, and the staff of the World Bank under the presidency of Robert McNamara on the other hand. In particular, the links with the research staff of the World Bank headed by Hollis Chenery were very close. As a result the Kenya Mission was instrumental in moving the World Bank to a strategy of 'Redistribution with Growth' (Chenery *et al.*, 1974). This grew directly from the Kenya Mission's proposed strategy of 'redistribution from growth'. The change from the 'from' to 'with' is significant: in the subsequent joint version with the World Bank, redistribution had advanced to become an integral part of the growth process, whereas in the original version of the Kenya Report, growth was put first as essential for providing the resources for redistribution. However, the concern for equity is common to both versions and the relation between growth and equity has remained a major feature of development economics ever since, merging more recently with the concept of human development. Issues of poverty reduction, income redistribution and growth were brought together in the RWG strategy.

The emphasis in the Report on redistribution *from* rather than *with* growth is related to the assumption of a very high growth rate of 7 per cent per annum. Such an assumption seemed justified in 1971/72 – Kenya was then considered to be one of the happiest economic stories of Africa. Projecting such a high growth rate, it was natural to rely on growth first for providing the resources for equity. In the event, this projection turned out to be widely over-optimistic. By the time the World Bank Report on *Redistribution with Growth* appeared, this had become apparent and understandably led to less emphasis on growth first as a provider of resources.

The assumption of a 7 per cent growth rate gave the ILO Report a generally optimistic flavour. Erik Thorbecke, in a subsequent critique, argued that the 7 per cent growth rate appears like a *deus ex machina* which makes the many suggestions of the Report capable of implementation (Thorbecke, 1973:60). In fact, the growth rate was derived as a *deus in machina*. The Kenya economic machine had for nearly a decade demonstrated its capacity to grow at 6.5–7 per cent, and it was argued that there was no reason to expect the Mission's proposals to lower this rate. But, as explained later, the Mission's proposals did not foresee the major changes which soon occurred in the international context.

The ILO Mission was in fact mostly concerned with the relationship between growth and the wider sharing of benefits, specifically through wider and more productive employment and raising the incomes of the 'working poor'. While recognizing the possibility of trade-offs between growth and greater equality, the report also pointed out areas of complementarity, i.e., where greater equality would help to increase output and growth. In this last respect the report foreshadowed some of the later discussions of 'human capital' and 'human development'. In the specific case of a newly independent country like Kenya, with dangerous regional, social, racial and individual disparities, an equity-oriented approach was also necessary for the national integration of the new state and its political stability. This last argument in favour of greater equality was very much in the mind of Philip Ndegwa and the other Kenyan counterparts (and members) of the Mission. It led the Mission to argue the case for regional quotas in access to civil service jobs, for access to secondary education and the establishment of new schools and for the allocation of government expenditure to offset urban biases.

The strategy of redistribution from (or with) growth must be sharply contrasted with trickledown strategy, which was still part of development orthodoxy at that time. Neither on the international nor on the Kenyan side was there a belief in anything like automatic trickledown – and this disbelief has been amply justified by subsequent experience. The redistribution required an active and specific policy, and much of the Report was devoted to spelling out the details of such a policy: rural public works, training and skill developments, greater efforts in educational and health provisions, credits for both small farmers and urban informal sector producers, encouragement of small-scale and labour-intensive technologies, etc. Such a policy would go much beyond the provision of social safety nets. With the broadening of the unemployment concept to include the working poor, there inevitably went a broadening of the concept of employment policy in the direction of an anti-poverty policy.

With hindsight, what can be learned from Kenya experience about the strategy proposed?

Implementation of the report's recommendations was to a considerable extent hampered by the explosive rise in oil prices a year later and its impact on Kenya which neither Philip Ndegwa and his Kenyan colleagues, nor the members of Mission could foresee.

The impact on the Kenya economy was severe. Growth slowed substantially under the impact of oil price increases and widespread drought in 1974–5. An unprecedented boom in world prices of coffee and tea boosted Kenya's growth in 1976–8, but recession then set in, and from 1978–85, income per capita fell. Economic growth, which had averaged 6.5 per cent per year over the six years before the Mission, slipped, and averaged no more than 2 per cent over the following two decades, as opposed to the 7 per cent assumed in the Mission's report.

Notwithstanding slower growth, important advances in health, education, literacy, life expectancy and child mortality were registered. Literacy more than doubled, from 32 per cent in 1970 to 77 per cent in 1990. The gross primary school enrolment ratio more than doubled from some 45 per cent in 1960 to about 95 per cent in 1990. Access to water increased from under a fifth in the 1970s to over half by the early 1990s, with over three-quarters of the population having access to health and basic sanitation. Such improvements were reflected in major advances in child mortality and life expectancy. Child mortality rates almost halved, from 202 in 1960 to 112 by 1980 and then declined, but at a slower rate, to 90 in 1994. Meanwhile, life expectancy increased from 45 years in 1960 to 54 years by 1994.

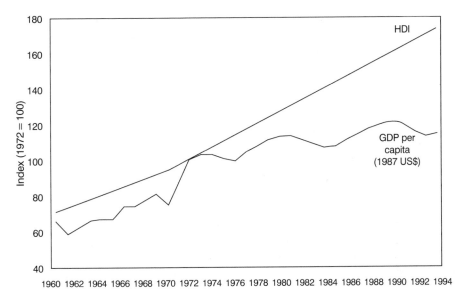

Figure 4.1 Economic growth and Human Development in Kenya

These human advances contrast sharply with the economic changes and set-backs, as shown in Figure 4.1. The human advances are captured by the steady increase in the Human Development Index of Kenya, which even shows a slight acceleration in the 1970s and 1980s over the 1960s. But as the figure brings out, the economic changes after 1972 were much slower than forecast and interrupted by the major economic setbacks over the lost decade of the 1980s.

What explains Kenya's failures to implement the RWG strategy? It is possible to adopt a worldly wise cynicism, or an analytical sceptical frame, to explain that those in power in Kenya at the time had no real interest in carrying through this part of the strategy proposed. A good deal of evidence could be marshalled to defend such a position, as indeed was done by Colin Leys in a brilliant and influential book issued soon after the Kenya Report. He wrote:

> The obvious puzzle presented by these proposals is what incentive the mission thought all these groups – the heart and soul of the alliance of domestic and foreign capital – might possibly have for making such sacrifices. Apart from anything else, there was at least a family resemblance between the mission's package of proposals and the essentials of the KPU's former programme. The KPU had not of course worked out a programme as fully or with as much sophistica-tion as the mission; but then the mission did not, for its part, seem to have pondered the significance of the suppression of the KPU. What did the mission think would induce the Kenyatta regime to do in the 1970s what it had not only not done, but had destroyed its opponents for advocating, in the 1960s?
>
> (Leys, 1975:262)

This uncompromising critique rested on strong arguments and many specific points and examples, not merely on a general ideological interpretation. It may well be that in the specific situation of Kenya in the early 1970s, with the economic and political hold of Kenyatta and those in power, there was no alternative.

But had the external circumstances of Kenya remained more favourable and Kenya's earlier growth rates of 7 per cent been maintained, what might have been the outcome? Certainly the constraints of conceding some measure of redistribution would have been greatly eased by higher growth rates. No one, of course, can say, but it is tempting to speculate.

With the benefit of hindsight, it is possible to speculate on how an alternative evolution might have looked in Kenya, using the example of Malaysia. Malaysia in 1970, beset by ethnic riots a year earlier, embarked on an explicit and far-reaching policy, with many elements of redistribution with growth. A twenty-year plan was prepared and adopted which involved explicit measures of redistribution: faster income growth for Malays of local origin, the poorer section of the population, with measures to expand their assets; large investments in education and health, including quotas to ensure fairer access (as the Kenya Report had recommended), targets for reducing poverty – and an acceleration of economic growth, with which to provide the resources needed for meeting many of the basic targets. The strategy was brilliantly successful. Malaysia's growth accelerated, to nearly 7 per cent per annum, many elements of redistribution were carried through and poverty was rapidly reduced. The proportion below the income poverty line in Malaysia fell from nearly 60 per cent in 1970 to 21 per cent in 1985 and to 14 per cent in 1993. The Gini coefficient fell to 0.45 and the share of the poorest 40 per cent of the population rose to nearly 14 per cent.

It is not our intention to argue that all this could simply have been repeated in Kenya. There were and are many, many differences between Malaysia and Kenya, not least in the political economy of the two countries, and of the interests and power base of those in position of leadership in the early 1970s.

But 25 years later, with the benefit of hindsight and the experience of redistributive strategies pursued in Asia, two important questions need to be raised, first in relation to economic growth, second in relation to leadership. Kenya's failure to sustain the 7 per cent growth meant that growth per capita fell from the assumed 3.5 per cent per annum, to 1.8 per cent per year until 1980, then became negative until 1985 with the second oil shock and the effects of stabilization. By 1994, per capita income in Kenya was barely 50 per cent higher than in 1972, over 25 years since the Mission. This provided a continual squeeze on resources over most of the period, instead of the margin of manoeuvre envisaged in the Kenya Report. In contrast, in the Asian tigers, poverty reduction and redistribution were successfully combined with rapid growth – and politically made easier by such growth.

Had the international context been more favourable, and Kenya's growth rates been maintained, might not the outcome in terms of incomes, redistribution and poverty been much more favourable? And had this occurred, might not the freedom of political manoeuvre been greater, even for some measures of redistribution?

The Kenya Report had called for enlightened leadership, for some sharing of the fruits of growth and wealth, and for the reduction of poverty and as a step to greater stability, politically and economically.

This again is an area where Kenya has experienced depressing problems, with inequality increasing and often political tensions increasing with it. What might have made the outcome different?

Philip Ndegwa continued throughout his career to call for enlightened leadership, and to demonstrate it in his own professional leadership. In one of his final books, he wrote about the role of political leadership. In this he said:

> The importance of political leadership in the process of economic development has sometimes been overlooked . . . Political leadership has a crucial role to play, akin in many ways to that of management at the level of the individual firm, in ensuring that the economic and social environment is conducive to development . . . a high degree of motivation can only be achieved through linking the interests of the people individually and collectively to the set of national objectives.
>
> (Ndegwa, 1986:145 and 148)

This perhaps should provide the final word on the situation and prospects in Kenya.

Note

1   We are indebted for research assistance to Mr Matthew Morris.

References

Chenery, H. *et al.* (1974) *Redistribution with Growth*, A Joint Study by the World Bank's Development Research Center and the Institute of Development Studies at the University of Sussex. Oxford: Oxford University Press.

ECLAC/CEPAL (1996) *Preliminary Overview of the Economy of Latin America and the Caribbean*. Santiago: ECLAC/CEPAL.

Hart, Keith (1973) 'Informal Income Opportunities and Urban Employment in Ghana', in Richard Jolly *et al.* (eds), *Third World Employment: Problems and Strategy*. London: Penguin.

IBRD (1963) *The Economic Development of Kenya*. Baltimore: Johns Hopkins University Press.

ILO (1972) *Employment, Incomes and Equality: A Strategy for Increasing Productive Employment in Kenya*. Geneva: ILO.

ILO (1973) *Strategies for Employment Promotion: An Evaluation of Four Inter-Agency Employment Missions*. Geneva: ILO.

Leys, Colin (1975) *Underdevelopment in Kenya*. Los Angeles: University of California Press.

Ndegwa, Philip (1986) *The African Challenge. In Search of Approach Development Strategies*. Nairobi: Heinemann Kenya.

Thorbecke, Erik (1973) 'The employment problem: a critical evaluation of four ILO comprehensive country reports', in ILO, *Strategies for Employment Promotion*. Geneva: ILO.

5

Civil Wars in Sub-Saharan Africa: Counting the Economic and Social Cost[1]

Frances Stewart

1. Introduction

Philip Ndegwa recognized that political stability was the most important precondition for sustained development (Ndegwa and Green, 1994). Unfortunately, violent internal conflict, or civil war, has been increasing in Sub-Saharan Africa (SSA). Conflict has been both a source and a consequence of underdevelopment, and any serious analysis of poverty and deprivation cannot neglect it. Of the ten countries ranking lowest in terms of income per capita or the Human Development Index, eight have experienced major conflict during the last quarter of a century. All the poor conflict-ridden countries are in SSA apart from Afghanistan.[2] While the end of the Cold War saw a diminution of conflicts which had been fuelled by Cold War tensions (conflict by proxy), such as in Mozambique and Angola, new eruptions occurred, such as in Somalia and Rwanda. The problem is without doubt an ongoing one.

The aim of this chapter is to present an overview of some of the economic and social costs of civil conflict in the last twenty-five years in SSA. The intention is not just to point to the heavy costs, but also analyse their nature and to identify mechanisms by which people and investments might be protected even in the midst of conflict.

The next section of the chapter provides an overview of the incidence and severity of conflict in SSA, putting it into the context of conflict worldwide. The third section presents a framework helpful in identifying the probable economic and social consequences of conflict, pointing to expectations about the nature, direction and magnitude of the effects of civil war, at macro, meso and household level. Section 4 reviews some empirical evidence of how major economic and social variables changed in the countries worst affected by conflict in the 1970s and 1980s. However, actual developments may not be indicative of the effects *due* to conflict, since many other changes were occurring simultaneously (e.g., the debt crisis and falling commodity prices) which affected what happened. Some attempt is made to allow for the counterfactual, by comparing performance in major variables in a conflict-country with that of developments in the region as a whole. Section 5 presents some conclusions about the magnitude of the effects and of possible domestic and international policies that might moderate them.

Clearly, the first-best solution is to avoid large-scale violent conflict; but if this is not possible, there is a need to analyse ways in which the costs of conflict might be reduced.

2. The incidence of violent conflict

The first issue to be dealt with is that of definition. Violent conflict occurs in all societies at all times: how does one differentiate what is commonly called 'crime' from 'civil war'? Two criteria are used: one is that the conflict challenges the government's authority, aiming to overthrow or change the regime, whereas crime, *per se*, is not directed towards political change. This challenge to government authority is usually organized. The second criterion is one of magnitude: only conflicts involving more than 1,000 deaths a year will be considered. Such deaths may be the direct outcome of the conflict (i.e., due to bullets, bombs, mines etc.), or indirectly caused as a result of some of the economic and social consequences of violence. When we come to an assessment of economic and social consequences, our investigations relate to countries that have lost 0.5 per cent or more of their 1990 population over the twenty years between 1970 and 1990. The reason is that smaller conflicts may not have visible consequences in the country-wide data which will be used. Once effects of the large conflicts have been identified, subsequent research may explore whether similar effects are to be found among countries experiencing smaller disturbances.

Data on pre-1960 conflicts[3] identifies no major African civil conflicts, but this is because of the way the data were compiled, as a number were excluded from the data base on the grounds that the countries concerned were not recognized states.

From 1960 to 1990, Africa was the region with the greatest number of conflicts in which more than 1,000 died per year of war, accounting for over a third of the total (Table 5.1). An estimated 6 million people died in SSA as a direct or indirect

Table 5.1 The incidence of conflict by region, 1960–90

Region	No. of countries in conflict	No. of countries in region	% of countries in conflict	Deaths from wars, 1960–90 (millions)	% of pop. in region who died in conflict
Africa	19	45	42	6.1	1.1
Asia	14	28	50	7.3	0.4
Middle East	8*	11	73	1.0	0.6
Latin America	12	24	50	0.5	0.1
Low-income	30	50	60	12.4	0.4
Lower-mid-income	17	33	52	2.4	0.4
Upper-mid-income	6	17	35	0.06	0.01
Total	53	98	54	14.9	0.4

* Includes Iran and Iraq international conflict
Source: Sivard (1991); World Bank (1995). A continent in Transition: Sub-Saharan Africa in the mid-1990s, Washington, DC., World Bank.

Table 5.2 Seven major conflicts in Sub-Saharan Africa: countries where over 0.5 per cent of population died, 1970s and 1980s*

	Deaths ('000s)		As % 1990 population		% civilian	
	1970s	*1980s*	*1970s*	*1980s*	*1970s*	*1980s*
Mozambique		1,050		6.7		95
Uganda	303	308	1.9	1.9	100	97
Angola		341		3.3		94
Sudan		506		2.0		99
Ethiopia		609		1.2		85
Somalia		55†		0.7		91
Liberia		15		0.6		93

* Includes war-related famine
† Excludes current problems
Source: Sivard (1991).

result of conflict. Although the African incidence is less than other regions when expressed as a proportion of the countries in each region, the number of deaths in Africa (direct and indirect) are the highest as a proportion of the population, exceeding 1 per cent, while deaths as a proportion of the population were 0.4 per cent in Asia and 0.1 per cent in Latin America (Table 5.1). (If India and China are excluded, however, the Asian incidence is comparable to that of Africa). Low-income countries had a higher incidence of wars (60 per cent of the countries, compared with 52 per cent among lower-middle-income countries and 35 per cent among upper-middle-income). The incidence of deaths was the same (0.4 per cent) among low and lower-middle-income countries, but much lower among upper-middle-income countries (0.01 per cent) and developed countries (almost zero from 1960–90).

In Africa, with over 40 per cent of the countries affected by conflict over these years, war has become a major obstacle to development. During the 1970s and 1980s, six countries in SSA suffered such extensive conflict that 0.5 per cent or more of the population died (Table 5.2). According to these estimates Mozambique was worst affected, with nearly 7 per cent of the 1990 population dying as a result of conflict in the 1980s. These seven countries – Mozambique, Uganda, Angola, Sudan, Ethiopia, Somalia and Liberia – will form our sample for the analysis of costs that follows.

3. An economic framework for analysis

A UNICEF Report on Cambodia graphically draws attention to the types of cost that can be sustained.

> In 1979 lack of food was exacerbated by people deserting the rice paddies and eating available food stocks, including seed and draught animals. Much of the

surviving population moved about the country in search of their family and homes. Few facilities for training and education remained. The country was without even a rudimentary health care system, and there was a lack of most medical supplies. The industrial infrastructure as well as most roads and bridges had deteriorated beyond use. There was no functioning administrative structure and personnel had to be found for the newly-established posts at a time when hardly anyone in the country had performed other than agricultural tasks since 1975, and when the majority of professional and technical cadres had been killed or fled the country.

(UNICEF, 1990:4)

Direct deaths in battle form only a small part of the costs of conflict. This is indicated by the high proportion of civilian deaths in the data in Table 5.2. Indirect deaths and suffering are caused by the workings of the economy during war, for example due to famine resulting from loss in agricultural production as people flee and agricultural land is mined, or the consequences of rapidly escalating inflation on those with fixed monetary incomes set off by deficit financing, or from epidemics caused by deteriorating health services combined with mass migration and malnutrition. The indirect costs are the main concern of this paper, since it is with respect to these that economic analysis can be most illuminating and policy measures most helpful.

The costs of war can be divided, somewhat artificially, into immediate human costs and longer-term development costs. The division is artificial because human costs, such as reduced nutrition and lack of education, also form development costs, while development costs (e.g., destroyed infrastructure) are among the causes of immediate human suffering. But analytically it is helpful to distinguish them.

The human costs of conflict

Mechanisms by which war can lead to human suffering of an 'indirect' kind occur at three levels: the macro (or aggregate level of output and incomes), meso (determining the allocation among sectors and groups) and micro (or at the level of the household or individual). Effects at each level interact with other levels.

To explore these indirect effects, two aspects of the economy are key: what happens to production, in total and its sectoral allocation; and what happens to entitlements (or household or individual claims over goods and services)? The two interact, as production failures (or gains) are generally reflected in some entitlement losses (or gains), but there can be major changes in entitlement without any significant production losses; conversely, vulnerable households can be protected from production losses if their entitlements are sustained. The concept of entitlements comes from Sen (1991). Entitlements were defined by Sen as legal claims over goods or services, which might either be direct (i.e., own-produced or subsistence) or market entitlements (or cash which 'entitles' people to buy goods and services). In this paper the concept is modified and extended. First, claims over socially produced and unpriced goods (e.g., health services) are defined as *public* entitlements (Stewart, 1993). The realization of public entitlements requires both provision of the goods and services and also access for individuals. Secondly, those entitlements which derive from civil society (the community, NGOs, or the family) are termed *civil* entitlements (O'Sullivan, 1997). Thirdly, illegal activities, such as theft, can be an important source of survival in conflict. For completeness, we shall describe these as *illegal entitlements*, although this oxymoron might seem objectionable, since people are not normally regarded as *entitled* to what they acquire by violence and theft. The level and distribution of entitlements are likely to change substantially during conflict, with severe reductions for many house-holds leading to deprivation and even death; and gains for others giving them a vested interest in the continuation of conflict.

Conflict can lead to negative effects at each level, macro, meso and micro, by having adverse effects on both production and entitlements in ways that can cause immense human suffering. But there are also compensatory mechanisms which can modify the costs somewhat.[4]

Clearly, the effects of conflict depend in part on its nature and duration, and the conditions (income levels, structure, external dependency, flexibility) in the economy concerned. For example, a conflict which involves the placing of mines in agricultural terrain on a large scale, as in Mozambique, will have significant negative effects on food and possibly export production, with highly adverse effects on the economy as a whole and the well-being of many people if a large proportion of economic activity and employment is agricultural based. In con-trast, an economy which is highly dependent on trade, such as an oil-exporting economy which imports most food, would be badly affected by a trade embargo, which might have little effect on the first type of economy.

Features of conflicts which are relevant to the economic effects include:

- the magnitude of the conflict, in terms of the proportion of the population actually fighting or being threatened – and hence potential deaths, migration and loss of trust;
- the duration of the conflict: in a short conflict, countries and households can call on various forms of reserve, but have little time to adapt. In a prolonged conflict, reserves are run down, but adaptation of various types is possible (e.g., new sources of income and employment may be created; new markets identified, etc.);
- the geographic spread of the conflict;
- the role and strength of the government and of quasi-governmental struc-tures introduced by opposition forces. If governments collapse (and are not replaced by strong quasi-governmental structures), significant adverse effects can be expected on revenue collection and government expenditure, on security and hence on trust and transactions;
- international reactions to the conflict in terms of financial flows (which may be increased in support of government or rebels or decreased as a result of the conflict) and trade policies (embargoes, etc.).

Characteristics of the economy which are relevant include:

- the extent, actual and potential, of subsistence production, especially of food, as a proportion of total activities; the higher the subsistence level the more might people (and the economy) be protected against large losses, unless inhabitants are forced to migrate from subsistence areas;
- the dependence of the economy on imports; a highly dependent economy will be particularly adversely affected by loss of export earnings and/or foreign finance;
- the dependence of the economy on a few large plants (e.g., power plants), which are vulnerable to attack;
- the dependence of the economy on modern institutions, including a legal framework and a modern banking sector, in which transactions are supported by a set of institutions and assumptions that lead to trust between strangers; this type of dependence is more likely in more developed economies (see Collier, 1995).
- the flexibility of the economy; flexible economies (as defined by Killick, 1995) will find it easier to adapt by substituting for imports, finding new markets, repairing or replacing damaged equipment, developing alternatives for formal sector institutions where these break down, etc.

Characteristics of the society which influence the human costs of conflict:

- how near to subsistence people are; when they are very near the survival limit, small changes can have devastating effects; the same changes might have only minor effects in richer economies (e.g., nutrition actually improved in wartime Britain, despite a cut in food availability, as rationing improved distribution);
- support networks available to people, through their own families, civil society or the state; in general societies with strong family or community networks are able to protect people better when the state and other civil networks break down;
- the strength of governments, quasi-governments and NGOs;
- policies adopted by governments, quasi-governments and foreign organizations to provide support for those adversely affected.

Bearing in mind the factors which determine economic consequences, we can suggest some general directions of change in economic variables that are likely to result from civil conflict:

1. Macro-effects

GDP per capita is likely to be adversely affected (i.e., either to fall or to rise less than it would have done in the absence of conflict) as a result of both direct and indirect effects.

Direct effects include output loss due to damage to physical assets, including destruction of plant, roads, etc. and mining of agricultural land; deaths and migration of people and diversion to military activities; damage to institutions leading to loss of trust. Unskilled men of prime working age are likely to be particularly hit by deaths and diversion; skilled labour is most likely to leave the country. How large these direct effects are will depend on how fully capacity was used prior to the conflict.

Indirect effects arise from the follow-on effects of the direct effects; for example, the loss of a power plant not only constitutes a loss in output in itself, but may cause other production facilities to close down or operate at lower levels. Reduced finance for (or access to) imports, arising from loss of export earnings, reduced external finance etc., may have a multiplier effect on domestic production. (see Di Addario, 1997)

Savings.   In absolute terms, domestic savings are likely to fall as incomes fall. It is difficult to predict, *a priori*, whether the marginal propensity to save will rise or fall: on the one hand, it might be expected to fall as people attempt to sustain their consumption levels in the face of unexpectedly falling incomes; on the other, precautionary reasons for sustaining savings will increase, and the non-availability of consumption goods may lead to forced savings (see Di Addario, 1997). 'Forced' foreign savings may also rise, at least in the short term, as people are unable to secure foreign exchange to pay for the goods they have bought. These forced foreign savings could also take the form of government or private sector failure to meet interest payments or repayments of old debt. Voluntary private lending from abroad is likely to fall with falling confidence; but government lending may either increase or fall, depending on political factors (for example, there was enormous US government lending to South Vietnam in the late 1960s).

Investment.   Investment is likely to fall. Both domestic and foreign private investment will be adversely affected by reduced confidence in the future, lesser trust and deterioration in transport and communications, raising transactions costs. Local investment is likely to find increasing difficulties in getting access to finance. Foreign investors will be concerned about the safety of their personnel and are likely to perceive a greater foreign exchange risk. Government investment is likely to be negatively affected by reduced revenue, and diversion of expenditure to military uses (see below). Falling investment will affect the growth of GDP adversely.

Government revenue is likely to fall absolutely and as a proportion of GNP as the government finds it more difficult to collect taxes and major sources of revenue (e.g. exports) fall away.

Government expenditure may be restrained by any fall in revenue, although probably not proportionately so that *budget deficits* are likely to rise.

Inflation.   The normal expectation is that inflation is liable to accelerate, as governments resort to deficit financing to support the conflict and finance other essential services.

2. Meso-effects

Within the economy, we may expect transaction-intensive activities to fall relative to less transaction-intensive ones (Collier, 1995). This means that activities involving a higher proportion of sales between agents, those needing a large amount of working capital and those with significant transport requirements are likely to be discouraged. This would mean relatively more subsistence production, reduced formal and increased informal sector activity and, proportionately, less manufacturing and less long-distance trading domestically and internationally.

Within *government expenditure*, we may expect increasing resources devoted to military uses, and hence a squeeze on other expenditures including economic and social.

3. Effects on households

Household composition is likely to change, with men joining the army, being killed or migrating. Women are likely to acquire greater responsibilities, often becoming head of household and chief income provider, while female opportunities may also increase as traditional attitudes are undermined by war.

Both market and public entitlements may decline on average, though not for all households. Market entitlements decline as a result of reduced employment and real wages, with the losses in production and rising inflation noted above. Entitlement losses can be dramatic and life-threatening in contexts where food prices escalate – as in the Bengal famine of the 1940s, attributed by Sen (1991) to war deficit financing. Public entitlements to social services may fall as absolute levels of government expenditure are curtailed and the share of the social sectors is reduced. The resulting deterioration in health conditions, with reduced immunization levels, worsening water conditions, and higher rates of infection arising from movement and concentration of people combined with low levels of resistance because of poor nutrition, can be a major cause of loss of life in some conflicts (de Waal, 1989). Civil entitlements may rise to offset the fall in other entitlements in contexts where civil society remains effective, but elsewhere, where society itself disintegrates, they may fall. In general, we would expect *illegal entitlements* to rise sharply for some, but these are not additional to the total entitlements of society but consist of a transfer from some people to others.

Indicators of human well-being – for example, mortality rates, nutrition rates and school enrolment – would be expected to worsen.

It must be emphasized that these expectations are for the population as a whole: some groups gain resources during conflict, sometimes making spectacular fortunes (see Duffield, 1992; Keen, 1994).

Development costs

These consist in the destruction of existing assets and the reduction of new investment. Table 5.3 identifies categories of capital which are most likely to be

Table 5.3   Development costs of conflict

Destruction of existing capital		New investment reduced
Physical production infrastructure	transport system irrigation power factories	Fall in private investment Government investment cut Development aid reduced
Social infrastructure	schools clinics hospitals	Government investment cut Development aid reduced NGOs switch to relief
Human capital	educated and skilled people killed or migrate	School enrolments fall, partly due to reduced physical and human capital in sector
Organizations	government machinery debilitated; banks, extension services, legal system undermined	New formal organizations /expansion of existing ones postponed
Social/cultural capital	reduced trust, work ethic, respect for property	Antagonistic groups formed; some development of informal sector substituting for formal organizations

adversely affected, including physical and social infrastructure, institutional cap-ital and, perhaps most critically, social and cultural capital, in the form of trust and social cohesion which is vital for the effective functioning of society and the economy.

Summary

The differing conditions in war-affected countries make it difficult to generalize about the consequences of conflict. However, broadly, the following seem likely to occur compared with what might have been expected in the absence of conflict: at a macro level reduced GDP per capita, lower export earnings and probably imports, a reduced investment ratio and probably savings ratio, reduced govern-ment revenue and expenditure, higher budget deficits and higher inflation. At a meso level, a switch to government expenditure on the military from economic and social sectors would be expected; and within economic activity, a switch from tradables to non-tradables, from production which is exchanged to subsistence production, and from formal to informal sectors. At a micro level, average levels of entitlements of all kinds are likely to decline, sometimes with catastrophic con-sequences for human survival. Indicators of well-being are likely to worsen. There is likely to be some destruction of existing capital of all types and reduced invest-ments leading to heavy development costs.

It needs to be emphasized that in predicting the consequences of conflict, as with natural disasters, there are two types of effect: the immediate consequences of the conflict, and the reactions to these effects. Humans are very ingenious, and while it is fairly straightforward to predict the immediate consequences, the reactions can be large, unexpected and often have compensatory effects, as has been shown in the realm of natural disasters (see Albala-Bertram, 1993).

4. The consequences of conflicts in Sub-Saharan Africa 1970–90: empirical evidence

This section of the paper attempts to assess actual changes that occurred in the SSA countries worst affected by conflict in the 1970s and 1980s, investigating whether they accord with the expectations about probable change just discussed.

There are two important reasons (among others) why it is extremely difficult to identify the consequences of civil conflict empirically. The first is that there is generally a lack of reliable data during conflict, itself partly a reflection of a weakening in government machinery for collecting and processing data, as bureaucracies are undermined and their focus is diverted to conflict-related issues. In addition, the tendency for the official economy to decline relative to the informal and subsistence economy during conflict means that those indicators that are available, normally relating to the formal economy, fail to capture a large and growing segment of activity.

The second reason is that even when the basic facts are established, this does not mean that what happened can be attributed solely to conflict since other developments, such as changing international terms of trade, were taking place simultaneously. It is therefore necessary to try and establish a 'counterfactual'. This is even more difficult than normal for three reasons: first, pre-conflict relationships that might be used to model the economy may break down;[5] secondly, the data deficiencies during conflict make it almost impossible to model the economy; and thirdly, comparisons with developments in similar but not war-affected countries may not be legitimate because often it is differences in initial economic conditions that gave rise to the conflict.

This paper adopts three approaches to this difficult issue. The first is to explore the direction of change in the major variables identified above. This simply records what happened and does not deal with the counterfactual. The second approach is to compare behaviour of the variables during the conflict with previous performance; if everything else is unchanged, any change provides an indicator of the effects of conflict. The third approach is to compare each conflict country's ranking on various indicators within the region before and during the conflict. This approach takes the counterfactual position to be the behaviour of the rest of the region. In addition, by calculating the difference between actual behaviour of a variable in a conflict-ridden country and the change in the variable on average in the region it is possible to come to a rough estimate of the magnitude of the effect. However, this would provide an underestimate of the effects of conflict since average regional behaviour is affected by the performance of war-torn economies within it.

The conclusions of all three approaches taken together provide a fairly reliable indication of the direction of the effects if not the precise magnitude, but none of the methods, of course, can get round the problem of data deficiencies.

Table 5.4 The macro-effects of conflict: GDP per capita, exports and imports

Variables	Number of countries increased during conflict	Number of countries decreased during conflict	Regional average (positive or negative)	Number improved compared to pre-conflict	Number worse compared to pre-conflict	Ranking change number improved	Ranking change number worse
GDP per capita growth	0	5	+ 70s − 80s	0	2	0	2
Food prod. per cap	0	6	+ 70s − 80s	0	6	2	3
Export growth, % pa	0	4	+	0	4	1 nc	5
Import growth, % pa	4	1	+ 70s − 80s	2	2	0	2
GDS as % GDP	6	0	+	0	6	2	2
GDI as % GDP	6	0	+	2	4	1	0
Gov. rev. % GDP	4	0	na	1	1	3	na
Gov. expend. % GDP	4	0	na	2 nc / 2	1	na	na
Budget surplus % GDP	0	4	na	1 nc / 0	4	na	na
Inflat. (Cons. prices)	not applic.	not applic.	na	1 lower compared to pre-conflict	4 higher compared to pre-conflict	1 nc	3

nc = no change; na = not available
Source: World Bank, World Tables, 1994; World Development Report (various).

Macro-changes

The findings with respect to macro-variables are summarised in Table 5.4, which provides as much evidence as available on the three methods. It shows whether countries in conflict experienced positive or negative performance and what happened in the region as a whole for comparison. It also indicates whether countries' performance improved or worsened in the conflict, compared with the pre-conflict situation. And finally, where there are sufficient data, it shows how the ranking of countries in conflict altered.

The indicators invariably suggest that the *GDP growth rate was reduced by the conflict.* All countries with data experienced falling GDP per capita. However, in most of the countries the conflict occurred in the 1980s which were, in general, a bad decade for economic growth in Africa. But for the two countries where we can rank countries within their region before and during the conflict, the ranks worsened. The average drop in rank for the two was large, from 19th to 35th.

For *food production per capita* there has been a negative impact for all countries. There was a drop of nearly 20 per cent, on average, in food production per capita during the war years compared with pre-war. This indicator is a particularly valuable one because, in principle at least, it should encompass non-marketed production. Moreover, food availability is a key element in determining human welfare, and indeed survival, especially with foreign exchange problems diminishing the capacity to import food. The universal, and often large, declines in food production confirm the negative impact on GDP per capita, since food production accounts for a large proportion of GDP, in most cases increasingly so during conflict;[6] this evidence also points to the heavy human costs of conflict.

The value of exports fell during the wars in all the countries for which data are available. The worst was in Somalia, where exports fell by 16 per cent. However, imports were not so badly affected, rising in dollar terms in four out of five cases while ranking was improved in two cases and worsened in two. The relative insulation of imports can be explained by rising foreign debt.

In section 3 we argued that the probable effect on the savings ratio was uncertain, although we would expect a negative effect on investment. For these conflicts, however, the gross domestic savings ratio fell in every case in SSA, with a quite dramatic fall in Ethiopia, Mozambique and Uganda, the ratio at least halving and sometimes becoming negative. The regional ranking worsened in two out of the three African countries for which there are data. Contrary to expectations, the negative effects appeared *less* marked for the investment ratio which rose in two cases, falling in four; and where it fell, it did so by much less than the fall in savings. Ranking indicators also show that the investment ratio, held up relative to regional performance in Africa, where the ranking rose in all three cases for which there are data (Mozambique, Somalia and the Sudan). This largely reflects the poor investment performance of countries in Africa as a whole over the 1980s. Still the results for investment are surprising, indicating a greater resilience than expected, perhaps in response to war damage and new economic opportunities offered by the war. Nonetheless, in absolute terms investment did poorly, falling per capita in each country.

Government revenue as a proportion of GDP *did not invariably fall* in conflict countries: it fell in one case, rising in one and showing no significant change in two. This is an indicator which reveals the biggest divergence in behaviour. For example, in Ethiopia the revenue ratio rose sharply, while in Uganda it fell dramatically. There are some indications of similar divergence among the countries without systematic data – with a large fall in revenue in Somalia, but sustained revenue collection, relative to GDP, in Mozambique. One explanation for these differences is that Mozambique and Ethiopia had 'centrally planned' economies with extensive state ownership and control of enterprises in the modern sector. In Somalia and Uganda the collapse of government explains failure to collect taxes – with massive smuggling of normally taxed commodities, especially coffee and cotton. In Sudan, the South, where the conflict was centred, accounted for a relatively small proportion of modern economic activity and Sudan also received considerable flows of aid which enabled her to sustain public expenditure.

Budget deficits increased in every country for which data are available. Massive deficits developed in Mozambique and Somalia – of more than 15 per cent of GDP. But Uganda ran only small deficits. Government expenditure mostly rose or remained unchanged as a proportion of GDP. But in some countries it fell dramatically – in Uganda and probably also Somalia. These were countries which lost their tax collection capability. Falling GDP per capita meant that only the countries with very large increases in their expenditure ratios were able to sustain real levels of government expenditure per head, such as Ethiopia. Elsewhere, and especially where the effects of falling GDP per head were compounded by falling expenditure ratios, like Uganda, there were large falls in government expenditure per head.

The inflation rate generally rose, as predicted. In Liberia, however, consumer prices apparently fell. Inflation rates of over 40 per cent a year were recorded in Mozambique, Uganda, Somalia and Sudan. Most of the conflict countries experienced inflation rates considerably above the regional norm. The impact on inflation may be a key variable determining market entitlements, especially in the short run, with sharp increases potentially having very damaging effects on well-being and even survival.

Meso-changes

Sectoral changes

Sectoral changes are difficult to capture accurately because data only cover the formal sector. Given this limitation we can detect some general changes in the conflict-affected countries. For the most part there was a decline in the proportion of output accounted for by *industrial activity* in African countries: it declined significantly in four countries (Uganda, Mozambique, Somalia and Liberia), remained unchanged in Ethiopia and rose in the Sudan. In parallel, the proportion of GDP accounted for by *agriculture* rose in most of those countries where the industrial proportion fell. For example, in Mozambique industry fell from 24 to 18.5 per cent of GDP and agriculture rose from 47 to 55 per cent. In most countries, the proportion of output accounted for by *services* also rose, Uganda being an exception. These changes would be greater if one included the switch to the informal and subsistence sectors, which tend to be much more concentrated on agriculture and services. Chingono has recorded the large rise in informal sector activity in Mozambique, while Green has documented its development in Uganda, which anecdotal evidence suggests occurred during all the conflicts.[7]

These sectoral changes are in the opposite direction to the changes for the regions as a whole: in Sub-Saharan Africa on average there was a large rise in share of industry from 1965 to 1990 and a fall in the share of agriculture, the service share increasing slightly.

The sectoral changes in conflict countries are consistent with the predictions for what might be expected with a breakdown in trust associated with conflict. They could also be due to a shortage of foreign exchange to finance imported inputs, which are used more intensively in industry than agriculture or services.

Government expenditure patterns

It is not possible to generalize about the consequences of conflict for government expenditure patterns, partly because of huge lacuna in the data, and partly because countries followed different paths. The syndrome predicted is of rising military expenditure financed by squeezing social and economic expenditures, thereby accentuating the social and economic costs of conflict. But this pattern rarely occurred. In fact, Table 5.5 shows only Liberia followed this pattern consistently with a reduction in both the share of health and education in government expenditure.

As expected, the share of military expenditure in GDP and in government expenditure rose in every case for which we have data (Table 5.6). The extent of the rise varied considerably. According to the Swedish International Peace Research Institute data, military expenditure rose to around 30 per cent of GDP in Angola and to 23 per cent in Mozambique. But in Uganda, the Sudan and

Table 5.5 Changes in patterns of government expenditure during conflict

	Share of military: war compared with pre-war	Share of education: war compared with pre-war	Share of health: war compared with pre-war	Share of H+E: war compared with pre-war	Share of economic services	Share of invest-ment
Angola	++	na	na	na	na	−
Ethiopia	++	−	nc	−	na	−
Liberia	+	−	−	−	nc	−
Sudan	+	nc	+	+	−	−
Uganda	+	−	−	−	−	−
SSA, 70s	−	+	+	+	+	+
80s	−	−	−	−	−	−

+ = increase   ++ = large increase   − = decrease   nc = no change   na = not available
Source: SIPRI; World Bank, *World Tables, World Development Reports* (various).

Table 5.6   Military expenditure as a percentage of GDP

Country	1970s*	Peak	1994[†] or latest year
Angola	14.0 (1979)	28.4 (1985)	8.7
Ethiopia	1.9 (1971)	9.0 (1984)	2.6
		17.9[†] (1985)	
Liberia	1.0 (1971)	4.8 (1981)	2.5
Mozambique	5.6 (1980)	12.1 (1984)	7.1
		22.5[†] (1985)	
Somalia	6.8 (1979)	1.8 (1986)	na
		6.2[†] (1985)	
Sudan	4.8 (1971)	4.8 (1971)	3.5
Uganda	2.9 (1975)	3.4 (1984)	2.4

* First date available in the 1970s   † Source is UNDP
Sources: SIPRI *Yearbook*, various issues (Stockholm:SIPRI); UNDP,
Human Development Report 1996 (New York: OUP).

Liberia it remained below 5 per cent of GDP. In Ethiopia and Angola the share of military expenditure in total government expenditure more than doubled in war years compared with pre-war, with moderate rises in Liberia and the Sudan. The share of health and education fell in three out of the four cases for which there are data, but rose in Sudan.

One uniform finding for the countries is a drop in the share of investment in total government expenditure (Table 5.5). Expenditure on economic services contracted as well, in the majority of cases, also pointing to a medium term development cost.

A similar fall in investment and in expenditure on economic services occurred in general among non-conflict countries, with the cutbacks in government expenditure associated with adjustment policies in Africa.[8] The falls in the share of health and education also paralleled falls among adjusting countries in the 1980s.[9] The rise in military expenditure as a share of government expenditure, however, contrasts with developments elsewhere, as its share fell over these years.

What matters for social and economic development, of course, are the absolute changes. On the one hand, the rise in the share of government expenditure in GDP, which occurred in the majority of cases, protected social and economic expenditures, but on the other, GDP itself was falling, as recorded above. The net effect varied as indicated in Table 5.7, with two countries in Africa – Ethiopia and Sudan – actually experiencing a *rise* in social expenditures and two countries – Mozambique and Uganda severe falls.[10] The situation in conflict countries as a whole in SSA is certainly worse than this because countries where evidence is lacking – e.g. Liberia, Somalia – are known to have had a very poor performance, with weakening governments, falling revenue and reduced ability to provide social services.[11] Countries which achieved a rise in social sector expenditure did so by increasing the share of government expenditure in GDP. The worst case was that of Uganda, where expenditure per head on the social sectors fell by around

Table 5.7 Factors underlying changing expenditure on social and economic services

	Change in GDP per capita	Change in share of govt exp.	Change in govt exp. per capita	Change in social allocation ratio	Change in economic allocation ratio	Change in social exp. per capita % pa#	Change in econ. exp. per capita % pa#
Ethiopia	–	+	+	–	na	+1.6	na
Mozambique	–	–	–	na	na	–3**	na
Sudan	–	+	+	+	–	+3.4	–0.9
Uganda	–	–	–	–	na	–9.1	na

** estimate for Mozambique assuming social allocation ratio was unchanged   # rough estimates calculated from ratios.
+ = increase   – = decrease
Source: World Bank, *World Tables*; *World Development Reports*.

9 per cent annually, due to a dramatic collapse in government expenditure as a share of income, so that absolute levels of government expenditure per head fell to less than a quarter of their previous level, and there was also some fall in the share going to health and education.

The large differences in behaviour among countries with respect to these variables underlines the importance of government policies. At times of conflict, expenditures on the social sectors, especially health and support for food security, become of even greater importance for human well-being than normal. Many of the 'indirect' deaths are due to malnutrition combined with disease, which may be preventable if health services and food interventions are effective. As noted, the worst case, from this perspective, was Uganda, where revenue collection collapsed in the 1970s and government expenditures could not be sustained. This was not a policy decision, but a reflection of the debilitating nature of the conflict on the government machinery. It has been paralleled, it seems, in other conflicts (for which data are lacking), including probably Somalia.

3.   Effects on human well-being

The insecurities, migration and deaths which were the direct outcomes of the fighting obviously had adverse effects on human well-being in all conflicts. Indirect effects caused by changing entitlements varied.

As far as market entitlements are concerned, the fall in GDP per person which occurred in all the conflicts made negative effects for many probable. Large changes in asset and income distribution protected some groups, while worsening the situation for others. In the majority of countries there was a rise in consumption as a proportion of GDP, reducing the negative effects on short-term living standards. Nonetheless, growth in consumption was reversed in most cases, with sharp falls in consumption per head in Mozambique and Uganda. The situation with respect to public entitlements was more mixed and better in some countries, as just noted.

It is possible to build a fuller picture of the household situation, extending to more countries, by looking at specific basic needs goods and services availability.

Table 5.8   The availability of basic needs goods and services during conflict

Country	Primary school enrolment %		Calories per head		Population per doctor ('000s)	
	c.1980 or pre-war	c.1990 or end-war	c.1980 or pre-war	c.1990 or end-war	c.1980 or pre-war	c.1990 or end-war
Angola	148	24	2230	1880	13.2 ('65)	25.0
Ethiopia	37	25	1735	1700	58.5 ('80) 79.0 ('84)	32.7
Liberia	71	35 ('87)	2390	2260	9.6	9.3 ('84)
Mozambique	104	60	2170	1810	18.9 ('70) 38.0 ('84)	33.3
Somalia	41	15 ('85)	1950	1870	14.3	16.1 ('84)
Sudan	51	50	2450	2040	8.9	10.1
Uganda	67 (65)	50 ('80) 77 ('90)	2385 ('65)	1760 ('80) 2085 ('85)	9.2 ('70)	26.8 ('80) 25.0 ('90)
SSA	50 (1970)	68	2065 ('177)	2170	31.8 ('70)	23.5

Sources: World Bank, *World Tables; World Bank World Development Reports*; UNDP, *Human Development Report 1995;* World Bank, *Accelerated Development in Sub-Saharan Africa* (1981).

Calorie availability per person fell in every case (Table 5.8). In some countries deficiencies became acute, attaining, on average, only 70 per cent of requirements in Mozambique, Ethiopia and Uganda for some years. There was a worsening situation with respect to doctor availability in Ethiopia where the ratio of population to doctors was 79,000 in 1984, compared with 70,000 in 1965, and deterioration also in Uganda, Angola and Mozambique. However, Sudan succeeded in improving its ratios during the conflict. Each country also saw worsened primary school enrolment ratios, with very sharp falls in Angola, Mozambique and Somalia. In Angola and Ethiopia the enrolment ratio fell to one quarter and in Somalia to just 15 per cent. But Sudan managed to keep its ratio broadly constant at half.

The deterioration in these indicators during conflict was virtually universal, and was worse than occurred among similar countries not at war. The data show average performance of each country taken as a whole. Undoubtedly some groups within any economy avoided the negative effects altogether and flourished, while others were able to protect their standards relatively – for example by retreating into subsistence activities. In some cases, the distributional effects were mediated by government policies: for example, Mozambique had food rations which reached the urban areas, although generally rural areas received little help. Outside Africa, Nicaragua and Iraq had strongly redistributive food subsidies and food rations which protected many from malnutrition.[12] However, collapsed governments were unable to pursue such policies, while other governments (e.g., in Sudan) did not want to.

Infant mortality rates (IMRs) are a sensitive indicator of human well-being. While there are strong forces making for improvements in these rates over time, notably rising levels of female education and higher levels of immunization, these forces were overturned at the peak of the conflict in most countries – all seven of

Table 5.9 Infant mortality rates among countries at war

	1965				1994	Change 94/65	Expected IMR 1994 if avg. region improvement	Infant lives lost in 1994	Est. cumul. loss in infant lives, 1965–94[d], ('000s)[c]	War years
Angola	193	152 (1981)	169 (1987)	170 (1992–4)	170	.81	108	62/1000 =33,000	235 (2.2)	70–90
Ethiopia	166	145 (1981)	154 (1987)	(1992–4)	161[a]	.97	93	68/1000 =174,200	1,200 (4.8)	74–90
Liberia	180	127 (1985)	87 (1987)	146 (1992)	144	.79	101	43/1000 = 5,900	39 (1.4)	85; 90+
Mozambique	172	113 (1980)	141 (1987)	167 (1992)	161	.97	96	65/1000 =45,400	346 (2.2)	65–75; 81–90
Somalia	166	145 (1981)	152 (1985)	126 (1990)	125	.75	93	32/1000 =34,500	102 (1.1)	88–90
Sudan	161	97 (1977)	112 (1985)		94	.58	90	4/1000 =4,300	32 (0.1)	63–72; 84–90
Uganda	122	96 (1981)	116 (1981)	111 (1992–4)	111	.91	68	43/1000 =45,400	295 (1.4)	71–79; 71–87
SSA	167	115	107		93[a]	.56				

[a] 1993 [b] 1992 [c] Bracketed figures are percentages of 1994 population [d] Assuming the difference between the actual and potential IMR increased steadily from 1965 to 1994

Source: UNICEF, State of the World's Children; World Bank, World Development Reports.

the SSA countries showed increasing IMRs at some point during the 1965–94 period (Table 5.9). The Angolan rate at 170 per 1,000 in 1994 was among the highest in the world.

5. Conclusions

An exploration of the economic and social consequences of civil war is a huge subject. A short paper cannot cover everything, and must appear at times super-ficial. Moreover, as frequently noted, data deficiencies are one of the adverse consequences of conflict, which make it difficult to find out what has happened on the basis of internationally available statistics, without in-depth country stud-ies. There is also, unavoidably, the problem of identifying what would have happened in the absence of conflict. Nonetheless, our survey permits some important conclusions. Two stand out.

First, there are *large economic and social costs over and above the direct battle deaths.* The economic costs are shown in falls in GDP, food production and exports. All the countries in conflict showed worsening performance on GDP growth, and a worsening in their rank in the region,where evidence is available. A similar sharp adverse performance was shown by food production per capita in every country. Another uniformly adverse change was falling export growth (negative in almost all cases). In all cases the budget deficit became larger and in all but one inflation accelerated.

Falling output per head was reflected in worsening market entitlements, with falling consumption per head and in food availability per capita. Negative social effects are shown by the impact on infant mortality, which rose for some period, against all trends, in all six countries.

Longer-run development costs were of two types: the destruction and/or migra-tion of existing capital of all kinds, including physical plant, infrastructure, human and social capital. No direct estimates have been made of this destruction here, but the loss of output is indicative. Secondly, additions to the capital stock did not occur, or were less than they would have been, as indicated by reduced levels of investment, both public and private, reduced allocation of government expenditures to economic services, and falling school enrolments.

Two summary measures of the costs of war can be calculated. One is economic, consisting of a measure of the loss in output due to the conflict, calculated by comparing actual output loss with an estimate of how output would have grown had it done so in each country at the rate of the average growth for the region. The other is an estimate of the human costs of war, estimated as the number of infants that would have been alive if the country had improved its IMR at the same rate as the region as a whole. Both these could be expected to be underestimates since the changes on regional averages were themselves pulled down by the behaviour of countries in conflict. However, weak development performance appears to be one factor that contributes to conflict[13] so the countries in conflict might be expected to perform below the regional average even in the absence of conflict.

Table 5.10 Estimates of cumulative GDP loss

Country	GDP growth, % pa		Loss in growth compared with region, % pa		Cumul. loss of GDP: 1965–90 as % 1965 GDP
	1965–80	1980–90	1965–80	1980–90	
Ethiopia	2.7	1.8	−1.5	−0.3	−28.8
Uganda	0.6	2.8	−70.0	+7.2	−58.6
Somalia	3.5	2.4	−11.0	+3.0	−7.8
Sudan	3.8	2.5*	−6.2	+14.4	+7.2
Liberia	3.3	−1.3*	−14.4	−18.1	−35.1**
Mozambique	na	0.7	na	−31.8	−31.8#
All SSA	4.2	2.1 (0.8)*	Not applicable	Not applicable	Not applicable

* 1980–88   ** 1965–88   # 1980–90   na not available
Source: World Bank, *World Development Reports.*

On this basis, output losses are shown in Table 5.10. Five of the six countries had below average growth rates, Sudan being the exception. Sudan's conflict was regionalized, mostly confined to the south; in this respect it was similar to Sri Lanka, which also did not suffer a fallback in economic growth in aggregate (O'Sullivan, 1997). The worst output loss cumulated for the whole period was that of Uganda, at 59 per cent of the 1965 GDP. According to this method of calculation, output losses of over a third were experienced by Liberia and Mozambique. Data for Mozambique are only available for 1980–88. The picture would undoubtedly look worse taking a longer period.

Estimates for the additional infant mortality incurred in conflict countries in 1994 are given in Table 5.9. The largest costs were borne by Ethiopia, where infant deaths were 174,000 greater than they would have been had Ethiopian improvement followed the regional average. The estimated total additional deaths cumulated over all the years, 1965 to 1994 are over one million in the case of Ethiopia or nearly 5 per cent of the 1994 Ethiopian and Eritrean population. In the other countries, the estimated additional infant deaths due to conflict range from 2.2 per cent of the 1994 population (Mozambique) to almost zero in the case of Sudan. For Ethiopia, Somalia and Liberia these exceed all the estimated deaths from the conflicts, shown in Table 5.2.

The *second* finding is the *divergent behaviour among conflict-affected countries in many areas*, with some countries better able to protect themselves from various economic and social costs than others. The rather crude estimates for GDP loss in Table 5.10 indicate that Sudan actually did better than the regional average, while in other countries GDP losses were extremely large. Another example is imports: despite falling exports, imports rose in more countries than they fell, financed by rising foreign debt. There was also divergent behaviour on government revenue collection, with some countries managing to maintain (or in one case even increase) the ratio of GDP it collected in revenue. While the military share of government expenditure invariably rose, one country also increased the share going to health and education. This meant that expenditure on health and education per head actually rose in Ethiopia and Sudan during the conflict, despite falling GDP per capita and rising military expenditure. The protection of public entitlements contributed to the reduction of potential social costs. In the Sudan the IMR was *lower* in 1994 than if the regional average improvement, 1965–94, had been achieved.

The differing costs of conflict are the product of the nature of the conflict and of government structures and capacity, which are themselves affected by the conflict. The worst costs were incurred where the conflict was pervasive geographically and the government severely undermined, to the extent of being unable to collect taxes or provide services. This seems to have been the case in Uganda in the 1980s. Negative effects on social capital are also likely to be greatest in this context. In contrast, Mozambique, for some part of its conflict, was able to extend education and health services, though subsequently this was undermined; and Sudan avoided significant deterioration in the availability of most social services. There was generally a downward movement in economic entitlements. Here people's own capacity to find alternative occupations was important in helping sustain livelihoods – in particular in subsistence agriculture and the informal sector. The extent of these activities has not been recorded here because of dearth of statistics, but other evidence emphasizes their importance. The fact that the effects on human indicators was less severe than it might have been is a reflection of human resilience in severely adverse circumstances.

Policy implications

The idea that policies might be designed to moderate the economic and social costs of conflict, while it is going on, is not widely accepted. Governments are usually primarily concerned with prosecuting the war, and do not want to pursue policies which might help the rebels. Aid donors tend to delay development aid until the conflict is finished, believing that to do otherwise would be to 'waste' the aid. Action is confined to emergency relief supplies. In long drawn out conflicts such neglect can be costly in economic and social terms, especially since so many of the costs of conflict are indirect, and appropriate policies can be effective in reducing them.

Many of the indirect deaths during conflict are due to entitlement failures, especially entitlements for food (from subsistence or the market) and health services (public entitlements). The earlier analysis traced why these entitlement failures occurred. The empirical evidence from the African experience, and also elsewhere, shows that these effects can be modified or even avoided. For example, in Mozambique and Ethiopia, government action at times sustained entitlements through food rations or works programmes. Preventative health networks were expanded during the conflict in Mozambique and sustained in Sudan.

To avoid unnecessary deaths it is essential for governments to make the maintenance of essential entitlements a central objective of policy. This may be achieved in a variety of ways, including food rations and subsidies, employment schemes and infant and child feeding centres, making use of clinics and schools.

The maintenance and extension of publicly provided health services, particularly immunisation and treatment of diarrhoea, is perhaps of even greater importance and could avoid more deaths than any other single policy.

It is sometimes argued that the aid community should focus on emergency relief and not undertake development projects as these would be 'wasted'.[14] Apart from raising the development costs of conflict, this view is wrong even from the perspective of effective relief. Development projects are often needed to facilitate relief (e.g., roads), and such projects contribute directly to maintaining entitlements through the employment and incomes they create. Sustaining people's livelihoods during conflict is essential to avoid mass migration, and the economic collapse and human tragedy this represents. Rather than eliminate aid, what is needed is to redesign it in such a way that it contributes directly to maintaining essential entitlements, and does not take a form (e.g., large power plants) which attracts immediate destruction.

This approach to policy can be in conflict with the political aims of foreign governments. They may refuse to deal with governments that suppress minority rights, for example. The judgement on whether this is justified is a fine one. In many cases economic and aid embargoes do not cause governments to change policy, but rather accentuate the suffering of people living in the conflict-ridden country. In this sort of situation, there is a very strong argument for eliminating military aid and the supply of arms. But there is rarely a convincing case for policies directed at increasing the economic and human costs incurred.

Economic costs can be lessened by:

- keeping international markets open to sustain export earnings;
- providing foreign aid flows to offset losses in foreign exchange and government revenue;
- providing project/reconstruction aid to support institutions that are key for providing the framework for market transactions, including the transport and communication system; the banking sector; energy. But the nature of projects may need to be altered towards small less visible and vulnerable projects.
- advancing policies that support the credibility of government.

Irrespective of what aid donors do, a country's government remains the most important actor for ensuring adequate public entitlements and monitoring market entitlements. Sustaining tax revenue is a key. Governments which succeed in this also generally manage to sustain public entitlements.

Government policies which may reduce the economic and social costs include:

- policies which, if possible, reinforce the credibility and predictability of government economic policy and thereby reduce some of the uncertainties associated with conflict;
- policies that build up (not destroy) key sectors, even in rebel held areas;
- rapid reconstruction of key sectors (again reducing, where possible, vulnerability by smaller-scale more decentralized projects);

- policies that support (or at the minimum do not conflict with) new economic ventures, as, for example, the thriving informal sector activities;
- policies to sustain government revenue and protect government economic expenditures (including government investments);
- policies that maintain a preventative health network as a first priority, and ensure access to adequate food supplies and entitlements. (The best way to achieve this will vary with the specific circumstances.)

Mechanisms for achieving these objectives depend on the state of the war and the authority of the government or alternative administrative channels. Where government machinery is extant, the main issue may be one of finding finance to support the infrastructure, personnel and transport needed. But where rebels are in control, then resources (from donors or even the government) may need to be channelled via their structures. The worst case is where no governing structures are in evidence. In this context NGOs may need to be used as a substitute for governments. But since, in general, it seems that the collapse of government is worst for both economic development and human welfare, external (official and NGO) policies should support government authority and revenue collection efforts.

There are examples of relatively successful government interventions to protect people during conflict from other regions of the world. Nicaragua succeeded in extending services and distributing food rations throughout the country during the conflict, even improving the situation of the war-affected zones, relatively. In Sri Lanka, the government supported services within the rebel-held zone, maintaining services there. In Afghanistan, NGOs have substituted for government structures but this has meant somewhat patchy coverage.[15]

While these policies are appropriate from the perspective of sustaining economic and social structures during conflict, they may be inconsistent with the underlying political economy of the country in question. Many studies have shown[16] that aid donors and governments frequently *use* economic and social policies and projects to pursue their war agenda. Hence to the extent that the policies recommended above conflict with this agenda, they are likely to be perverted in practice. This occurred for example with food relief in the Sudan, which has been used to strengthen government forces rather than to reach those in need. A more subtle and sophisticated set of policies is needed which (a) takes into account the forces of political economy – which of course will vary from context to context; (b) provides an incentive for powerful warring groups to end the war rather than, as sometimes happens, an incentive to prolong it; and (c) also reaches the primary target of protecting economic and social development.

We are still at an early stage in delineating such alternative policies. The first requirement in any conflict is to understand the forces of political economy and their interaction with the conflict. In the light of this, it should be easier to devise policies which meet the three requirements noted above. Ones that might do so include:

- food or medical supplies that are sufficiently abundant so that they lose their power as a 'weapon of war';

- extensive works programmes, if they can be organized, may simultaneously meet three objectives – reconstruction of roads, dams etc., entitlement distribution, and providing people with an economic alternative to war; relief schemes should be carefully monitored (possibly by NGOs); where the relief is not reaching those for whom it is designed, the agencies involved should use alternative channels, including rebel forces.
- international agencies (e.g. UNDP) should monitor the activities of bilateral aid agencies to ensure that their own policies/projects are supporting development, not the war.
- leverage presented by the need for foreign finance can be used for a type of *war conditionality*, which would include ensuring the government gives priority to social programmes.[17]

These must be regarded as tentative policy conclusions, which will be filled out, or indeed altered, as our knowledge expands. The important conclusion is that economists should not wait for the conflict to finish before formulating policies to reduce suffering and sustain development.

Notes

1 This paper draws on work conducted for a Queen Elizabeth House research programme on the economics of conflict. I am grateful to Frank Humphreys, Nick Lea and Taimur Khan for very helpful assistance, and to Dharam Ghai for helpful comments on an earlier draft.
2 Among the lowest GNP per capita for mid-1994, are Rwanda, Mozambique, Ethiopia, Tanzania, Burundi, Sierra Leone, Malawi, Chad, Uganda and Madagascar: only Madagascar and Tanzania have been conflict free. For HDI in 1993 the list includes Niger, Somalia, Sierra Leone, Mali, Burkina Faso, Afghanistan, Ethiopia, Mozambique, Burundi, and Angola. Burkina Faso (and possibly Niger) are the non-conflict countries in this list.
3 Small and Singer (1982). Outside Africa their investigation identified 54 international conflicts, from 1816 to 1960, with battle-deaths of more than 1,000 per nation year. Over the same period there were 71 civil conflicts with more than 1,000 battle deaths per year, of which nine conflicts caused the deaths of over 0.5 per cent of the population. The data set excludes what are described as 'massacres', as well as conflicts with less than 1,000 deaths. This leads to some odd exclusions including the holocaust, which is not an event referred to in the list of conflicts that are known to be excluded; and the Muslim/Hindu massacres during Indian partition, noted as among the 'excluded' conflicts.
4 There is a growing theoretical literature analysing the costs of conflict. See e.g., Sen (1991); Stewart (1993); Collier (1995); Bruckman (1996); and the special issue of *Oxford Development Studies*, 25(1), 1997.
5 For evidence that this did occur in Nicaragua see Di Addario (1997).
6 As indicated by the data for the change in agricultural share of GDP.
7 See Chingono (1996); Green (1981); Duffield (1992).
8 A comprehensive analysis of countries whose overall government expenditure fell in any year between 1970–84 indicates that when government expenditure was cut, capital expenditure was cut more severely than current (Hicks, 1991). See also Pinstrup-Andersen *et al.* (1987).
9 Stewart (1995: Chapter 3).
10 It must be emphasized that these are estimates pieced together out of patchy and possibly unreliable evidence.

11   In Liberia, data show that both education and health expenditure fell as a proportion of GDP, although government expenditure as a whole was maintained. Data are lacking for GDP per capita growth, though it seems almost certain that this was falling. In Somalia, the government has lost control of much of the country.

12   See Utting (1987); Dreze and Gazdar (1991).

13   See Auvinen and Nafziger (1997).

14   'Efforts to begin reconstruction now would be a waste of effort and resources,' according to Lancaster, writing of the Horn of Africa in Lake *et al.* (1990:40).

15   For Afghanistan, see Marsden (1996); and for Sri Lanka, O'Sullivan (1997).

16   Keen (1994); Duffield (1992).

17   Boyce (1995) suggests the use of war conditionality, somewhat on these lines.

References

Albala-Bertrand, J. M. (1993) *The Political Economy of Large Natural Disasters*. Oxford: Clarendon Press.

Auvinen, J. and W. Nafziger (1997) *Economic Causes: The Political Economy of War, Hunger and Flight*. Helsinki: WIDER.

Boyce, J. (1995) 'External assistance and the peace process in El Salvador', *World Development*, 23(12):2101–16.

Bruckman, T. (1996) *The Economic Effects of War*. M.Phil. thesis, University of Oxford.

Chingono, M. (1996) *War, Economic Change and Development in Mozambique: The Grass-roots War Economy of Manica Province* (mimeo). London: Queen Elizabeth House.

Collier, P. (1995) *Civil War and the Economics of the Peace Dividend*, CSAE Working Papers, 95–8. Oxford: CSAE.

Di Addario, S. (1997) 'Estimating the economic costs of conflict: an examination of the two-gap estimation model', *Oxford Development Studies*, 25(1).

Dreze, J. and H. Gazdar (1991) 'Hunger and poverty in Iraq, 1991', *World Development*, 20(7): 921–46.

Duffield, M. (1992) 'Notes on the parallel economy, conflict and relief in the post Cold War era', in C. Petty *et al.* (eds), *Conflict and Relief in Contemporary African Famines*. London: Save the Children Fund and the London School of Hygiene and Tropical Medicine.

Green, R. (1981). *Magendo in the Political Economy of Uganda: Pathology, Parallel System or Dominant Sub-mode of Production?* IDS Discussion Paper 164. University of Sussex: Institute of Development Studies.

Hicks, N. (1991) 'Expenditure reductions in developing countries revisited', *Journal of International Development*, 3(1):29–37.

Keen, D. (1994) *The Benefits of Famine: A Political Economy of Famine and Relief in Southwestern Sudan, 1983–1989*. Princeton: Princeton University Press.

Killick, T. (1995) *The Flexible Economy: Cause and Consequences of the Adaptability of National Economies*. London: Routledge

Lake, A. *et al.* (1990) *After the Wars*. ODC Policy Perspectives, 16. Washington, DC: Overseas Development Council.

Marsden, P. (1996) *The Conflict in Afghanistan: The Economic and Social Impact (mimeo)*. Oxford: Queen Elizabeth House.

Ndegwa, P and R. Green (1994) *Africa to 2000 and Beyond: Imperative Political and Economic Agenda*. Nairobi: East African Educational Publishers.

O'Sullivan, M. (1997) 'Household entitlements during wartime: the experience of Sri Lanka', *Oxford Development Studies*, 25(1).

Pinstrup-Andersen, M. Jaramillo and Frances Stewart (1987) 'The impact on government expenditure', in G. Cornia, R. Jolly, and F. Stewart (eds), *Adjustment with a Human Face*. Oxford: Oxford University Press.

Sen, A. K. (1991) 'Wars and famines: on divisions and incentives', STICERD, Discussion Paper 33. London: London School of Economics.

Sivard, R. L. (1991) *World Military and Social Expenditures 1991*. Washington, DC: World Priorities.

Small, M. and J. D. Singer (1982) *Resort to Arms: International and Civil War, 1816–1980*. Beverly Hills: Sage.

Stewart, F. (1993) 'War and underdevelopment: can economic analysis help reduce the costs?' *Journal of International Development*, 5(4):357–80.

Stewart, F. (1995) *Adjustment and Poverty: Options and Choices*. London: Routledge.

UNICEF (1990) *State of Women and Children in Cambodia, 1990*. Phnom Penh: UNICEF.

Utting, P. (1987) 'Domestic supply and food shortages,' in R. Spalding (ed.), *The Political Economy of Revolutionary Nicaragua*. London: Allen & Unwin.

Waal, A. de (1989) *Famine that Kills: Darfur, Sudan 1984–5*. Oxford: Clarendon Press.

World Bank (1995) *A Continent in Transition: Sub-Sahran Africa in the Mid 1990s*, Washington, DC: The World Bank.

6

Social Dynamics of Environmental Change in Africa

Dharam Ghai[1]

Summary

There has been a tendency in Africa, as elsewhere, to view the environmental problem in ecological, physical and technical terms. The social aspects of environment have been largely neglected both in analysis and policies. This has contributed to the high failure rate of official conservation programmes and policies in most African countries both in the colonial and the post-independence period. The purpose of this paper is to provide a social perspective on the extent, emergence and amelioration of the environmental crisis in Sub-Saharan Africa.

The available indices point to a grim picture of environmental degradation in Africa as expressed in soil erosion, deforestation, desertification and sedimentation and pollution of waterways. Although there are serious doubts about the reliability of these data, circumstantial evidence and in-depth micro studies corroborate this picture. There is even greater paucity of information on the social manifestations of the environmental crisis. The problem is further compounded by the difficulty of isolating the impact of environmental factors from the many variables which impact on social conditions.

Natural disasters provide the most dramatic illustration of the social impact of changes in environment. The great droughts of the early 1970s and the 1980s resulted in the deaths of hundreds of thousands from starvation and malnutrition. Tens of millions were forced to abandon their homes in search of food. There was a large-scale decimation of livestock that contributed further to the impoverishment of the rural people. The cumulative degradation of natural resources has jeopardized the livelihood sources for scores of millions of farmers, herders and forest dwellers. The effects have been felt through declines in yields and food production, dwindling access to forest produce and game, declining productivity of grazing land and increasing scarcity and cost of wood fuel. The environmental crisis has reinforced urban migration, disrupted community life and provoked local, national and regional conflicts. Women and girls have been especially adversely affected because of their role in food production, family upkeep and fetching of water and wood fuel.

In the pre-colonial period, the local communities had by and large succeeded in evolving systems of resource use and management which combined livelihood security with resource conservation. These systems were disrupted during the colonial period by the expropriation of land for white settlers and for plantations, commercialization of agriculture, inappropriate macro-economic policies and ill-conceived infrastructural projects. Many of these policies were continued in the post-independence period. Rapid and accelerating population expansion in recent decades has greatly increased the pressure on resources.

The past patterns of economic development are socially and ecologically unsustainable. There is urgent need for new approaches designed to integrate resource conservation with livelihood improvement. A key element of this approach is the progressive transfer of responsibility to local communities and organizations for the management of natural resources. There is impressive historical evidence of the ability of pre-colonial societies in Africa to adapt production systems and livelihood strategies to local ecological conditions with environmental sustainability. There are also numerous contemporary experiences from different ecological zones of the ability of local communities to restore and improve degraded resources through technical innovations, social mobilization and institutional and organizational improvements.

For a locally based resource conservation strategy to work, it will be necessary to transfer responsibility and resources to local communities, initiate property reforms relating to ownership, use and access to resources, and strengthen the technical and managerial capabilities of organizations of rural producers. Because of the enormity of the challenge, these efforts can only succeed if they are supported by sympathetic individuals, organizations, national authorities and the international community. External assistance will be required to solve technical problems, elaborate programmes for raising labour and resource productivity, conduct field research and furnish food, materials and cash. But it is important that such assistance should reinforce local efforts, enhance local capabilities, build upon indigenous knowledge and skills and respect community priorities.

Introduction

Concern with environment is not a recent phenomenon in Africa. Already at the turn of the century there were serious debates and learned discussions about the deteriorating soil conditions and excessive deforestation in the Cape Colony in South Africa (Grove, 1987). Likewise the British, German and French colonial authorities were preoccupied with this problem in the 1920s and 1930s and took a variety of preventive measures (Darkoh, 1987; Korir-Koch, 1991). Many of these measures were of a coercive nature, often relying on forced labour for construction of structures for soil conservation and compulsory destocking to ease the pressure on rangelands. They were deeply resented by farmers, pastoralists and forest dwellers. It was therefore not surprising that governments which came to power after independence decided to abandon them. However, after a period of benign neglect in the early years of independence, African governments have become increasingly alarmed by the state of the environment and are now setting in motion wide-ranging measures to arrest and reverse its degradation.

Throughout much of this period, there has been a tendency to view the environmental problem in physical, ecological and technical terms. The problem is defined as loss of soil, disappearance of forests, extinction of wildlife and plant species, spread of deserts, pollution of waterways and sedimentation of dams and irrigation facilities. The villains of the piece are the nomadic herder, the subsistence farmer and the forest dweller whose galloping numbers and primitive methods of earning a livelihood are portrayed as putting intolerable pressure on limited and fragile resources. The measures devised to cope with the problem have focused on technical solutions involving land use and alleviation of human and animal pressure on resources. Conceived by government officials and international experts, they have been imposed upon a largely passive if not an outright hostile populace. It is not surprising that most of these measures have failed to achieve their objectives.

In recent years, some attempts have been made to view the environmental problem in a holistic framework integrating physical and ecological with social and political processes. This is an important advance but the full implications of this approach continue to be largely neglected or insufficiently reflected in the design and implementation of measures for environmental rehabilitation and conservation. The purpose of this paper is to present a social perspective on the environment problem and to outline an approach to resource conservation informed by this perspective.

A social approach to environment focuses on issues of ownership, control and management of natural resources. It addresses questions of power and conflicts of interest (Redclift, 1987, 1992; Vivian, 1992). It brings out the complex and multiple interactions between social and natural systems. It pays attention to institutions, motivation and incentives. And it stresses the vital links between resource conservation and human needs. Thus a strategy for environmental improvement is unlikely to succeed if it neglects the social dimension. Reliance upon purely ecological, technical or economic approaches is undoubtedly one of the reasons for the failure of many conservation programmes and policies.

The next section looks at some indices of environmental stress in Africa. Starting with the conventional physical measures, the paper discusses the principal social consequences of environmental degradation. Section 2 contains an analysis of the dynamics of environmental deterioration. Special attention is paid to the traditional systems of resource management and their breakdown under colonial rule, the processes of modernization and population expansion. Section 3 outlines an approach to conservation based on livelihood security and community empowerment. This approach is built around a strategy promoting a progressive restoration of sovereignty over natural resources to local communities and a strengthening of their capabilities in partnership with the state and the international community.

Given the vast scope of the paper in terms of both the region and the issues covered, it has not been possible to provide detailed empirical and analytical justification of the propositions advanced. The sources cited furnish further support to the points made here. This paper should rather be seen as providing a broadbrush social perspective on the extent, emergence and amelioration of the environmental crisis in Sub-Saharan Africa. The focus is on natural resources and the rural sector. No attempt has been made to discuss industrial and water pollution or urban environmental problems.

1. Environmental degradation from a social perspective

There is a close relationship between indices of environmental stress and the extent of social hardship and suffering. The data on such physical and social indicators are often incomplete or unreliable but in conjunction with other evidence they point to a dramatic picture of environmental damage in the continent.

Some physical indices of environmental deterioration

From all accounts the environmental crisis in Africa is serious and getting worse. The available indicators point to an alarming deterioration in the quality and quantity of natural resources. Just to mention a few commonly cited figures, Africa's 703 million hectares of forests are being cleared at the rate of 3.7 million hectares (or 0.6 per cent) each year; deforestation outstripped the rate of new tree planting by 29 to 1 (World Bank, 1989); more than 63 per cent of the original wildlife habitat has been lost (McNamara, 1990).

Soil erosion has assumed serious dimensions. The affected areas are experiencing soil loss at the rate of 10 to 200 tons per hectare. More than 35 per cent of the land north of the Equator is affected by either erosion or salinity (FAO, undated). It is reported that 80 to 90 per cent of Africa's rangelands and 80 per cent of cropped land in the dryland areas may be affected by soil degradation (World Bank, 1989). Nearly 34 per cent of African land is under threat of desertification (FAO, undated). There is growing pollution of waterways and sediment levels in rivers have been increasing at 5 per cent per annum in countries like Nigeria, Tanzania and Zimbabwe.

Most of the above figures are averages for the continent as a whole or for Sub-Saharan Africa. For certain countries the situation is much worse. The Sahelian countries are suffering more acutely from the encroaching desert. In Ethiopia, annual loss of topsoil has been estimated at a staggering figure of 3.5 billion tons (Harrison, 1987). Nearly 50 per cent of the land area in Tanzania is subject to soil erosion and requires remedial action (Blackwell *et al.*, 1991). The following countries have lost more than 80 per cent of their original moist forests: Angola, Burundi, Côte d'Ivoire, Ghana, Guinea-Bissau, Kenya, Liberia, Madagascar, Nigeria, Senegal, Sierra Leone, Sudan, Tanzania, Togo and Uganda. The area under wetlands and marsh has declined by more than 60 per cent in Cameroon, Chad, Malawi, Niger and Nigeria. Mangroves have declined by 60 per cent or more from their original levels in Côte d'Ivoire, Djibouti, the Gambia, Ghana, Guinea, Guinea-Bissau, Kenya, Liberia, Mozambique, Somalia and Tanzania (World Resources Institute, 1990).

The data cited above are admittedly rough estimates of the magnitude of the problem. Terms such as deforestation, soil degradation and desertification raise conceptual problems (Barraclough and Ghimire, 1990; Blaikie and Brookfield,

1987), and the actual measurement of these phenomena in African countries is fraught with all kinds of difficulties. There are few countries which can boast of accurate statistics on most dimensions of the state of environment. After looking at the literature on land degradation, one commentator came to the conclusion:

> Any honest reviewer of the current situation would have to come to the same conclusion as a 1986 IFAD review which stated bluntly that the 'extent of erosion in Africa south of the Sahara cannot yet be quantified'.
>
> (Fones-Sundell, 1989)

While it is not possible at this stage to make an accurate quantitative estimate of the dimensions of the environmental crisis in Africa, there is considerable circumstantial evidence from various micro studies and from indicators such as declining soil fertility and growing scarcity of fuelwood which points to both the seriousness of the situation and worsening trends over the past few decades. Nevertheless, for more effective planning and monitoring, there is an urgent need for an evaluation of the reliability of the currently available data and for gathering priority information on environmental indicators through low-cost methods including local field level surveys and inquiries.

Social impact of environmental crisis

Imperfect as the data on the physical indicators of environmental degradation are, there is even greater paucity of information on its social impact. Part of the problem arises from the difficulty of separating the impact of environmental changes from those of other events and policies. For instance, it is tempting but hardly justified by the present state of knowledge to attribute the catastrophic economic performance of Sub-Saharan Africa over the last 10 to 15 years to accelerating degradation in the environment. There is little doubt that environment in all its facets has played some part in the prolonged economic crisis of the 1980s, but it would be foolhardy to attribute a quantitative dimension to this role. A more accurate idea of the nature and extent of the human impact of environmental deterioration is provided by in-depth local studies in African countries.

The social consequences of environmental degradation are pervasive and wide-ranging, extending from death to pauperization, from hunger to ill-health, from community disruption to family break-ups, from massive migration to inhuman workloads for women and from local conflicts to national and regional wars. This section looks first at the social effects of natural disasters before turning to a consideration of the impact of environmental stress on production, incomes and consumption, health, migration and work patterns. It concludes with a brief discussion of the political and armed conflicts provoked by resource degradation and scarcity.

Natural disasters provide the most dramatic illustration of the social impact of changes in environment. Earthquakes, floods and droughts occur periodically in different regions of the world and take their toll in human lives, destruction of property, loss of livelihood, impoverishment, physical disabilities and disruption of communities. Africa has been ravaged more by droughts than by other forms of natural disasters. They have occurred periodically and affected large parts of the region. The last two decades have been especially deadly.

The great drought of the early 1970s struck the Sahelian and the Sudano-Ethiopian regions. Between 100,000 and 250,000 people died in the Sahel, according to a report prepared for the United Nations Conference on Desertification. Millions were reduced to destitution, provoking mass migration to urban areas in search of work and relief. According to FAO, an estimated 3.5 million head of cattle, 25 per cent of the total, died in the Sahel in 1972–3 alone (Grainger, 1990). The social tragedy was enacted on an even grander scale in the Sudano-Ethiopian region with much bigger numbers of human deaths and decimation of livestock.

The 1983–5 drought hit 30 countries in western, eastern and southern Africa. In March 1985, the peak of the crisis, it was estimated that 30 million were affected by the drought. Ten million of them were forced to abandon their homes in search of food. In Niger, half the population suffered from the effects of drought. In Ethiopia and Sudan, eight and ten million people respectively were affected. In Botswana, over half the population was dependent on food aid (Harrison, 1987). Millions in other countries, especially Angola and Mozambique, survived through food aid.

This is not the place to discuss the important question of the extent to which environmental disasters such as the drought are purely 'natural' phenomena and the extent to which they are 'man-made'. There is a growing technical literature and a considerable amount of controversy on the subject. Less contested are the pattern of and responsibility for the social consequences. It is the poorest farmers and herders and the assetless poor, in other words those with the least or most vulnerable entitlements, who are the most exposed to hunger, famine and starvation. Likewise, the experiences in Africa and elsewhere show that there is no inherent link between drought and famine. The ultimate responsibility for famine and starvation must rest on social and economic structures, tragic errors of policy and criminal negligence by national and international authorities (Franke and Chasin, 1980; Glantz, 1987; Mortimore, 1985; Sen, 1980; Watts, 1983).

While natural disasters bring out in a spectacular manner the link between environment and human welfare, it is the social impact of gradual cumulative changes in environment which has dominated policy discussions. These changes affect the quality and quantity of resources available to individuals, families and communities. Since natural resources directly or indirectly form the basis of livelihood for a great majority of the population in most African countries, their characteristics and distribution affect human welfare and social relations. Environmental degradation affects incomes and consumption through its impact on agricultural and livestock production and availability of forest produce and wildlife.

It is widely believed that environmental degradation has contributed to the poor agricultural performance of African countries over the past decade and a half, though it is impossible to quantify its impact. The principal mechanisms are stated to be decline in land fertility through soil erosion and monocropping, loss of cultivable land through desertification, reduction in the quality of pasture lands through over-grazing, cultivation of low potential, semi-arid lands and disappearance of forests.

One measure of the impact of land degradation is the effect on yields of food crops. According to the data put together by FAO and ECA, 14 African countries experienced declining yields of maize, 12 of millet and sorghum and 15 of rice over the period 1971–80 or 1983 (ECA–FAO, 1992). While suggestive, such aggregate figures cannot accurately reflect the impact of land degradation. Not only do they combine production data from many countries with differing performance but they are also influenced by factors such as weather and national and international policies bearing on agriculture and food. It is therefore necessary to have recourse to national and micro studies to obtain more precise estimates of the effect of land degradation on yields and production.

There are few studies which attempt to quantify the economic costs of soil erosion and land degradation either at the level of individual farmer or the society as a whole (Fones-Sundell, 1989). But some partial estimates have been made. In Ethiopia, soil erosion is estimated to result in an annual loss to grain production of 1 million tons (Blackwell *et al.*, 1991). In Zimbabwe, the nutrient loss through soil erosion was valued at US $1,500 million in fertilizer equivalent in 1985 (FAO, undated).

Through its impact on fertility, soil erosion has reduced yields of foodcrops. In the tropics as a whole, erosion on shallow or impoverished soils reduces maize yields by 30 to 70 per cent (Blackwell *et al.*, 1991). Sometimes farmers have had to substitute less nutritious crops, such as cassava for millet in Zambia. Likewise, the move to marginal areas has resulted in lower yields. The effect has been a declining or stagnant production of food and cash crops for millions of small farmers throughout the continent. The consequent inadequacy of food and cash has led to a search for supplementary income-earning opportunities through casual, part-time jobs and migration to urban areas.

The crisis has been more severe for the 15 to 25 million nomadic herders who have been hit by a series of disasters – armed conflicts, prolonged droughts, encroaching desert, settlement schemes that squeeze on pasture lands, creation of protected areas, expansion of cultivated area and degradation in the quality of the land available for grazing. Some nomads have been forced to abandon their traditional way of life to seek livelihood as subsistence farmers, wage workers or recipients of relief aid. For the rest, environmental degradation has reduced animal productivity and increased food insecurity.

Millions of people in Africa derive all or part of their subsistence requirements and cash income from the forests. The forests furnish them with food, medicines, building materials and household equipment, raw materials for agricultural processing and fuelwood. In West Africa, bushmeat, palm products such as oil and wine, medicines, fuelwood and building materials are the most highly utilized forest products (FAO, 1990). Bushmeat, fruits, nuts, vegetables, palm wine, medicines and fuelwood are also an important source of cash income. Poor households and women are especially dependent upon the forests for their subsistence and cash needs (FAO, 1990). Forest products are an important source of nutrition, providing protein, energy, fibre, vitamins and essential minerals (FAO, 1989). The accelerating deforestation, demarcation of areas for national parks and protected forests and other measures of exclusion have deprived large numbers of people of their traditional access to forest products, thus threatening their sources of livelihood (Ghimire, 1991; Koch *et al.*, 1990).

In many ways women in the rural areas have been the most affected by the environmental crisis. Nearly 80 per cent of the economically active women in Sub-Saharan Africa are in agriculture, and they are responsible for 70 per cent of food production in Africa. In their capacity as food producers, they have seen the returns to their labour reduced by declining soil fertility and cultivation in marginal areas. The migration of male members of the household induced by scarce or degraded resources has further contributed to their responsibilities and workloads. An indication of the scale of the problem is given by the growing numbers of female-headed households, which now amount to 20 per cent in Africa with an even higher proportion in rural areas. In Botswana, female-headed households are estimated at 45 per cent, in Malawi at 29, Zambia at 28 and Ghana at 27 (United Nations, 1991).

Labour force surveys estimate the total working time for women in Africa at 67 hours per week. Small-scale studies suggest that women and girls spend on average 5 to 17 hours per week collecting and carrying water (United Nations, 1991). The growing scarcity and escalating price of fuelwood has further increased their workload. Women and girls spend long hours in collecting fuelwood with adverse effect on family nutrition and health (Cecelski, 1987). Women in the Transkei in South Africa cover 6 to 9 kilometres each day, scouring the bush for firewood and collecting loads of about 30 kilograms (Koch *et al.*, 1990). The additional work burden carried by women and the increasing scarcity and cost of fuelwood have negative effects on family welfare and health, especially of children. Less nutritious food may be chosen; it may not be cooked properly. The water may not be boiled.

The discussion so far has been concerned with the impact of resource degradation on individual and family welfare. Environmental crisis has also provoked social unrest and conflict. Several governments, most notably the Haile Selassie regime, have been swept from power by the suffering and unrest associated with drought and famine. With continuing degradation and increasing scarcity of natural resources, the struggle and competition for them are likely to become a potent source of conflicts among communities and countries. The movements of farmers, herders, forest dwellers and the landless away from dwindling resources toward areas less subject to environmental stress has intensified conflicts in several countries and can be expected to further exacerbate ethnic and national tensions and animosities (Hjorst af Ornäs and Mohamed Salih, 1989).

2.   Dynamics of environmental degradation

Environmental change is a complex phenomenon. It is the result of intricate interactions among social, ecological and physical systems. This section focuses on the impact of policies, institutions and human activities on the state of environment. Environment in Africa, perhaps even more than in other regions, is highly varied, with infinite local specificities. The account given here is necessarily selective in highlighting critical mechanisms and important tendencies. It begins with an analysis of the traditional systems of resource management that reflect centuries of adaptation in the search for secure livelihood. It then examines the environmental impact of the establishment of colonialism and European settlement. This leads to a discussion of the role of modernization and state policies in resource degradation. The section then considers the impact of population expansion, concluding with some observations on the sustainability of the current patterns of development and resource use and management.

Environment and livelihood under traditional systems

Environmental stress is a relatively new phenomenon in Africa's long history. It is true that African soils are more fragile, the timing and quantity of rainfall more variable and that there is greater predominance of arid and semi-arid areas than in other regions of the world. It is also true that African communities have from time immemorial been periodically ravaged by droughts, floods and diseases. But it is a measure of their tremendous social achievement that pre-colonial African societies had evolved systems for the use and management of natural resources that by and large ensured both environmental integrity and secure livelihood. Evidence from different parts of the continent bears testimony to ingenious and sophisticated adaptation of the production systems to the unique characteristics of the African environment (Watts, 1983; Kjekshus, 1977; Franke and Chasin, 1980; Molutsi, 1988; Wamalwa, 1991).

The continent possesses an extremely varied topography, comprising most major ecological systems. These include tropical forests, cool highlands, humid coastal areas, riverine and marshy zones, extensive savannahs, semi-arid regions and vast stretches of desert. The soils and rainfall are also highly variable. The principal pre-colonial activities comprised cultivation, herding, hunting and gathering. The land tenures showed a great deal of variation, generally combining communal ownership with private use. Some resources were allocated for the use of families while others were reserved as common property.

This ecological diversity gave rise over time to an extraordinary variety of production systems which sought to exploit the local and regional specificities to assure secure livelihoods. Thus, as illustrated below, intensive cultivation, shifting agriculture, organic fertilizers, intercropping, mixed farming, hillside, wetlands and dry plains cultivation, water harvesting and irrigation, soil and forest conservation, nomadic and transhumance pastoralism, all have formed part of the traditional production systems of different African communities.

Running through the diversity of ecological and production systems were some common characteristics of resource use and management. Nature in all its manifestations constituted an organic part of the world view of most communities. It was treated with reverence and respect. This attitude has been described as 'living in nature' (Wamalwa, 1991; Turton, 1989). It is manifested in the designation of certain rivers, hills, mountains, forests, groves and trees as sacred places for worship and burial. Perhaps one of the most beautiful examples of the reverence for nature is provided by the custom of the Tembe-Thonga people of Kosi Bay in South Africa of showing newborn babies to the moon and taking them down to the beach and allowing a wave to wash over them (Koch *et al.*, 1990).

Secondly, the customary systems were based on an extensive use of resources. This was necessitated by technology and made feasible by abundance of resources in relation to population. Even in areas of dense population there were adequate resources to sustain a system of extensive exploitation. The population was held in balance by a regime of high fertility and high mortality. This characteristic of the African system of resource use was illustrated by the widespread practice of shifting agriculture under which land was cleared and cultivated for a certain period before being abandoned for regeneration through natural processes. The same principle was evident in the practice by nomadic people of constantly moving their herds to take advantage of water and grass for their livestock. Seasonal mobility across ecological regions was a central feature of herding communities in most regions of the continent. It served both to conserve resources and provide insurance against loss of livestock through disease, raids or lack of nourishment.

The third common characteristic of the African systems was a set of institutions and rules which governed the use and management of natural resources. It is too often assumed that the traditional systems were characterized by a free-for-all anarchic exploitation of resources. While it is possible that in some exceptionally richly endowed regions with very sparse populations, the regulatory mechanisms may have been minimal or even non-existent, most communities had evolved systems which, in varying degrees, conserved resources and ensured their equitable distribution among households.

The fourth widespread feature of the system was highly localized adaptation of agricultural, herding, fishing and gathering practices to fully exploit the extraordinary ecological diversity characteristic of many regions in Africa. Its corollary is very considerable experimentation and innovation undertaken by peasant farmers with inputs and methods of production (Richards, 1985). This finding, supported by a growing body of evidence, contrasts with the widely held view of static and uniform techniques of production handed down through the generations.

The general points made above may be selectively illustrated with examples of customary systems of resource management chosen from different regions and ecological zones. The Tembe-Thonga people of Kosi Bay coast and the neighbouring area in South Africa live in an ecological paradise and derive their livelihood from fishing and forest produce. Their holistic approach to resource conservation includes aspects of land tenure, taboos, myths, gender roles and harvesting techniques. Some species of indigenous fruit trees are preserved through privatization by allocating them to individuals in the community. Sites where palms are tapped for the juices used in palm wine, as well as fish trapping locations, are granted to individuals for supervision and protection against over-exploitation. When fresh water stocks are low, the more efficient methods of fishing are banned by the local headman or even by the fishermen themselves. Likewise seasonal restrictions are placed on gathering and hunting (Koch *et al.*, 1990).

Examples of the development of intensive and environmentally sound methods of cultivation come from several parts of Africa. The Konso of south-west Ethiopia have developed a complex and sophisticated form of agriculture that has allowed them to subsist in a mountainous area with fragile soils and an irregular rainfall. Their farming is based on an elaborate system of terracing, a variety of soil and water management practices, the integration of livestock and forestry with the rest of their agriculture, and the use of manure and compost to maintain soil fertility (FAO, undated). The Kikuyu in Kenya also relied on a mixed farming system combining animal husbandry with multiple cropping in a careful spatial pattern to conserve water and reduce soil erosion (Korir-Koch, 1991).

In south-eastern Nigeria, forest farmers have developed sophisticated systems of tree and crop farming that mimic the multi-storeyed vegetation of the rain-forest that surrounds them. The Chagga who farm the southern slopes of Mount Kilimanjaro have for more than a century made careful use of melting snows, tapping the water of high mountain streams into networks of skilfully aligned irrigation channels. Apart from practising stall feeding and using organic material to improve soil fertility, they also developed their own system of multi-layer farming, growing intercropped yams, sweet potatoes, maize, beans and peas among coffee bushes, with banana palms providing shade (Harrison, 1987). A similar system was developed in the western Usumbaras in Tanzania with a multi-storeyed agricultural system and integration of agroforestry with crop cultivation (Mascarenhas and Maganga, 1991).

Numerous examples of agricultural innovation and experimentation have been documented in West Africa (Richards, 1985). Intercropping occurs in 80 per cent of all farms in West Africa. It results in better and more reliable yields, a smoother labour input profile and better control of pests, weeds and diseases. Wetlands agriculture is another area where West African smallholders have been especially inventive with rice cultivation in flood plains and swamps, utilizing a variety of small-scale irrigation schemes. After considerable experimentation, the Itake farmers in western Nigeria moved to a gradual substitution of cassava for yams in response to changed ecological conditions, labour supply constraints and new market conditions. In the Mogwamama area alone in Sierra Leone, 78 farm households planted a total of 59 distinct rice varieties!

The herding communities had also developed intricate and efficient systems for exploiting rangelands while conserving the environment. In the Ferlo region in northern Senegal, the Peul tribe practised a well-organized system of cultivation and grazing based on transhumance (Toure, 1988). The cattle were moved to take advantage of the rainy season and after the harvests left to graze on the fields, supplying manure to the soil. The symbiotic relationship between the herding and farming communities was mutually beneficial and quite widespread in the Sudano-Sahel region. Ecological imperatives as well as husbandry and commercial considerations imposed perpetual motion on cattle and their herders. The system required strict administration of access rights to water and grazing land.

Customary law guaranteed free access to the bush zones but imposed strict management rules for agro-pastoral areas.

Similar systems were developed by the herding communities in East Africa. The Barabaig of the Hanang plains in Tanzania have devised a seasonal grazing rotation that exploits the forage regimes at different times of the year (Lane, 1992). Open rangeland is regarded as the property of the whole community. The Barabaig used a variety of arrangements to protect land. Some groups are assigned the duty to protect their land against intruders. Within the commons, rights to property range from communal access to exclusive private possession. The Barabaig regulate rights of use and access to land through a tripartite jural structure, each with its own sphere of interest and authority: the community, the clan and individual households. Likewise the Maasai of the Kajiado district in Kenya had evolved an elaborate system of range management involving reserved and sequenced grazing, neighborhood based controls on grazing, collective action against invaders and punishment and fines for infringement of customary rules (Brokenshaw and Little, 1987).

Colonial roots of environmental degradation

The establishment of colonial rule in the nineteenth and early twentieth centuries in most parts of Africa set in motion a series of developments with profound implications for the environmental balance. The principal mechanisms disturbing the equilibrium were expropriation of land for settlement and plantations, assumption of state sovereignty over natural resources, commercialization of agriculture, development projects and policies and population growth.

Large tracts of grazing and crop lands were expropriated either for European settlement, as in many eastern and southern African countries, or for plantations, as in several central and west African countries. This was accompanied by the demarcation of land as colonial territories of different European powers. These developments not only disrupted the long established systems of shifting cultivation and nomadic pastoralism, but also confined indigenous populations to restricted areas often of low agricultural potential. A number of methods using varying degrees of coercion were employed to secure labour for European farms, plantations and mines (Brett, 1973; Palmer and Pearson, 1977). This established the migratory system, which resulted in prolonged periods of absence of male members and consequent neglect of their role in sound resource management practices, apart from greatly adding to women's workload. The overcrowding of croplands, the closing off of seasonal pastures and the absence of males effectively undermined the traditional systems of resource management in many areas, thus laying the foundations of environmental degradation.

The adverse effect on effective resource management was reinforced by the assumption of sovereignty by the colonial states over forests, mountains and hills, lakes and rivers and grazing and crop lands. The situation varied by regions and colonial authorities but the general trend was toward increasing central control and growing disenfranchisement of local communities. For instance, in 1930 the French colonial authorities expropriated all common lands and established a forestry code which extended state rights to all forest areas (Lawry, 1989). The process was continued after independence from colonial rule. In the Sudan, the state took control of range regulations from local authorities in the 1960s, while in Botswana local grazing and water management systems have been supplanted by District Land Boards (Brokenshaw and Little, 1987). In Ghana, rights in the forest lands invested in the traditional groups and governed by customary rules were transferred to the central government in the early 1970s (Repetto and Gillis, 1988).

While the state took over formal responsibility for the management of commons and other resources previously governed by customary rules, it was rarely able to exercise effective control. This created the worst possible situation from the point of view of resource conservation: the traditional system of resource management was effectively undermined but nothing was put in its place. The result was uncontrolled and short-sighted exploitation of common property resources that further accelerated environmental degradation.

The commercialization of agriculture, whether through the establishment of large farms and plantations or the cultivation of cash crops by peasant farmers, was an additional source of environmental stress. The search for profits brought an ever-increasing area of land under cultivation. Some of the earlier practices of crop rotation, intercropping, mixed farming and shifting cultivation were either abandoned or restricted. While tree crops such as cocoa, coffee and tea have beneficial effects on soil conservation, the growth of export commodities such as cotton and groundnuts reduced soil fertility and increased its vulnerability to erosion. This was especially the case with continuous monocropping. The deleterious effects on soil fertility have also been observed with continuous monocropping of food crops such as maize, even when fertilizers are used. In Zambia, for instance, maize yields have been declining in some areas by 20 per cent per annum even with fertilizer use (Blackwell *et al.*, 1991).

Development projects and policies

There are many other elements of official policies, both in the colonial and in the post-independence period, which have contributed to environmental deterioration. The agricultural sector has been heavily taxed directly or indirectly, especially since the Second World War (World Bank, 1981). The farmers have thus been deprived of means which might have contributed to beneficial investment in resource conservation and improvement. Some other aspects of macro policies such as commodity and natural resource pricing, subsidies to inappropriate technology, harmful pesticides and large-scale commercial ventures have had detrimental effects on the environment (Repetto and Gillis, 1988; Lane, 1992).

Many large-scale development projects, financed for the most part by multilateral and bilateral donors, have been designed and implemented without regard to their impact on the delicate ecological balances or the complex social systems of resource management and securing livelihood. These include construction of dams as in Jabel el-Awliya in the White Nile Province in Sudan (Horowitz and Salem-Murdoch, 1987); creation of irrigation facilities such as the Gezira in Sudan or Bura on the Tana River in Kenya (Mohamed Salih, 1989; Hughes, 1987); integrated river basin development schemes, such as the Awash Valley Authority in Ethiopia (Gamaledinn, 1987); large-scale resettlement and villagization schemes, as in Ethiopia, Tanzania and Mozambique; commercial exploitation of tropical forests, as in Côte d'Ivoire and Cameroon. Such projects have intensified resource degradation through disruption of traditional cultivation and grazing systems, concentration of population on limited land, water and forests and changes in the level and direction of water flows.

Population expansion

There is a complex relationship between population growth and environmental change. There is a tendency to attribute the main if not total responsibility for environmental damage to rapid population growth. The preceding discussion has identified many other forces which have been operating on the environment in Africa. Thus even when population is the 'proximate' cause of environmental degradation, the 'ultimate' causes may lie elsewhere, e.g., in inequitable distribution of resources, inappropriate macro-economic policies or droughts, conflicts and wars (Shaw, 1989). It is also clear from historical evidence and contemporary experience that major increases in population are compatible with environmental preservation and improvement because of changes in technology, production systems, land tenure and social institutions (Repetto, 1987). For example, several of the most densely populated parts in Burundi, Kenya and Malawi are characterized by impressive practices of soil conservation, while some of the more thinly populated regions in the Sahelian countries are faced with formidable problems of desertification. There are also of course some densely populated regions, as in parts of Ethiopia and Lesotho, which are suffering from acute problems of soil erosion.

It was noted earlier that historically the systems of resource use and management in most parts of Africa evolved in response to a relatively favourable balance between population and resources. This situation is however changing rapidly with the high rates of population expansion experienced in most African countries in recent decades. The population in Africa has increased nearly threefold over the past four decades alone. It is set to double again over the next two decades, although these projections may be affected by some of the recent developments, such as the spread of AIDS, falling incomes and declining health services. In the absence of rapid adaptation of technologies, production systems and social institutions, it is clear that population expansion of this order of magnitude cannot be accommodated within the framework of the current systems of resource use and management without a massive aggravation of the environmental crisis.

If the options of migration abroad and employment in the non-agricultural sectors are absent or inadequate, a rapid increase in the rural labour force will result in use of the surplus land, sub-division of holdings, opening up of new land through encroachment of forests and grazing land and migration to areas of low potential. These indeed are the principal ways in which increased rural populations in African countries have been accommodated (Bilsborrow and Okoth-Ogendo, 1991). In all these cases the pressures exerted by increased human and animal populations are likely to intensify the processes leading to resource degradation. Significant and long-lasting damage can only be averted by an accelerated shift to more intensive and sustainable methods of resource use.

Alternative approaches to conservation and development

The current patterns of economic development are fundamentally unsustainable in the long run for two reasons. First, they have failed to reduce poverty. On the contrary, the past decade and a half has been characterized by impoverishment of a rising proportion of the population. Second, the past growth patterns have been accompanied by a vast degradation of natural resources. In economic terms this is equivalent to a huge decumulation of capital. It is as if the factory owners use up the machines and buildings in the production process and fail to make provision for their replacement. The degradation of resources amounts to a gradual destruction of the productive base of the economy. By the same token, because the loss in the quality of natural resources is not reflected in prices, any sale of resource-based products, whether in domestic or foreign markets, is inherently subsidized, in most cases from the poor rural producers to more affluent domestic and foreign consumers (Dasgupta and Mäler, 1990).

The move to sustainable development will require wide-ranging changes in property systems, consumption patterns, production methods, technologies, products, institutions and lifestyles both in the rich and the poor countries. Changes of this nature and magnitude can only be achieved over long periods of time. It is not the intention here to go over this ground, which has been covered in a number of well-known reports (Brundtland Commission, 1987; IUCN, 1989).

It is, however, necessary to stress that no conservation strategy is likely to succeed if it does not give a central place to livelihood improvement for the impoverished. This requires wide-ranging changes, *inter alia* in access to and use of resources, investment patterns and organization and composition of public services. Changes of this nature are unlikely to be forthcoming without political and economic empowerment of marginalized groups. Thus democracy and strengthening of popular organizations are an integral part of a strategy linking resource conservation with poverty amelioration. The rest of this paper focuses on one critical component of a strategy along these lines: strengthening the resource management capability of rural producers and their communities and organizations.

3.   Conservation, livelihood and democracy

This section argues the case for a conservation policy based on local-level management of resources, considers some principal obstacles in its implementation and outlines its key features.

Necessity of a locally based conservation strategy

A conservation strategy centred on people's participation is supported by compelling logic and impressive evidence (Ghai and Vivian, 1992). The fate of the environment in Africa, even more than elsewhere, will be determined by the interactions between hundreds of millions of peasants, herders, nomads, forest dwellers and fisherfolk and the natural resources from which they derive their livelihood. They have a greater interest in the health and integrity of environment than any outside parties, for their very existence and way of life are at stake. The fact that many of their activities contribute to the impoverishment of these resources is a powerful indictment of the situation they have often been pushed into. One of the principal reasons for this, as argued earlier, has been the breakdown of the customary systems of resource management and the consequent loss of local autonomy and responsibility in this domain.

The indigenous communities have a deep and intimate knowledge of the local ecology, the flora and the fauna, a knowledge born out of centuries of constant interaction with the environment and handed down from generation to generation. In view of the incredible complexity, diversity and specificity of plant and animal habitats, such knowledge and skills are indispensable in evolving responses to changing material conditions to preserve and enhance environmental quality. Few of the interventions from the national and international agencies take local conditions into account and thus fail to respond to the real needs of the local people and often end up by doing more harm than good.

The local communities are in a very good position to assess the relevance and validity of the solutions to environmental problems devised by outsiders. For these solutions and interventions to succeed it is not enough for them to be technically sound. They must also be economically and socially efficient for the small farmer or nomad, taking into account their resource constraints and opportunities and responding to their concerns for livelihood security. An effective participation of the local people in devising and implementing programmes and policies for resource conservation provides the best guarantee for the achievement of these objectives. All this is not to argue that outside assistance can make no contribution to resource conservation. As shown later, such assistance has a vital role to play, but it must be geared to building up local capabilities and must respond to the priorities established by local communities.

The case for reliance on local communities and grassroots initiatives in resource management and conservation is further strengthened by the evidence provided earlier on indigenous inventiveness and creativity in devising environmentally harmonious adaptations in production systems to changes in social and material conditions. There is also abundant evidence of the success of environmental projects which combine external resources with community initiatives and participation (Conroy and Litvinoff, 1988; Egger and Majeres, 1992; Harrison, 1987; Ledea Ouedraogo, 1990; Pradervand, 1990; Reid *et al.*, 1988; World Bank, 1989).

Kenya and Rwanda have achieved major gains in soil conservation and agricultural production through programmes which combined community participation with government commitment and sustained donor support. In Kenya, half a million farms had been terraced already by 1985. In Rwanda, communal forests, village nurseries, tree planting and agroforestry have helped to provide fuelwood, fodder and erosion control for the rural poor. By 1985, 63 per cent of the farms were protected by terraces, infiltration ditches or bunds of deep-rooted fodder grasses. Large-scale rural works were undertaken in Ethiopia through peasant associations involving soil and water conservation through terracing, small dam construction, planting of trees and rehabilitation of degraded forests. Although successful in many respects, the programme did not prove sustainable without food aid because of the excessive extraction of resources from the peasantry to finance wars and the lack of participatory structures, with consequent adverse effects on peasant motivation and incentives (Ståhl, 1992).

The importance of community participation is also brought out in the successes achieved in soil and water conservation, vegetable and food crop production and reforestation by Six-S in Burkina Faso and other Sahelian countries; by the mass planting of trees by women's organizations under the leadership of the Green Belt movement in Kenya; and by the successful combination of wildlife conservation with enhanced incomes, employment and local capabilities in the Purros Project in Namibia (Jacobsohn, 1991). It is not difficult, on the basis of these and other experiences, to isolate the factors which contribute to the success of local level projects. These include meaningful democratic participation by the local people; an adequate preparatory period; emphasis on livelihood concerns; the existence or creation of community organizations; reliance on locally available tools, materials and skills; low-risk activities with very attractive pay-offs; an effective system of marketing and extension and government and donor support and commitment (Cruz, 1991; Harrison, 1987).

Environmental rehabilitation and preservation cannot however be based on projects alone. By their very nature they can reach only a limited number of people. Their major role is to test new approaches and techniques, working in close co-operation with the local farmers and herders. While a lot more can be done to draw lessons from failures as well as successes and to ensure a speedy extension and replication of successful experiences, projects cannot substitute for overall approaches and strategies for resource conservation through people's participation.

Strengthening community resource management capabilities

For a participatory approach to environmental conservation to work, a number of changes will be required in the current practices and policies in African countries. These will vary in accordance with differences in ecology, natural resources, social institutions and customary practices between and within countries. However, some key reforms are likely to be relevant across a broad spectrum of ecological and institutional diversity. The first requirement is for a progressive devolution of power and responsibility for resource use and management from the centre to the local communities. Currently, while the formal powers and responsibility are vested in the state and its organs, in reality there is a great deal of uncertainty on the ground about access to and use of resources. The result often is a short-sighted and destructive exploitation of resources. In order to rectify the situation, the powers and responsibilities of the different parties involved – the individual users, the customary authorities, the new local government bodies, the political organizations, the state and the bureaucracy – need to be defined clearly and precisely.

A reform of property rights has to be an integral part of a policy seeking to restore local autonomy over natural resources. The present situation in this respect is unsatisfactory in most African countries. The objective should be to ensure equity in access to resources and incentives for their conservation and improvement. It is necessary to establish clear rules on the access, ownership and use of resources. In some cases, this may require individual title deeds; in others the formalization and effective enforcement of traditional systems of land tenure and use. Under some circumstances, it may be necessary to evolve new property regimes and build new institutions to ensure their implementation.

This approach is illustrated by the Communal Areas Management Programme for Indigenous Resources (CAMPFIRE) in Zimbabwe. The CAMPFIRE programme is designed to smooth the transition from communal ownership of land to more formal structures. Initially the programme will set up an institutional structure to enable local co-operatives to develop management schemes for land use, wildlife, forestry, grazing and water in specific areas, and to maximize returns from them. The income from these operations will go to subsidized loans for villagers and community investment and for shareholder dividends (Reid *et al.*, 1988; FAO, undated).

The third requirement is for a strengthening of local institutions and organizations. Experience has shown that such organizations are most successful when they consist of people with homogeneous socio-economic backgrounds, evolve democratic and participatory working methods and respond to the priority needs of their members, which often concern livelihood security and basic needs provisioning. Such organizations can simultaneously empower local communities, foster grassroots democracy and promote a broad-based development effort focused on livelihood improvement through resource regeneration (Ghai, 1990).

There are many ways of promoting grassroots organizations. In some cases, the traditional groups can be revitalized and given new roles and responsibilities. An outstanding example of this is the Six-S, an association of small peasants, operating in several Sahelian countries (Ledea Ouedraogo, 1990). Six-S is based on the traditional Naam groups and has pioneered a series of highly successful initiatives on soil conservation, reforestation, water harvesting and turning back the encroaching desert. Reliance upon traditional modes of co-operation is also the basis for the highly successful Organization of Rural Associations for Progress (ORAP) in Zimbabwe, which seeks to strengthen food security and improve living conditions for poor peasant households (Kempadoo, 1991).

In other cases the village councils or elected local authorities can provide the institutional base for a broad-based effort at improvement of livelihood through resource conservation. This is illustrated by the Mwenezi experience in Zimbabwe (Gaidzanwa *et al.*, 1987). The newly elected district, ward and village authorities pioneered an innovative approach to resource conservation and livelihood improvement comprising land reform, village resettlement, separation between grazing and arable land, creation of fish ponds and protection of wildlife. Sometimes it may be necessary for the local people themselves to create new organizations to take on responsibility for local development. An interesting example is provided by the experience of Utooni in the Machakos district in Kenya (Mutiso, 1991). Starting with an informal grouping of families, the initiative evolved into a complex organization with a membership of 20,000 persons with departments for different activities but retaining a democratic decision-making process. Combining traditional knowledge with modern science, the organization overcame soil erosion and declining yields through terracing, planting of trees and construction of sub-surface dams, water tanks and river barrages. The activities comprise horticulture, dairy cattle, poultry, flour mill, crop storage and pest control, improved sanitation and health centres.

The fourth requirement is to strengthen the technical, organizational and managerial capabilities of rural communities and their organizations. The latter cannot undertake the vast task of resource rehabilitation and conservation without support from sympathetic individuals, organizations, the national authorities and the international community. The positive role played by such external support has been crucial in the successes achieved by many grassroots initiatives for environmental improvement (Ghai and Vivian, 1992). External assistance will be required to solve technical problems, to elaborate programmes for raising labour and resource productivity, to conduct field research and experimentation and to furnish food, materials and cash. But it is important that such assistance should reinforce local efforts, enhance local capabilities, build upon indigenous knowledge and skills and respect community priorities.

Such assistance is in the interest of all parties: the local communities stand to benefit from strengthening of capabilities and improvement of living standards and the natural resources, the national authorities will profit from a prosperous economy and reversal of negative externalities generated by resource degradation, and the international community will see a progress in the realization of its objectives of sustainable development, preservation of global environment and conservation of the unique forest and wildlife resources of Africa.

Democratic reform and environmental conservation

The existence of participatory initiatives with a successful record in resource and livelihood improvement shows that the approach set out above is feasible and viable. The failure of this approach to spread rapidly to embrace major parts of the region is an indication of the formidable difficulties encountered in transforming it into national policy. Apart from problems of finance, technology, knowledge, skills and organization mentioned above, there are serious problems of a political nature.

The transfer of power, responsibilities and resources to local institutions and organizations runs into powerful vested interests at many levels. These include politicians and bureaucrats at the centre, commercial enterprises and even international agencies and bilateral donors. The difficulties are further compounded in many situations by the existence of sharp inequalities in wealth and organizational and political power at the local level. The objective of resource and livelihood improvement cannot be achieved if the transfer of power and resources from the centre results in further accentuation of inequalities and marginalization.

The existence of democratic space at the national level and freedom of association for all groups are crucial to the success of a locally based strategy of resource conservation. Recent democratic reforms in a number of African countries provide a favourable setting for the multiplication of grassroots initiatives and movements. Ultimately it is the presence of strong, democratic and self-reliant organizations of rural producers and their communities which alone can ensure equitable and sustainable patterns of development. A primary objective of an environment policy must therefore be the strengthening of such organizations.

In view of the difficulties outlined above, the progress in implementing a locally based conservation strategy is likely to be slow and halting. But there are also a number of considerations which provide a favourable context for the adoption of locally based strategies. These include a growing perception of the social and ecological unsustainability of present patterns of development, heightened awareness of the disastrous consequences of environmental degradation at local, national and international levels, mutuality of interests in environmental integrity among different sectors and social groups from the local to the global levels and a powerful global momentum for democracy and human rights.

4. Conclusion

Environmental degradation in Africa is widespread and continuing. It is undermining the productive potential of the region thus threatening the livelihood security of scores of millions of peasants, herders and forest dwellers and creating serious ecological problems at local, regional and perhaps global levels. A number of processes have contributed to environmental deterioration. At different periods and in different zones, these have included expropriation of resources, breakdown of the customary systems of land use and management, commercialization of agriculture, rapid population expansion, inappropriate macro policies and ill-conceived infrastructural and settlement schemes.

The past policies to rehabilitate and conserve degraded resources have for the most part failed because they neglected the social dimensions of the environmental problems, the solutions to which were seen largely in physical, ecological and technical terms. There is growing evidence that a holistic approach sensitive to people's problems, and priorities can successfully combine resource conservation with livelihood improvement. A key element of this approach is the progressive transfer of responsibility to local communities and organizations for the management of natural resources. The national authorities and the international community can play a vital role in this process through assistance designed to reinforce local efforts, enhance local managerial and organizational capabilities and build upon indigenous skills, knowledge and inventiveness.

An approach to sustainable development based upon local management of natural resources faces enormous difficulties of conflicts of interest amongst different groups at local, national and international levels. But there are also common interests among diverse groups and organizations in poverty alleviation, preventing the disastrous ecological consequences of resource degradation and initiating a process of environmental rehabilitation and preservation. The current struggle for democratic reform in Africa provides an exceptional opportunity for expansion and strengthening of grassroots organizations of rural producers – a crucial component of a locally based approach to sustainable development.

Note

1   This is a revised version of a keynote address given at the third assembly of the African Academy of Sciences on 'Environment and Development in Africa', organized jointly with the University of Swaziland and held in Swaziland in November 1991. I am grateful to Thomas Odhiambo, President of the Academy; Peter Anyang' Nyong'o, then Director of Programmes; and Ne Ngangu Massamba, Secretary for International Affairs, for the invitation to deliver the address. In revising the paper I have benefited from comments by participants at the general assembly. I am especially grateful to the following UNRISD colleagues for material, comments and editorial assistance: Adrienne Cruz, Krishna Ghimire, Veena Jha, Heiko Schaper, Peter Utting, Jessica Vivian and David Westendorff. I would also like to thank Rhonda Gibbes, Françoise Jaffré and Irene Ruiz for assistance with typing, proof-reading and formatting the paper. The paper originally appeared as UNRISD Discussion Paper No. 33.

References

Barraclough, Solon and Krishna Ghimire (1990) *The Social Dynamics of Deforestation in Developing Countries*, UNRISD Discussion Paper No. 16. Geneva: UNRISD.

Bilsborrow, Richard and H. W. O. Okoth-Ogendo (1991) *Population-driven Changes in Land Use in Developing Countries*, mimeo.

Blackwell, Jonathan M. *et al.* (1991) *Environment and Development in Africa*. Washington, DC: World Bank.

Blaikie, Piers and Harold Brookfield (1987) *Land Degradation and Society*. London: Methuen.

Brett, E. A. (1973) *Colonialism and Underdevelopment in East Africa: The Politics of Economic Change 1919–1939*. New York: Nok.

Brokenshaw, D. and P. Little (1987) 'Local institutions, tenure and resource management', in David Anderson and Richard Grove (eds), *Conservation in Africa: People, Policies and Practice*. Cambridge: Cambridge University Press.

Brundtland Commission (1987) *Our Common Future*. London: Oxford University Press.

Cecelski, E. (1987) 'Energy and rural women's work: crisis, response and policy alternatives', *International Labour Review*, 126(1).

Conroy, Czech and Miles Litunoff (eds) (1988) *The Greening of Aid*. London: Earthscan.

Cruz, Adrienne (1991) *Grassroots-based Environmental Rehabilitation Projects*, mimeo. Geneva: UNRISD.

Darkoh, M. B. K. (1987) 'Socio-economic and institutional factors behind desertification in southern Africa', *AREA*, 19(1).

Dasgupta, Partha and Karl-Göran Mäler (1990) 'The environment and emerging development issues', *Proceedings of the World Bank Annual Conference on Development Economics*. Washington, DC: World Bank.

ECA–FAO (1992) *Land Degradation and Food Supply*. Addis Ababa: ECA–FAO.

Egger, Philippe and Jean Majeres (1992) 'Local resource management and development: Strategic dimensions of people's participation', in Ghai and Vivian (1992).

FAO (1989) *Forestry and Nutrition: A Reference Manual*. Rome: FAO.

FAO (1990) *The Major Significance of Minor Forest Products*. Rome: FAO.

FAO (undated) *The Conservation and Rehabilitation of African Lands*. Rome: FAO.

Fones-Sundell, Melinda (1989) *Land Degradation in Sub-Saharan Africa*, mimeo. Uppsala: Swedish University of Agricultural Sciences.

Franke, Richard W. and Barbara H. Chasin (1980) *Seeds of Famine: Ecological Destruction and the Development Dilemma in the West African Sahel*. Montclair: Allanheld & Osmun.

Gaidzanwa, R. *et al.* (1987) 'Involving the people in soil and water conservation: the Mwenezi experience', *People's Participation in Soil and Water Conservation*. Maseru, Zimbabwe: SADCC.

Gamaledinn, Makunun (1987) 'State policy and famine in the Awash Valley of Ethiopia: the lessons for conservation', in David Anderson and Richard Grove (eds), *Conservation in Africa: People, Policies and Practice*. Cambridge: Cambridge University Press.

Ghai, Dharam (1990) 'Participatory development: some perspectives from grassroots experiences', in Keith Griffin and John Knight (eds), *Human Development and the International Development Strategy for the 1990s*. London: Macmillan.

Ghai, Dharam, and Jessica M. Vivian (eds) (1992) *Grassroots Environmental Action: People's Participation in Sustainable Development*. London: Routledge.

Ghimire, Krishna B. (1991) *Parks and People: Livelihood Issues in National Parks Management in Thailand and Madagascar*, UNRISD Discussion Paper No. 29. Geneva: UNRISD.

Glantz, Michael H. (ed.) (1987) *Drought and Hunger in Africa: Denying Famine a Future*. Cambridge: Cambridge University Press.

Grainger, Alan (1990) *The Threatening Desert: Controlling Desertification*. London: Earthscan.

Grove, Richard (1987) 'Early themes in African conservation: The Cape in the nineteenth century', in David Anderson and Richard Grove (eds), *Conservation in Africa: People, Policies and Practice*. Cambridge: Cambridge University Press.

Harrison, Paul (1987) *The Greening of Africa: Breaking Through in the Battle for Land and Food*. London: Palladin.

Hjorst af Ornäs, Anders and M. A. Mohamed Salih (1989) *Ecology and Politics: Environmental Stress and Security in Africa*. Motala: Scandinavian Institute of African Studies.

Horowitz, Michael M. and Muneera Salem-Murdoch (1987) 'The political economy of desertification in White Nile Province, Sudan', in Peter D. Little *et al.* (eds), *Lands at Risk in the Third World: Local-level Perspectives*. Boulder, CO: Westview.

Hughes, Francine (1987) 'Conflicting uses for forest resources in the lower Tana Basin of Kenya', in David Anderson and Richard Grove (eds), *Conservation in Africa: People, Policies and Practice*. Cambridge: Cambridge University Press.

IUCN (1989) *World Conservation Strategy for the 1990s*. Gland, Switzerland: International Union for the Conservation of Nature and Natural Resources.

Jacobsohn, Margaret (1991) 'The crucial link: conservation and development', in Jackelyn Cock and Eddie Koch (eds), *Going Green: People, Politics and the Environment in South Africa*. Cape Town: Oxford University Press.

Kempadoo, Peter (1991) *Zenzele: The O. R. A. P. Way*. Bulawayo: ORAP.

Kjekshus, H. (1977) *Ecology Control and Economic Development in East African History*. Berkeley: University of California Press.

Koch, Eddie *et al.* (1990) *Water, Waste and Wildlife*. Johannesburg: Penguin Books.

Korir-Koch, Michael (1991) 'History of environmental management in Kenya', in Amos Kiriro and Calestous Juma (eds), *Gaining Ground: Institutional Innovations in Land Use Management in Kenya*. Nairobi: Acts Press.

Lane, Charles (1992) 'The Barabaig pastoralists of Tanzania: sustainable land use in jeopardy', in Ghai and Vivian (1992).

Ledea Ouedraogo, B. (1990) *Entraide villageoise et développement*. Paris: L'Harmattan.

Lawry, Steven W. (1989) *Politique de tenure et gestion des ressources naturelles en Afrique de l'ouest sahelienne*. Madison: Land Tenure Centre, University of Wisconsin.

McNamara, Robert S. (1990) *Africa's Development Crisis: Agricultural Stagnation, Population Explosion, and Environmental Degradation*, mimeo.

Mascarenhas, Adolfo and F. P. Magana (1991) *Land scarcity and Deforestation in the Western Usambaras*, mimeo. Geneva: UNRISD.

Mohamed Salih, M. A. (1989) 'Political coercion and the limits of state intervention: Sudan', in Hjort af Ornäs and Mohamed Salih, (1989).

Molutsi, Patrick P. (1988) 'The state, environment and peasant consciousness in Botswana', *Review of African Political Economy*, no. 42:40–7.

Mortimore, Michael (1985) *Adapting to Drought: Farmers, Famines and Desertification in West Africa*. Cambridge: Cambridge University Press.

Mutiso, Gideon Cyrus (1991) 'Managing arid and semi-arid areas in Kenya', in Amos Kiriro and Calestous Juma (eds), *Gaining Ground: Institutional Innovations in Land Use Management in Kenya*. Nairobi: Acts Press.

Palmer, Robin and Neil Pearson (1977) *The Roots of Rural Poverty in Central and Southern Africa*. London: Heinemann.

Pradervand, Pierre (1990) *Listening to Africa: Developing Africa from the Grassroots*. New York: Praeger.

Redclift, Michael (1987) *Sustainable Development: Exploring the Contradictions*, London: Routledge.

Redclift, Michael (1992) 'Sustainable development and popular participation: a framework for analysis', in Ghai and Vivian (1992).

Reid, Walter V. *et al.* (1988) *Bankrolling Successes: A Portfolio of Sustainable Development Projects*. Washington, DC: Environmental Policy Institute and National Wildlife Federation.

Repetto, Robert (1987) 'Population, Resources, Environment: An Uncertain Future', *Population Bulletin*, 42(2).

Repetto, Robert and Malcome Gillis (eds) (1988) *Public Policies and the Misuse of Forest Resources*. Cambridge: Cambridge University Press.

Richards, Paul (1985) *Indigenous Agricultural Revolution*. London: Hutchinson.

Sen, A. (1980) *Poverty and Famines*. Oxford: Clarendon Press.

Serageldin, Ismael (1990) *Saving Africa's Rainforests*. Washington, DC: World Bank.

Shaw, Paul (1989) 'Rapid population growth and environmental degradation: ultimate versus proximate factors', *Environmental Conservation*, 16(3).

Ståhl, Michael (1992) 'Environmental rehabilitation in the northern Ethiopian highlands: contrasts to people's participation', in Ghai and Vivian (1992).

Toure, Oussouby (1988) 'The pastoral environment of northern Senegal', *Review of African Political Economy*, 42.

Turton, D. (1989) 'The Mursi and national park development', in David Anderson and Richard Grove (eds), *Conservation in Africa: People, Policies and Practice*. Cambridge: Cambridge University Press.

United Nations (1991) *World's Women: Trends and Statistics 1970–1990*. New York: United Nations.

Vivian, Jessica M. (1992) 'Foundations for sustainable development: participation, empowerment and local resource management', in Ghai and Vivian (1992).

Wamalwa, Betty Nafuna (1991) 'Indigenous knowledge and ecological management', in Amos Kiriro and Calestous Juma (eds), *Gaining Ground: Institutional Innovations in Land Use Management in Kenya*. Nairobi: Acts Press.

Watts, Michael (1983) *Silent Violence: Food, Famine and Peasantry in Northern Nigeria*. Berkeley: University of California Press.

World Bank (1981) *Accelerated Development in Sub-Saharan Africa*. Washington, DC: World Bank.

World Bank (1989) *Sub-Saharan Africa: From Crisis to Sustainable Growth*. Washington, DC: World Bank.

World Resources Institute (in collaboration with UNEP and UNDP) (1990) *World Resources, 1990–91*. New York: Oxford University Press.

7

Environment and Sustainable Development in Africa

Maurice Strong

When in December 1972 the United Nations General Assembly took the decision to establish the United Nations Environment Programme (UNEP) and locate its headquarters in Nairobi, Kenya, my first act as the Executive Director of the new organization was to fly to Nairobi to begin the process of establishing it there. On arrival I immediately sought out Philip Ndegwa, who at that time was Permanent Secretary of Finance. I had come to know him in his earlier capacities as Permanent Secretary, Planning and Agriculture, when I was President of the Canadian International Development Agency. In his characteristically candid manner he told me that no provision had been made to finance the arrangements for hosting the UNEP headquarters and that the Ministry of Foreign Affairs had proceeded on its own in offering to host the UNEP in Nairobi without consulting the Finance Ministry. Nevertheless, he said he would do everything possible to be helpful but insisted first that I make the case for why this would be good for Kenya and for Africa.

We then launched into an extensive discussion of the substantive nature of the environmental issues which had led to the establishment of UNEP and their relationship with the primary development priorities of Africa which were at the core of Philip's own deepest interest and for which he was such an eloquent and persuasive advocate. What evidence was there that the more developed countries were prepared to give more than lip service to the underlying causes of environmental degradation in Africa – poverty and underdevelopment? Why should African countries give any priority to co-operating with the more developed countries in dealing with global environmental problems which these countries had created, especially as they had themselves only started to address these problems after they had reached an advanced stage of development? Was there not a real tendency on the part of the more developed countries to impose standards and conditions which would constrain development in developing countries and distort their own priorities? Was the agreement by the more developed countries to headquarter UNEP in Nairobi a mere symbolic gesture designed to co-opt African countries to the northern environmental agenda?

My dialogue with Philip Ndegwa was a continuing one, in which his well-honed intellect and penetrating insights broadened my own knowledge and understanding of these issues, while at the same time deepening his interest in them. This led to my recruiting him as Assistant Executive Director for Policy at UNEP, the only time he had been prepared to accept any of the many invitations he had received to serve at the senior levels of international organizations. In this capacity he became the prime mover in the development of UNEP's own policies and their attunement to the interests and aspirations of developing countries. Philip's primary commitment was always to Kenya and to Africa and it is to the issues bearing on the relationship of the environment to Africa's development that he made his greatest contribution. While the views I express in this chapter are my own, they bear the deep imprint of the seminal contribution that Philip Ndegwa made to my own thinking and understanding.

1.   The potential of natural resources

Africa is a large and diverse continent which includes the world's largest area of arid lands as well as some of its principal tropical rainforest areas. It is made up of nation states whose borders were imposed on it by colonial powers and which divide tribal groups and natural ecosystems in ways which compound the problems of political and economic management. Most African countries have been experiencing severe economic problems exacerbated by the world's highest rates of population growth, recurrent natural disasters and internal conflicts. This has produced a proliferation of bad news from Africa which has conditioned the world community to see Africa as beset by perennial and seemingly unresolveable problems.

More recently there has been good news from Africa. At the political level, the momentous and peaceful transition of South Africa from a racially divided apartheid system of government to a democracy that has empowered the country's black majority has ushered in a new era of political stability and regional co-operation in Southern Africa. And since 1994 Africa's economic performance has been steadily improving. While it is still too early for this to have effected any significant relief from the poverty which continues to make Africa the world's poorest region, it provides a basis for greater optimism that Africa's recovery can move it beyond the abyss to a new era of sustained and sustainable development.

The economies of the African countries continue to depend largely on their natural resource endowment and their export earnings from the sale of commodities, to which crude oil is now making an increasing contribution. More African governments are making progress in overhauling the management of their economies. Economic management in Africa is even more closely related to the environment than in many other regions of the developing world because of Africa's almost total dependence on natural resources. Although African leaders have become increasingly sensitized to the need for sustainable development of their natural resources, institutional and attitudinal inertia have combined with more immediate economic and political pressures to frustrate the implementation of policies and practices that would mitigate environmental degradation and drive the transition to sustainable development. As a result, environmental conditions in most African countries have continued to deteriorate, accompanied by massive depletion of soils, vegetation and wildlife.

For the majority of Africans who remain in the grip of a systemic poverty it is a vicious circle in which the day-by-day struggle to meet their bare survival needs drives them to undermine or destroy the very resources on which their future survival and well-being depend. Degradation of arable lands is particularly threatening to the livelihoods of the peasant farmers who depend on them as well as to the economies of the countries which already produce less food than they consume and face the prospect of an increasing dependence on imports to meet the basic food requirements of their people. A UNEP study estimated that in 1990 some 500 million hectares in Africa were moderately to severely degraded, amounting to one-third of all crop land and permanent pasture (UNEP, 1991). In some countries the degradation is even more severe. It results primarily from over-grazing, clearing of forest areas and grasslands for cultivation, and the working of marginal lands, compounded by inadequate management and recurrent drought conditions. Population pressure in some areas is leading to a reduced availability of land, accelerating trends to more intensive farming methods and the opening up of new areas not suited to sustained cultivation. This is particularly ominous because many African countries have now become dependent on food imports at a time when food aid is becoming increasingly hard to come by.

This underscores the importance of the initiative of FAO Director-General Jacques Diouf in calling for higher priority to be given to the issue of food security, particularly in Africa. Although the deficit in food production is growing, agriculture continues to produce some 55 per cent of the exports of Sub-Saharan Africa, except for the countries which are oil exporters. But the future of these export crops is also clouded by the prospect that the dramatic advances in biotechnology and genetic science will give rise to major changes in the patterns and economics of production for some of Africa's most important export crops.

From the earliest stages of our relationship, Philip Ndegwa had impressed on me the fundamental importance of agriculture to Africa's development future. He was largely influential in developing the policies which led to the diversification of Kenya's agricultural economy. This was based on a twin-track approach – support for the small peasant farmers who constitute the majority of Kenya's farming community while at the same time Kenyanizing many of the larger farms and ranches which contribute disproportionately to export earnings.

Deterioration of the resource base has its most immediate impacts in rural areas in which most people continue to live at the level of bare subsistence. Loss of soil and vegetation cover reduces the productivity of land and drives people to exploit it even more intensively and to move into marginal areas, which rapidly degenerate into unproductive waste lands.

Nothing is more important to the sustainable development of rural areas than water management. The recurrent droughts to which much of Africa is susceptible require that water resources be carefully husbanded and watersheds protected. Experience in some of the particularly drought-prone areas has demonstrated that careful management of water resources can prevent droughts from turning into famines and enable agricultural productivity and soil quality to be maintained.

The Great African Famine of 1984–6 provided dramatic evidence of how natural phenomena combined with unsustainable human practices can turn lands that have been farmed for generations into unproductive wastelands. Most of the some thirty million people affected by the famine were rural peoples, who had led self-reliant lives without the support of their national governments or international aid agencies. But after seventeen years of below-average rainfall, their own reserves were exhausted, they had to sell their meagre possessions and had no alternative but to leave their homes in search of food and sustenance.

Droughts are inevitable; famines are not. They are the result of human failings – failures of policy at the national level; misallocation of resources which deny support to rural areas in favour of the more politically active urban populations. And failure, too, of international development assistance agencies in deploying their resources in ways that reinforce the traditional self-reliant skills and practices of peasant farmers.

But the human tragedy of famine is also a product of the limits that nature itself imposes when the needs of the human and animal populations of an area exceed its capacity to meet these needs on a sustainable basis. With more access to capital, information and training, co-operative efforts at the community level can raise the 'sustainability thresholds' of these areas to levels at which they can meet the needs of their people without destroying or undermining the resource base required to meet these needs on a continuing basis.

There is an intrinsic, systemic relationship between the condition and prospects of Africa's forested areas and its agriculture. Africa's forested areas account for some 38 per cent of its total land area – some 1.14 billion hectares (FAO, 1995). Of this, about half is tropical forest, representing only some 30 per cent of the original forested area (UNEP, 1994). The temperate forests of Africa are also declining at a rate greater than that of any other of the world's regions (FAO, 1995). Harvesting of fuel wood combined with the pressure to open up new areas for cultivation provide a strong motivation for continued deforestation.

Some 90 per cent of household energy and 70 per cent of total energy consumed in Sub-Saharan Africa is derived from fuel wood (WCMC, 1992), which is already in short supply, adding to the pressures on existing forested areas. Indeed, concerns by Kenyans themselves for the continued encroachment on the country's forestry resources led to establishment of a grassroots movement, the 'Green Belt Movement' headed by a remarkable and dynamic Kenyan lady, Wangari Maathai, one of the best examples of citizen-level environmental action in the developing world. The initial goals of this organization were focused on combating desertification, but they later expanded to include empowerment of women, economic development and related social goals. Its primary focus was on tree-planting activities at the community level stimulated by a national mass-media campaign. The movement was strongly supported by the Kenyan Forestry Department, but later became involved in political controversy which strained its relations with government. Nevertheless it served as the model for the establishment in 1992, following the Earth Summit, of the Pan African Green Belt movement (Michaelson, 1994).

The resource that most of world identifies most specifically with Africa is its wildlife, especially the large mammals of which Africa is the principal habitat. But Africa's wildlife is rapidly disappearing. Of an original habitat of some 20,800,000 square miles, it is estimated that 65 per cent has now been lost through logging and conversion to agriculture or other uses (WRI, 1989). Hunting and poaching for ivory and rhino horn has also contributed to a severe reduction in the population of elephants and rhinoceros. From an original population of some 10 million, only 700,000 elephants remain and these are being depleted at the rate of more than 10 per cent per year (IUCN, 1989). The black rhinoceros population has declined to less than 4,000 from an estimated 60,000 during the past twenty years (*Bio Science*, 1990). And there are similar precipitous declines in the numbers of other species of wildlife that are indigenous to Africa.

Africa's wildlife resources are the basis of a thriving tourist trade which both provides economic incentives for their preservation and exerts additional pressures on their habitats. The conflict between maintaining the habitats of the animals and the needs of expanding local populations for creating more grazing and cultivable land has inhibited measures for conservation of wildlife. This has led to the initiation of new methods of wildlife management based on the participation by local peoples on a basis which gives them economic incentives to help maintain wildlife populations.

As the world has come to recognize the economic potential as well as the environmental value of biodiversity, there is increasing awareness that the continuing degradation of Africa's biological resources represents a loss and a risk, not only to Africa, but to the entire world community. The remaining forests of Sierra Leone, the Ivory Coast and Liberia contain the last remaining vestiges of the species-rich forests of Upper Guinea Zone (UNEP, 1994). Some of the major watershed areas, the Niger, Gambia and Senegal River Systems, are exceptionally rich in biodiversity and these too, as the World Bank points out in a 1995 report, are at risk.

The greatest concentration of Africa's biodiversity resources is in the vast tropical rainforest area of the Congo Basin. This region has one of the highest levels of urbanization in Africa, yet one of its lowest population densities. The main threats to the rainforest come from exploitation of its timber resources as well as development of its mineral potential. Political instability, poverty and the corrupt and ineffective policies of governments have combined to make development of the tropical forest areas much more environmentally destructive than it need be, and this will ultimately exact a high cost in economic terms. The mountain and highlands areas of Africa, Mount Kenya, Mount Kilimanjaro, the Aberdares and the Rwenzori and the Rift Valley in East Africa, Mount Cameroon and the highland areas of Ethiopia and Southern Africa are also rich in biodiversity. But all are also subject to increasing population pressures, giving rise to shortages of cultivable land and living space which are undermining the biological resources of these areas and compromising their sustainability.

Not all of Africa's biological resources are concentrated in the tropical forest and highland regions. The wetlands areas of the Lake Victoria and Chad Basin, the swamps of the Congo and the Sudd in the Upper Nile Region and the deltas of some of the major rivers are home to a diverse range of plant and animal life, including many rare and endangered species. Africa's extensive coastal regions provide the habitats for a diversity of fish species, and the contiguous land areas have some of its richest and most productive soils as well as forest and wetland areas. All of these resources are being severely impacted by the high concentration in coastal areas of urban and industrial development and tourism.

The vast savannahs of Africa constitute one of the richest grassland regions in the world and provide the habitat for a wide range of unique flora and fauna, including the world's greatest concentration of large mammals. As these areas are the home for a major portion of Africa's human population, they are also subject to the pressures of extensive cultivation and livestock grazing.

Much of Africa receives relatively low levels of precipitation and is subject to frequent droughts. UNEP, in a 1985 study, cites evidence that Africa's annual rainfall has diminished since 1968, and the effects of this have been exacerbated by the disruption of watersheds resulting from deforestation and the erosion and degradation of soils. Africa's ground water resources are not substantial; in Sub-Saharan Africa some 75 per cent of the population relies on ground water, which represents only some 15 per cent of renewable water resources and is subject to deteriorating water quality. The great river systems of Africa – the Niger, Volta, Zambezi, Nile and Lake Victoria – constitute valuable water resources which require a degree of management, often involving co-operation across national boundaries, which is so far largely lacking.

Much of the world's untapped hydro-electric power potential exists in the river systems of Africa. The fact that some 54 rivers or large bodies of water are shared by more than one country in Africa offers both a mounting potential for conflict and a major opportunity for co-operative management. Even in areas of high rainfall, water quality is a growing problem. The majority of the countries in the world with the highest percentage of their people denied access to safe drinking water are in Africa (WRI *et al.*, 1996).

2. People and environment

Although Africa continues to be the least urbanized continent in the world, its urban growth rate is among the highest. Migration from poverty-stricken rural areas is responsible for some 40–60 per cent of urban population growth (McGee and Griffiths, 1994: 60). Most migrants exchange their rural poverty for a marginal urban existence detached from their traditional culture and family support systems. Internal migration has been exacerbated by conflicts as well as by the severe drought and famine conditions that have afflicted Sub-Saharan Africa, which has also had to accommodate an estimated 35 million international migrants.

The number of cities with population of more than a million has increased from only one in 1960 to eighteen by 1990 (UNDP, 1996). With limited resources,

African cities have not been able to provide basic health, sanitation services, physical and social infrastructure to meet the needs of these growing populations. The result has been a continued deterioration of the urban environment and the proliferation of slum areas, which have become festering centres of poverty, disease, crime and social disintegration. The contrast between the rapid emergence of modernization in Africa and the small but growing elite who monopolize its benefits with the plight of the majority of the poor, dispossessed and marginalized is nowhere more evident than in Africa's cities. The high-rise buildings that define the skylines of the cities, their teeming shopping areas and traffic-congested streets, often with more Mercedes in evidence than in most western cities, co-exist with spreading slum areas. In the daytime in the busy city centres, the wretched and the poor look longingly into shop windows and beg for help from the well-dressed business people and foreign tourists who mingle with them in the streets. Nowhere is this more evident than in Nairobi, where the local authorities periodically bulldoze the unauthorized suburban shanty towns, leaving their hapless residents to fend for themselves.

Africa's population, now some 700 million, is growing at a rate of approximately 2.9 per cent per year, one of the world's highest population growth rates. This will produce a total population of over one billion people by 2005. While in theory Africa's resource base could sustain this level of population, in practice growth is concentrated in the areas in which population density is already highest, while there are still vast areas of relatively sparse population. But providing even the most basic level of services and livelihoods for twenty million new people each year is beyond the capacity of an Africa already struggling to meet the basic needs of its existing population with meagre financial resources and a paucity of skills and institutional capabilities. The result is that progress in improving economic performance on an aggregate basis is offset by the effects of population growth and its concentration in existing urban centres.

Paradoxically, encouraging progress in improving human health in Africa has contributed to the high population growth by extending average lifespans significantly. This is a very positive and promising trend in human terms, despite the additional economic pressures to which it contributes. Even so, most suffering and deaths result from preventable causes, notably water-borne disease and lack of basic sanitary facilities and health care services. All of this underscores the fact that development is a multi-faceted, integrative process in which there must be progress on all fronts to ensure that development produces the improvement in the quality of life and standards of living that are its primary goal. This is what sustainable development is all about.

In a world in which knowledge is the primary source of comparative advantage and added value, Africa is particularly disadvantaged. In this context, the reduction in educational enrolment during the 1980s, which has still not been reversed (UNDP, 1996), is one of the most ominous portends for Africa's future. Reductions in government budgets for education resulting from the recent period of budgetary austerity that virtually all governments have faced will exact a heavy price on Africa's future. With nearly half the population constituting children below the age of 16, the prospects of their obtaining the kind of education and skills they will need to compete in an increasingly competitive job market are indeed slim. Employment prospects are bleak for this generation of young people unless there is a sustained acceleration of economic growth.

Africa's need to move to a new generation of accelerated development is also severely strained by a debt burden that is higher than that of any other developing region. The World Bank describes about 40 countries as 'heavily indebted' – that is having debt service payments at least twice as large as what they earn each year from exports. Eighty percent of the most severely debt-burdened low-income countries identified by the World Bank are in Sub-Saharan Africa, where the average per capita debt servicing load is some US $43 – as compared with US $35 average per capita expenditures on health and education. Mozambique spends more on debt service than on health, education, police and judicial systems combined. Some two-thirds of the money that foreign donors provide goes straight back out to foreign bankers.

Even with recent measures for debt forgiveness, many of the poorest countries of Africa will continue to face debt burdens that are beyond their capacity to service. The international community has responded to Africa's needs with an increased flow of Official Development Assistance as well as some debt relief. While welcome, this has deepened Africa's high dependence on foreign assistance at a time when most donor governments are reducing their ODA levels. Africa continues to need ODA and must be accorded the highest priority by donors. Nevertheless it seems evident that Africa must look to private investment for most of the external capital it will require in future. Yet Africa has been largely bypassed by the major increases in foreign and direct investment that the Asian and Latin American regions have experienced in recent years. Some 35 African countries have undertaken structural adjustment programmes accompanied by economic and management reforms which improve the climate for private investment. Some of these measures have also served to exacerbate social tensions and the gaps between rich and poor. Nevertheless, there is no question that Africa must attract more foreign direct investment in future and that efforts to provide a more hospitable and profitable environment for private investment will pay off.

Professor Thomas Homer-Dixon has produced some compelling evidence as to the relationship between environmental factors and conflicts which is particularly relevant to Africa. His work demonstrates that what he describes as 'environmental scarcity' arising from high population densities leading to scarcity of water, land, declining soil fertility and deforestation is a source of threats to the socio-economic well-being of Africans in the areas concerned, and was a contributing factor to the recent conflicts in Rwanda (Homer-Dixon and Percival, 1995a) and to social instability in South Africa and in Rwanda (Homer-Dixon and Percival, 1995b). As the pressure on scarce resources continues to grow, so will the potential for social instability and conflict.

3. Towards sustainable development

Africa is a continent of immense diversity and contrast to which a brief overview of this kind cannot possibly do justice. But it is against this background that sustainable development must be seen as the only viable pathway to the future of Africa. When the Stockholm Conference put the environment issue on the international agenda, environmental concerns were seen primarily as a disease of the rich, the by-product of the same processes of urbanization and industrialization that had produced the unprecedented wealth of the industrialized countries. The initial response of developing countries was that if economic growth is accompanied by environmental impacts, this would not only be acceptable, but welcome – that, like the industrialized countries, they must concentrate first on economic growth and leave environmental problems to be addressed at a more advanced stage of development. At the international level, developing countries expressed their suspicions that the environmental preoccupations of the industrialized countries would divert attention and resources from the priority development interests of developing countries and that the environment issue would be invoked to impose constraints on their development. They insisted that, as industrialized countries had been largely responsible for creating global environmental problems, they should accept primary responsibility for addressing them and should provide to the developing countries the 'new and additional financial resources' they would require to participate in international environmental co-operation.

The location of the headquarters of the United Nations Environment Programme in Nairobi, as the first global UN organization to be headquartered in a developing country, gave African nations a special incentive to take an active part in discussion and negotiation of environment-related issues in international fora. The strong representation of Africa in the membership of the United Nations and its specialized agencies lends particular weight to the positions of African countries. Illegal trade in wild fauna and flora in Africa has been a major factor in the severe depletion that has occurred of Africa's unique wildlife resources. Despite the fact that more countries have adhered to and are implementing the 1973 Convention on International Trade in Endangered Species of Wild Fauna and Flora (CITES), illegal trade has proliferated to the point where Interpol estimates its annual value at a level of some US 5 billion dollars, second only to the value of world trade in narcotics. On the initiative of the African countries primarily affected by this trade – Botswana, Kenya, Mozambique, South Africa, Swaziland, Tanzania, Uganda and Zambia – an agreement was reached in a conference in Lusaka, Zambia in 1992, the Lusaka Agreement on Co-operative Enforcement Operations, directed at stemming illegal trade in wild fauna and flora and providing for cross-border co-operation for this purpose. This represented an important African initiative in dealing with the African environmental issue that had significant international dimensions.

African governments were particularly active in the negotiations on the elaboration of the Basel Convention on environmentally sound management and disposal of hazardous wastes and their trans-boundary movements, which were led by the United Nations Environment Programme. Guidelines were developed at a conference in Cairo in 1985, and subsequently approved by the Governing Council of UNEP, as a basis for negotiation of a convention. African countries, particularly concerned at the tendency of more developed countries to export hazardous waste for final disposal to Africa, convened a meeting in Dakar in January 1989 under the auspices of the Organization for African Unity. It called for the incorporation into the Basel Convention of explicit provisions banning the export of hazardous waste to countries which had banned their import. When they were unable to obtain agreement to incorporate the ban into the final text of the Basel Convention, African countries negotiated and concluded a separate regional agreement, the 1991 Bamako Convention on the ban of the import into Africa and the control of trans-boundary movement of hazardous waste within Africa. This was an important example of African leadership on an environmental issue in which it had previously been assumed that Africa had limited interest.

African countries joined the consensus achieved at the UN Conference on Environment and Development held in Rio de Janeiro, Brazil, in June 1992. The regional consultations leading up to the 1997 Rio +5 Civil Society Forum noted that a considerable amount of progress has been made in the African region in implementation of the Rio agreements, particularly Agenda 21 and the conventions on bio-diversity, climate change and the subsequent convention on drought and desertification. Over 40 African governments are at various stages of preparing or implementing a national conservation strategy, a national environmental action plan, or national sustainable development plan. Egypt, Tunisia, Togo, Benin, Burkina Faso and Uganda have all taken steps to prepare their own national Agenda 21 based on Rio's Agenda 21. And 15 African countries have established multi-stakeholder national councils for sustainable development, or equivalent bodies.

A particularly encouraging development has been the establishment of environmental funds in Uganda, the Gambia, Benin, Ghana and Madagascar, with support both from government and the private sector. Comprehensive environmental education programmes are being implemented in Swaziland, Ethiopia, the Gambia, Uganda, Zambia, Egypt, Senegal, Benin and Ghana. And the Africa 2000 network programme has developed a series of grassroots and community level initiatives which are lending practical impetus to the sustainable development movement in Africa. An independent evaluation of the programme done for UNDP in July 1995 gave high marks to its innovative approaches and methods, which yield multiplier effects in the fight against poverty and for environmental protection. It points to the flexibility shown by the programme in its ability to adapt to each national situation and to evolving objectives and strategies, its contribution to promoting democratization at the local level, to the revival of the use of traditional skills and knowledge and to enabling a genuine break with the old donor culture.

All this helps demonstrate both the feasibility and the benefit of sustainable development. But overall it has to be said that sustainable development has not yet taken root in Africa under conditions that would enable African countries to make the transition to a sustainable development pathway.

Why should they do so? And how should they go about it?

Virtually every aspect of Africa's development is environment-related. The heavy dependence of African economies on their natural resource endowments clearly dictates that the care and responsible development of these resources is essential to the development future of these countries. This is what sustainable development is all about – in the words of the Brundtland Commission: 'Development that meets the needs of the present without compromising the ability of future generations to meet their own needs.' While reliable figures are not available, there is no question that a substantial proportion of the economic growth being generated by African countries today is based upon unsustainable development practices that represent a drawing down of the natural capital which constitutes the primary asset base of these countries, and on which their future development depends. The situation is especially ominous in that there is extensive 'mining' of renewable resources such as soil, forested areas and wildlife which can and should be developed on a renewable basis. Thus, the rate at which precious renewable resources are being depleted is robbing African countries of the capital on which their hopes and aspirations for a better future must be based.

Paradoxically, the unsustainable development of African resources also short-changes African countries in economic terms. The highly competitive international marketplace still does not price most of the commodities which constitute the bulk of Africa's exports on a basis that reflects their real environmental and social costs. One of the most important challenges facing the international community in the period ahead is to make the transition to an economic regime in which the environmental and social costs of products, particularly renewable resources, are internalized and incorporated into their prices. This is especially important to developing countries whose economies are disproportionately dependent on exports of such resources. Such changes will be resisted by the more developed countries whose importers would need to be bear these costs. Accordingly, it would be in the interest of developing countries to take a lead in negotiating these changes. Africa would be one of the principal beneficiaries of these changes, and this gives Africa special reasons to concert its efforts in leading the international movement we require to achieve agreement on these measures.

African nations are not yet able to realize the added value potential of localizing the processing and upgrading their products. All of this requires capital, as well as manufacturing, technical and marketing skills that are in short supply in Africa. So in developing its renewable resources on an unsustainable basis, Africans are not only selling their development future, they are selling it far too cheaply.

Philip Ndegwa was a strong believer that Africa must not become overdependent on foreign aid, and that it was entirely feasible for Africans, through better management of their economies, to achieve self-reliance and sustainability. But this also requires a more hospitable and supportive international economic environment. The role of the international community must shift to a system which requires that the environmental and social costs be incorporated into the price of both natural and manufactured products. This must be done by governments on a generalized basis, as it would not be feasible to apply it only to the commodities that Africa produces. Unfortunately we are far away from such a system at present. But there is more and more awareness that the global transition to a sustainable development pathway can only be achieved when environmental and social costs are internalized. Under such a system, Africa would have access to the resources it requires to make its own transition to sustainable development on a basis that would be more dependable and equitable than foreign aid, which is not a satisfactory or a satisfying basis for the continuing relationships between developing and more developed countries.

Economic reform and improvements in economic policy and management in many developing countries are providing an important stimulus to both domestic and external private investment. Oil and mineral development is providing impetus to the development of some countries. Higher prices for some of the major export commodities are also giving many African countries a much needed boost. Economic growth in Sub-Saharan Africa rose to almost 4 per cent in 1995 and 1996, and is predicted to continue at this rate or more through 1997–2006 (World Bank, 1997).

Most of all, the capacity to become more self-reliant requires more effective utilization and deployment of domestic resources. A recent study commissioned by the Earth Council indicates that developing country governments spend several billion dollars per year in subsidies in four sectors of their economies – transport, water, energy and agriculture – subsidies that in large part provide incentives for unsustainable practices and benefit primarily the high income minority of their populations at the expense of the poor. These subsidies are much greater than the amount of Official Development Assistance that Africa receives. While subsidies can be a useful instrument for achieving certain policy objectives, it is clear that to a great extent many of them have become perverse in their real effects, imposing high costs on both taxpayers and consumers, while imposing severe constraints on the generation of the new capital required to extend these services to those who need them most.

Many infrastructure projects supported by external development assistance also serve to undermine progress towards sustainability and lead to the misuse of scarce resources. This is particularly true when the funding of the capital cost of the project is not accompanied by measures to ensure long-term operating and maintenance costs. A recent study estimates that nearly one-third of the 150 billion dollars invested in roads in Africa has already been lost because of inadequate management and maintenance. This not only hampers economic development in the regions which depend on the roads, but imposes an accumulating burden on future resources. The same study estimates that to restore only those roads that are economically viable would require an expenditure of some 1.5 billion dollars annually over the next 10 years (de Moor and Calamai, 1997).

Virtually all African governments have established environmental ministries or agencies accompanied by supporting legislation and policies. But sustainable development cannot be achieved merely through assigning responsibility to ministries of environment, for most of the policies and activities that impact on the environment and natural resources are the responsibility of other ministries. Thus it requires a total commitment of governments to sustainable development, for which Rio's Agenda 21 provides a valuable set of guidelines. This must be accompanied by a complete review and reorientation of government fiscal, economic and sectoral policies and the institutions which administer them to develop a comprehensive system of incentives and penalties which provide positive incentives for sustainable behaviour on the part of industry and individuals. There are enough positive examples in our experience to date to know that this is feasible. But individual examples, as welcome as they are, will not be sufficient to enable societies to make the fundamental transition to sustainable development. This must be a systemic change in which governments have to take the lead.

Governments cannot do this in isolation – but fortunately, they do not have to. In many respects people are already ahead of their governments. In the African countries there has been a remarkable proliferation of non-governmental organizations and civil society groups with a commitment to various aspects of sustainable development at both the policy and practical levels. The sustainable development ethos is not foreign to Africa. It is intrinsic to the traditional cultures and commercial practices that have enabled African societies to survive, and many of them to thrive, in the many centuries that preceded the modern era in Africa. There is a great potential in marrying this traditional knowledge and experience with modern technologies and techniques to forge a distinctively African approach to sustainable development.

It may seem something of a paradox, and perhaps even a utopian dream, to envisage Africa as the world leader in the transition to sustainable development. This requires a reversal of the conventional wisdom that unconstrained economic growth must precede the movement to sustainable development. Surely it is clear from the experience and current trends in African development that Africa will not be able to meet the needs and aspirations of its people unless it develops sustainably. Sustainable development is an imperative – not an option. And in Africa the transition to sustainability will become more difficult, more costly and less likely the longer it is delayed.

Of course, African countries cannot be expected to make this transition alone. First they would need to develop a framework for the commitment and co-operation of all, or at least the majority, of African countries through establishment of an African alliance for sustainable development. The international community and the multi-lateral development agencies, notably the World Bank and the United Nations Development Programme, can be expected to lend their full encouragement and support. But the initiative must come from Africans themselves.

Philip Ndgewa's conviction that Africa can and must move to a development pathway that is self-reliant and sustainable was based not just on his strong emotional attachment to Africa, but on the objective analysis and exceptional policy insights of one of Africa's most brilliant minds and experienced practitioners. What he saw as feasible is now more than ever imperative. Indeed, in opting for sustainable development as the pathway to its own future, the world's poorest region could lead it into a new era of security, prosperity and well-being for the entire human family. If it chooses this pathway, all the friends of Africa must join in providing their strong and sustained support.

References

Bio Science, Vol. 3 (3), March 1990.

FAO (Food and Agriculture Organization of the United Nations) (1995) *Forest Resources Assessment 1990: Global Synthesis*, FAO Forestry Paper 124. Rome: FAO.

Homer-Dixon, Thomas and Valerie Percival (1995a) *Environment Scarcity and Violent Conflict: The Case of Rwanda*, Occasional Paper, American Association for the Advancement of Science and University of Toronto. Toronto: Centre for Peace and Conflict Studies, University of Toronto.

Homer-Dixon, Thomas and Valerie Percival (1995b) *Environmental Scarcity and Violent Conflict: The Case of South Africa*, Occasional Paper, American Association for the Advancement of Science and University of Toronto. Toronto: Centre for Peace and Conflict Studies, University of Toronto.

McGee, Terence G. and C. J. Griffiths (1994) 'Global urbanization: towards the twenty-first century', in *Population Distribution and Migration* (Draft proceedings of the United Nations expert meeting on population distribution and migration, Santa Cruz, Bolivia, January 1993). New York: United Nations.

Michaelson, Marc (1994) 'Wangari Maathai and Kenya's Greenbelt Movement: exploring the evolution and potentialities of consensus movement mobilization', *Social Problems*, 41(4): 540–61.

Moor, André de and Peter Calamai (1997) *Subsidizing Unsustainable Development: Undermining the Earth with Public Funds*, Toronto/San José, Costa Rica: Earth Council.

UNDP (1996) *The United Nations System-Wide Special Initiative on Africa*. New York: UNDP.

United Nations Environment Programme (1991) 'Global Digital Datasets for Land Degradation Studies: A GIS Approach', GRIC Case Studies Series, No. 4. Nairobi: UNEP.

UNEP (United Nations Environment Programme) (1994) *The Convention on Biological Diversity: Issues of Relevance to Africa* (Regional Ministerial Conference on the Convention on Biological Diversity). Nairobi: UNEP.

World Bank (1997) *Global Economic Prospects and the Developing Countries*. Washington, DC: World Bank.

WCMC (World Conservation Monitoring Centre) (1992) *Global Biodiversity: Status of the World's Living Resources*. London: Chapman & Hall.

World Resources Institute (WRI), UNEP, United Nations Development Programme (UNDP) and World Bank (1996) *World Resources: A Guide to the Global Environment, 1996–97*, New York: Oxford University Press.

Part II

Agenda for Political and Economic Reform

8

Democratization, Equity and Stability: African Politics and Societies in the 1990s

Yusuf Bangura

Introduction

The 1990s have witnessed remarkable changes in the way African societies are governed. What Samuel Huntington (1991) has described as 'the third wave of democratization' has been strongly felt in most African countries since 1990.[1] A large number of military and one party dictatorships have collapsed in the face of mass civil protests and demands for political change. An interesting aspect of the new wave of democratization is the increasing recognition of political equity as an important aspect of institution-building. Significant steps have been taken to craft political systems that would reflect the plural character of African societies. But democratization has not followed a uniform pattern, and there have been significant setbacks which have raised questions about the viability of the democratic experiments. Problems of instability have thus forced issues of regional and political stability onto the agenda of democratic change.

This paper seeks to examine recent patterns of democratization by focusing on actual political reforms that have emerged in the various countries. It stresses the need to analyse concrete political processes, rather than relying on standard socio-economic determinants of, or preconditions for, democracy, in order to understand the nature of the reforms that have been underway in each country. Standard theories of democratization, which often focus on such issues as levels of economic development, the nature of economic enterprises, formation of modern classes, civic values and social structures are surely relevant in studying the experiences of individual countries, but do not account for the location of countries in the patterns that have emerged. It is important to note that African societies share many things in common: they are largely multi-ethnic and agrarian, with small-holding farms and informal economic enterprises providing the dominant form of employment and livelihood for most people. These economies are also heavily dependent upon the world economy for trade and financial capital. The differences that have emerged among countries in such areas as levels of industrialization, state formation, methods of public administration, and the development of modern social classes have not been significant enough to determine the patterns of political change. The paper emphasizes the need for detailed studies on the political dynamics of each country in order to make sense of current trends in democratization.

The first part of this chapter discusses conceptual issues relevant to democracy and equity; the second provides an overview of the discourse and patterns of authoritarian rule; the third analyses the main issues of political reform; the fourth focuses on patterns of democratization; and the fifth explores the different types of actions taken on security by external powers and African governments to regulate the problems of democratization.

1. Democracy and equity: conceptual issues

In its most fundamental sense, democracy is concerned with people's rule, or popular control and management of power in the public sphere. In short, it is a form or method of rule that embodies the popular will, or 'people's power'. In small city-state pre-modern Athenian conditions or in pre-colonial African village republics, such power was exercised directly by free adult males. Direct democracy is possible under such conditions because of the homogeneity of the societies, the smallness of their population size, their limited division of labour, common patterns of time use, and overlapping interests. Participation rates are thus likely to be high and problems of free riding[2] and non-accountability,[3] which may occur in more complex societies, minimized.

In contrast, large modern-day societies, which are highly differentiated, require the principle of representation to make democracy or 'people's power' feasible. Not everyone may have the time, resources or interest to actively participate in public affairs. In other words, the 'people' must delegate their power to professional politicians or interested elites if public policies are to be formulated and implemented. However, the principle of representation may approximate 'people's power' when it is linked to another important principle – that of accountability. In short, a modern democratic system is one in which the 'people' are able to hold their representatives accountable for the policies they pursue or the decisions they make in the public sphere.

Most students of modern democratic theory would agree that a representative and accountable government must have four important elements to qualify as a democratic polity. The first is the organization of *periodic, free and fair elections* in which all parties or candidates enjoy relatively equal access to, and protection by, the rules. The second is the existence of a *plural civic and political culture*. This refers to competitive political parties and civic or community organizations that enjoy some degree of autonomy. A legislative organ that is made up of multiple parties, in which the leading party does not have a large majority, can be an important indicator of political plurality. The third is the *separation of the state from ruling political parties*. In other words, the institutions of the state – viz. parliament, the judiciary, the military and the civil service – should be relatively separated from the programmes and activities of the political parties in power. Such institutions must serve the governments in power in ways that do not make it difficult for them to constructively relate to the wider public and opposition parties.

The fourth element is the constitutional *guarantee of basic human and political rights*. This calls for the protection of the fundamental rights of expression, assembly and organization – necessary for holding political representatives accountable. One may wish to add a fifth element, which may be important for countries that are in transition from authoritarian to democratic rule: the principle of *the alternation of power*. In order to preserve or develop the neutrality of the state in the exercise of public authority, as well as to prevent the abuse of power by incumbent governments, it is important for power to regularly alternate between contending political parties. Indeed, respect for the principle of the alternation of power helps the development of three additional values that are central to the consolidation of democracy: the necessity for political parties to recognize *the limits of power*, including the readiness to surrender power to democratically elected opponents without fear of the consequences; acceptance of the principle of *moderation and compromise* in political bargaining; and a commitment to live with and support *plurality* in social and political life.

These five elements deal essentially with the *forms* of a democratic polity. They do not directly address distributional issues: i.e. how power is allocated among groups in society. Formal democratic governance may indeed reproduce, even create, social and economic inequalities – in class, ethnic, racial, or gender terms, for instance; and it may not necessarily produce the best leaders. The policies and programmes of political representatives may better reflect the interests of ruling elites or powerful business oligarchies – who have more resources, networks, and capacities to influence public policies – than those of workers, petty traders, artisans or smallholders who occupy the lower rungs of society. Similarly, in situations where a single ethnic or racial group enjoys an absolute demographic majority, it is very possible for formal democracy to produce all, or a disproportionate number, of its political representatives from the dominant ethnic or racial group. In such situations, the votes of the minority groups may not carry the same weight as those of the majority. In other words, formal democratic systems of government, like markets, though non-discriminatory in the juridical sense, are not necessarily just or equitable.

Non-equity outcomes may affect the cohesion and stability of formal democracies, especially in developing countries that do not have the economic strength or state capacity to manage or control social differences and dissent. Excluded groups may opt out of the democratic process and seek redress through non-constitutional or violent means. These limitations explain why Marxists, or revolutionary movements, and minority rights groups often question the *democratic* character of formal democratic institutions: to the former, formal democracy appears as 'bourgeois democracy'; and to the latter, democracy is seen as ethnic discrimination, racism or patriarchy. How to improve the institutions of representation and accountability by introducing equity issues in political systems has, therefore, been central to the concerns of societies whose democracies have been troubled by problems of socio-economic and political exclusion.[4]

The social class exclusion aspect of the democratic debate has been most systematically addressed, especially in Western societies, by the institutions of state welfare provisioning. By providing relatively 'free' and reliable education, health services, minimum income support, unemployment benefits, subsidized housing and food security to disadvantaged groups, the revolutionary pressures that threatened to sweep much of Europe between the late nineteenth century and the immediate post-Second World War period were contained. Excluded groups that are now dependent on the state for their welfare could, in theory at least, defend their interests through the evolving democratic institutions. Political inequality issues, on the other hand, such as those based on ethnicity and race, have been addressed by reforming the formal political systems themselves. These include changes in electoral rules to allow for more proportional representational outcomes; the introduction of special rules of equity or social balance in the formation of political parties and governments; formal power-sharing arrangements in legislative and executive organs of government; rotational presidencies; decentralization; special seats for minorities or disadvantaged groups; and constitutional provisions that protect minority rights.

Across the world, the record of crafting democratic institutions that reflect the ethnic, racial or religious make-up of societies has been uneven. It is instructive that in this area, the experiences of the leading western societies, the pioneers of modern democratic rule, have not been helpful, since their democratic arrangements have been largely guided by eighteenth- and nineteenth-century ideologies of the nation state. Such states are assumed to be homogenous in language, culture, history, religion and race. Most, therefore, are not tailored to handle the equity problems that arise in heterogeneous social settings. Only multi-ethnic societies like Switzerland and Belgium have been sensitive to political equity issues in crafting their democratic institutions. In most developing countries, which received their democratic institutions from European colonial powers, issues of political equity were not central to their decolonization programmes, and are only now being addressed to contain the problems of instability that have accompanied democratization.

2.   The discourse and patterns of authoritarian rule

An understanding of the ways in which African countries have responded to the issues of equity in their current democratization programmes requires analysis of the discourse and patterns of rule that preceded the democratic transitions of the 1990s. Equity issues did not feature strongly in the constitutional arrangements of the independent states in the early 1960s. Although the departing colonial powers were already making significant advances in the promotion of welfare programmes in their own countries, only limited welfare systems were introduced in the colonies at the terminal stage of colonial rule. These included subsidized education, health and pensions for a small, largely urban, elite – but not basic income support or unemployment benefits. The new states not only retained this conservative approach to social policy, but copied the colonial powers' centralized nation state institutions and majoritarian first-past-the-post (FPTP) and two round (TRS) systems of electoral rules.[5] These proved unsuitable for the ethnically plural, largely agrarian and underdeveloped societies of the new democracies. Although most independent governments reflected the ethnic diversity of the respective societies, these were mostly formed on an ad hoc basis, and depended mainly on the preferences of those in power rather than on any rational and objective set of principles that recognized plurality and equity as institutional imperatives. The political outcomes, therefore, tended to be volatile and open to abuse as individuals competed through ethnic group networks for hegemony.[6]

Much of the debate about the democratic potential of Africa in the 1960s focused on the unsuitability of its socio-economic structure and low levels of economic development. Authoritarian rule was justified or rationalized as a necessary option for rapid development and nation-building. The debate highlighted three main issues. The first two were often merged into a single argument that posits a virtuous linkage between modernization and democratization: democracy is assumed to be a product of market-based industrialization, secularism, mass education and the development of professional middle classes. Market industrialization fosters competition and helps the growth of autonomous groups in civil society. And democratic values, such as respect for the rule of law, personal accountability, and tolerance are assumed to be essentially middle-class values. It was argued that democracy has survived in Western societies because of their high levels of market industrialization and well-entrenched professional middle classes (Dahl, 1971; Lipset, 1960; Cnudde and Neubauer, 1969).

In contrast, except for countries of European settlement – such as Kenya, Rhodesia and South Africa – African economies were largely agrarian, with smallholding agriculture accounting for the dominant form of land tenure. Although much of the output from agriculture was marketed domestically and externally, a substantial proportion was for immediate household consumption. What is more, many of the markets were either oligopolistic, like those dominated by the export-oriented commodity boards, or clientelistic, as were many of the domestic food markets and informal petty trade and artisanal activities – hardly the right economic conditions, it was believed, for the exercise of autonomous individual choice and the development of a secular-libertarian civil society (Apter, 1965; Huntington, 1968; Bauer, 1981). The limited industrialization that existed was largely concentrated in the mining sector, with foreign firms as the leading investors. It was argued, especially by neo-Marxists, that the expansion of capitalism on a world scale created socio-economic polarization, which made it impossible for democracy to grow in the peripheral economies of the Third World (Amin, 1987, 1991; Baran, 1957). Some theorists within this framework even postulated that a national entrepreneurial or bourgeois class was needed for the growth of democratic institutions (Beckman, 1992b).[7] Since Africa was economically dependent on the world market and its local business enterprises were dominated by foreign corporations, critics contended that it was impossible for any democratic or bourgeois form of development to take place.

A related issue in the debate was the route which the burgeoning local business classes were said to have adopted to extend their grip on the national economies: this was largely done through the state by lobbying for contracts, import licences, subsidies, loans and preferential treatment, thereby encouraging large-scale corruption and inefficiency. On this score, both neo-Marxist and neo-liberal writings on the subject were in agreement: the overwhelming dependence of the business classes and ruling elites on the state led to an overextended state and fierce, often bloody minded, competition for the control of the state and the stifling of opposition groups and civil liberties (Ake, 1987; Diamond, 1988; Sandbrook, 1985; Joseph, 1987; Osoba, 1978). Professional middle classes did not grow rapidly enough to impose on the emerging societies their assumed values of accountability, tolerance and respect for the law. Instead, these classes, where they emerged, grew up in, and helped foster, the dominant culture of patronage and authoritarianism.[8]

The third argument focused on the assumed authoritarian culture and ethnic cleavages of African states – the point being that democracy requires a high degree of individual autonomy and civic, not primordial, values to function (Pye and Verba, 1965). Given the low level of the development of markets and the social division of labour, African societies were said to be largely collectivist, or tribal; individual initiative was not fully rewarded; and individuals were only able to pursue their self-interests when they followed, or structured their interests through, communal or group norms and practices. Relations of affection, rather than those based on individual rational calculation, were said to be the defining features of such societies (Nyerere, 1967; Hyden, 1985). This meant that Africans were unable to exercise one of the most fundamental principles of democratic rights and obligations – that of individual political choice and personal accountability. A related point is the view that African societies contained too many ethnic groups to allow for the development of a coherent national identity. Instead, individuals were likely to support ethnic parties and pressure groups rather than those based on cross-cutting socio-economic interests. Ethnic-driven or primordial politics, when fully ignited, could threaten social cohesion and political stability. The dominant forms of political behaviour that were likely to emerge out of these two experiences were said to be clientelism and neo-patrimonialism – not democracy.[9]

There is much to be said for the three arguments in capturing aspects of African social realities, which serve as serious constraints to the development of democracy in the continent. Socio-economic conditions, historical processes and forms of accumulation are important in understanding the constraints and opportunities for stable long term democratization in Africa and elsewhere. It seems, however, that many of the points about Africa's unsuitability for democratic governance were overplayed by the critics. At bottom, it would seem that an idealized western experience was used as the yardstick to evaluate the democratic potentials of African countries. It is a method of analysis that Mamdani has described in a different context as 'history by analogy rather than history as process' (Mamdani, 1996:12). Standard socio-economic theories on democracy are good in pointing to the long-term structural constraints to democratic rule, but offer little help in understanding the concrete types of rule, democratic or otherwise, that have emerged in Africa and other developing countries. Why, for instance, were Mauritius, Senegal, Botswana and Gambia able to practise some form of pluralist politics in the pre-1990 period when the rest of Africa was mired in one-party or military forms of authoritarian rule? And what accounts for the renewed interest in democratic rule across Africa in the 1990s?

To start with, there is no incontrovertible reason why agrarian societies should not support variants of democratic government, especially as the link between democracy and industrialization has not been a unilinear one even in the history of democracy in western societies: much of the US was agrarian when it embarked on its democratic route; and democracy did not emerge in Western Europe only after it had attained a high level of industrialization (Therborn, 1977). Indeed, in a recently published, well researched book on Italian democracy, Putnam (1993) has shown that the civic traditions of the northern regions, which could be traced to the country's pre-industrial past – not economic development – were central in explaining the strength of democratic governance in those regions when compared with those of the south, which did not have similar civic traditions. Civic consciousness was a very powerful factor in the subsequent push for economic development in the north. Indeed, there is much to be said for the democratic potential of smallholder African agriculture and informal economies, with their relatively egalitarian distribution of assets and incomes, and absence of oligarchic landlords (Nyerere, 1967).[10]

One can also question the argument that posits a positive correlation between national entrepreneurial autonomy and democracy. This link can hardly be defended with any degree of seriousness today, especially when one takes into account current processes of economic globalization and the democratization experiences of countries in Latin America and parts of East Asia that are heavily dependent upon global economic processes. The critics also failed to take into account the emergence of vigorous professional middle classes and industrial labour movements in Africa – two developments which tended to undermine clientelist arrangements and patrimonialism in African politics, and which kept alive the democratic alternative in the continent. Indeed, the history of trades unions and professional groups in several parts of Africa suggests that these groups played leading roles in the burgeoning democratic projects at independence, and continued to do so in the democratization wave of the 1990s (Damachi *et al.*, 1979; Sandbrook and Cohen, 1975; Bangura and Beckman, 1991; Olukoshi, 1989, 1993; Hashim, 1994; Jega, 1994).

One should also add that although communal bonds and ethnicity are important factors that shape social behaviour and choice in Africa (and, indeed, elsewhere), it is unhelpful to ignore the wide-ranging socio-economic differentiation that has occurred, including the significance of individual choices in large areas of social life even when these are made within the context of broadly shared norms. Households are relatively independent agents in the acquisition and disposal of incomes, commodities and non-land assets. They also, in the main, take personal responsibility for their actions, although in more traditional settings, kinship-based social bonding can be very strong. However, group bonding for the pursuit of political objectives exists even in highly individualistic Western societies. People vote ethnic in Belgium, Northern Ireland and Spain; and racial bonding plays a key role in US elections, especially at the state and city level, and is significant in debates on burning public issues. And clientelism does not always prevent the growth of democracy, as the case of Italy so clearly demonstrates, even though it can act as a constraint on its full realization (Putnam, 1993).[11]

The politics of the Cold War and rabid elite competition for control of the state undervalued the latent democratic impulse that was associated with decolonization and ultimately led to authoritarian forms of rule. With hindsight, it seemed that the views of the professional theorists and the actions of the political actors fed each other to create a mutually fulfilling prophesy: the democratic experiments failed because the political actors learned from the professional theorists that democracy would not work in Africa; and the theories became vindicated because the political actors behaved the way the theories said they would. Almost everywhere, ruling elites became more concerned with promoting 'nation-building' and 'economic development' than with promoting democracy.

Two main patterns of authoritarian rule emerged out of the nation-building and national development processes – military dictatorship and one-party government. The two were often influenced by the dominant global ideologies of the time – 'socialist-inspired populist politics' and 'free-market capitalism'. These produced two additional subsets of authoritarian rule, bringing the number to four. In the first type of military dictatorships – such as those of Mathieu Kerekou in Benin, Nguesso in Congo-Brazzaville, Mengistu in Ethiopia, and Sankara/Compaoré in Burkina Faso – attempts were made to fashion the political systems along Soviet-style institutional arrangements, although they did not incorporate the additional elements of central economic planning and the universal provision of social welfare that were central to the Soviet model. In such countries, political parties were created by the military to subordinate, control and suppress civic groups and opposition parties. In the second type of military rule, such as those in Nigeria, Mali, Niger, Ghana, Lesotho, and Uganda, rulers simply governed by decrees without the trappings of 'popular' civic institutions. The same bifurcated experience occurred in the case of one party regimes: those of Mozambique, Angola, Somalia, Tanzania, Zambia, and Guinea experimented with grassroots structures that were integrated to those of the ruling political parties; whilst other one party regimes like those of Kenya, Sierra Leone, Côte d'Ivoire and Cameroon failed to incorporate in a systematic way most civic groups and associations into the ruling party structures.

Interestingly, if one adjusts for prior historical advantages, performance rates in economic and social development have not been very different among countries in the four groups. And if countries are placed in a two-dimensional figure of authoritarian rule (i.e., using the four subsets or variables of 'military–populist'; 'military–non-populist'; 'one party–populist'; and 'one party–non-populist'), no clear or consistent pattern will emerge. Standard variables, such as colonial experience, regional location, state dependence on mineral rents or agrarian export surpluses, distribution of ethnic groups, and formation of professional classes or labour unions, are not significant in determining the location of regimes in the four authoritarian slots.

Authoritarian rule had several attributes: political power was monopolized by the army or the single party, with the leader enjoying near-absolute authority; there were no freely competitive and fair elections; no separation of powers existed between the governing military councils, ruling political parties and other arms of the state; civic organizations and opposition parties were either controlled or not allowed to canvass for alternative forms of government; basic freedoms of expression, association and assembly were circumscribed, although this varied across regimes; and the principle of alternation of power was non-existent – indeed, governments were removed from power largely by military means. It is instructive to note that 61 military coups occurred in Africa between 1963 and 1989. Only three leaders of one-party regimes died in office (Sekou Touré, Jomo Kenyatta, and Augustino Neto); and four gave up power voluntarily (Julius Nyerere, Leopold Senghor, Siaka Stevens and Amadu Ahidjo), and were succeeded by members of their ruling parties.

3. Issues in political reform

Authoritarian rule came under considerable strain during the late 1970s and throughout the 1980s. And by 1990, most countries were in the throes of major social and political upheavals which ushered in various movements for democratization and changes in governments. These upheavals were linked to the long-running economic recessions in the 1970s and 1980s, and the adoption of deflationary stabilization and adjustment programmes that increased, at least initially, the economic downturn of countries. Recession and restructuring meant that the limited resources that were available at independence for state-led development, when these economies showed positive, if lopsided, rates of growth, became further squeezed – affecting incomes and livelihoods, social provision in education and health, public sector administration, the building of infrastructure, and the development of classes in the formal sector (Mosely and Weeks, 1993; Bangura, 1994; UNDP, 1997). The social and political networks that had held together the authoritarian regimes became highly unstable and ungovernable. Increased poverty and weak performance rates in the macro economy rendered all four varieties of authoritarian rule illegitimate. In much of Africa, the early 1990s were indeed a period of mass industrial strikes, extensive street demonstrations, urban economic and political riots, and armed conflicts (Bratton and van de Walle, 1992; Rudebeck, 1992).

It is interesting to note that the pendulum on the discourse on authoritarianism and democracy swung in favour of the latter as a result of these economic and political developments. Most theorists now argued the case for democracy in Africa even though the socio-economic conditions for the support of democratic rule were much worse in the early 1990s than they were in the 1960s. Three virtuous linkages were identified in the debate. The first states that Africa can only get out of its economic crisis if it is ready to embrace democracy – this is often referred to as the development and democracy linkage (Anyang' Nyong'o, 1988; Mkandawire, 1988; Gutto, 1988; Ake, 1996; Chalker, 1991; Woodward, 1994; Leftwich, 1996). The second posits that the wave of instability in the 1990s can only be stabilized, and the decaying political institutions revived, properly managed, and made to respond to the needs and aspirations of the populace, if African countries become fully democratized – this is the democracy, stability and good governance debate (Joseph, 1990; Hyden and Bratton, 1992; World Bank, 1992; Ibrahim, 1993). And the third linkage is that which posits that democracy is only possible in Africa if it can dismantle its statist approach to economic management and embrace the neo-liberal or market policies of structural adjustment recommended by the World Bank and the IMF – this is the democracy and structural adjustment debate (Diamond, 1988; Chazan, 1988; Bratton, 1989; World Bank, 1989, 1992; Beckman, 1992a; Bangura and Gibbon, 1992). All three debates tended to coalesce into a single framework that celebrated economic and political liberalization, or 'good governance', although there were significant dissenting voices in each sub-set of the discourse.

Like the early post-independence debate on the inevitability of authoritarianism, the post-1990 debate on the potentials of democracy tell only a partial story. On the first linkage on democracy and development, the most current statistical analysis (for all it is worth), which reviews nine previous quantitative studies on the subject, does not find a stable, long-term relation between democracy and economic growth or between democracy and economic inequality. However, Errson and Lane (1996), the authors of the study, do find a strong relationship between democracy and human development or quality of life for more than a hundred countries that included Africa. There have not been any systematic statistical studies on the other two linkages. On the democracy, good governance and stability linkage, it is worth noting, however, that the enthusiasm that greeted the democratic upheavals of the early 1990s has given way to much scepticism among theorists and international donors about the stabilizing, peace-yielding and good governance properties of current forms of democracy. The occurrence of many large-scale wars and democratic reverses in the 1990s has led policy-makers to place more emphasis on stability as an independent variable that needs to be pursued in its own right. We take up this issue in the last section of this paper. And the linkage between democracy and structural adjustment has been challenged by a host of authors who have argued that it is the resistance to structural adjustment rather than adjustment itself that is responsible for the democratization wave of the 1990s (for the most robust argument on this issue see Beckman, 1992a).

If any strong point can be deduced from these swings in theorization on democracy it is this: the trends and patterns of democratization and authoritarian rule have not always conformed to the assumptions and postulations of mainstream theorists and policy-makers. This conclusion calls for an intimate understanding of the *political* processes of democratization.[12] Democratization has not been the project of any single social group, nor has it been more successfully pursued in countries with higher levels of market liberalization or economic development.

And different colonial experiences have very little, if anything, to do with the outcomes, except, of course, for the institutional forms used to structure the reforms. Countries have responded to the agenda of political reforms differently. There have been gains and losses, advances and reverses – even failures. The real political reforms have focused on five main issues: constitutionality; electoral reform; civil liberties and political pluralism; power sharing; and decentralization. They help to throw light on the relevance and applicability in Africa of the five elements of democratization highlighted in section one.

The quests for *constitutionality* and *political pluralism* are at the core of the political reform processes. The two deal with attempts to subject African political processes to constitutional rules. The four types of military and one party regimes had either operated outside of constitutional legality, as could be seen in the constant recourse to military decrees, or paid limited attention to constitutional procedures, as was the case with the one-party administrations. Pressures for constitutionality have assumed two forms. The first has been a top-down process: i.e. cases where incumbent military or one-party regimes have been strong enough to preside over revisions of existing constitutions or the writing of new ones. Examples in this category include Tanzania, Nigeria, Zaire, Ghana, Sierra Leone and Kenya. Special representatives may be appointed or elected into specially created constitutional assemblies (as in Nigeria, Ghana and Zaire), or governments may simply form broad based committees with mandates to write new constitutions or revise existing ones. Such committees would receive petitions from the general public, publicize their work, stimulate debates and gauge citizen preferences. The end of the exercise has often been accompanied by referenda, whose outcomes incumbent governments have been expected to respect. However, in practice, governments have enjoyed much leeway in influencing the final product.

The second process has assumed a more bottom-up approach: this represents cases where autonomous national conferences have been held with the explicit objective of reforming existing constitutions or writing new ones. The national conferences have been established after long periods of militant political demonstrations in which the powers of incumbent governments to maintain public order and trust have been thoroughly weakened. The conferences or assemblies have, therefore, been given autonomous powers to deliberate on new constitutional directions, which the incumbent governments have not been able to veto. This bottom-up approach has been largely followed in the Francophone countries, although Sierra Leone also copied some aspects of it in its celebrated Bintumani Conferences in 1996 when the military changed its top leadership and tried to obstruct the elections that an earlier Bintumani conference had slated for 26 February 1996 (Abraham, 1997). The military was forced to respect the verdict of the Conference, which took place in the context of mass nationwide demonstrations. The Republic of Benin has been the torch bearer in the use of autonomous conferences to change the authoritarian regimes of Francophone countries (Diop, 1991; Allen, 1992; Decalo, 1997). However, the practice has not been uniformly successful in these countries: in a number of cases, the opposition movements have not been strong enough to impose their will on the incumbent regimes – such as in, for instance, Zaire, Togo, Cameroon, Gabon and Côte d'Ivoire.

The key issues in constitutionality relate to the demilitarisztion of the institutions of government, the return to legality and the rule of law, and the removal of pre-existing provisions that granted ruling parties the sole right to form parties and governments. The links between ruling political parties and organized interest groups, such as trade unions, professional associations, and community organizations, are often terminated to allow for the autonomous development of such groups, and to give competing political parties equal chances to relate to groups in civil society. Constitutionality also deals with the distribution of power between the various institutions of the state, the forms and responsibilities of government, and the provision of basic human and civic rights. Most constitutions call for clear divisions of power between the legislative, executive and judicial arms of the state; the existence of plural political parties; and the separation of the interests of the state from those of incumbent governments. Undoubtedly, much progress has been made in the formulation of new constitutions and in getting leaders to respect them, but in a large number of cases what Okoth-Ogendo (1993) refers to as the paradox of a high incidence of 'constitution-making without constitutionality' remains a serious problem.

Political pluralism deals with efforts to create a relatively autonomous civil society and political culture. There has been a proliferation of autonomous interest group organizations, political parties, civic associations, non-governmental organizations and a plural press in virtually every country. Although these developments remain distinctly urban in most countries, with varying degrees of participation, African societies have made much more progress in this area of political reform than in others. In the absence of good comparable quantitative data on the development of civic culture, I have decided to use two proxy indicators to measure the extent of political pluralism across countries: these are the percentage share of seats enjoyed by political parties other than the largest party in a legislative assembly; and the number of political parties that are represented in such an assembly. The first measures what can be called the *intensity of plurality* and the second that of *absolute plurality*. Taken together they do give some indication of the nature and extent of political pluralism in Africa today.

Table 8.1 provides data for 36 countries that have had competitive party elections in the 1990s. Plurality is much more pronounced for the indicator on parties in parliament than for the one that measures the relative strength of the leading parties. The average number of parties in Africa's 36 parliaments is 6.4. In four parliaments, those of Madagascar, Benin, Chad and the Central African Republic, party representation ranged from 13 to 17. Not surprisingly, these are also among the countries in which the leading parties received less than 50 per cent of the seats in parliament. Only Lesotho, Djibouti and Burundi have had parliaments in which party representation has been two and below. In the case of Lesotho, which has only one party in parliament, the result reflects the distortion that is inherent in that country's first-past-the-post electoral system. Although the leading party scored only 54 per cent of the votes, it ended up winning all the seats. And in

Table 8.1 Political plurality in Africa's party competitive parliaments in 1997.

Countries	Intensity of plurality (% share of seats held by parties other than the largest party)	Absolute plurality (number of parties in parliament)
Benin	74.7	17
Madagascar	66.7	17
Sierra Leone*	63.9	6
Central African Rep.	60.0	13
Chad	66.0	15**
Togo	55.6	5
Malawi	52.0	3
Sao Tomé & Principe	50.2	3
Mozambique	48.4	3
Mauritius	47.0	6
Kenya	46.8	7
Angola	41.4	12
Cameroon	39.5	7
Guinea-Bissau	38.0	5
Guinea	37.8	9
South Africa	37.4	7
Niger	35.0	10
Ghana	34.0	4
Botswana	32.5	3
Cape Verde	30.6	3
Senegal	30.0	6
Gabon	29.2	5
Gambia	26.7	4
Namibia	26.4	5
Liberia	23.5	6
Djibouti	23.3	2
Tanzania	22.3	5
Burundi*	19.8	2
Seychelles	18.2	3
Côte d'Ivoire	15.5	3
Equatorial Guinea	15.0	4
Comoros	14.5	3
Mali	13.1	8
Mauritania	10.9	3
Burkina Faso	9.1	4
Lesotho	0.0	1
Average intensity of plurality; and average of absolute plurality	34.8	6.4

*The governments and parliaments of these two countries have been overthrown by the military.

** This is a rough estimate; there are four large parties in parliament and an assortment of smaller ones share a total of 24 seats.

Sources: Raw data for this table obtained from Wilfred Derksen Political Websites, 'Elections Around the World'; http://www.geocities.com/derksen/election/country/lt.htm; *Europa World Year Book*; and Klipsan Press, 'Recent Election Results', http://www.klipsan.com/index/httml.

Burundi, whose parliament had two parties, the outcome reflected the country's two-tier ethnic social structure. However, the intensity of plurality, which is arguably the more powerful of the two indicators, or the percentage share of seats held by parties other than the largest party, seems to be much more limited. The average intensity of plurality for the 36 countries is only 34.8 per cent. This is very close to the critical threshold of a minimum of one third of parliamentary seats plus one (the opposite of a two thirds majority) that is often required to prevent a ruling party from changing fundamental clauses of a constitution. Seventeen, or almost half, of the countries have parliaments in which the largest party enjoys more than a two-thirds majority. And there are only eight, or 22.8 per cent of countries where the ruling party does not control the majority of seats in parliament.

When compared with other regions of the world that have multi-party parliaments, the African average turns out to be the lowest for both indicators on intensity of plurality and absolute plurality. The interesting thing about Table 8.2 is that performance tends to correspond to conventional, indeed specialist, knowledge of the state of democratization in the five regions: Western democracies lead, followed by Latin America and East/Central Europe, and then South and East Asia. It is important to note that the absolute plurality measure can sometimes distort parliamentary realities. A party can command an overwhelming majority of the seats in a parliament that may still boast of a high number of party representation. This has been the case, for example, in Mali, with a mere 13.1 per cent score on intensity of plurality, but a high absolute plurality score of 8. Despite Africa's relatively low scores in the league table, a few countries have shown levels of plurality that are comparable to those of the other regions with high scores.

Table 8.2 Political plurality in Africa, Latin America, East/Central Europe, South & East Asia and Western Democracies (average figures)

Regions	Intensity of plurality (percentage share of seats held by parties other than the largest party)	Absolute plurality (number of seats)
Sub-Saharan Africa	34.8	6.4
South & East Asia	46.3	8.7
Latin America	56.9	9.4
East & Central Europe	56.7	9.4
Western Democracies	59.8	8.5

Notes: For Sub-Saharan Africa, N = 36
          South & East Asia, N = 13
          Latin America, N = 16
          East & Central Europe, N = 20
          Western Democracies, N = 22
Sources: Raw data for this table obtained from Wilfred Derksen Political Websites, 'Elections Around the World'; http://www.geocities.com/derksen/election/country/lt.htm; *Europa World Year Book*; and Klipsan Press, 'Recent Election Results', http://www.klipsan.com/index/httml.

Electoral reform has been high on the agenda of political reforms. This deals with two main issues. The first is the efforts of opposition parties and groups in civil society to eliminate the advantages which incumbent governments have enjoyed in the use of state institutions and public resources, as well as the application of discriminatory or oppressive laws to influence electoral outcomes. Top on the agenda is the question of the neutrality of the electoral office, the right to appoint party officers as polling agents to oversee the electoral process, and the creation of a credible electoral register. In countries where autonomous conferences were held and allowed to influence the content of the electoral system, such as Benin, Congo-Brazzaville, Mali, Burundi, and Niger,[13] there was some success in producing fairly neutral electoral regimes during the transitions. The same applies to Sierra Leone, where the military was largely discredited, and the electoral office was headed by a well respected ex-UN bureaucrat who was determined to ensure that the elections were free and fair. Where national conferences failed to impose their will on incumbents – Cameroon, Togo, Gabon, Burkina Faso, and Côte d'Ivoire, for instance – the electoral systems were compromised. The results were thus militantly challenged, sometimes violently, by opposition groups. The same applies to the top-down regimes of constitutional change – Tanzania, Kenya and Ghana, for instance.

Indeed, in the case of Ghana and Kenya, the struggles to make the electoral systems fair and autonomous have been at the centre of their national politics since the democratic transitions started in the early 1990s. The Ghana opposition boycotted the 1992 parliamentary elections on the grounds that the rules for the presidential elections, which preceded the parliamentary ones, were weighted in favour of the incumbent: complaints were made about the excessively bloated character of the electoral register and the composition and partiality of the electoral officers. Despite an initial uncompromising stand by the ruling party of the ex-military ruler, Jerry Rawlings, some progress was made in correcting the lop-sidedness of the electoral regime to give opponents a relatively fair chance in the 1996 elections. And Kenya has witnessed some of the most violent pro-electoral reform protests in recent years. In this case, the opposition parties and civic groups were concerned about not only the composition and neutrality of the electoral office but also the question of the gerrymandering of electoral boundaries that gave the incumbent party an advantage; they were also concerned about the government's use of archaic laws on public order, rights of assembly and demonstrations, to intimidate and harass opposition parties and critical individuals. The government was forced to concede to many of the demands of electoral reform in anticipation of the general elections of December 1997, although several problems remained unresolved.

The second issue relates to the types of electoral system chosen to express representation in parliamentary and presidential organs. Both deal with the question of political equity. With regards to parliamentary representation, the electoral reforms produced five systems, which are summarized in Table 8.3. Under the *first-past-the-post* electoral rules, an electorate is divided into constituencies, and the candidate with the largest number of votes in each constituency wins, even if he/

Table 8.3 Electoral systems in Africa

First-past-the-post	Block vote	Two round system	Parallel	List PR
Botswana	Djibouti	CAR*	Cameroon	Angola
Zambia	Mauritius	Chad	Niger	Benin
Gambia		Congo	Senegal	Burkina Faso
Ghana		Gabon	Seychelles	Burundi
Guinea		Mali		Cape Verde
Côte d'Ivoire**		Mauritania		Equatorial Guinea
Kenya		Comoros		Guinea Bissau
Lesotho		Togo		Liberia
Malawi				Madagascar
Tanzania				Mozambique
Zimbabwe				Namibia
				Sao Tomé
				Sierra Leone
				South Africa
11	2	8	4	14

*Central African Republic
**Côte d'Ivoire's FPTP is combined with a block vote system.
Source: Adapted from IDEA, *The International IDEA Handbook of Electoral System Design*; International Institute for Democracy and Electoral Assistance, Stockholm, Sweden. Handbook Series 1/97, 1997.

she does not have the majority of the votes. In the *two round system*, if a candidate fails to win an overall majority in the first round, a second round is held, in which candidates who score less than a stipulated percentage of the votes are excluded. The *block vote* system is similar to the first-past-the-post rule, except that in the former, constituencies are much larger, and more than one candidate is eligible to be elected. The number of ballots given to a voter are equal to the number of candidates to be elected in each constituency. Voters are free to choose candidates across party lists. However, if party loyalties are strong, and voters choose candidates from a single party, the system can produce an extreme form of disproportionality. The *list proportional representational* system seeks to ensure that popular votes gained are proportional to the seats allocated in parliament. The country is divided up into one single constituency or very large electoral districts. The electorate votes for parties, and not for individuals. The parties draw up a list of ranked candidates, corresponding to the number of seats to be filled. Seats are allocated according to the proportion of votes gained by each party, and are filled by the candidates in a descending order in each list. The *parallel* voting scheme combines the first-past-the-vote system and the list proportional representational system.

As the table shows, eleven countries adopted the first-past-the-post majoritarian rule (FPTP) system; two adopted the block vote system (BV); eight adopted the two round system (TRS); four adopted the parallel FPTP/PR systems (Parallel); and 14 adopted the list proportional systems (List PR). The first two can produce serious discrepancies between the proportion of votes won and the number of seats gained; and the second can give larger parties an unfair advantage in the second round of voting since smaller parties are likely to be eliminated. Significantly, about a third of the countries opted for an electoral system that was explicitly aimed at providing proportional outcomes. And a little more than 40 per cent had systems with some degree of proportionality. Thus, as far as the legislative organ is concerned, there is clearly a trend away from the colonially bequeathed majoritarian electoral schemes in favour of proportionality.

But the majority of countries (21 out of 39) still preferred the majoritarian FPTP, TRS and BV systems. It is important to note, however, that because of the very large number of ethnic groups in most African countries and the tendency of many voters to vote ethnic, most majoritarian systems produced very plural parliamentary outcomes, although the proportion of seats enjoyed by different political parties did not reflect their relative voting strengths. There are at least eleven countries where the proportion of seats gained by leading parties was much higher than the proportion of votes won. The List PR system was efficient in ensuring that total votes cast were roughly equal to the proportion of seats obtained in the parliaments where the system was used. But it did not always produce a high degree of plurality, as the elections in Liberia demonstrate. In Liberia, voters largely ignored ethnic factors and voted overwhelmingly (75.3 per cent) for the party that they thought was likely to ensure non-renewal of the war – the party of the strongest warlord, Charles Taylor. In one exceptional FPTP case, Malawi, where the electorate voted ethnic and produced three main political parties, the proportion of votes cast was roughly equal to the proportion of seats gained in parliament.

In the case of presidential elections, most countries have opted for electoral systems that would produce a president with a majority of the national votes. In this regard, the TRS, Parallel and List PR systems converged as elections for presidents in all three systems required a second round to produce a winner with the majority of the votes. This is not a requirement for the FPTP countries. In Kenya, for instance, Daniel Arap Moi was returned to power in 1992 with 36.4 per cent of the popular vote. Thus, none of the five electoral systems was structured to produce proportional outcomes in the executive branch of government. It may be argued that the attempt to produce majoritarian outcomes in the presidential organs of government is a major limitation in the current efforts to introduce political equity issues in the governance of African countries. Except in a few cases where coalition governments have been formed to help with the passage of government bills in parliament, majoritarianism in the executive organ has given substantial powers to leading parties, which in most cases did not enjoy the confidence of the majority of the voters as parties of first choice. Ministerial, top-level parastatal, and ambassadorial appointments have tended to reflect the majoritarian outcomes of the second rounds of presidential elections. This has been a major source of instability in the fledgling political systems. It is only South Africa's electoral system that has been sensitive to the issue of proportionality in the executive organ of government.[14]

Reforms that are aimed at *decentralization* and *power sharing* represent additional attempts to broaden the plurality of politics and prevent the concentration of power in a few hands or regions. Much of the decentralization that has taken place has been carried out as part of wider programmes of public sector reforms. These enjoy World Bank, UNDP and other principal donor support. Decentralization involves the creation or reactivation of local governments, the devolution of the powers of central ministries to regional and local areas, attempts at the devolution of fiscal or tax-raising powers in certain areas of governance, and establishment of formulae for sharing centrally derived revenues between various levels of government. In most cases, decentralization has not led to real transfer of power and autonomy to regions, municipalities and rural local authorities. This is the case even in the bold decentralization programme of Ethiopia, in which power was devolved to ethnically-defined regions within a federal structure, and a constitutional principle was affirmed that respected the rights of nationalities to secede from the federation. A strong centralization impulse has informed all decentralization programmes that have been attempted in Africa. Governments are often more willing to decentralize line ministries, which they may still be able to control, than to devolve real tax-raising powers and political authority to regions and local areas.

Reforms that are aimed at power sharing have largely been promoted by countries that have been racked by civil war or long-running conflicts. Such wars and conflicts have often been inconclusive. They have thus required the interventions of outside powers or agencies to create agreements for peaceful coexistence between parties. Agreements often focus on the creation of new armies and internal security systems that reflect the relative powers and interests of the main combatants; joint representation in national electoral bodies; and formation of broad-based governments that will also reflect the electoral strengths of the contending parties. The latter represents an extension of the principle of plurality to the executive arm of government.

A key example in power sharing is the Lusaka Accord for peace and governance in Angola. This accord gave a number of cabinet seats, parastatal directorships, ambassadorial appointments, and regional governorships to Jonas Savimbi's rebel UNITA movement, which lost the elections to the ruling MPLA government.[15] Mozambique, another war-torn country, also practises a modified form of power sharing, especially on issues dealing with national security. But unlike in Angola, the losing armed opposition, Dlakama's RENAMO, is not represented in government. However it controls about 44.8 per cent of the seats in the national parliament and a good number of regional governments, although not the critical offices of the governors, which have been a bone of contention between the two parties. Under the Abidjan Accord of November, 1996, some kind of power sharing mechanism was also recommended as a solution to the six years of war in Sierra Leone. Power sharing in this case was limited to participation of the rebel Revolutionary United Front in newly created institutions dealing with the management of the peace, the reconstruction of the army and the police, and the formation of a new national electoral commission. The peace treaty was signed in the context of a new constitution, which had ushered in a new multi-party government and parliament in which the rebel movement did not participate. In the case of

South Africa and Nigeria, the new power sharing regimes were not facilitated by outside powers, no doubt because of the relative capacities of the two govern-ments to oversee their respective transitions – even though the Nigerian transition happens to be deeply flawed. In South Africa, parties that scored 5 per cent of the votes were expected to be part of the national government; and in Nigeria, a rotational principle was introduced as an effort to break the stalemate which had dogged that country's politics since the annulment of the elections of 12 June 1993.

As Bayo Adekanye (1996) has noted, power sharing arrangements that have been born out of wars seek largely to solve short term problems of security. They do not always succeed in promoting the goals of democracy. Although they have opened up the political systems to new actors, they often tend to create new state-centred 'power sharing' oligarchies. More importantly, most such reforms have proven to be very unstable: actors are still guided by the logic of war and zero-sum calculations rather than the logic of compromise that the power sharing regimes seek to cultivate. This has led to a manipulation of the rules of power sharing by both government and opposition parties and the collapse of several of the power sharing agreements.

4.   Patterns of democratization

In this section, I discuss five patterns of democratization that have emerged out of these experiences. The first represents the small number of countries that practised some form of multiparty rule even before the democratization pressures of the 1990s. These are Botswana, Mauritius, Senegal, Gambia and Zimbabwe. This is a mixed set of countries, with different colonial histories, levels of development and social structures. Botswana and Mauritius are among the African countries that have grown rapidly since independence and have largely avoided the painful stabilization programmes of the IMF because of their respectable macro-economic performance records. Smallholding agriculture is still prevalent in most of the countries, although large-scale commercial agriculture is very prominent in Zim-babwe, and Botswana's development has largely been driven by its diamond sector and beef exports; and Mauritius is noted for its successful manufacturing export zones.

All five countries have very small populations: Gambia, Mauritius and Botswana have populations of roughly one million, and Zimbabwe and Senegal about nine million. All five countries are multi-ethnic, although Zimbabwe and Botswana have a smaller number of ethnic groups. Before the 1990 transitions, these coun-tries held competitive multi-party elections; key interest groups in society were not tied to the reigning political parties, although civil society itself was poorly developed; and civil liberties were reasonably protected, even if not comprehens-ively. Of course, not all five countries' elections can be said to have been free and fair – those of Senegal, Gambia and Zimbabwe were often hotly contested by the losers. Mauritius was the only country among this group which experienced a change of government: a coalition of opposition parties defeated the incumbent government in elections in 1982. However, due to the long tenure of the government parties there was hardly any separation of powers between the state and ruling parties in this set of countries.

In the post-1990 period, Mauritius has continued to enjoy competitive politics and periodic alternation of power between parties. Electoral plurality has increased in Botswana, with the opposition parties now enjoying a much higher representation in parliament than hitherto. Others have not made much progress. The elections in Senegal have consistently been challenged by the opposition parties and groups in society, leading to very serious levels of street violence (Diop, 1994). The government also has to contend with a growing civil war in one of its regions – the Casamance. Gambia became a military regime in 1994 and its new ruler, Yahaya Jammeh, quickly legitimized his regime by organizing flawed elections (Kandeh, 1996); and Zimbabwe was well on the road to becoming a one party state in the early 1990s, if it were not for the resistance of civic groups and the difficulties which the president, Robert Mugabe, faced in making a case for one-party rule against the tide of democratization that was sweeping Africa and the rest of the world (Sachikonye, 1995).

The second set of countries represent those that were able to change incumbent governments in the post-1990 period through successful multiparty elections. These were Zambia, Benin, Malawi, Congo-Brazzaville, Burundi, Mali, Cape Verde, Niger, Lesotho, Namibia, South Africa, Madagascar, Burundi, Sierra Leone and Liberia. Again, this is a mixed group of countries, which does not allow any general set of explanations for the different outcomes. Each country may have to be analysed separately to understand the dynamics at play. Like the first group, they scored highly on electoral competitiveness, the separation of ruling political parties from organized interest groups, and – in some countries – the promotion of civil liberties. Winning parties continue, however, to exercise the tradition of party domination of the state. Four countries – Zambia, Benin, Mali and Cape Verde – have held second elections after those that ushered in the multi-party changes. The Zambian elections were boycotted by the leading opposition parties because of constitutional changes introduced by the new government that undermined the nationality and political rights of one of the leading opponents,[16] as well as complaints about electoral malpractices. In the second election for the presidency in Cape Verde, which was held in February 1996, the new incumbent president was returned unopposed. In Mali, there were very serious allegations of electoral malpractice against the government, which led to the boycott of the elections by the main opposition parties. The new president was re-elected by an incredible 95.9 per cent of the popular vote in 1997. Benin had a successful second election in 1996, which the incumbent, Soglo, a former World Bank official, lost to Mathieu Kerekou, a former military ruler who himself had lost the first multi-party elections in 1991.

Indeed, Benin is the only other country in Africa, after Mauritius, that has experienced an alternation of power between political parties without the intervention of the military or a constitutional crisis. In the case of Madagascar, which has also changed its government twice during the current transition, the democratically elected president, Albert Zafi, was impeached in 1996 by parliament over allegations of constitutional violations relating to his dismissal of the Prime Minister. The Supreme Court upheld the impeachment; and in the elections held in 1997, Zafi lost the presidency to Didier Ratsriraka in a closely fought contest. Sierra Leone, Burundi and Niger lapsed back into military rule, although in Niger, the new military leader organized very flawed elections, which his party won; Congo-Brazzaville's government was overthrown after a four month civil war in which the military government of the former ruler, Denis Sassou-Nguesso, was reinstated; soldiers briefly took power in Lesotho in 1994 before they were prevailed upon by regional leaders to hand it back; and Zambia experienced an abortive coup in November, 1997. Liberia's elections took place only in July 1997 after seven years of a viciously fought civil war.

The third pattern of democratization refers to cases where pre-1990 ruling regimes still retain control of the state, even though many of the elements of formal democratization – such as multi-party elections, non-homogenous legislatures, growth of independent interest groups in society and a relatively free press – are discernible. These countries include Mauritania, Guinea Bissau, Guinea-Conakry, Togo, Côte d'Ivoire, Ghana, Burkina Faso, Cameroon, Central African Republic, Gabon, Djibouti, Tanzania, Kenya, Mozambique, and Angola. In this set of countries the principle of free and fair elections still remains a highly contested issue; opposition parties and civic organizations have been unable to wrest power from the governing parties through the medium of elections; and the activities of ruling parties are still very much inseparable from governmental practices. This means that governments enjoy considerable powers to limit the scope of participation, representation, organization and expression. As a result, extra-judicial forms of protest, such as politically inspired riots, are very prevalent in many of these countries.

The fourth pattern of democratization deals with cases where military regimes are still in place or have recently been installed following the overthrow of newly elected governments; it also includes countries that have been stateless or that are governed by armed militia men. Examples include Nigeria, Burundi, Sudan, Sierra Leone and Somalia. In this set of countries, national legislatures are largely non-existent; regimes rule by decrees or the personal dicta of leaders; and arbitrariness and state or militia-sponsored violence are rife. Sudan has a 'non-party' parliament which was elected in 1996 by a combination of direct and indirect methods. Islamist parties loyal to the regime dominate the parliament. As is the norm in most transitions to democratization, however, an independent media has grown in this set of countries even though it works under extremely hazardous conditions. Newspaper closures and harassment of journalists, politicians and social activists are routine. Despite their authoritarian character, these regimes continue to face persistent demands from the populace to democratize (Ibrahim, 1992; Mustapha, 1993). Some, like Nigeria, have even set up elaborate, though tightly controlled, processes of democratization (Othman and Williams, 1997). In the case of Sierra Leone, the ousted government and the mass public have led a very effective campaign to restore constitutional legality and the democratic institutions of the country. The military rulers of Burundi have also faced isolation and sanctions from neighbouring countries, including calls for the return of constitutional rule.

The fifth pattern is that of the new populist regimes – Uganda, Ethiopia, Rwanda, Eritrea, and Congo-Kinshasa – which came to power through armed struggle and civil wars. They have refused to organize multi-party elections although other elements of democratization are discernible: these are a relatively free press (especially in Uganda); existence of several autonomous organizations in civil society despite the impulse to regulate them through old-style single party structures; the organization of elections, although these are either non-party competitive or tightly controlled by the ruling parties; and varying commitments to the protection of human rights. These countries, especially Uganda and Ethiopia, have attempted to set up very elaborate decentralization programmes and what they have called 'grassroots' or 'cell-based' systems of rule. The power of the central administration and ruling parties is, however, still unquestionable. Alternative parties are not allowed to contest elections for state power under the 'grassroots' or populist systems of rule. In Uganda's 'non-party' elections-derived parliament, 39 seats were reserved for women, 10 for the army, 5 for the youth, 3 for trade unions and 5 for the disabled. Ethiopia's two-chamber parliament, formed on the basis of nation wide elections, provides for some form of ethnic representation, in addition to the popular mandates of individuals who are mostly allied to the ruling party. Eritrea's parliament is made up largely of appointed and indirectly elected members. Rwanda also has an appointed parliament, although in this case members were chosen from previously existing political parties.

What comes out of this review is a mixed picture of democratization. Contrary to popular belief, there is no single pattern of democratization in Africa, but several. If one can draw any general conclusion from the review, it is this: most countries in Africa now have budding pluralist political systems; and much progress has been made in the area of civil and political rights. The latter can be discerned from the rapid expansion of independently controlled newspapers in most countries – manned by an equally rapidly growing university graduate population, which has gone into journalism because of the limited opportunities for employment in the wider economy and public sector. There is still much arbitrary rule in many parts of Africa, including in countries that have made much progress in instituting the rule of law as a cardinal principle of statecraft. But much of the arbitrariness is conducted in a context of legitimate political competition and an independent press – an outcome that is different from the pre-1990s period. Much needs to be done in the crucial area of separating ruling parties from the institutions of the state, the organization of free and fair elections, and the alternation of governmental power by the political parties.

Despite this evidence in the growth of political pluralism, one other significant trend is also visible across Africa – i.e. the problem of political instability and important reverses in several of the programmes of democratization. In general, as Table 8.4 shows, a large number of incumbent regimes of the pre-1990 period

Table 8.4 Patterns of democratization in Africa

Pre-1990 multi-party political systems	Post-1990 multi-party political systems with new govts	Post-1990 multi-party political systems with pre-1990 govts	Post-1990 military regimes	Post-1990 populist political systems formed through wars
Botswana	Benin	Mauritania	Nigeria	Uganda
Mauritius	Zambia	Guinea-Bissau	Sudan	Ethiopia
Senegal	Malawi	Côte d'Ivoire	Burundi	Eritrea
Zimbabwe	Namibia	Togo	Sierra Leone	Rwanda
Gambia**	Mali	Cameroon	Somalia	Congo-Kinsasha
	Congo-B**	Burkina Faso		
	Burundi**	Seychelles		
	Madagascar	Kenya		
	Sierra Leone**	Djibouti		
	Niger**	Tanzania		
	Cape Verde	Mozambique		
	South Africa	Gabon		
	Liberia	Ghana		
	Lesotho	Sao Tomé & Principe		
	CAR**	Equatorial Guinea		
	Comoros**	Chad		
		Angola		
5	16	17	5	5

** Later relapsed into military rule. The military rulers of Gambia and Niger later organized elections, which they 'won'.
Some countries appear in more than one group because of their different experiences in democratization. It is useful to include them in multiple groups to show the details of the trends that have been underway.
Swaziland, the only Sub-Saharan African country not included, is run by an executive monarchy. Its national assembly, the *Libandla*, is composed of individuals elected by traditional councils or appointed by the monarch.

are still in power, and continue to face tough, sometimes violent, opposition from sections of the public for a fairer application of the rules of political contestation; several countries that held successful elections have reverted to military rule, or have experienced aborted military uprisings; and civil wars are a major feature of the political landscape of many countries in the region. Figure 8.1 provides a comparative picture of the problems of instability in the pre-1990 and post-1990 periods. The indicators used are numbers of military coups, civil wars, and setbacks in democratization. There have been eleven military coups between 1990 and 1997. This translates as about 1.6 per year, slightly lower than the 2.1 average for the pre-1990 period. Twenty-one (or 42.5 per cent) of Africa's current 47 leaders first came to power by means of a military coup d'état. An additional nine came to power through civil wars or armed struggles. This means that 63.8 per cent of current African leaders have strong links with the military.

An interesting development in African politics has been the use of elections by both old and new military rulers to legitimize their grip on politics. Democratization

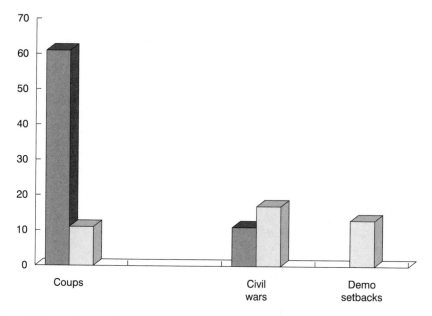

Figure 8.1 Trends in military coups, civil wars and democratic setbacks: 1960–89; and 1990–97.

Note: The dark colour represents the period 1960–89; and the light colour the period 1990–97.

Coups: 1960–89 (61); 1990–97 (11). Some of the civil wars in the post-1990s are carry-overs from the pre-1990 period. Only those which were still unresolved when the wave of democratization started in 1990 are included. Many of these wars, both pre- and post-1990, have now been resolved.

Civil wars: 1960–89 (11); 1990–97 (17).

Democratic setbacks: 1990–97 (13).

Democratic setbacks include successful military coups and those that were subsequently reversed; they also include cases where second post-1990 elections were either boycotted by the opposition parties or an incumbent president was returned unopposed.

Source: *Africa Contemporary Record; Africa South of the Sahara,* Country Reports of the *Economist* Intelligence Unit; as well as Reuters and Agence France news agency reports have been used as primary data sources to calculate the number of coups, civil wars and democratic setbacks.

has not checked the impulse for coup-making among the military: instead, the latter have adjusted their political strategies to accommodate the popular demands and donor pressures for democratization. In addition to the continued occurrence of military coups, there have been 17 civil wars in the 1990s, as opposed to 11 in the pre-1990s (figure for post-1990 includes some of the wars that started in pre-1990). And 13 countries have experienced setbacks in their democratic programmes. We may conclude from this analysis that if the 1990s can be described as the decade of democratization, it is also true to call it the decade of political instability. In other words, democratization and political instability have been products of the same processes of change.

5.   Responses to instability

Political instability has led to population displacement, acute personal insecurity and considerable human misery in several countries. Not surprisingly, there has been intense debate, both within and outside Africa, about ways of responding to the humanitarian crisis that has emerged in the context of democratization and political change. The responses have been twofold, and emphasize the primacy of security in regulating the processes of change. The first is external, and deals mainly with the policy initiatives of the United States, France and Britain – the main foreign powers that have influenced events in Africa. In the early 1990s, these powers had signalled an intention to make democracy and human rights cardinal principles of their foreign aid programmes. Working in conjunction with other major bilateral donors and, to some extent, the Bretton Woods institutions, they sought to tie aid flows to progress made in democratization. François Mitterrand had announced at the Franco-African summit at La Baulé in 1990 that French aid would henceforth be linked to democratization (O'Toole, 1997). Indeed, Douglas Hurd, the British Foreign Minister, and Linda Chalker, the Minister for Overseas Development, had made similar pronouncements during the same period (Leftwich, 1996). In a new empirically researched book, William Robinson reports the rise of 'political aid' in US foreign policy as a tool for the promotion of a particular form of democratization in developing countries (Robinson, 1996).

During the early 1990s, these three powers intervened directly at critical conjunctures to force the hands of incumbent governments to accede to the popular domestic demands for elections. The most celebrated cases were those of Kenya and Malawi in 1992, and the Central African Republic in 1993. In Kenya and Malawi, the Western aid consortium suspended aid negotiations and eventually forced the incumbent governments to heed the demands for elections and political reforms. In the Central African Republic, French officials were withdrawn from the special security organ of the president, Kolingba, in order to force him to hold elections; and the French government further threatened to withdraw aid when he tried to cancel the elections which he had lost (O'Toole, 1997).

This unqualified enthusiasm for democratization did not last more than four years. As the scale of instability deepened, external powers expressed interest in military intervention schemes as solutions to the problems of democratization. France, which has 9,000 troops in, and a series of bilateral military agreements with, its ex-colonies, reverted to its long-standing policy of intervention in Francophone Africa. However, its failure to prevent the fall of the Hutu-dominated regime in Rwanda, its inability to influence the events leading to the overthrow of Mobutu's regime in Zaire, and the problems it has experienced in policing the peace in the Central African Republic, where a number of French soldiers have been killed, have forced a rethink in policy. The new policy seeks to reduce the number of French troops in Africa as part of a wider programme which places emphasis on the development of peace-keeping equipment at French bases, and the recruitment of a multinational African peacekeeping force to maintain order in troubled spots. In the Central African Republic, where this new policy is being tested, an 800-strong African force, under a Malian commander, is helping to protect the democratically elected government of Patassé against sections of the military that mutinied three times in 1996, plunging the capital city into chaos. The programme is administered by France, including the payment of the salaries of the peace-keeping force (*Economist*, 1997).

Similarly, the failure of the American intervention force in Somalia in 1993, and the abortive effort to put together a Western-led intervention force for the Great Lakes region in 1996, have produced a new policy initiative from the US. This is the African Crisis-Response Force, which was launched in 1996, and renamed African Crisis-Response Initiative, when it was criticized by African leaders as a disguised form of neo-colonialism. Under the programme, the US, Britain and France would train ten battalions from several African countries; the troops would remain with their national armies but would be called upon to participate in humanitarian interventions when the peace and security of specific countries were threatened. Preliminary training, which has been largely provided by the US, has been conducted in Senegal, Uganda and Malawi.

This new focus on 'African' solutions to the continent's troubled democratization programmes has received a major boost, in the form of three autonomous regional initiatives, within Africa itself. They partly reflect what Ali Mazrui has called a new impulse for a *Pax-Africana* (Mazrui, 1997).The first concerns the major effort which the Economic Community of West African states (ECOWAS) has made in restoring order and organizing successful elections in war-torn Liberia; as well as their intervention in Sierra Leone in May 1997 to overturn the violent and unstable military coup that ousted the democratically elected government of Ahmed Tejan Kabbah. ECOMOG (ECOWAS' Monitoring Group), the organ responsible for the regional operations, was first deployed in Liberia in 1990 as a humanitarian force, but it increasingly took on the functions of a peace-enforce-ment or peace-making force – coercing the various warring factions to heed the call for a cease-fire and the organization of elections. The driving force of ECOMOG is the regional power, Nigeria, which supplies at least 60 percent of the troops, and a much higher percentage of the cost of the operation. Acting under Chapter VII (enforcement) and Chapter VIII (regional arrangements) of the United Nations Charter, ECOMOG has been able to get the approval of the United Nations Security Council for a comprehensive sanctions regime against the junta in Sierra Leone. It signed a peace agreement with the junta on 23 October 1997, in which the latter agreed to restore the ousted government to power in April 1998, following a comprehensive disarmament programme (Gberie, 1997). An ECOWAS meeting in Lomé on 17 and 18 December 1997 agreed to transform ECOMOG into a permanent institution.

The second initiative has come from Southern Africa, which also boasts of a regional economic organization, the Southern African Development Cooperation (SADC). This region has experienced two long-running wars in Angola and Mozambique, wars of national liberation in Zimbabwe and Namibia, and an oppressive racist regime in South Africa. Like in other regions of the continent, democratization has also been uneven, with threats of, and actual, military interventions to reverse the political reforms, as in Lesotho and Zambia; and there are real dangers of renewed wars in Angola and Mozambique. Regional security has emerged, therefore, as an important issue in the democratic evolution of SADC (Mandaza, 1994; Goncalves, 1995), although the organization has yet to intervene in any country in the region. The coup in Lesotho, in 1994, was reversed by informal pressures exerted by regional leaders, rather than by the use of force. However, in 1996, the organization established the SADC Organ for Politics, Defence and Security, which seeks to respond to the problems of peace, security and defence in the region (Campbell, 1997).

The third initiative has emerged in East and Central Africa. However, in this case, there is no clearly recognized regional power or economic organization that deals with common problems of economic integration and security. Responses have, therefore, tended to be *ad hoc*. Interestingly, it is war-torn Uganda that has played a central role in the security dynamics in the region. What may be called the 'Tutsi phenomenon' helps explain the Ugandan initiative. Yoweri Museveni of Uganda, believed to be half Tutsi, has had cordial relations with Tutsi exiles in Uganda, who had fled their country in 1959 after the bloody anti-Tutsi, Hutu-led military coup. These Tutsi exiles played a crucial role in Museveni's armed campaigns and eventual seizure of power in Uganda in 1985. In return, Museveni offered support for their struggles to oust the Hutu-dominated Rwandan government, which culminated in the genocide of 1994 and their final take-over of power. A massive refugee crisis was created on the borders of Rwanda, Zaire, Burundi and Tanzania. More than a million Hutus, who had fled Rwanda in anticipation of revenge by the advancing Tutsi army, were scattered in several camps, in which were found members of the Interahamwe, who had carried out the genocide. The new Tutsi-led Rwandan government felt threatened by the activities of the Interahamwe in the refugee camps and the Zairean dictator's stridently anti-Tutsi position especially in eastern Zaire, where Tutsis (the Bayamulenge) have been resident for centuries. Rwanda and Uganda armed the Bayamulenge Tutsis, who later teamed up with Laurent Kabila, a long-standing opponent of Mobutu, to take over the reins of power in Zaire. This initiative later had the backing of some of the regional governments, such as Angola, Zambia, Zimbabwe and South Africa.

A similar *ad hoc* response to crisis was also evident during the four month civil war in Congo-Brazzaville in 1997. In Congo-Brazzaville, the democratically elected government of Pascal Lissouba was challenged by armed militias loyal to the ex-military ruler, Denis Sassou-Nguesso, when the former tried to disarm the latter in anticipation of general elections slated for July 1997. The capital city, Brazzaville, was devastated by the four-month stand-off between the two armies. The regional governments were powerless. Through the initiative of France and the Organization for African Unity, an attempt was made to deploy to the country an African-led United Nations peacekeeping force, with troops from eight African countries. The initiative stalled at the Security Council. Angola, which was worried about Pascal Lissouba's links with his own country's rebel leader, Jonas Savimbi, and secessionist tendencies in one of its oil enclaves, Cabinda, decided to intervene decisively on the side of the former military ruler, Nguesso. In this case, intervention led, not to the protection of democratic reform, but to its reversal.

Regional initiatives are likely to become prominent in the quest for stability in Africa's troubled democratization programme. Their effectiveness depends, however, upon the presence of regional powers that are ready to take risks. A regional power clearly exists in West Africa, although French influence in the region is likely to act against a proper institutionalization of the ECOMOG initiative. It must be stressed that ECOMOG is the first truly autonomous regional security force in the developing world. Improving its technical, logistical and institutional capacity should go a long way in helping to stabilize the conflict-ridden West African societies. The democratization and stability of the regional power, Nigeria, is also essential if it is to continue to provide effective and credible leadership in the region. In the long run, SADC should be able to provide real regional security in Southern Africa, given the democratic character of the leading regional power, South Africa, and its high technical, industrial and administrative capacity. The real challenge in this case is the deracialization of the South African military, which is necessary if it is to play the kind of interventionist, peace enforcement role that the Nigerian military has been able to play in West Africa. East and Central Africa lag behind in the institutionalization of regional security initiatives, yet two of Africa's most serious and intractable conflicts are located there – Rwanda and Burundi. If the new Congo stabilizes, and links up with other potential powers like Ethiopia, Tanzania, Kenya and Uganda, more long-term solutions could be found to that region's security problems. It is significant to note that that the potential power in Central Africa, Congo-Kinshasa, has been admitted into SADC.

6. Conclusion

Democratization will continue to be an uneven enterprise in Africa. There is not likely to be one uniform pattern of change, but several. Conventional theories on the socio-economic determinants of democracy may be useful for explaining political dynamics and outcomes in individual countries, but not for classifying countries and analysing group patterns of change. Rather than treat democratization as an abstraction, this paper has shown that theorists and practitioners can make progress in understanding and advancing the phenomenon by focusing on the core elements of political reform as they have been articulated in different countries. These are the issues of constitutionality, civic and political plurality, electoral reform, decentralization, and power sharing. As we have seen, these issues have been central to current efforts in Africa to introduce political equity issues in the way their societies are governed.

We have not attempted to assess the degree of accountability and quality of governance in the different countries. This requires analysis of group or community level demands for effective governance and public policy issues that affect the welfare of citizens. The policies of economic adjustment that have underpinned the democratization programmes have not given sufficient weight to the other important aspect of equity – that of social welfare provisioning. African societies that are interested in consolidating their political reforms need to pay much more attention to this issue than they have hitherto done. They also need to invest much time and substantial resources in deepening and broadening the political reforms, which seek to provide equitable representational systems that will allow the populace to hold leaders accountable for their public policies. Such reforms should be buttressed by appropriate regional security institutions to police the difficult transitions. In the final analysis, it is the political dynamics in each country that will determine the growth or stagnation of democratization.

Notes

1 The first wave refers to the pressures for democratization that started with the French and American revolutions of the eighteenth century. The second wave is associated with the decolonization and democratization movements that emerged after the Second World War.
2 This refers to people not taking an interest in public policy issues (like voting, or petitioning public officials, for instance), but enjoying the benefits that may be associated with effective civic vigilance and activism from others.
3 This refers to situations where public officials enjoy unearned benefits, or rents, as a result of the positions they occupy.
4 In communist societies, the problem was addressed by nationalizing economic enterprises, setting up central planning systems, and providing universal welfare programmes. Political democracy in the sense used here was seen as a trade-off for the wide-ranging economic welfare programmes enjoyed by the population.
5 FPTP was British-inspired; and TRS was French.
6 It is important to note, however, that despite the problems of ethnicity, most countries succeeded in creating a sense of nationhood among the different ethnic groups. This explains why movements for national self-determination were relatively few. Only Biafra (in Nigeria), Eritrea (in Ethiopia), Katanga, now Shaba (in Congo), and Southern Sudan (in Sudan) produced ethnic movements which called for autonomy or independence. In the rest of Africa, ethnic competition and conflicts focused on improving access to the state's resources and public offices within a unified state.
7 Beckman (1992b) provides a powerful critique of this linkage.
8 This argument was largely made by modernization theorists.
9 This is the dominant perspective of a large number of theorists who write about African societies and politics.
10 There are, of course, authoritarian relations in African rural power structures as expressed through the rule of chiefs, rural money-lenders, colonial trading companies and parastatal enterprises (Mamdani, 1996). Mamdani's recent study on citizenship has shown the imperative of locating democratization at the local rural level in order to draw the peasantry into the mainstream of African life, and convert them from subjects into citizens – the latter seen as a status long enjoyed by social classes in the city, and a critical factor in democratic rule.
11 See also Bangura (1992) for an analysis of clientelist types of democracy in Africa.
12 Leftwich (1996) arrives at a similar conclusion in his 'On the Primacy of Politics in Development' *Democracy and Development*, Cambridge: Polity Press, 1996. His main focus was, however, on the politics of donor governments.
13 This applies only to the national conference that produced the first multi-party government.
14 The National Party, the party of apartheid, later pulled out of the national government in order, as their leader, F. W. de Klerk stated, to provide an effective opposition to the ANC-dominated government.

15   This agreement has stalled because of the reluctance of Savimbi's UNITA movement to hand back to the central government the territories that it controls. These territories are very rich in diamonds.

16   This was the country's first president, Kenneth Kaunda.

References

Abraham, A. (1997) 'War and transition to peace: a study of state conspiracy in perpetuating armed conflict', *Africa Development*, XXII(3/4).

Adekanye, B. (1996) *Disarming Ethnic Guerrillas, Power-Sharing and Transition to Democracy in Africa: Ethiopia, Mozambique, South Africa and Uganda as Comparative Cases*. Interim Research Report. International Peace Research Institute. Oslo: PRIO.

Ake, C. (1987) 'The Nigerian state: antimonies of a peripheral formation', in C. Ake (ed.), *The Political Economy of Nigeria*. London: Longman.

Ake, C. (1996) *Democracy and Development in Africa*. Washington, DC: Brookings Institute.

Allen, C. (1992) 'Restructuring of an authoritarian state: "democratic renewal" in Benin', *Review of African Political Economy*, 54 (July).

Amin, S. (1987) 'The state and the question of development', preface to P. Ayang' Nyong'o, *Popular Struggles for Democracy in Africa*. London and New Jersey: Zed and UNU.

Amin, S. (1991) 'The issue of democracy in the contemporary Third World', *Socialism and Democracy*, 12 (January).

Anyang' Nyong'o, P. (1988) 'Political instability and the prospects for democracy in Africa', *Africa Development*, 13(3).

Apter, D. (1965) *The Politics of Modernization*. Chicago: University of Chicago Press.

Bangura, Y. (1992) 'Authoritarian rule and democracy in Africa: a theoretical discourse', in P. Gibbon *et al.* (1992).

Bangura, Y. (1994) 'Economic restructuring, coping strategies and social change: implications for institutional development in Africa', *Development and Change*, 25:787–827.

Bangura, Y. and B. Beckman (1991) 'African workers and structural adjustment: the Nigerian case', in D. Ghai (ed.), *The IMF and the South*. London: Zed Press, UNRISD and UWI.

Bangura, Y. and P. Gibbon (1992) 'Adjustment, authoritarianism and democracy in sub-Saharan Africa: an introduction to some conceptual and empirical issues', in P. Gibbon, Y. Bangura and A. Ofstad (eds), *Authoritarianism, Democracy and Adjustment: The Politics of Economic Reform in Africa*. Stockholm Scandinavian Institute of African Studies, UNRISD and CMI.

Baran, P. A. (1957) *The Political Economy of Growth*. New York: Monthly Review Press.

Bauer, P. T. (1981) *Equality, The Third World and Economic Delusion*. London: Methuen.

Beckman, B. (1992a) 'Empowerment or repression: the World Bank and African adjustment', in P. Gibbon *et al.* (1992).

Beckman, B. (1992b) 'Whose democracy? Bourgeois versus popular democracy', in R. Rudebeck (ed.), *When Democracy Makes Sense: Studies in the Democratic Potential of Third World Popular Movements*. Uppsala: AKUT, University of Uppsala, Sweden.

Bratton, M. (1989) 'Beyond the State: Civil Society and Associational Life in Africa', *World Politics*, 41(3):407–30.

Bratton, M. and N. van de Walle (1992) 'Toward governance in Africa: popular demands and state responses', in G. Hyden and M. Bratton (eds), *Governance and Politics in Africa*. Boulder and London: Lynne Rienner.

Campbell, H. (1997) 'SADEC heads at loggerheads?', *Southern African Political and Economic Monthly* 10(12).

Chalker, L. (1991) *Good Governance and the Aid Programme*. London: Overseas Development Administration.

Chazan, N. (1988) 'Ghana: problems of governance and the emergence of civil society', in L. Diamond, J. J. Linz and S. M. Lipset (eds), *Democracy in Developing Countries, Vol. 2: Africa*. Boulder, Colorado: Lynne Rienner.

Cnudde, C. F. and D. Neubauer (1969) *Empirical Democratic Theory*. Chicago: Markham.

Dahl, R. A. (1971) *Polyarchy: Participation and Opposition*. New Haven: Yale University Press.

Damachi, U., H. Seibel and L. Trachman (eds) (1979) *Industrial Relations in Africa*. London: Macmillan.

Decalo, S. (1997) 'Benin: the first of the new democracies', in J. F. Clark and D. E. Gardinier (eds), *Political Reform in Francophone Africa*. Boulder, Colorado: Westview Press.

Diamond, L. (1987) *Class, Ethnicity and Democracy in Nigeria: The Failure of the First Republic*. London: Macmillan.

Diamond, L. (1988) 'Roots of failure, seeds of hope', in L. Diamond, J. J. Linz and S. M. Lipset (eds), *Democracy in Developing Countries, Vol. 2: Africa*. Boulder Colorado: Lynne Rienner.

Diop, M. C. (1991) 'Statutory political successions. national conferences: democratic transition or alternative to civil war?', *CODESRIA Bulletin, No. 3*.

Diop, M. C. (1994) *Senegal: Essays in Statecraft*. Dakar: CODESRIA.

Economist (1997) 'An African answer to Africa wars', *Economist* 18(24).

Errson, S. and J.-E. Lane (1996) 'Democracy and development: a statistical exploration', in A. Leftwich (ed.), *Democracy and Development*. Cambridge: Pluto Press.

Gberie, L. (1997) 'The May 25 coup d'état in Sierra Leone: a 'militariat' revolt?' *Africa Development*, 22(3/4).

Gutto, S. B. (1988) 'Social revolutions – the preconditions for sustainable development and people's democracies in Africa: a contribution to the Anyang' Nyong'o/Mkandawire Debate'. *Africa Development*, 13(4).

Goncalves, F. (1995) 'Southern Africa: in search of a common security?' *Southern Africa Political and Economic Monthly*, 8(7).

Hashim, Y. (1994) *The State and Trade Unions in Africa*. Ph.D. dissertation, Institute of Social Studies, The Hague, Holland.

Huntington, S. P. (1968) *Political Order in Changing Societies*. New Haven: Yale University Press.

Huntington, S. P. (1991) *The Third Wave: Democratization in the Late Twentieth Century*. Norman: University of Oklahoma Press.

Hyden, G. (1985). *No Shortcuts to Progress: African Development Management in Perspective*. London: Heinemann.

Hyden, G. and M. Bratton (1992) *Governance and Politics in Africa*. Boulder and London: Lynne Rienner.

Ibrahim, J. (1992) 'The state, accumulation and democratic forces in Nigeria', in L. Rudebeck (1992).

Ibrahim, J. (1993) 'History as Iconoclast: Left Stardom and the Debate on Democracy', *CODESRIA Bulletin. No. 1*.

Jega, A. (1994) *Nigerian Academics Under Military Rule*. Stockholm: Department of Political Science, Stockholm University.

Joseph, R. (1987) *Democracy and Prebendal Politics in Nigeria*. New York: Cambridge University Press.

Joseph, R. (1990) 'Political renewal in Sub-Saharan Africa: the challenge of the 1990s', in Carter Center, *African Governance in the 1990s*. Atlanta: Carter Center.

Kandeh, J. (1996) 'What does the militariat do when it rules? Military regimes: The Gambia, Sierra Leone and Liberia', *Review of African Political Economy*, 69.

Leftwich, A. (ed.) (1996) *Democracy and Development*. Cambridge: Polity Press.

Lipset, S. M. (1960) *Political Man*. New York: Doubleday.

Mamdani, M. (1996) *Citizen and Subject: Contemporary Africa and the Legacy of Late Colonialism*. New Jersey: Princeton University Press.

Mandaza, I. (1994) 'Southern Africa: towards a common foreign and security policy (CFSP)', *Southern Africa Political and Economic Monthly*, 8(1).

Mazrui, A. (1997) 'Africa's own trusteeship system: 'Pax Africana' has begun', *CODESRIA Bulletin. No. 3*.

Mkandawire, T. (1988) 'Comments on democracy and political instability', *Africa Development*, 13(3).

Mosely P. and J. Weekes (1993) 'Has recovery begun?: Africa's adjustment in the 1980s revisited', *World Development*, 21(10):1583–99.

Mustapha, A. R. (1993) 'Ever decreasing circles: democratic rights in Nigeria', in O. Nnoli (ed.), *Dead-end to Nigerian Development*. Dakar: CODESRIA Books.

Nyerere, J. (1967) *Socialism and Rural Development*. Dar es Salaam: Tanzania Publishing House.

Okoth-Ogendo, H. W. O. (1993) 'Constitutions without constitutionalism: reflections on African political paradox', in D. Greenburg *et al.* (eds), *Constitutionalism and Democracy*. New York and Oxford: Oxford University Press.

Olukoshi, A. (1989) 'Nigerian Marxist perspectives to the formation of the Nigerian Labour Party (NLP)', paper to conference 'Philosophy, Ideology and Society in Africa'. Vienna: African Studies Group (ZAST), University of Vienna.

Olukoshi, A. (ed.) (1993) *The Politics of Structural Adjustment in Nigeria*. London: James Currey.

Osoba, S. (1978) 'The deepening crisis of the Nigerian bourgeoisie', *Review of African Political Economy*, 13.

Othman, S. and G. Williams (1997) 'Politics, power and democracy', in J. Hyslop (ed.), *Democratic Movements in Contemporary Africa*. London: James Currey.

O'Toole, T. (1997) 'The Central African Republic: political reform and social malaise', in J. F. Clark and D. E. Gardinier (eds), *Political Reform in Francophone Africa*. Boulder, Colorado: Westview Press.

Putnam, R. D. (1993) *Making Democracy Work: Civic Traditions in Modern Italy*. Princeton, New Jersey: Princeton University Press.

Pye, L. W. and S. Verba (eds) (1965) *Political Culture and Political Development*. Princeton, New Jersey: Princeton University Press.

Robinson, W. I. (1996) *Promoting Polyarchy: Globalisation, US Intervention and Hegemony*. New York: Cambridge University Press.

Rudebeck, L. (ed.) (1992) *When Democracy Makes Sense*. Uppsala: AKUT, Uppsala University.

Sachikonye, L. (ed.) (1995) *Democracy, Civil Society and the State: Social Movements in Southern Africa*. Harare: SAPES Books.

Sandbrook, R. (1985) *The Politics of Economic Stagnation*. Cambridge: Cambridge University Press.

Sandbrook, R. and R. Cohen (eds) (1975) *The Development of an African Working Class*. Toronto: Longman.

Therborn, G. (1977) 'The rule of capital and the rise of democracy', *New Left Review*, 103.

UNDP (1997) *Human Development Report*. New York and Oxford: Oxford University Press.

Woodward, P. (1994) 'Democracy and economy in Africa: the optimists and the pessimists', *Democratization*, 1:116–32.

World Bank (1989) *Sub-Saharan Africa: From Crisis to Sustainable Growth*. Washington, DC: World Bank.

World Bank (1992) *Governance and Development*. Washington, DC: World Bank.

9

Africa in an Interdependent World: A Partnership of Vision and Principle[1]

Dunstan M. Wai

1. Introduction

By whatever standard is used, poverty and human suffering are intolerably extensive in Africa. The region suffers from poor infrastructure, a lack of appropriately trained and skilled professionals, limited technology, weak institutions, and deficient health and education services; its economy is over-dependent on a few products and exports and is insufficiently integrated into the global economy.[2] While the rest of the world has become increasingly interconnected and interdependent, Africa remains marginalized. Consequently, African countries are highly susceptible to negative international trade fluctuations, they are heavily indebted to external creditors, and they lack market clout. As a result, development efforts in almost every sphere have been ineffective. Indeed, given Africa's recent history and its record of decline – although one may continue to look for hopeful signs – expectations for progress are fading. In a region where arbitrary and capricious rule has led not only to economic and social decay but also to vacillation regarding development objectives, even the rare bright spots seem less illuminating on closer inspection.

On the positive side, Africa's structural deficiencies are not as ingrained as they appear. But while it must be said that condescension and paternalism on the part of outsiders are no help to Africans, by the same token it is both glib and unhelpful to blame Africa's negative circumstances on colonialism and neo-colonialism. More often than not, the tendency in Africa is to turn to the past when Africans wish to maintain their illusions. The fact remains, however, that most of Africa's predicaments today are of its own creation. Since the achievement of Uhuru[3] by African countries, there has been a tendency to hide private agendas inside public ones.

What can be done? Africa needs responsive leadership and good governance, and a new partnership with its development partners. The latter is particularly urgent because existing development partnerships have not produced significant tangible results on the ground.

Building new partnerships for development requires identifying key problems, building consensus around priority policy areas, and agreeing on solutions. New and effective partnerships must be forged on the basis of a clear vision and a set of principles which can underpin the pursuit of sustainable development with equity. But then, what is a *vision* in this context?

A vision is an image of a better world. It is not a projection of what is or has been, but a view of what might be. A vision is forward looking; it breaks away from patterns and ideals accepted in the past. Often enough, change in the course of human development starts with a new vision. A vision is not a hallucination. As we shall use the term, it is a conceptual framework that is based on a continuous reassessment of experience in the light of new ideas.

The vision for Africa's future includes countries with market-oriented economies in which producers have the right to earn and freely invest their profits, where there is full opportunity for individual economic advancement, a high mobility of the factors of production, and free movement of capital and technology across borders. It is also part of this vision that Africa be endowed with the requisite political, social and regulatory environments so that such economies can flourish.

Constructing a vision for Africa by Africans is a vital first step towards new and improved development policies. All too often policies are designed simply according to a criterion of 'feasibility' – that is, in reference to past experience. While the lessons of experience, resource constraints, and so forth, should be taken into account – and it is prudent to do so – it is all too easy to let such an approach *govern* policy design,[4] with the result being the reinforcement of the status quo. The fundamental purpose of visionary thought is to avoid this trap. A *vision of development* implies a strategy for *change*.

In what follows, we shall identify and analyse the main challenges which face African countries, as well as the opportunities which are available to them. Then we shall make suggestions about the strategic focus necessary to achieve sustainable development in an interdependent world.

2. Challenges and opportunities

The scope and severity of the crisis facing Africa is unique in the developing world: low levels of income-generating growth, declining per capita income, intense poverty, food shortages, unsustainable debt, and neglect of capacity building and environmental protection.[5] At least six mutually reinforcing challenges underpin the continuing crisis facing the region in what remains of the 1990s and beyond into the twenty-first century:

- improving the quality and efficiency of the state;
- focusing on capacity building;
- modernizing agriculture, avoiding a population explosion, and preventing environmental degradation;
- pursuing political liberalization and economic reforms;
- increasing economic co-operation and integration;
- escaping marginalization for interdependence.

Improving the quality and efficiency of the state

First, how to improve the quality and efficiency of the African state by promoting good governance remains a major challenge (Wai, 1985). Ways must be found to improve the links between governance and economic development. Such improvements may be achieved by enhancing the economic competence of the government so that it can respond better to the expressed needs of its people; strengthening government instruments (e.g., institutions, policies and personnel) to promote development; and providing a clear definition of what should be the government's vision and its development objectives.

The quality of governance is another problem of the African state (Wai, 1994). The fundamental virtues of modern statehood, namely the practice of accountability, transparency, openness, predictability and rule of law, have been notably absent from many African countries, replaced by clientelism, corruption, ethnic favouritism, secretiveness, and arbitrary rule. Kleptocratic states have not been rare in Africa.

Good governance must be a primary goal for African governments, and should lead to a more efficient and equitable allocation of resources. For national resources to be used both efficiently and responsively, they must be employed in the public, rather than private interests of government officials, and they must be put to the best possible economic use through open planning and capable implementation by government agencies. Bad governance is responsible for a phenomenon in Africa in which those countries which are best endowed with natural (particularly mineral) resources are generally the worst economic performers, because the state has institutionalized the squandering of wealth on patronage, corruption and poor economic decisions. Bad governance is equally responsible for the flight of investable resources to safer havens abroad.[6]

The practice of good governance creates legitimacy for public authorities and justifies their claim to make demands on citizens in the interest of development. A society must believe that its government will fulfil its end of the bargain – that it will guard against the diversion of national savings for the private uses of individuals, that it will ensure that property will be safe from arbitrary seizures or damage, and that it will ensure the impartial adjudication of disputes between economic partners. Good governance also promotes market-led economic growth by increasing trust between groups and individuals. Under good governance, individuals can enter into economic interactions with confidence because they can be reasonably sure of impartial adjudication by the judicial arm of the state. They can also trust in the maintenance of steady interest rates where credit is involved. Employees in both the state and the private sectors have the assurance that productive effort will be rewarded. In effect, the presence of an accountable, professionally-run public service lowers the cost of economic transactions.

Improved governance will be powerful catalyst for Africa's development because it will promote the efficient, equitable and responsive distribution of resources, it will legitimize the government's development efforts and it will help get Africa's fledgling private sector off the ground (see Callaghy,1990:258; Diamond, 1988:

23; Bratton,1989). Improved governance is essential for strengthening political liberalization and economic reform programs, as well as for reducing the dangers of continued marginalization in an increasingly interdependent and global economy. Successful management of political and economic reform programmes will provide a major breakthrough in efforts to end the cycle of stagnation in the region.

Focusing on capacity building

Second, capacity building should be made an integral part of the process of development (World Bank, 1996). If local capacities are not built and sustained, there is no likelihood that Africa will develop as it should and as it must if it is to achieve take-off early in the next century. Closely related to the issue of capacity building is the urgent need to improve the quality of education in Africa. Education should not be treated as a luxury, but rather as a necessity with a direct impact on the quality of the development achieved. As Alfred Marshall and the classical economists discerned long ago: 'Knowledge is the most powerful engine of production.'

'Capacity', in its most restrictive usage, refers to the human and institutional qualities which permit countries to analyse, plan and implement development policies (ibid.). Leadership – whereby political authorities show integrity, vision and dedication to the public trust – is an essential component of capacity. Penetration, the degree to which the state is able to exercise its political, administrative and juridical responsiveness and effectiveness, is also a central element of capacity. Likewise, human capabilities, including skills, training and experience, in the staff of public institutions is also a necessary ingredient of capacity. The lack of appropriate education, 'brain drain', or failure on the part of higher political officials to identify and use skilled and trained manpower reduces these capabilities. Professionalism is also central to capacity as it implies a standard of behaviour among public officials that is goal-oriented, merit-based and untainted by personal connections. Finally, the autonomy of public institutions is essential to capacity. Public officials must be able to perform their duties unhindered by requests for political or personal favours from outsiders to prevent public services and resources from being captured by special interests. Such contextual factors are often important in determining the effectiveness of capacity, and hence must be addressed in capacity building efforts in Africa.

The features of the institutional environment that have hindered capacity building may be traced to the neopatrimonialism endemic to many countries in the region. This gives politics priority over economics, personalizes power and breeds patron-clientelism, and encourages the overexpansion of the state. The result of these related processes has been atrophy of institutions. Perverted by leaders' pursuit of personal power, public institutions have lost their autonomy, and management systems, practices and procedures have fallen into disuse as politicians repeatedly intervene for political gain. In addition, institutions have been weakened by corruption and nepotism.

Against this background, it is easy to understand the dismal capacity building performance in Africa. Hence, capacity building must be taken seriously as the core of development, and African countries should be thinking in terms of a capacity building approach to development.

Modernizing agriculture, avoiding population explosion and preventing environmental degradation

A third set of challenges facing Africa encompasses the need to modernize agriculture, to stop the inevitability of population explosion and to prevent further environmental degradation (Clever and Schreiber, 1994). In this connection, Africa must anticipate the special capacity requirements which will emerge as a consequence of the dramatic acceleration of the HIV epidemic. These concerns should be at the core of national policies. For if African agriculture is not made more productive and competitive, if population growth is not stalled and if environmental destruction is not reversed, then Africa's future development is indeed bleak.

The slow development of agriculture is one of the principal reasons for Africa's slow economic growth, and it is hard to understand the persistence of bias in economic policy and investment against agriculture and against rural areas in general. But urban bias has been evident in most African countries, and in addition to slowing economic growth, it has also contributed to the failure to deal with poverty, since the great majority of poor live in rural areas.

The key to rapid growth and swifter alleviation of poverty lies with increasing production in the rural economy. For the foreseeable future, the task of providing productive employment for the growing labour force of African countries must rest with the agriculture sector. Within the agricultural sector, the long term goals of growth and poverty alleviation are best served by concentrating resources and policies in favour of smallholder agriculture. The details of smallholder agricultural strategy will vary across countries, but there are some principal elements that are common to all: the elimination of incentive bias against agriculture in policy frameworks; the institution and encouragement of oxen cultivation and new tools and implements; a reduction in the transport and marketing margins between the farmer and the final point of sale; and more intensive land use, such as greater husbandry and greater use of 'technical packages', including fertilizer and seeds. Population growth is inducing a transition from resource-based, land extensive farming to science-based, land intensive practices; however, adverse effects of population growth may be witnessed in shortened fallow periods, resulting in soil fertility problems.

Population growth presents a great challenge to long-term development. Sub-Saharan Africa has the highest fertility and mortality rates in the world. While mortality rates have been declining, there have been no significant change in fertility rates. Thus, the rate of population growth is likely to accelerate before it declines. Parents' recognition that they cannot afford education for large numbers of children is probably the best hope for future population decline. Very few African governments presently endorse family planning programmes, though in some countries such programmes are being incorporated into the maternity–child health component of national health services. Thus, the outlook for the next two decades is one of continued population growth. Ultimately, as improvements in child mortality reduce the number of births, and education offsets strong pro-natal feelings, population growth can be expected to decline. In the meantime, African economic policy makers must plan on high levels of population growth.

Pursuing political liberalization and economic reforms

Fourth, the simultaneous twin endeavours of political liberalization and market economy reforms must be continued without interruption (Bratton, 1993; Call-aghy, 1993; Herbst, 1993; van de Walle, 1994; Sandbrook, 1993; Hyden and Bratton, 1992; Lipumba, 1994). Political liberalization, which started in the late 1980s, and the programme of economic reform policies that seek to stimulate growth and encourage entrepreneurs and companies to be productive and effici-ent, have both produced positive results so far. This trend in the continent is important, because the achievement of economic growth with equity must be a goal for every concerned African government. Coupled with the growing con-sensus on economic reforms, African governments have a rare opportunity to come to grips with economic issues that were previously beyond their control. But both of these twin endeavours need to be carefully managed to make sure that they have the desired impact.

Widespread hope and enthusiasm greeted the wave of pronouncements by African leaders, beginning in 1989, that they intended to relax long-standing restrictions on the rights of political association and expression. This optimism embodied more than an appreciation for the intrinsic merits of political liberal-ization; it reflected a widespread belief that political liberalism was a precondition for economic reforms, which was generally believed to be the only way out of Africa's seemingly chronic stagnation. The generally upbeat view in the West about this spreading political opening was punctuated with pronouncements of support by major donor country governments. And official enthusiasm found further support and confirmation in Western intellectual scholarship.

The mixed success of African countries in achieving political liberalization, and the frequently disappointing economic progress of those that have made the transition to multi-party democracy, led to a backlash of pessimism regarding the benefits of political liberalism. Thus debate continues over the viability of political liberalization in Africa today. Two fundamental issues are at the core of this controversy. One relates to whether political liberalization is sustainable in African countries, many of which are beset with chronic ethnic and regional strife, weak central political authority, and corrupt, inept governing elites. At the same time, there is very little sense of a national political community within the population at large. An opposing viewpoint maintains, however, that some level of political liberalization is itself a prerequisite for economic growth, social matur-ity and political stability.

Another issue relates to whether liberal political structures are propitious for African economies. A political opening – so it is commonly maintained – only empowers and creates expanded opportunities for the very organized groups (often depicted as 'rent seeking coalitions') which were largely responsible for economic stagnation in the first place. A contrary viewpoint holds that, even if negative economic forces are given a freer hand in a politically open regime, their impact is offset by the likely emergence of more accountable and responsible governance under the greater public scrutiny afforded by more liberal political structures.

Although the sustainability of multi-party democracy within Africa remains in question, it cannot be denied that there has been significant and irreversible political liberalization. The end of apartheid in South Africa marks only the best-known case of this trend. Elsewhere, political prisoners have been freed, states-of-emergency lifted, and civil rights much more widely respected. Freedom of expression has also grown in recent years. This is particularly important as African journalists have been a driving force for further political liberalization. Most important of all, however, has been the remarkable upsurge of freedom of association, as evidenced by the establishment of large numbers of independent organizations in African countries. It was these forces, frequently coalescing into broad movements (such as the National Conferences in several Francophone countries) that fuelled African political liberalization.

Africa's remarkable up-swell of democratic rights and freedoms has enormous potential to wash away the abuses of power and economic mismanagement that have marked the tenure of the continent's authoritarian regimes. Yet there is also the danger – always present at times of political transition – that political opportunists will exploit popular fears and misconceptions about the effects of economic adjustment measures to delay economic reform.

Notwithstanding these problems, simultaneous economic and political transformation carries great opportunities. Critics of political democratization often fail to recognize that authoritarian regimes have to legitimize themselves too. They have often done so by pandering to the short-term interests of forces opposed to sustainable development, with the same result as that predicted by those who believe democracy is harmful. Development theory has recently rediscovered that interest groups can serve beneficial purposes. Research done on Europe's development, for example, demonstrated the importance of co-operation and economic responsibility on the part of economic interests for reaching national accords on development planning.

But development nowadays does not just depend on national achievements. In an increasingly interdependent and competitive world, it also depends on the successful integration into a world economic system.

Increasing economic co-operation and integration

The fifth challenge is increasing economic co-operation and the integration of African economies into the world economic system.[7] This is an urgent matter. Without economic co-operation it will be almost impossible for Africa to compete in the global economic system. Africa is one of the most fragmented continents in the world. It has 165 borders which separate the region into 51 countries, 22 of which have a population of 5 million or less, and 11 of which have a population of under 1 million. African countries have similar economic problems; however, they also often compete with one another for foreign resources and markets. If the region's economic policies and projects were better co-ordinated, the opportunities for faster growth would increase, because the synergies of different countries could be exploited and gains would be made in trade with economies of scale. Consider agriculture and food security, for instance – two obvious areas where increased regional co-operation in regional grain marketing and drought early-warning systems could benefit virtually all African countries. Substantial savings could also be made through regional co-operation in education and training programmes, and in institutions.

Africa has a positive role to play in global affairs if it can harness its vast economic potential as a continent of consumers and exporters. This can be accomplished by creating a favourable economic environment through structural changes, such as attracting sufficient capital, and removing negative trade barriers that dampen Africa's export potential.

Escaping marginalization for interdependence

The sixth challenge is that of escaping marginalization for interdependence. The global economic system has resulted in more and more interdependent countries, meaning they are subject to reciprocal gain and mutual susceptibility. Several mutually reinforcing factors have contributed to this process of increasing global interdependence. First, the switch to market-oriented economies has revolutionized economic management. Second, capital markets have greatly expanded and become a growing force for discipline in the global economy. Third, the world trade system has become increasingly important and is now decisive for a developing country's economic prospects. Fourth, the triumph of democratic pluralism has had far-reaching intellectual and attitudinal implications worldwide.

But Africa remains marginal at a time when most of the rest of the world has become increasingly interdependent. It has been far too dependent on a limited number of external partners. Lacking a diverse base of production, African countries are highly susceptible to negative international price movements. Heavily indebted to external creditors, and without significant market clout, most African states are in the position of supplicants for greater access to markets, foreign investment and credit.

Yet the global economy increasingly affords new opportunities for trade and investment. Africa needs a visionary, pro-active development strategy if it is to take advantage of these opportunities and avert the danger of falling behind in international trade. The African countries' international dilemma has a political side as well. For the first thirty years of independence, the Cold War relations of the great world powers loomed over Africa, creating a logic of rewards and punishments for national leaders in accordance with their willingness to support one side or another. However, since 1989, the major criterion by which Western donors have judged the aid-worthiness of African countries has come to be economic performance. The need for African countries to show results on the ground is also important because of the growing indifference and scepticism of public opinion in Western donor countries. Public views of Africa within Western countries are increasingly influenced by the Western media's focus on Africa's disaster areas and by reports on scandals involving corrupt African officials.

These international economic and political changes have brought about a shift in the attitudes and priorities of Western aid officials. Whereas in the past international assistance for Africa could be obtained without reference to a country's performance, the current trend among both bilateral and multilateral donors is to insist on merit, which is measured in terms of real changes in the economic and political policies of the state – or at the very least in terms of efforts to reform. This change has been accompanied by a shift in intellectual attitudes, and by a reconsideration of the role of the state in development. While once the debate was polarized between advocates of state-led development and those in favour of a more-or-less complete withdrawal of the state from productive activities, now there is a growing consensus on the need for states to play a limited, but nurturing role in market-oriented development.

This view implies that state capacity must be improved, and it puts emphasis on the competence and integrity of political leaders and top government officials. Western donors are no longer willing to protect African political elites from political opposition within their own societies, nor do they feel obliged to protect African countries from the pressures of international competition. It is an international normative order in which Africa is increasingly expected to interact with other sovereign entities on terms of equality.

3. The quest for sustainable development

Changing focus and priorities

Africa now stands at the crossroads: between the era of easy options and hard options; between adjusting to the changed economic environment of the 1980s and 1990s, and maintaining the discredited policies of the 1970s. For many countries, there is in fact no choice. Change is imperative. The easy sources of growth which sustained some development in the 1960s and the 1970s have now been exhausted. The adverse terms of trade, reductions in aid and in levels of foreign direct investment, as well as the increased competition facing many African commodities in world markets, have made it harder for many governments to maintain levels and rates of investment comparable to those of the 1960s and 1970s. Meanwhile, demands on African governments for services have increased. They include demands for more education, health and farming services, and that is quite apart from the need to create productive employment. African governments have been faced with these growing demands at the same time that the capacity to supply and maintain such services is diminishing. The question of choice is therefore uppermost. Doing more of the same is unlikely to generate the economic growth that is essential to fulfil the expectations and aspirations of the African people. A change in the style of development management is indispensable.

It is for this reason that the present initiative on a *Partnership for Capacity Building in Africa* is so timely (World Bank, 1996). Whereas in the first era of easy options the focus of policy analysis could be on the management of the development process, the focus now must shift to the development of management. The styles and systems of management of the first phase of African development must change from preoccupation with creating physical capacity in many sectors to developing human capital; from concerns with broad economic programming to the micro elements of resource allocation and efficiency in a context of scarcities. The distribution and the use of limited resources in a society create tensions. The management of development must therefore increasingly concern itself with the management of change in unstable, rapidly evolving and largely unpredictable conditions. Economic growth helps make changes smoother because the beneficiaries of change are able to compensate the losers without losses to social welfare. It is possible, therefore, for governments to design compensating measures at times of economic growth which ensure that growth with equity prevails. In times of growth there is room for mistakes in planning and resource allocation, but this is not the case during periods of economic decline and stagnation. At such times, neither the resources nor the consensus on economic and political goals are there to assure routine management functions and styles of governance.

Scarcities imply change and adjustments in resource allocation and use, and hence the importance of policy analysis and professional advice by governments. During periods of recession, maximizing the returns from resources is crucial. Meanwhile, the emphasis on allocative and technical efficiency requires different skills from general macro-economic planning. It implies putting more emphasis on criteria of efficiency when planning government investments. Hence the emphasis on public expenditure and investment review in the World Bank's funded structural adjustment programmes aimed at increasing the efficiency of general government investments as well as the cost effectiveness of specific sectoral programmes. Adjusting and adapting to adverse economic change requires special analytical skills to design compensatory and targeted policies as well as programmes to mitigate the destabilizing effects of such conditions. To stimulate the private sector, it is necessary to shift the managerial emphasis in state bureaucracy and the attitudes of African policy makers from regulation and control to competition; the need for more rapid growth in Africa calls for increases in private sector productivity just as much as it calls for improvements in government efficiency. To increase the returns to private sector investments means reducing business operating costs. This can be done by improving government management systems in their dealings with the private sector.

All these changes call for fundamental shifts in the skill composition, styles of management and institutional arrangements within government and society at large, as well as for new relations between these entities. The emphasis on technical efficiency and analytical skills needs to be backed up by an understanding of the micro-economics of policy by decision makers at all levels of government. High-level decision makers must be able to handle complex specific analysis without losing sight of the broad social and political goals. Managers must be innovative, and management systems flexible enough to accommodate changes in policies. But they must also be sufficiently resilient to sustain reform. Indeed, the challenge posed by Africa's lingering economic crisis calls for a total overhaul of the civil service rather than its mere restructuring. However, the capacity to put these new systems in place is lacking in several countries. In fact, by focusing on this major constraint in Africa's development, capacity-building in Africa is going to occupy the centre stage of development efforts, which in future must be based on a coherent vision and set of principles.

Fostering a market-friendly economy

There is no longer an ideological debate as to whether market-friendly policies are the quickest and most effective means of achieving economic prosperity and growth. Rather, it is recognized that the only way for countries to maximize their material and human resources potential is by permitting market forces to work. African countries need to construct a market-centred base for competing in an increasingly interdependent world economy. But what are the principal features of a market-friendly economy in Africa that would facilitate sustainable economic growth (World Bank, 1995a and 1995b; Helleiner, 1986; Alesina and Perotti, 1994)?

First, in order to achieve their highest potential, markets must be free from political interference. African state interventions in markets and attempts to control the allocation of economic resources have been notoriously connected with wastage, corruption and declining productivity. Even after years of economic reforms, government subsidies for state-owned and mixed enterprises are still one of the principal ways in which national resources are used up. Yet such resources are now desperately needed for investment in productivity-enhancing projects such as infrastructure. By contrast, countries that have effectively allowed the free interplay of market forces have seen almost immediate improvements in their overall economic performance.

A second basic right in a market economy is that producers be allowed to earn and invest profits. But all too often African states have killed economic initiative by overtaxing the most productive members of their societies – typically farmers. Indeed, a frequent response of African farmers is simply to 'drop out' from the formal economy, either by switching farm production into production of food for their own exclusive consumption, or by producing cash crops which they sell on parallel 'informal' markets. In either case, Africa's comparative advantage in the economic sector concerned is lost. Furthermore, there is ample evidence that price incentives produce a quick productive response. The right of private individuals to invest their profits, especially through efficient financial markets, has also been shown to be a factor of major importance in achieving industrial self-sufficiency. In East Asia, for instance, private investment has been a key element in the region's rapid economic transformation.

Third, for a market economy to thrive there must be economic equality and/or democracy. In other words, there must be equality of opportunity for personal economic advancement. When such opportunities do not exist, or when it is uncertain whether advances made can last, then a kind of fatalism is likely to set in; the personal motivation that lies behind high productivity will vanish.

Fourth, there must be mobility in the factors of production between economic activities and sectors. Such mobility allows for rapid shifts of productive resources in and out of various economic sectors according to changing conditions in the international economy. Such flexibility has been recognized as an underlying reason for the prosperity of Europe's smaller industrial nations as well as for the East Asian 'miracle' economies.

Fifth, there must be a flow of technology, capital and know-how into Africa from the North, for such flows help change economies. They would also facilitate a rapid equalization of economic disparities with Africa's trading partners and specialization of production in a diversified economy.

Sixth, old patterns of trade and investment should be replaced by increasing regional integration and mutual reliance between African partners. This will help develop the economic potential of all countries in the various sub-regions of Africa, and will help break continuing patterns of dependence on trade and technical assistance from a small number of external partners.

Creating an efficient facilitating state

Having outlined the goals and ends of the vision of economic development for Africa, it is time to consider the means. Clearly, a growth-oriented market economy cannot simply be willed into being. Development takes place in an environment of different factors, some of which constrain growth and some of which facilitate it.

Any vision of Africa's economic development must come to terms with the matter of the state. What is the proper role of the state in an economy? How can this role be achieved? To what extent and in what manner should the state be involved in economic activities?

With these questions in mind a vision for Africa's future should include a developmental role for the state (see Wai, 1995; World Bank, 1997a). The recreated African state should base its actions and policies on the following:

- First, the priority of state officials should be economic development perceived in terms of long-term growth, productivity and competition. Such a state operates in a strategic framework which is based on market principles. Within this framework, the country's economic leaders differentiate between long- and medium-range proposals, and anticipate and manage policy changes. They also draw up a list of priorities according to their political feasibility, and anticipate what the benefits and early payoffs will be in the programme of reforms.
- Second, the state should limit its interventions to protecting the rights of private property and enhancing the workings of the market. A country's political authorities should focus on policies that provide for the accumulation of physical and human capital; the acquisition of technology and skills from abroad; and international competition. However, political leaders should not try to dominate or control the domestic market.
- Third, the state should provide guidance in the market with the help of instruments which are developed by teams of managers. These teams could be drawn from the top graduates from the national education system. As

such, many of them will have received advanced training or graduate-level qualifications from abroad. These economic managers could/will study, plan and implement national development policies.

- Fourth, the state should exercise its political authority to mobilize domestic resources and to direct them where they will do the most to increase the quantity and quality of the nation's physical and human capital. The government should mobilize national savings and direct its investment in universal education, health care, rural infrastructure and access to clean water – all areas which contribute to national productivity. These are economic investments; they contribute to the human and physical capital that will be vital for development in future. They also have the added advantage of building up the government's popular legitimacy which will help it when it comes to introducing even more difficult stages of the economic reforms.

- Fifth, state officials should practice good governance; that is, they should operate on principles of accountability, transparency, openness, predictability and the rule of law. In this way they can contribute to a stock of popular good will which is necessary if the population is to co-operate with development programmes. With good governance practices established, economic agents have their faith restored in the good intentions and impartiality of government. Investors will invest, and entrepreneurs will undertake long-term projects. Economic growth is also a consequence of good governance.

- Sixth, the state should make capacity-building and capacity-use a top priority. It should make long-term investments in education and training for the entire workforce, and focus on building up a cadre of skilled individuals capable of analysing, formulating and implementing development policy. The state should concentrate on building up high-calibre civil services by ensuring that recruitment and promotion is based on merit and the result of completion; that remuneration in the civil service is competitive with the private sector; and that top employees are provided with incentives to remain in public service. In addition, the civil service must be insulated and protected from political and social pressures.

An efficient African state apparatus is a crucial factor that can promote or inhibit growth and development, but it is not the only factor. Others include the political situation, the social scenario, and the degree of integration in a global economy.

Nurturing an enabling political kingdom

The realm of political interaction – meaning, at the most basic level, the struggle for control over the state and the uses of state power – also constitutes a critical element of the political kingdom[8] and the enabling environment. Local tradition, past political events, and other idiosyncratic factors can play a major role in defining the character of political interaction in a given political situation. Political behaviour – on the part of governments, interest groups and individuals – can either increase or diminish the chances for achieving sustainable economic development. This difference in economic possibilities is most obvious depending on whether the political contention is a source of political conflict and/or violent conflict, or whether it takes place in an atmosphere of co-operation and peace. For economic development simply cannot occur in conflict-ridden national or regional settings.

Political reform, however, is possible even in the most conflict-ridden of situations. Africa has experienced a wave of political liberalization that has affected large numbers of regimes that were formerly more authoritarian. Therefore, this vision for Africa's economic future includes a political scenario in which fundamental reforms have succeeded in changing the political situation from one beset by discord to one characterized by stability and co-operation. Such a situation has several aspects:

- Establishing basic political freedoms is vital for political stability. Fortunately the trend in Africa recently has been in the direction of more rather than less political liberty. This is very important for economic development, as incentives for productive economic activity tend to be stifled when arbitrary regimes show no concern for political or human rights. Furthermore, investors who find they have no guarantees of a minimum of personal security and protection from unpredictable state action will not make long-term investments of the kind that are essential for growth.

  Another set of political freedoms – those that guarantee the rights of association and participation in elections – can help prevent the state from deteriorating into a personalized and corrupt power. This is because well-organized political organizations can serve as watchdogs on behalf of their constituencies and make otherwise non-accountable political leaders answerable. When political organizations can function freely and in the light of day they are also more likely to do so in a non-violent, non-conspiratorial way. In such circumstances political organizations contribute to, rather than detract from, political stability.

- Establishing valued political institutions is also crucial. As vital as basic political freedoms are, it is equally critical that political interaction take place in an environment that has well established political institutions which have norms, structures, and rules regulating political action. To be effective, political institutions must be widely respected. The institutions must conform not only to political necessity but to the established norms and ethics of the society in which they are placed. Conversely, political interaction in an arena devoid of institutions would be chaotic; it would undermine the political stability that is so crucial for the enabling environment for economic development. Political institutions that are inappropriate to local circumstances can also be destabilizing.

While admitting local variations in the shape and content of political institutions, there are nonetheless features which are generally considered essential for political stability. These are:

- A government should consist of separate and independent branches. Having separate executive, legislative and judicial branches of government in Africa is vital for guaranteeing the independent rule of law. Each branch of the government serves as a check and a balance on the other. The existence of 'rubber stamp' legislatures and judiciaries has been a major source of corruption in African societies in the past.
- Regular elections should take place to renew the mandate of national and local officials. These are vital to ensure both the accountability of government and the legitimacy of political institutions in general. It is critical, however, that elections in Africa be considered a legitimate undertaking by both candidates and electors; elections which are not accepted as binding by losers as well as by winners are a formula for conflict.
- Mechanisms should exist for communication between government and interest groups and individuals, but they should ensure bureaucratic insulation from undue political and social pressure. One of the important lessons of the economic success of East Asia is that government officials and economic leaders were in constant communication, sharing vital information and participating together in national planning (World Bank, 1994b). At the same time, government institutions in Africa should have built-in devices to protect civil servants from excessive influence by vested interests.

The social realm constitutes another critical element in the enabling environment for sustainable growth. Beyond the arena of the state, and of interaction between the state and society, there are many Africans who are organized into groups depending on their sense of social identity and/or their economic interest. These associations, which constitute 'civil society' according to the common use of the term, can interact in ways that contribute to economic development and growth, or which detract from it. Of course social conflict, which in the African context typically implies ethnic discord, has to be considered in relation to political and economic structures, as these often exacerbate ethnic tensions.

Social identity is not 'primal', but it is inextricably rooted in local experience. Nonetheless, social identity exists; usually it has strong roots, and it is deeply embedded in local history. It is one more factor in the environment with which policy makers who are intent on bringing about economic development must cope.

The achievement of a visionary goal for African development requires four social conditions to prevail. First, there must be an end to communal conflict. Relations between communally defined groups (ethnic, religious, regional and so on) should be co-operative. This means that political elites and entrepreneurs alike should resist the temptation to consolidate their personal power by manipulating and/or stirring up ethnic hatred.

Second, it is imperative to have co-operation between economic groups in Africa. Organized economic interest groups – for business, labour, government, and so on – should take a co-operative approach to national development goals. In the late twentieth century, the factor which is common to all successful cases of rapid economic change is that such organizations have accepted sacrifices, or at least deferred the demands of their members. This has been as true of Northern Europe's small industrialized democracies as of East Asian and Latin American countries. Such associations are, moreover, participants in national development. They often collaborate in national planning, even while remaining critical of the government in other respects. Currently, most such organizations in Africa behave in a 'rent-seeking' manner; that is, they appear to be more concerned with claiming as large 'a slice of the pie' of national wealth as possible – to the exclusion of competing groups. Interestingly, this often occurs when such groupings come under the category of being government or ruling party-dominated organizations. Thus being co-opted as an organization is no guarantee against irresponsible behaviour, and indeed, the reverse is often true. Autonomous interest groups, lacking the protection of the state, often behave with greater responsibility than co-opted organizations and their leaders. Whatever the case, it is essential that organized interest groups in African countries start regarding development in terms of an 'expanding sum' game, in which both they and the government can benefit from co-operation, rather than regarding development as a 'zero-sum' game based on confrontation.

Third, there is an urgent need for a change in the structure of social relations of authority in Africa. Personalistic, patron–client type relations of authority should be replaced by contractual relations. Clientelism feeds on and helps keep in place the self-interest of the few, because it depends on secretive, two-way relations. A contractual relationship, on the other hand, is open for all to see, and makes it possible for economic benefits to be distributed to entire groups.

Fourth, strenuous efforts must be consistently pursued to decrease gaps between rich and poor. A society that is rigidly divided between rich and poor is doomed to chronic instability. One of the critical lessons of the East Asian economic success is that public authorities made sure that such gaps were reduced by social policies such as universal primary education, public housing and the development of rural infrastructure (World Bank, 1994b). This was a major help in reducing social friction and it also gave greater legitimacy to government efforts in economic reform.

Overcoming asymmetry

Any vision for sustainable development in Africa has to include an idea of Africa's place in the global economy. Africa is inevitably linked to that system, so the vision must take account of Africa's role in, and contribution to, an increasingly interdependent world economy. Interdependence means that there is potential for mutual vulnerability and potential for mutual gain: for instance, the burdens of a worldwide recession are shared by all actors in a global economy; but so are the benefits of worldwide growth. Africa has fallen behind while the rest of the world – including most of the developing world – has become increasingly integrated in the global economy. Most African countries remain marginal and even subservient in the global realm. To overcome this and give Africa a new international role would have to involve at least the following:

- First, asymmetries in international relations, which relegate Africa to a subordinate position, need to be broken. These would be replaced with a positive role for Africa in an interdependent world economy. While such a change can certainly be facilitated by international actors, it is up to African countries themselves to initiate and sustain the transformation. This effort means that Africans themselves should bring about a reform of their internal institutions and processes to at least the same degree as other developing countries have done.
- Second, economic vulnerability must be decreased through diversification of production and trade. African countries would be less subject to economic shocks – such as occurred during the oil crises of the 1970s – if they were able to engage in more diverse productive activities, and could greatly expand their market outlets.
- Third, African countries should become more open to the international economy by opening their borders fully to the free flow of trade and investment. They should also avoid price distortions by letting the costs of the factors of production find their own level, and by allowing their currencies to float freely to find their real market value.
- Fourth, world markets must become more open to African goods and services. Increasing global integration means that the international community must behave responsibly vis-à-vis Africa. The international community should make a commitment to help African countries in their transition to market-oriented economies by lifting barriers to African products and by helping Africa open new markets.
- Fifth, approaches to technical assistance must be rethought. Such assistance should be reoriented away from functions that Africans can do themselves, and towards assistance with capacity building and utilization that is aimed at increasing African ownership in the development process.
- Sixth, there must be greater partnership in the development process, and more co-operation between the major international donors, non-governmental organizations (NGOs) and African governments, so that scarce development resources can be used better on agreed priorities.

Integration in a world economy, although an important step, is not sufficient to lift Africa out of its present poverty and widespread marginalization. What is needed above all is a shared vision of development and a consensus among Africans on how this vision can become reality.

4. The World Bank's response

Groping for an effective role

How does the World Bank, the most important development partner assisting Africa, fit into Africa's vision for sustainable economic development in the region? An effective partnership role for the Bank in Africa is one in which the Bank is a dynamic, proactive multilateral institution (see World Bank, 1989). The Bank would remain a major international catalyst for both resources and ideas on African development. It would also base its operations in Africa on a new partnership; that is, it would engage in a continuous ongoing dialogue with, and be responsive to, its African partners. Such a development strategy would include a program to seize the opportunities now available for attracting international capital flows, for reducing outstanding debt, for lowering barriers to trade and investment, and for investing in capacity building (human and physical capital) for a diversified, export-based economy.

It is virtually a truism that large bureaucratic entities respond slowly to changes. But the challenge for the Bank or any organization of its size is to structure itself in such a way that it can listen, learn, synthesize and perpetually enhance its policies in response to Africa's development needs.[9] Fortunately, the Bank has avoided intellectual atrophy because it is constantly reviewing its policies and procedures, and is publicly self-critical. Yet, if it is to help Africa meet the challenges it will be facing in coming years, the Bank must go beyond even these positive practices when it comes to elaborating a development vision and defining its role with its African partners. That is precisely what the Bank is doing at present through its 'renewal programme.'[10]

The challenges facing Africa discussed above have implications for the World Bank's approach to African development. An additional challenge is that of developing and supporting effective partnerships between Africa and the development community. These partnerships should be based on a shared vision, mutual interests, joint actions and consultations and respect. Such partnerships are indispensable if Africa's current lack of competitiveness in an interdependent world is to be halted.

There are at least three reasons for the ineffectiveness of most aid partnerships in Africa. First, bilateral aid is predicated on donors' concerns for their national interest, which invariably results in differing perspectives among donors, and between donors and recipients on the purpose of aid. The political motivation of aid has made forging a common agenda for economic development difficult. Second, at the local level, aid co-ordination among donors and with national officials has been problematic partly because of inadequate attention to local management and absorptive capacity. Consequently, a good deal of developmental resources have been wasted (Berg, 1996). Third, more often than not, there has been insufficient consensus among the key actors: the government, the bilateral agencies and multilateral institutions and the private corporations.

The Bank started its operations in Africa in the early 1950s in Ethiopia, and its operations increased in the 1960s as the rest of the region gained independence. Since then there have been major changes in the scope of activities in which the Bank is involved, and in the degree of the Bank's financial commitment. The hallmark of this approach has always been an ability to analyse and reflect on the lessons of experience and adapt policy strategies and instruments accordingly.

How can the Bank position itself in what remains of the 1990s and beyond, to deploy all the considerable resources (monetary, technical and intellectual) it has so that its assistance makes a real difference in Africa? The experience of the changes that have taken place in Africa and in the world – and in the Bank itself – since the 1980s will give rise to several new general principles in the Bank's approach to African development.

The Bank's approach to Africa's development challenges must be *strategic*; that is, it must start with an identification and analysis of the various factors – economic, political, social, cultural and international – that have an influence on development policies and their outcomes. The technical aspects of development policies and programmes should be based on this analysis, rather than be created in a piecemeal fashion, without coherent relation to the national enabling environment. One of the first lessons of experience in Africa is that problems of development in Africa should not be viewed in isolation, and that it is a mistake to try and solve them in a unidimensional way or with purely technical solutions. Frequently, the solution to one sort of problem requires approaching it on several fronts. The problem should be seen as one in a complex series of interconnecting phenomena (for instance, the following problems may all be connected: overpopulation, inadequate national, social and economic policies, soil-eroding farm practices, malnutrition and poverty). Focusing on just one aspect of a problem while ignoring the related elements often results in little, if any, progress.

The enormity of the development task in Africa over the last two decades has prompted the World Bank to re-emphasize that sustainable growth and development in the region is its number one priority. Despite new responsibilities in other areas of the world, the Bank's commitment to Africa is unwavering. Consistent with this, the Africa Region has become the Bank's single largest department with some 30 in-country Resident Missions. Lending to Sub-Saharan Africa amounts to between two and four billion dollars annually. In the current portfolio for FY97, there were a total of 31 active operations for a total commitment of $2.7 billion in 22 countries. The Bank is also the principal mobilizer of resources for Africa. This is largely because of the stamp of approval provided by its lending program and through forums like the Special Program of Assistance to Africa (SPA). Furthermore, the Bank now has a dominant intellectual position on African economic issues. For instance, it is involved in roughly 90 percent of the analytical economic research that is currently done on Africa.

The strategic agenda

The Bank has tried to respond flexibly in a variety of ways to Africa's development challenges: it has diversified its lending instruments, shifted sectoral allocations and types of projects, intensified its catalytic role in mobilizing resources and increased its co-operation with other agencies, notably the Fund, and instituted a more systematic exchange with governments on policy issues.

Proportionately, the amount of external assistance the Bank provides is large. Given Africa's dismal economic condition, such aid may be a fact of life. The Bank is working in an environment where African governments often have not been able to meet their development commitments either to their own people or to donors. For their part, donors have also had difficulties acting effectively and sustaining their commitments. Thus the Bank has become the focal point of discussion about aid to Africa.

The Bank's role has helped forge a consensus within Africa, and between Africa and the donor community, on Africa's development objectives and on how these objectives may be realized. This consensus forms the basis of the Bank's objectives over the long term for African development. The framework, spelt out in the Bank's 1989 Long-term Perspective Study Report, has served as the basis for Bank policy in Africa in the 1990s. The strategic agenda outlined in the report has three fundamental goals:

- reducing poverty and the suffering that typically accompanies it;
- promoting market-oriented economic growth as the surest and most sustainable way of achieving development;
- building human and institutional capacity, especially in government entities that are responsible for analysing, planning and implementing development policy.

In addition to these three development goals, there are seven building blocks in the Bank's strategic agenda for Africa that evolved in the late 1980s:

- First, economic policy and institutional reforms that encourage productivity and efficiency must be implemented.
- Second, investment in capacity building, and, above all, in the development of human resources, must increase. Through the promotion of education, health and family planning services, for instance, women should receive particular attention. Once human resources are developed, it is equally important to ensure that they are put to good use. Using talent and capacity efficiently and effectively is indispensable.
- Third, increasing agricultural production is vital, in order to reduce poverty, to provide food security for rapidly growing populations, and to produce the resources needed for further investment in development. In addition, it is important that policies to develop agriculture target smallholders and small farmers, address the nutritional needs of women and children, and encourage environmentally conscious farming practices.
- Fourth, an enabling environment for Africa's private sector must be created in order to allow this sector to realize its potential as the engine of the continent's future growth. A significant jump in investment can take place only after African governments allow their citizens to take advantage of business opportunities, reinvest the profits from their labour, and demonstrate success.
- Fifth, infrastructure must be developed and maintained. If African agriculture and businesses are to grow, they will require transport and communications systems to link them with markets and suppliers. Investment in infrastructure must include rehabilitating maintenance capabilities, and a careful consideration of the most efficient ways of managing infrastructural development and upkeep.

- Sixth, regional integration must be encouraged as the framework for economic growth through trade and productive specialization. The establishment of market, monetary and investment links between African countries will improve the viability of the region's small open economies. Efforts in this area should take place within the framework of existing bilateral and regional groupings, and should emphasize exchange rate harmonization and currency convertibility; the shared use and training of manpower; the upgrading and expansion of transport, telecommunications and energy connections; the promotion of a rational agricultural policy; and the identification of joint ventures and cross-border investments.
- Seventh, donor co-ordination is extremely important in all reform efforts. An excellent example of donor co-ordination at work is the Special Programme of Assistance (SPA). This programme benefits from being highly focused. It also provides a forum for discussion in which any and all issues may be raised. It is a means for filling gaps in financing, so that no important programme ends up being under-funded. But it is exclusively a donor's club, notwithstanding occasional efforts by the Bank to invite African economic leaders to share experiences with the SPA Group.

Poverty alleviation

The overriding mission of the World Bank is to alleviate poverty in developing countries. The World Bank's agenda for Africa's development is aimed first and foremost at assisting African governments to improve the quality of life for the majority of Africans who live in abject poverty. The pursuit of economic growth through adjustment policies became one of the main pillars of the Bank-funded operations in Africa. Since the Bank started structural adjustment lending in Sub-Saharan Africa in 1980, it has loaned over $15 billion. But, according to the 1997 Bank Operations and Evaluation Department (OED) study, the impact of adjustment on economic performance and poverty alleviation in the thirty-seven beneficiary countries has been fairly marginal growth, limited financial stability and insignificant reduction in levels of poverty (World Bank, 1997b).

As the Bank's OED study shows, only half of the countries that received adjustment lending improved their economic performance, and fewer made substantial progress towards poverty alleviation and sustainable growth as a result of their improved performance. Several factors account for poor compliance by the majority of the countries undergoing adjustment and for the weak results even among the best complying countries.

First, many countries did not achieve the expected improvements because they did not comply with conditions they had agreed to – they did not perform. During the first five years of adjustment lending, between 1980 and 1985, the number of countries with adjustment operations increased rapidly from 2 to 16, and to 32 in FY91. In the process, it is pointed out, the Bank approved poorly prepared operations in countries unwilling or unable to adjust. However, the ratio of satisfactory numbers has improved since 1991, when the Bank started reducing the number of countries receiving quick-disbursing support – by FY96 the number had been scaled down to 22.

Although there has been some improvement in compliance, arguably attributed to better selectivity and preparation, the results have not improved dramatically. Poor achievements are the result of poor borrower ownership of adjustment operations and the poor quality of adjustment programs agreed with the countries. Poor borrower ownership continues to be the most important factor negatively affecting performance. The countries with poor compliance are also the ones with poor borrower ownership.

In addition to ownership and design, implementation issues have also been significant factors in poor performance. Implementation problems include excessive ambitiousness, poor sequencing of reforms, insufficient attention to macroeconomic stability, poor attention to institutional reforms, and poor supervision, monitoring and evaluation.

Underlying the unsatisfactory result of adjustment operations are severe capacity constraints that are not usually identified in the review of these operations and therefore do not receive sufficient attention in the design of operations. Yet the lack of capacity for policy formulation and implementation, budget control and debt management are not sufficiently addressed in adjustment lending operations. Adjustment operations require countries to comply with strict conditions but pay little attention to the capacity for compliance with these conditions.

Ideally, countries should be doing their own analysis and diagnosis and should design reform measures. However, that is not yet the case. No doubt Bank policies and practices may unwittingly tend to exacerbate poor ownership, but the lack of capacity in adjusting countries is often the reason why Bank staff tend to take over the design and implementation of adjustment operations. It is not enough to exhort Bank staff to involve adjusting countries in the design and implementation of operations when they lack the capacity to do so.

Studies elsewhere suggest that the problems with monitoring and supervision of projects can also be traced to lack of capacity in borrower countries. This is a problem that the Bank has encountered in its other operations in Africa. The solution is usually to enhance Bank monitoring and supervision of projects. But this is only a partial solution because without the capacity for countries to successfully implement projects, closer monitoring and supervision only make project implementation more cumbersome without significant improvements in outcome. The OED study suggests that the countries that had a poor record of compliance with adjustment conditions also had a higher incidence of poor supervision.

There is an enormous difficulty in measuring the impact of adjustment operations on poverty alleviation because of the paucity of data. This is yet another area where capacity deficiency has a direct impact on the success of adjustment operations. Adjusting countries often lack the capacity to collect and maintain the data necessary to monitor the impact of adjustment operations. Without the ability to measure performance against indicators, it becomes difficult to achieve the ultimate objectives of adjustment lending.

Generally, there have been significant improvements in adjustment operations, particularly as they become more selective, the quality of conditionalities are improved and the design incorporates many of the lessons learned in the last decade and a half. But as the review of recent operations indicates, the results are still far from satisfactory. Increased capacity for compliance and for better implementation and monitoring is needed to make more lasting gains in adjustment operations. The Bank needs to pay more attention – and indeed, it is giving more attention – to capacity building in adjusting countries as an integral component of adjustment operations. There should be a better analysis of capacity building issues in the design of adjustment operations, and the findings of the analysis should be incorporated as a condition for the operation together with specific monitorable benchmarks and targets to record progress.

Almost everything the Bank does in Africa is directly or indirectly related to poverty alleviation. The Bank's lending in structural and sectoral adjustment serves to promote economic growth. But growth alone is not sufficient to reduce poverty. The pattern of growth is as important as the rate of growth. The Bank's strategy is therefore to encourage efficient, labour-intensive growth which provides employment and income opportunities for the poor. The Bank's smallholder focus in African agriculture, for example, serves to empower the rural poor who comprise the majority of Africa's citizens. Promoting an enabling policy environment, encouraging the transfer and creation of technology, developing rural infrastructure, and introducing natural resource management all impact positively on rural poverty. The Bank also invests directly in people: it helps provide social services, especially primary education, basic health, family planning and nutrition services; it works to improve living conditions and to increase the capacity of the poor to respond to income opportunities when they occur as a result of economic growth. Protecting the environment is another important element in the Bank's poverty-reduction strategy.

Even with all these efforts, it will take longer for some of Africa's poor to benefit in growth and social investments, while some will not benefit at all. Therefore, an important part of the Bank's agenda includes targeting particularly vulnerable groups, especially women, who play a critical role in African development.

In defining its approach to Africa's development challenges, the Bank will have to continue to study the successes and failures of economic adjustment efforts. This will make it possible for the Bank to promote best practices, and to identify problems in economic policies when they are implemented, as well as problems that may arise in the environmental, political, institutional or other spheres. Political and social realities are increasingly being taken into account in the Bank's operations. A consequence is that the Bank now reaches out to organized groups with the influence either to promote or block development efforts. Changing African reality makes it imperative that the Bank listens to and understands Africa's own vision for the continent's development.

The Bank has changed considerably over the years in its approach to African development. In doing so, it has benefited from an ongoing process of review and evaluation that seeks to incorporate into development policy both African and other intellectual currents.

The Bank has also recognized making mistakes in its African assistance. For instance, poor project implementation has not always been the fault of the client governments. The Bank, however, is constantly analysing such shortcomings and creatively searching for responsive solutions. Indeed, bearing these past oversights in mind, the Bank as much as Africa is striving to achieve a *new partnership* based on joint efforts to reach a common goal: sustainable and equitable economic growth to free Africa from marginalization. The Bank understands that the new partnership can be realized if it enhances the mechanisms for dialogue with its African partners. Ultimately, of course, the success of the Bank's efforts depends on how responsive they are to Africa's development vision, strategy and commitment.

5. Conclusion

This paper has sought to outline an attainable path of economic development in Africa through which the human suffering associated with poverty may be eradicated. With this strategic perspective, the paper also discussed the factors underlying an enabling environment that can lead to economic growth and sustainable development. Finally, the paper has discussed how the World Bank has approached development in Africa, and what it can continue to do to help its African partners achieve their development vision.

The World Bank has a role to play in partnership with Africa in achieving its development goals. It has financial, technical and human resources and a comprehensive approach toward solving the challenges of African development. In addition it is possibly the only organization at present that has the wherewithal to analyse and to quickly adapt its approach in the face of the breathtaking changes that are occurring in Africa today. Nevertheless, the key to the Bank's success in contributing to Africa's development in future will be to continue and extend its practice of listening to, and learning from, both its clients and its critics, and being unafraid to change its approaches as Africa's realities dictate.

Africa's destiny, however, lies squarely with Africans. In fact, as the world grows ever more interdependent, Africa's huge potential as both a producer and a market is going to require more, rather than fewer efforts to integrate into the global economy. The Bank is at the centre of this transformation process. How it goes about supporting Africa's efforts to make the required changes can make a big difference in the results. Furthermore, we believe both the challenges and the changes taking place in Africa today provide an unprecedented opportunity to achieve positive results.

Meanwhile it cannot be over-emphasized that the Bank's contribution to a future African development must be based on *partnership*. It is only through partnership that the vital motivating power of ownership of the development process and agenda can be preserved. Africans – governments and private citizens alike – must consider *themselves* to be the owners of the development process. The World Bank's management has frequently emphasized that the Bank will facilitate and help support the economic reform process in Africa, but it will not dictate it. Ongoing dialogue and two-way communication must be at the heart of the Bank's contribution to the vision for Africa's development.

Finally it must be re-emphasized that *the vision just outlined is attainable*. Too often in the past, development in Africa has been hindered by disbelief in its possibilities, by a lack of confidence by African leaders and society alike, and by ideologies which seem to be more interested in giving reasons for Africa's economic failures than in proposing cures. These factors together have resulted in a gloomy fatalism about Africa's future. Yet such fatalism has no foundation; too much of it is based on ideas inherited from the past. All the more reason to launch a new approach to development in Africa based on a vision of sustainable development: one that provides both a sense of direction to be pursued and an end to be achieved.

Notes

1 Although the author is a staff member of the World Bank, the views expressed in this paper are solely his own, and do not necessarily represent those of the World Bank.
2 The daunting development challenge in Africa is reflected in the following statistics: 583 million Africans, or 10 per cent of the world's population, produce only 1 per cent of the world's GDP; 262 million Africans, or 45 per cent, live on less than $1 a day; 290 million Africans, or 50 per cent, are illiterate (and 62 per cent of women are illiterate); 200 million Africans, or 35 per cent, are without access to health services; 274 million Africans, or 47 per cent, do not have access to safe water; and national expenditures on agricultural research typically amount to less than 1 per cent of agricultural GDP. See World Bank (1977). I am also deeply indebted to Professor David E. Apter for his insightful reflections on the changing political scene in Africa in the last forty years. I have unashamedly absorbed and borrowed phrases from his various communications to me in the last five years in the introduction of this paper. For a penetrating perspective on political changes in Africa see Apter and Rosberg (1997) and World Bank (1981, 1983).
3 Uhuru is a Swahili word for 'independence'.
4 The point to emphasize here is that feasibility studies must be done in the context of a development vision.
5 See Ndegwa and Green (1994).
6 This was certainly the case of Zaire under Mobutu Seso Seko.
7 African countries have expressed interest in regional integration through OAU Heads of States' revolutions, but notwithstanding the Abiya Treaty on Economic Co-operation not much has been done.
8 The concept of *political kingdom* was first used by David E. Apter (see Apter, 1961).
9 The President of the World Bank Group, Mr James D. Wolfensohn, has emphasized this point to Bank Staff at various times (Jaycox, 1992; World Bank, 1994a, 1995b).
10 The renewal programme of the Africa Region of the World Bank was launched as part of a reorganization of the World Bank in 1996.

References

Alesina, Alberto and Roberto Perotti (1994) 'The Political Economy of Growth: A Critical Survey of the Recent Literature', *World Bank Economic Review* 8(3):351–71.
Apter, David E. (1961). *The Political Kingdom in Uganda*. Princeton, New Jersey: Princeton University Press.

Apter, David E. and Carl G. Rosberg (1997) 'Changing perspectives', in D. E. Apter and C. G. Rosberg (eds), *Political Development and the New Realism in Sub-Saharan Africa*. Charlottesville and London: University of Virginia Press.

Berg, Elliot (1996) 'Dilemmas in donor aid strategies', paper prepared for workshop on External Resources for Development, Netherlands Economic Institute, Rotterdam, May 13–14.

Bratton, Michael (1989) 'Beyond the state: civil society and assimilational life in Africa', *World Politics*, 41(3):407–30.

Bratton, Michael (1993) 'Political liberalization in Africa in the 1990s: advances and setbacks', paper presented at the workshop for SPA Donors, *Economic Reform in Africa's New Era of Political Liberalization*, April 14–15. Washington, DC: USAID.

Callaghy, Thomas M. (1990) 'Lost between state and market: the politics of economic adjustment in Ghana, Zambia, and Nigeria', in Joan M. Nelson (ed.), *Economic Crisis and Policy Choice: The Politics of Adjustment in the Third World*. Princeton: Princeton University Press.

Callaghy, Thomas M. (1993) 'Political passions and economic interests: economic reform and political structure in Africa', in Thomas Callaghy and John Ravenhill (eds), *Hemmed In: Responses to Africa's Economic Decline*. New York: Columbia University Press.

Clever, Kevin M. and Gotz A. Schreiber (1994) *Reversing the Spiral: The Population, Agriculture, and Environment Nexus in Sub-Saharan Africa*. Washington, DC: World Bank.

Diamond, Larry (1988) 'Introduction: Roots of Failure, Seeds of Hope', in L. Diamond, J. J. Linz and S. M. Lipset (eds), *Democracy in Developing Countries*, Vol. 2: *Africa*. Boulder: Lynne Rienner.

Helleiner, Gerald K. (ed.) (1986) *Africa and the International Monetary Fund*. Washington, DC: International Monetary Fund.

Herbst, Jeffery (1993) *The Politics of Reform in Ghana, 1982–1991*. Berkeley: University of California Press.

Hyden, Goran and Michael Bratton (eds) (1992) *Governance and Politics in Africa*. Boulder, CO: Lynne Rienner.

Jaycox, Edward V. K. (1992) *The Challenges of African Development*. Washington, DC: World Bank.

Lipumba, Nguyuru H. I. (1994) *Africa Beyond Adjustment*, Policy Essay 15. Washington, DC: Overseas Development Council.

Ndegwa, Philip and Reginald H. Green (1994) *Africa to 2000 and Beyond: Imperative Political and Economic Agenda*. Nairobi: East African Educational Publishers.

Sandbrook, Richard (1993) *The Politics of Africa's Economic Recovery*. Cambridge: Cambridge University Press.

Wai, Dunstan M. (1985) *Governance and the Crisis of the State*, unpublished manuscript.

Wai, Dunstan M. (1994) *Governance and Economic Development*, unpublished manuscript.

Wai, Dunstan M. (1995) 'The essence of capacity-building in Africa', The James S. Coleman Memorial Lecture, UCLA, May.

Walle, Nicholas van de (1994) 'Political liberalization and economic reform in Africa', *World Development*, 22(4).

World Bank (1977) *Rural Development in Africa: The World Bank's Perspective*. Washington, DC: World Bank, Africa Region.

World Bank (1981) *Accelerated Development in Sub-Saharan Africa: An Agenda for Action*. Washington, DC: World Bank.

World Bank (1983) *Sub-Saharan Africa: Progress Report on Development Prospects and Programs*. Washington, DC: World Bank.

World Bank (1989) *Sub-Saharan Africa: From Crisis to Sustainable Growth*. Washington, DC: World Bank.

World Bank (1994a) *Learning from the Past, Embracing the Future*. Washington, DC: World Bank.

World Bank (1994b) *The East Asia Miracle*. Washington, DC: World Bank.

World Bank (1995a) *Global Economic Prospects 1995*. Washington, DC: World Bank.

World Bank (1995b) *A Continent in Transition: Sub-Saharan Africa in the Mid 1990s* (Draft Report, 11 January 1995). Washington, DC: The World Bank, Africa Region.

World Bank (1995c) *Global Economic Perspective and the Developing Countries, 1995.* Washington, DC: World Bank.

World Bank (1996) *Partnership for Capacity Building in Africa: Strategy and Program of Action.* A report of the African Governors of the World Bank to Mr James D. Wolfensohn, President of the World Bank Group, 28 September 1996. Washington, DC: World Bank.

World Bank (1997a) *The Role of the State in a Changing World: The World Development Report, 1997.* Washington, DC: World Bank.

World Bank (1997b) *The Impact of Adjustment on Economic Performance; An OED Study.* Washington, DC: World Bank.

10

Structuring Economic Reform in Africa

Edgar O. Edwards with Wilson Kinyua[1]

This essay seeks to identify the principal economic factors that have hindered development in Africa and to explore the elements of economic reform that will need to be introduced if the current trend is to be reversed. The essay is divided into three substantive sections. The first describes the visions entertained upon the achievement of independence, largely during the decade of the 1960s, about the nature of future development in Africa. The second relates the stark realities that have succeeded the earlier visions, and the third attempts to come to grips with the difficult choices that must be made in Africa if substantive economic reform is to be realized. A short conclusion completes the essay.

1. The promise of independence in Africa

Independence for many countries in Africa held a promise that really had two parts – to escape the tyranny of colonialism and to write a new script for future economic development. The promised escape has been only partial and the script for the new play turned out to have many faults.

The colonial inheritance

Most of the African countries, with the notable exception of Ethiopia and Liberia, which were not colonized, attained their political independence in the period 1960–70. Sudan and Ghana obtained their independence in 1956 and 1957, respectively, while a few countries, such as Zimbabwe, Angola and Mozambique, attained freedom after the end of the decade.

As African countries were basically creations of the Berlin conference of 1884, they share some common colonial legacies. One of these legacies is the definition of borders that bear little relationship to geographical or cultural features of the African landscape. At independence, African leaders decided to maintain the borders inherited from their colonial masters even though, in some instances, there were pressures for their revision. A major problem with the inherited borders is that people belonging to the same family, clan or tribe live in two or more states, e.g., the Maasai in Kenya and Tanzania, the Somalis in Kenya and Somalia, and the Banyankole in Uganda and Rwanda. As a result, many countries in Africa are not truly unified nations in a cultural sense, but comprise people with differing identities and aspirations. This is one of the major causes of instability and bloody conflicts in Africa.

Another colonial legacy that has had a negative effect on African development is the economic, social and political linkages established in colonial days with the colonial powers. On the economic front, for example, most of domestic production, whether in agriculture or mining, was designed to produce raw materials for industries located outside of Africa. Railways, roads and air routes were designed mainly to link African countries with cities in Europe. Similarly, consumption patterns copied from the former colonial powers have influenced the composition of industrial output in Africa even though such patterns may not be sustainable.

As a result, transport linkages between African countries are practically non-existent. For example, to travel from West Africa to East Africa, it is usually necessary, faster and safer to travel to Europe first. Consequently, the movement of people and goods between African countries is very limited, a factor that continues to limit intra-African trade and regional co-operation.

Many African countries attained their independence in the midst of the Cold War and were encouraged to choose between alliances with their former colonial masters in the West or socialist bloc countries in the East. The choice was made more difficult because in their fight against colonialism, some African countries received arms and training from Eastern bloc countries, which made them sympathetic to the policies of those countries. To resolve the dilemma, most African countries joined the Non-Aligned Movement, even though their economies remained firmly dependent on the West.

There are a few other interesting legacies from the colonial powers. African nations had observed that democracy, to the extent that it was practised at all in the colonies, was limited to the privileged few. They also learned that detention without trial was an acceptable practice, and that prohibiting some members of society from participating in selected economic activities was not necessarily discriminatory.

The newly independent nations in Africa did find a number of their colonial legacies useful. The colonial nations developed substantial infrastructures in the form of ports, roads, power generation and water supplies. While these were intended to serve the mother country and its settlers in Africa, the facilities were left in place as the colonial governments departed.

The colonial governments and the missionary institutions that entered with them also left an inheritance in the form of educational and health care institutions that assisted the newly independent nations to begin the task of educating and caring for their growing populations. Social services were not non-existent.

Perhaps the most valuable legacies were in the forms of legal structures, civil service organizations and systems of operation. The legal system was focused on law and order as opposed to economic development, but it also rested on an established judicial system which would serve the new governments well. The civil service was organized along functional lines and its lower levels of staff had been well trained in managing orderly filing systems, writing memos, organizing seminars, and sending their children to appropriate schools. Complaints would surface, but the basics were there.

Despite the diverse colonial experience, most African countries found themselves at independence with certain unfavourable, but common characteristics. First, the bulk of the population lived in poverty. Second, the level of illiteracy was very high, which made it difficult for governments to implement their development programmes and to obtain inputs from the people in the design of their own development projects. Third, in most of Africa frequent outbreaks of famine and disease kept the bulk of the population in poor health, which undermined both their survival and their productivity. Some of the social traditions, such as the preference for large families, made population management difficult in Africa as parents sought to overcome the insecurity associated with high infant mortality. At independence, therefore, nearly all African countries were entrapped in poverty, ignorance and disease.

The vision of the future

Political independence gave the new African governments the opportunity to define a better future for their peoples. Most governments seized upon this opportunity with enthusiasm and optimism and began planning for rapid and equitable growth. Potential donors shared their enthusiasm and encouraged the production of formal development plans as a basis for justifying foreign aid.

It was widely recognized that governments would have to play a major and active role in the development process. Private domestic saving was practically non-existent; private enterprise was heavily dominated by expatriate parent companies; African entrepreneurs with experience were few and far between; basic financial services and the financial markets were in their infancy; agriculture was geared towards subsistence, except for a few cash crops and large cattle herds controlled largely by expatriate farmers and ranchers; and because teachers and medical personnel were in very short supply, many expatriates had to be retained in these professions.

Africanization became an early priority. It was quickly evident in the civil service and only a little more slowly among teachers and nurses. Opportunities for employment burgeoned and governments understandably permitted quality and training to take a back seat in the drive towards greater African participation.

Africanization was also an important motivating force in the formation of central, development and commercial banks; the creation of national currencies; the organization of settlement schemes; and the establishment of governing bodies and marketing agencies as African farmers entered into the production of cash crops.

Large amounts of money and great faith were invested in the creation of parastatal organizations. These were viewed as means for developing African entrepreneurial talent, diversifying the industrial production base and the location of industry, and promoting import substitution. Many countries, at the outset, viewed parastatals as a way station to a vibrant, domestically owned and managed private sector. All of these were regarded as desirable objectives requiring government initiative and investment to make them possible.

Import substitution was really part of a larger concern. The realization that their economies were highly dependent on external forces made African leaders think that their political independence could only be safeguarded by embracing policies for economic self-sufficiency. Self-sufficiency in the production of food was typically given a high priority. With substantial amounts of uncultivated land, potential for irrigation and ample room for increasing productivity on both farm and range land, self-sufficiency seemed readily achievable.

The intent to provide food for all was accompanied by a desire to achieve other social goals as quickly as possible. Free and universal primary education was a respected objective along with reduced infant and child mortality and a more disease resistant population through improved and more widespread preventive health care. While local authorities were given some responsibilities in addressing these problems, central governments, on the whole, retained major control over social programmes.

Party manifestos and public statements by many African leaders suggest that most governments wanted to create welfare states in which their societies were free from want, ignorance and disease. This objective was reflected in their willingness to embrace many features of socialism in planning the development of their economies. Having only recently escaped from the western colonial powers, many African nations welcomed both verbal comfort and financial assistance from the socialist nations. But their economic ties were still primarily with the West and the former colonial powers were rapidly becoming the primary source of foreign aid. Interestingly enough, these donors provided major support for the production of development plans as a basis for foreign aid.

In practice, nearly all countries opted to provide free primary education and basic health care. Spurred by foreign aid, massive investments were made in education, health and infrastructure in order to redress colonial neglect and also to stimulate growth.

The development path followed by most governments was to put their faith in the modern monetary sector. Its growth would wean people away from subsistence agriculture as they found better livelihoods in the modern sector. In the meantime, settlement schemes were necessary to provide subsistence for growing populations.

The modern sector embraced much of agriculture as well as industry and services. Cash crops, such as cocoa, coffee, tea, and sugar, and modern ranching would bring more and more agricultural production into the monetary world. In industry, governments focused on promoting large-scale enterprises as a means of modernizing their economies most quickly. This was, of course, entirely consistent with the import substitution strategy, and required protection through high tariffs and overvalued exchange rates. Interest rates, on the whole, were deliberately kept low in order to stimulate private sector investment.

Most nations recognized that the small size of their economies could not attract private investment in industries that required larger markets to achieve efficiency. Many sought to join forces with neighbouring countries in order to create larger markets. These economic communities were expected to lure private foreign investors into forming joint ventures to serve large and rapidly growing economic areas. It was also thought that industries could be shared spatially so that all participating countries could be seen to gain from regional co-operation.

The African vision of rapid and equitable growth was expected to be realized through a combination of domestic entrepreneurship and foreign capital. The continuing dependence on foreign capital, largely in the form of concessional money from the former colonial powers, did not worry most governments who felt they could exercise effective control over the expenditure of those funds. Indeed, without foreign aid the realization of many of their ambitious objectives would not be possible within any meaningful time frame.

2. Emerging realities

Few of these visions have materialized. Institutional and financial shortcomings inherited from the colonial powers have been alleviated in some cases, have worsened in others and new institutional and financial problems have emerged. Population has continued to grow rapidly; the demand for social services and the perceived need for defence establishments have limited the allocation of resources to investment and employment creation; the quality of education, health care and other social services has remained low; unemployment has climbed persistently; domestic savings have withered rather than bloomed; parastatals have become empires rather than fading away; many foreign resources have been misdirected and badly managed; corruption has raised costs and reduced international competitiveness; and economic growth has stagnated while income distribution has worsened.

The brighter spots include recent evidence that fertility rates are declining; infant mortality rates have been falling; the percentage of infants that have been immunized against major diseases has been increasing; life expectancy has been improving; and the average level of education has been rising for both males and females. In some respects, however, these bright spots are a reflection of the substantial allocation of resources to the provision of social services – at the expense of investment and employment creation – that has been required by rapid population growth. Most of these social indicators would be even more favourable if the rate of population growth had declined at an earlier date.

Social indicators and resource imbalances

In Sub-Saharan Africa, which excludes countries bordering on the Mediterranean Sea, the growth of real gross domestic product has fallen from 4.5 per cent per annum in the 1965–73 period to 2.4 per cent in the 1975–84 period, and since then to 0.9 per cent in the 1990–94 period. At the same time, population, which was growing at 2.6 per cent per annum in the earlier period, was growing at 2.9 per cent per annum in each of the two later periods. As a consequence, gross national product per capita grew by only 2.9 per cent per annum in the 1965–73 period and actually *fell* by 1.8 per cent per annum in the later period. These figures reflect the heavy allocation of resources, public and private, to the provision of social services, the meagre resources allotted to investment and employment creation, and the weakness or ineffectiveness of both voluntary and governmental family planning programmes. Moreover, slow economic growth today, relative to population growth, means slower growth in the future because investment in innovation and physical and human capital must necessarily be less than it would otherwise be.

The important role of population growth

Rapid population growth has been reflected in rapidly growing numbers of people of working age, and of those able and willing to work, the labour force. Because it takes an infant 15 years to reach working age, the labour force will continue to grow rapidly for a considerable time after the rate of population growth subsides. The serious problem of creating job opportunities for those seeking work in Africa will clearly extend well into the future. Efforts to create jobs will help but the longer-term solution must lie in a reduced rate of population growth, which will both free resources for the creation of more job opportunities and eventually reduce the rate of growth of the labour force.

With rapid population growth, governments have faced the agonizing choice of providing social services for larger and larger numbers of people or rationing scarce social services in order to allocate more resources to improving the quality of those services. Focusing on quantity at a very clear cost in terms of quality was the choice that most governments made.

The quality question

Data on the numbers of people receiving or having access to social services are readily available but indicators of the quality of services are less quantitative and greater reliance must be placed on anecdotal evidence. Hence, while it is easy to point out that the percentage of school-age children enrolled in primary school in Sub-Saharan Africa has grown from 50 per cent in 1970 to 79 per cent in 1993, we rely primarily on anecdotal information to allege that the quality of primary education is substantially inferior to the quality of primary education in the more advanced industrialized countries. Similarly, we can document that for many of those countries in Africa for which data are available, a larger percentage of the population had access to health care services in the 1990s than was the case in the 1980s, but the quality of those services defies measurement.

Opting to respond to quantity demands at the expense of quality has, in retrospect, tended to widen the gap between the rich and the poor. The elites have increasingly turned away from government institutions providing social services, choosing instead to seek schooling and medical services in private and foreign institutions.

Basic needs

Other difficult social choices have had to be made, especially with respect to education and health care. Within each of these sectors, serious questions have arisen about the internal allocation of resources – in education, between higher and lower levels, and in health care, between curative and preventive health.

Numerous economic studies have shown that additional resources invested in lower levels of the educational system will earn a significantly higher return than if the same resources were invested in higher levels of education. Despite this evidence, the allocation of resources within education continues to favour the higher levels. Political evidence suggests that it is the elites that benefit most from higher education, including the civil servants who make the policy recommendations favouring higher education. Hence, the powerful political lobbies approve subsidies for higher education that are financed by widely disbursed taxes, but the benefits of which accrue to the elites.

Similar arguments can be applied to the allocation of subsidies between curative and preventive health care measures. The elite benefit significantly more from curative medicine than the very poor, while subsidies for curative medicine are financed by taxes that are widely disbursed. Moreover, while it is economically less expensive to provide infrastructure services in areas of high population density, even within the urban areas the provision of such services is biased toward those areas in which the elites live.

Development and recurrent expenditure imbalances

Sacrificing quality improvements in the interest of serving larger numbers of people has its counterpart in the trade off in government budgets between development expenditure and current expenditure, in the priority given to building facilities at the expense of operating and maintaining them efficiently. Indeed, the priority given to development expenditure over current expenditure extends beyond social service facilities and is perhaps even more noticeable with respect to infrastructure, such as roads, power, and water and sanitation facilities. Visual evidence of potholes, missing shoulders, power rationing, and water shortages points to the serious and widespread neglect of repair and maintenance. It is our contention that in most Sub-Saharan African countries, governments have been allocating excessive amounts of their budgets to capital expenditure and too little to current expenditure in just about every sector.

The seemingly irresistible favouritism accorded development expenditure reflects two very strong forces. First, capital spending for the most part results in visible and often large physical facilities, which make their contribution to national development much more apparent than spending on current costs, much of which disappears in the form of wages and salaries. Political leaders seem to have a natural propensity to build buildings, not to mention monuments, for which cornerstones can be laid and on which plaques can be hung.

Second, many donors share that propensity. Certainly, most foreign aid in the form of grants and concessionary loans has been restricted to capital spending. While resisting requests to finance some types of capital spending, donors are certainly aware that many governments complain that while they can get foreign aid to build schools, health clinics and highways, very little foreign aid is available to help finance current operating costs. This has meant that governments have been encouraged to build physical capital because it is easily financed, but, as a consequence, have had to use much of their domestically generated revenues to finance the current costs of operating and maintaining these projects. The commitment to finance current costs is long-term in nature. If foreign aid declines as a proportion of government budgets, and for some countries in Africa such declines have been precipitous, the continuing commitment to finance current costs necessitates sharp reductions in capital spending or an even sharper deterioration in the quality of social, economic and infrastructural services.

Excessive costs and inefficiencies

The difficult and related choices between quantity and quality of social services and between capital and current expenditure can not be allowed to disguise the pervasive problem of excessive costs and inefficiencies. These have arisen in many ways, but we will focus on the dominance of the public sector, economic management, parastatals, foreign aid and corruption.

The dominating role of governments

The transfer of power from colonial to African governments was a visible, indeed an electrifying, event. The private sector, however, continued much as it had under colonialism until steps were taken by governments to open up markets to Africans and to establish settlement schemes for African farmers. In every case, however, the initiating force was the government, the public sector. The apparent need for the public sector to direct, modify and control private sector activities was reinforced in several ways. First, many of the most able, well educated and talented Africans became political leaders and civil servants in the new governments. The confidence of these elites in their own abilities was abetted by their suspicion of the many non-African managers and technicians who continued to dominate private sector activities and of those few Africans who moved into prominent positions on the grounds that they were mere figureheads. Second, support for an aggressive public sector was readily forthcoming from those foreign nations that favoured communism or socialism as means for organising economic activity. Finally, most bilateral and multilateral donors who rushed to rescue Africa from underdevelopment preferred to deal with governments, and viewed planning within governments as essential for identifying projects and programmes that might qualify for concessional financing.

The dominance of the public sector over the private sector had its parallel in the commanding role central governments played with respect to their local authority counterparts. Following independence, local authorities and municipalities were, for the most part, poorly staffed and financed, and focused, as part of their colonial inheritance, on the maintenance of law and order rather than on economic development, the new priority. For these reasons, the few early efforts at devolution were generally quickly reversed. As things have developed in Africa, most local authorities have been given limited responsibilities and inadequate revenue bases, making them irresponsibly dependent on deficit grants from the centre. Central governments are reluctant to decentralise expenditures and increase access to self-generated revenues in the face of visible inefficiencies and corrupt practices at local and municipal levels.

Economic management

It is easy to be critical of economic management in Africa, and for most countries it is appropriate to be so. It is necessary, however, to distinguish between stated policies and observed practice, between published plans and revealed preference. We shall not dwell on this distinction, however, because our concern lies with emerging realities, not distant visions.

The mismanagement of which so many governments in Africa have been accused runs the gamut from poorly designed policies to inefficiencies in implementation. Criticisms of policy range from the early reluctance to put in place appropriate family planning guidelines to the excessive reliance on import substitution as the dominant force for economic development.

Import substitution seemed an easy and quick road to self-sufficiency and hence to development. Having attained political independence, the attraction of import substitution as a means of pursuing economic independence was, for all practical purposes, irresistible, It has, in fact, taken decades for most African nations, and many of their economic advisers, to learn that self-sufficiency and isolation did not automatically result in food security and economic growth. Instead they can mean high and rising prices and economic stagnation.

The goal of protecting local, often thought to be infant, industries led many governments to promote and maintain overvalued currencies, high tariffs and licensing and quota schemes that graduated into major sources of corruption. While these techniques did protect local industries and their inefficiencies from foreign competition, they also meant higher prices for consumers and for producers who required the goods and services of protected industries as intermediate inputs.

Protecting inefficiency has stifled economic growth, widened income differentials, limited exports to primary products, and raised costs and prices. Moreover, the practice has generated strong forces for maintaining and, indeed, fostering import substitution. These forces include labour unions that choose to protect those already in employment rather than gamble that export promotion might create more and perhaps higher paying jobs; those who benefit from the rationing process that necessarily accompanies quantitative restrictions; the many business firms that might not survive in a more competitive environment; and governments that have become accustomed to depending on revenues from import duties and licensing fees. These powerful lobbies make fundamental change a very difficult proposition.

With rapid population growth and disappointing economic development, hopes of achieving full employment were dashed almost universally throughout Africa. Some countries attempted to alleviate widespread unemployment by creating make-work jobs in the civil service only to discover that inefficiency became the norm and productivity fell to alarmingly low levels. Moreover, once shoddy work habits became ingrained, reversing course was made much more difficult. Some governments resorted to coercion in order to create jobs. In Kenya, for example, on several occasions the government required all public and private employers to increase employment by 10 per cent. The well documented outcome has been that public sector employment tended to be maintained, but in the private sector excessive employment in one year was quickly offset in the following year as employment in that sector returned to its normal trend line, presumably reflecting marginal productivity in the sector. While governments exhibited some concern for unemployment, many at the same time adopted minimum wage legislation in order to ensure that those in employment could be assured of a minimum standard of living. In the event, such legislation seems to have had the effect of reducing job opportunities in the formal sector and has had little effect on the standard of living of those employed in small-scale agriculture and the informal sector. Hence, the numbers unemployed appear to have increased and the minimum wage has not affected any of them favourably.

Parastatals

The idea that parastatals would prove to be a way station to African-owned and managed private enterprises has been misguided. Instead, parastatals have become a prominent and disillusioning feature of the economic landscape, and divestiture is proving to be an extremely difficult and sensitive challenge. Certainly public enterprises have turned out to be a greater public sector responsibility than was originally envisaged, and the public sector has been reluctant to give their parastatals the degree of independence that they needed to have a chance at success.

Explicit evidence in many countries in Africa reveals that very few parastatals have earned a positive return on the very substantial investments made in them, and the sector as a whole probably has a cumulative record of negative earnings. Moreover, many parastatals have either been exempt from income taxes or have succeeded in avoiding them. Finally, in those industrial sectors where parastatals and private enterprises have competed, such as textiles and food processing, the private sector typically has outperformed its state-owned competition.

Many parastatals were saddled with heavy debts incurred from the outset, often for outmoded and/or overpriced technologies, that limited their potential for years to come. Some parastatals were established in industries or at locations that gave them no chance at success. The boards of most public enterprises have become entangled between representing government interests and promoting the efficiency and profitability of their enterprises. As a consequence, many parastatals have been required to provide some services below cost and to relieve national unemployment problems by taking on redundant employees. In addition, parastatals have often had their management teams packed with political appointees having little knowledge of the business under their control and little concern for efficiency and profitability.

These external pressures have restricted the freedom of management to function effectively, have encouraged management to seek government aid to overcome any problems that might arise, and have retarded rather than stimulated the development of entrepreneurial talent. Africa's experience with parastatals has demonstrated that most so-called infant industries never mature, and government protection and intervention breeds inefficiency.

Foreign aid

The expectation that foreign aid, together with direct private sector investment, would supply the missing ingredient – capital – needed to set African nations on a sustainable development path is another vision that has not materialized. Shortages of complementary resources, particularly of well educated and motivated human capital, even when supplemented with technical assistance and modern and appropriate technologies, have demonstrated that capital has not been the only missing ingredient. But even the provision of capital on concessionary terms has not meant easy access to it as an effective factor of production.

The negotiation of foreign aid turned out to require a lot of talent on both sides of the table. While donors had talent to spare, newly independent African governments had to divert very scarce talent from the formulation and implementation of development policies to the task of negotiation, and later to the tasks of monitoring, reporting and accounting for foreign aid. For the most part, donors insisted on dealing directly with governmental agencies, posing additional problems of co-ordination, duplication and the danger that foreign aid would overpower absorptive capacity. Budgets became difficult to construct, expenditures became difficult to control, and deficits began to exceed expectations.

Problems arose from both sides of the table. While some aid came in the form of grants, much of it came in the form of loans requiring amortisation. The bulk of reported foreign aid can be treated as commercial lending with only the present value of interest foregone (reflecting concessional interest rates) taking the form of grants. Moreover, most large bilateral donors quickly learned that foreign aid could be used to promote exports to the developing nations receiving aid. So-called aid was often used to finance imports of defence equipment, materials for infrastructure, transport equipment, machinery and factories from high cost sources with implicit commitments to finance future high cost replacements on commercial terms. Tied aid became a typical condition of bilateral donors.

In principle, funds borrowed from external or domestic sources on commercial or concessionary terms should be used in ways that enable borrowers to repay the loans with interest on schedule. World Bank data reveal, however, that total external debt of counties in Sub-Saharan Africa relative to nominal gross domestic product rose from 19.7 per cent in 1980 to 70.7 per cent in 1994. Perhaps more compelling, the ratio of scheduled debt service in Sub-Saharan Africa to exports of goods and services was 48 per cent in 1994, while the debt service ratio using debt service actually paid stood at 18 per cent, the difference being accounted for by debt forgiveness and arrears.

These data suggest, if they do not prove conclusively, that significant amounts of foreign aid have been used in unproductive ways. First, substantial foreign aid has been lent directly to, or onlent by governments to, parastatal organizations, whose inefficiencies we have noted above. Second, much of it has been allocated to the provision of infrastructure, such as power plants, water and sewerage systems, paved highways and telecommunication facilities, built at unnecessarily high cost, to inappropriate scales or standards, or in costly locations. Third, many funds that have apparently been used wisely have freed other government revenues for allocation to monument building and unproductive projects. To the extent that foreign aid has contributed to the higher cost of infrastructure and parastatal services, it has also served to reduce the international and domestic competitiveness of local industries who must pay higher prices for services that are essential to them. At best, bilateral foreign aid, as it has in fact been administered, must be scored as a mixed blessing. Even food aid, while serving the needs of the poor and the famine stricken, has sometimes discouraged domestic farmers from producing food because of the depressing effect food aid can have on farm prices.

Corruption

Corruption is widely considered to be an important contributing factor to the progressive impoverishment that has characterized Africa in the last two decades. Moreover, corruption in Africa is a much more serious and costly issue than elsewhere in the world if it is viewed in relation to the total incomes being generated in Africa and elsewhere. Corruption in Africa is pervasive, extends to both public and private sectors, has substantial direct and indirect costs that inhibit development and limit competitiveness, and makes both bilateral donors and private foreign investors reluctant to participate in development opportunities in Africa.

Corruption has many forms, ranging from petty types to malversation, the violation of positions of trust. In most forms, corruption involves two or more parties. Hence, in transactions involving external parties, such as private foreign investment or foreign aid, a guilty party in Africa will usually be matched with a guilty party abroad. But guilt is a legal matter, a matter of law enforcement. For the economist, it is the cost of corruption that is significant.

The direct costs of corruption can be measured, if the facts can be uncovered, by the bribe a businessman pays for an import license, to exclude a competitor from the competition, or to win a contract, or by the kickback a politician or civil servant demands for awarding a contract or providing another service. But the direct costs of corruption, large as they are alleged to be, are probably dwarfed by the indirect economic costs that corruption inflicts on African economies. It is in this context that corruption in Africa is more costly than elsewhere in the world simply because it raises the costs of production and distribution in Africa by a much larger percentage.

If the costs of infrastructure services – power, water, highways and telecommunications – are higher by 10 per cent because of corruption, the costs of firms using these services will be higher by a fraction of that percentage that is determined by the ratio of those costs to the firm's total costs. If the firm uses inputs from other firms that are affected by higher infrastructure costs, it will suffer even larger cost disincentives. Input costs of business firms may also be affected if corruption eliminates competition, enabling a supplying firm to charge higher prices. Direct costs aside, these indirect costs can destroy a country's export promotion programme, especially if these cost effects are greater in Africa than they are for companies that are competing from other locations.

There are ongoing efforts to curb corruption in both the public and private sectors in Africa. These will have to be considerably strengthened if Africa is to compete successfully in world markets on a scale that will truly enhance development.

Regional co-operation

It is widely understood that most national markets in Africa are too small to support those industries that require large scale to be efficient. There have been, therefore, many efforts to promote regional co-operation in Africa, but most of them have failed largely because governments have been unable to agree on the issue of industrial location. It is a sad commentary that governments have been unable to recognize that industrial location is not a political matter, but an economic one on which the private sector should be consulted. It is business firms that must decide where their activities can be most economically conducted within the conditions and policies established by governments or regional authorities. Until governments are prepared to grant business enterprises the freedom to choose their locations and technologies, it is unlikely that efforts to promote regional co-operation in Africa will be successful.

3.   Accelerating development in Africa

Accelerating development in Africa has not been and will not be a simple task. Success in this endeavour will require sound development strategies, political commitment, and a softening of resistance to change by entrenched elites and influential organizations. We attempt, in this section, to indicate the magnitude of the task, its dimensions, and the essential ingredients of needed economic reform in Africa. While many will not agree with us on some specific issues, we hope that the positions we take will stimulate constructive discussion. If reforms are more readily embraced and implemented in times of stress, hardship and adversity, the time is now ripe for extensive reform in Africa.

The structure of reform

Stabilization and structural adjustment, as commonly understood, are at best partial responses to the economic reforms now required in Africa. The early focus of the International Monetary Fund on stabilizing exchange rates and money supply, on establishing positive real rates of interest, and on achieving smaller budget deficits identified monetary and fiscal problems and related reforms, but was heavily criticized for its narrow boundaries and short time frame. The World Bank's approach to structural adjustment centred on its support of the IMF prescriptions, but added to these adjustments intended to liberate the major economic sectors from the heavy hand of government. The criticisms levelled at the stabilization and structural adjustment programmes advocated by these two international institutions have focused on the short-term consequences for people and families of the prescriptions being offered, on their failure to address social dimensions and on the inability of governments to achieve specific targets and to implement complex policies and programmes.

There are clearly some underlying economic issues that also must be addressed, including the perceived conflict between growth and equity, the need to enhance productivity, the failure of economies to draw idle resources into productive pursuits, and the overly modest priority given by governments to the expansion of market size and the freer movement of labour and capital across national boundaries. Moreover, while economic policies matter, and matter a great deal, so too does overcoming resistance to change, improving the institutional base, and developing entrepreneurial and management skills.

Human development and family welfare must also have a place in economic reform. Perceived balances between demands for quality and quantity in education and health care must be re-examined; trade-offs between higher and lower levels of education and between curative and preventive health care must also be revisited; the sharing of costs between beneficiaries and providers, between local and central governments, and between the public and private sectors must be reconsidered; and the powerful role of elites and political lobbies in diverting subsidies in their own favour must be more openly exposed to public scrutiny.

The prescriptions of the IMF and the World Bank are necessary conditions for effective economic reform, but they are not sufficient. Newly opened markets will not be efficient if the institutional base on which these markets must rest is not relevant and well developed. Efficient markets require asset titles, physical and legal access to them, cultural acceptance, and other types of institutional accommodation that require time to create or develop as the case may be.

Economic reform must also embrace the social sectors and policies that address human development and family welfare. Without this dimension, there is a serious risk that structural adjustment of the financial and economic sectors alone will fail in the face of social resistance. The greater breadth suggested by this approach must be accompanied by greater depth. Manipulating exchange rates without addressing the underlying problem of low productivity will not accelerate genuine development in Africa. Introducing and maintaining positive real interest rates and reducing budget deficits while neglecting the basic problem of employing idle resources may excite antagonism rather than enthusiasm. Income distribution and poverty are not issues that can be safely ignored in any comprehensive economic reform programme.

African economic reform in a global context

Some of the features of economic reform in Africa must be addressed in a global context if the nature of the required reforms is to be fully appreciated. These features include population, the role of government relative to the private sector, international trade, and foreign aid. We discuss each in turn.

Population

The human race claims to be the most intelligent species on the face of the earth. If that is so, the human race has a responsibility to ensure reasonable access to resources by all species, to allow fair competition among species so that the fittest survive, to conserve resources and preserve the environment for future generations, to bank genes of plants and animals for possible future use, and to view the planet as a holistic system involving all species and resources. This broad planetary responsibility has not always been given a high priority by the human race, if we are to judge by the ways in which the race has chosen to apply its intelligence.

First, as all economists know, the objective of economic policies is to maximize the welfare of the human population, or a national segment of it. Presumably, this may be done without considering the impact of these policies on other species unless their welfare has a direct or indirect, current or future relevance to the welfare of the human race. Most discussions of environmental conservation also place the human race at the centre of the environmental universe.

Second, many of our intellectual resources have been allocated to the task of promoting or protecting the growth of the human population, often at the expense of the quality of human life and the survival of other species. Predicting, preventing and recovering from natural disasters is directed largely to the human population. Medical research directed at prolonging life, reducing infant mortality and improving fertility has had the effect of increasing population size. Moreover, many religions have actively argued against family planning, and particularly against some methods of controlling family size such as abortion, RU486 and the pill. These and other groups take sharp issue with those who contend that intelligence should be directed toward reducing the rate of human population growth. Finally, competition among tribes, nations, religions and ethnic groups often rests on which of the competitors can increase its population most rapidly.

The self-centred nature of the uses to which human intelligence has been directed is reflected in choices made amongst the human population itself. Research has commonly been directed to the needs of those who can pay for the results, the rich, rather than to the broader needs of the race as a whole; much more research has been focused on prolonging life than on improving its quality; and the care of the aged, who are no longer productive, has demanded far more attention than has been given to ensuring that infants, whose productivity lies ahead of them, get a healthy mental and physical start in life.

If the human race has been negligent in applying its intelligence to the task of achieving global symmetry, some of the consequences of that failure are beginning to force their presence upon us. Rising population densities are contributing to the growing social, tribal, ethnic and religious tensions and the conflicts to which these give rise. It now seems clear that those who predicted that such problems would arise as a result of rapid population growth were not given a fair hearing. Perhaps the time has now come to ask the United Nations, our umbrella global institution, to set population growth targets that are intended not only to stabilize population growth but to bring population size down to a level that is more symmetrical with other species with whom we must share the planet and its resources.

We also reject the argument that the relationship between population growth and the economic welfare of families remains unsettled. Rapid population growth in Africa has contributed to the pervasive poverty that is common throughout the continent and has served to reduce the otherwise attainable rates of growth in per capita incomes. People and families, and other species as well, would be better off today if the human population had grown more slowly in the past. The challenge for the future is to alleviate the asymmetry that misdirected intelligence has created for us in the past. Specifically, in Africa, we need strong, effective family planning programmes supported by educational programmes and well-publicized political will.

The role of the public sector

Governments all over the world are reassessing their roles, their functions and, indeed, their *raison d'être*. They are facing the twin problems of growing globaliza-tion, on the one hand, and the threats of fragmentation that social tensions are generating on the other. The collapse of communism and the difficult adjustment to freer markets that many countries have initiated are creating even more polit-ical and economic uncertainty. Africa is not alone in this turbulent world.

Globalization, especially in the business world, was proceeding at a rapid pace even before the collapse of communism. Since then, access to larger numbers of freer markets has spurred the movement toward corporate globalization. This trend is shrinking the role of national governments because national efforts to control and regulate business activities have become significantly less effective. Many businesses can move to new locations overnight, and the global reach of others makes any national activity a minor part of their total operations. More-over, the ease with which funds can now be moved around the world means that domestic saving is being transformed into global saving, and attracting foreign direct and portfolio investment is also becoming a global exercise. The scope for national public policies in these areas is rapidly diminishing. Clinging to tight national controls in these circumstances can only contribute to isolation and slower domestic economic growth.

The weakening of national controls and regulatory authority over corporate business activities does not mean that the need for control and supervision is diminishing. Rather, it means that the locus for control and regulation must change. If nations can no longer exercise effective control over corporate activi-ties, it seems logical that the United Nations, our only truly international author-ity, should assume a more supervisory role. This will require an expansion of its present terms of reference and an acknowledgement by its member nations that they are no longer able to regulate global business activities when their authorities are limited by national boundaries.

Most national boundaries in Africa reflect expedient agreements between com-peting colonial powers and this has meant that these national boundaries are fragile at best. Some political analysts would suggest that they should be redrawn to reflect tribal groupings in a more reasonable way. Social tensions suggest, however, that the more potent danger may be further fragmentation, the creation of even smaller states so that each tribe or religious group can have its own compound.

It is, however, the move towards freer markets, coupled with globalization in the business world, that is causing governments to review their roles in economic affairs. Knowing how pendulums swing, there is a danger that, as greater freedom is given to the private sector, the need to prevent abuses of freedom and to protect consumers and the environment from those abuses may be neglected.

International trade

As developing countries in Africa open up their economies and put greater emphasis on promoting exports, economic growth in those countries will depend increasingly on gaining freer access to international markets. This will mean, however, that domestic growth will necessarily be more closely related to growth in international trade. If economic growth worldwide diminishes, efforts to grow more rapidly in Africa may face severe handicaps. African nations will fare better in a setting of rapidly growing international markets.

The current trend towards the formation of larger trading blocs may not augur well for the freer access to international markets that African nations will need. The trend is well established, if one is to judge from the strong support being given to the formation of such trading blocs as the North American Free Trade Association, the European Union, the Latin American Free Trade Association and the ASEAN Free Trade Area. Freer trade within these emerging trading blocs may not result in freer access to trading bloc markets for countries in Africa. Moreover, there is little promise that Africa itself will soon form a trading bloc that might be able to bargain on stronger terms with these other larger and more dominant blocs.

The World Trade Organization promises freer trade internationally, and its success should produce a setting in which international trade can grow more rapidly. But Africa itself has contributed little to the thinking that has produced the WTO and has been consulted infrequently during the negotiations that resulted in the WTO. Enhancing Africa's voice in global affairs must be given a higher priority, not only on the global stage but in Africa itself.

Foreign aid

The first thing that should be done with foreign aid is to measure it properly so that recipients of that aid and taxpayers in the countries that are financing it, directly or indirectly, understand the true value of the aid that is being given and received. Three things need to be done. First, so-called aid that is really financial support for defence and military expenditures should be eliminated from the aid figures that are compiled and published. Aid should be defined as assistance directed to development only. Second, concessional aid given in the form of loans should be separated into its loan element (using a commercial rate of interest) and its grant element. Only the latter should be reported as aid. Third, grant aid given in the form of commodities should be valued at international market prices, not at market prices in the donor country. Rice given by Japan, for example, takes on very different values depending on the price chosen for valuation.

The second characteristic of foreign aid that should be addressed is those forms of conditionality that restrict the recipient country's freedom to buy from low-cost, competitive sources. Genuine aid should allow, indeed insist upon, the use of free competitive bidding in the expenditure of aid funds.

Finally, the cumbersome procedures that now characterize the procurement, collection and monitoring of foreign aid need to be streamlined and standardized. Insufficient attention has been paid in the past to the substantial costs borne by recipient nations through the diversion of their scarce talent to these tasks. Development planning, financial prudence, and project implementation have all suffered as a result.

Much of the talent diverted to the procurement and management of foreign aid might have been more usefully directed to export promotion and the expansion of international trade, which, in retrospect, should have been given a much higher priority by both donors and recipient countries. If that lesson has been learned, Africa may be able to accelerate its development in the future. There is a legitimate and much needed place for genuine foreign aid, but its management should not be allowed to displace the rightful priority of trade.

Growth and equity: compatible or contradictory?

Economic growth, as pursued by many developing nations in Africa, has widened income disparities and left many families in abject poverty. Many argue that pursuing economic growth as an objective will necessarily affect equity adversely. Others, like ourselves, feel that economic growth, properly defined and appropriately pursued, should also alleviate poverty and yield a reasonable degree of equity.

The measurement of gross domestic product and its components leaves much to be desired. It includes as positive production of goods and services many items, such as private security arrangements, that reflect economic deterioration, and fails to adequately take into account environmental considerations and value added in the so-called underground economy. The United Nations is taking the lead in remedying these and other measurement deficiencies, but in the meanwhile, economists have problems in the use of this measure of economic output and the rates of growth it reveals.

Wrong tracks

Efforts to promote growth in Africa since independence have suffered from over-simplification, poor guidance from donors and advisers, and, in many cases, being shunted by inappropriate policies onto the wrong tracks. Early ideas about the dual economy led governments to focus their attention on growing the so-called modern or monetary economy. The traditional sector would presumably grow as it was absorbed into the monetary sector. This simplification was accompanied by another – the idea that capital was the principal missing ingredient in the recipe for development.

Related efforts saw African nations giving high priority to import substitution and supporting policies such as high tariffs, over-valued exchange rates, and negative real interest rates. The heavy emphasis given to parastatals as a means of promoting import substitution and African ownership has also, in retrospect, turned out to be a strategy that has retarded rather than accelerated economic growth.

The emphasis on growth as an objective was failing to enhance living standards for many groups in the economy. This perception diverted the attention of many donors and policy makers from growth to the provision of basic needs. Unfortunately, this attempt to solve the problems of the very poor stressed the provision of subsidized services and other forms of transfer payments rather than the more fundamental issue of creating income-earning opportunities as a means of promoting both growth and equity. It is this approach to achieving growth and equity that we think will improve living standards for larger numbers of smaller families.

Enhancing the productivity of the labour force

Employing idle resources, especially labour, should enhance both economic growth and equity by increasing national output and distributing earned incomes more widely. This suggests that social productivity should be measured with respect to the entire labour force, not just with respect to those in employment. This has the interesting result that drawing someone into employment at very low, but positive, productivity will raise the average productivity of the labour force while it reduces the average productivity of those in employment.

From a policy point of view, a focus on the productivity of the labour force suggests that a much higher priority should be given to creating income-earning opportunities even at low levels of productivity than is given to protecting the incomes of those in employment through such devices as the minimum wage and collective bargaining. This approach also suggests that legitimate concerns about working conditions should not preclude children, the aged, the handicapped, and indeed the unemployed from entering low-productivity income-earning opportunities. The incomes earned may not cover subsistence but they do add to national output and reduce the need for transfer payments whether through the extended family or from other sources.

Access to credit

Drawing idle resources into production will also be facilitated if access to credit can be improved. In many countries in Africa, access to credit depends on title to land and other assets, and when title is ambiguous, credit is not available. Clear and unambiguous titles to property, titles that are not subject to political caprice, would enhance the flow of credit, provided that the right of creditors to foreclose is fully respected. The individual loss associated with bankruptcy should not be confused with a social loss. Foreclosure proceedings usually result in a transfer of assets from one owner to another within the economy. The economy as a whole still has access to those assets and they are probably in more productive hands after the transfer than they were before.

The limited participation of women in the development process can be traced in part to the difficulties they encounter in gaining access to credit. Many of these difficulties can be traced to laws and traditions that limit women's access to property titles whether through inheritance or otherwise. Eliminating discrimination of these kinds should enhance the participation of women in economic affairs and hence the productivity of the economy as a whole.

Efforts to involve the formal banking system in direct lending to small-scale enterprises have usually failed because the system is not geared to evaluate, monitor and collect loans to small-scale, often mobile enterprises. What is needed is an intermediary, a middle entity that knows the small-scale clientele and can also satisfy the formal banker's security concerns. The Grameen Bank in Bangladesh found such an intermediary in the organization of peer groups. While these may not be workable in other cultures, the search for alternative intermediaries, such as co-operatives, parent-teacher organizations, or respected community business people, should be widened and intensified.

The scale of economic activity

Allowing some members of the labour force to work at low-productivity jobs does not mean that such income-earning opportunities will automatically be available. Policies must support the creation of such opportunities and accord low-productivity jobs the respect they are due.

This means, among other things, a more even-handed approach to large- and small-scale economic activities and, in particular, a reduction in the past misplaced bias favouring large-scale activities. The formal sector bias may have led statisticians to underestimate the actual rate of economic growth where the informal sector is growing at a more rapid rate than the formal sector. More worrisome, however, is the likelihood that the bias has led to a misallocation of resources in favour of the formal sector when the marginal rate of return is much higher in the informal sector. As a result, growth would not have been maximized and income distribution would have been worse than it might have been.

This change in approach to small-scale entrepreneurs will not easily be accomplished. The larger firms are in positions of influence; they employ the elites; their unions protect established jobs and incomes; and governments cater to their interests. Micro-enterprises, like the poor themselves, must depend on the philanthropic outlook of those with greater lobbying clout.

There are, however, growing pressures favouring a more level playing field for small-scale economic activities. In particular, the movement toward greater democracy in Africa is giving the poor and the small-scale a greater say in government affairs. Secondly, multi-lateral and bi-lateral donors are giving significant support to the accession of democracy and to the need to bring small-scale enterprises into the development process in sustainable and environmentally responsible ways.

Divestiture

Escaping from the parastatal trap is proving difficult for most African nations, but the abysmal record of most public enterprises testifies to the need to divest. The reluctance of governments to let parastatals go reflects an unwillingness to admit failure, to recognize the losses that have been incurred, to accept the fact that prices that are well below historical costs, to give up control over prestigious jobs, and to allow foreign capital to compete for the ownership of the assets involved.

Selling off parastatals should not revolve around winners and losers, but rather around prospects for the future. The serious losers should be allowed to go bankrupt. If governments continue to bail out the serious losers, the losses will only mount and eventual disposition will prove to be even more costly. Winners should be sold if the private sector can achieve even better results. If some basic needs are being met at subsidised cost by the parastatal, similar subsidies can be channelled through the privatized corporation for the performance of similar functions.

The dynamic character of developing economies

Those developing countries that have found the strategies, the policies and the political will to grow rapidly are experiencing rapid and dynamic change. They also have legal systems that accommodate change, systems that have avoided excessive regulation and intervention, systems in which justice prevails over favouritism and is administered within a reasonable time frame. For many more African countries to achieve rapid economic growth, they will need to review their legal systems to ensure that they do not obstruct the dynamism that will characterize rapid and equitable development.

The legal system is not the only institution whose rigidity tends to obstruct change and dynamism. Trade unions, associations of manufacturers, retailers and wholesalers, and lobbies for farmers, doctors and civil servants all seek to improve their lot in life, usually by protecting the status quo. These lobbies seem to be unaware that improving their own welfare depends on sharing in everyone's prosperity. Even religions seem to do more to obstruct change than to facilitate it.

More open economies

It is now widely recognized that more open economies must be established in Africa if the task of accelerating development is to be completed. Large economies may survive under the cover of protectionism, but the smaller the economy, the more costly import substitution as a strategy for development will turn out to be.

Export promotion

The IMF and the World Bank seem to us to have the right prescription for dealing with this aspect of economic reform in Africa. It is necessary for the many small countries in Africa to abandon import substitution in favour of export promotion. This will entail the political will to eliminate overvalued exchange rates, protective tariffs, negative real interest rates, and the resistance of those with an entrenched interest in import substitution.

Foreign investment

Opening up domestic markets for goods and services to international competition should stem inflationary pressures, give consumers access to a wider choice of consumer goods at competitive prices, give workers an incentive to become more productive in order to earn higher incomes, and stimulate business firms to compete more effectively in international markets. But openness must be extended to the capital markets as well. If foreign direct and portfolio investment is to be attracted into the many small African markets, arbitrary restrictions on equity participation by foreigners must be eased and suspicion of foreign investment replaced by a more welcoming attitude.

Regional co-operation

Foreign sources of private capital would also find direct investment in Africa much more attractive if the domestic markets such investment might serve could be enlarged. This means that efforts to initiate and extend economic integration in Africa must be given the serious attention they deserve. Lip service and frag-mented efforts will not suffice. Governments must overcome temptations to tell foreign investors where they should locate, what they should produce, where they should buy their materials and components, who they should employ, what they should pay their workers, and where they should sell their goods and services. Governments must recognize that their comparative advantage in areas such as these is no better than their demonstrated inability to predict the demand for future labour skills through manpower planning.

Too often, discussions of regional integration have focused on administrative structures rather than on the removal of barriers to the movement of people, capital, goods and services. Governments have also been unduly concerned about the sharing of benefits. Which country should get which industry? Which country should supply the parts? By how much will employment increase in each country? How much will each country gain or lose in other dimensions of devel-opment? The concentration on such issues makes regional integration highly unlikely. If regional integration will stimulate growth throughout the region, all countries belonging to the region should benefit. The benefits of regional growth should be the focus of attention, not the competitive aspects of sharing a fixed and immediate return. Lowering tariff barriers and making them more uniform is the essential prescription.

Curbing corruption

The benefits of getting economic policies right with respect to openness will be relatively small unless specific, strong and successful efforts are made to curb corruption and renew infrastructure. Corruption raises the cost of production and reduces the international competitiveness of firms seeking to compete in the domestic market with imports or in international markets. This effect is especially true of corruption that increases the costs of infrastructure services, such as power, water and telecommunications. Firms in which these services account for a large proportion of total costs are especially hard hit. Moreover, relative costs can be badly distorted, with serious consequences in terms of misleading price signals and a bad allocation of resources.

Repairing infrastructure

The poor maintenance of infrastructure and the waste of resources this entails has similar consequences, and even the moral stigma may be similar if the poor maintenance represents poor management and outright neglect. High costs will inevitably be accompanied by a lot of down time so that both total output and productivity suffer. It is also quite likely that poor quality and erratic delivery of infrastructure services will affect small-scale enterprises more adversely than larger businesses simply because small firms are less able to provide for themselves substitute self-generated services through such means as generators, bore holes and mobile phones. On the other hand, shortages of services may benefit those who are accustomed to operate without them. Power shortages, for example, may benefit carpenters who work with mechanical tools and restrict the activities of those who rely on power equipment. These occasional benefits are probably out-weighed by the negative effects mentioned above for the small-scale sector as a whole.

Efficiency and equity in the social sectors

The globalization phenomenon, most evident in the corporate world, can also be found in the social sectors, especially in education and health. On the supply side, new technologies are changing the ways in which these services can be delivered. To the extent that these technologies (television and computers, for example, in education, and lasers and viewing equipment in medicine) are more expensive than the older technologies, developing countries are being put at a disadvantage with respect to more advanced countries. Moreover, given greater global mobility, the demand for education and health services is increasingly being spread around the globe, as those who can afford to do so seek quality education and health care wherever those services can be found.

Some difficult choices

Given limited resources, governments in Africa cannot continue to provide heav-ily subsidized education and health care to all those who apply and still expect to enhance the quality of the services being provided. Numerous studies have shown that the economic returns to investments in basic education and preventive health care exceed returns from investments in higher education and curative health care. Political forces continue to offer the largest subsidies to those least in need. Reallocating subsidies more favourably to basic education and preventive health care may occur as democracy begins to take root and the devolution of revenue and expenditure responsibility to the local authorities proceeds.

Greater efficiency in the delivery of education and health services must also be sought by focusing more sharply on essential services, using simpler but effective techniques, and sharing more responsibilities with junior staff. Basic education should seek to instil in students problem-solving skills and self-learning tech-niques that will assist them to continue learning after leaving the formal educa-tion system. Public health care should be devoted in larger measure to ensuring that infants and children develop fully their capacity to benefit from their later years of education and employment.

Increased efficiency should be matched by more equitable cost sharing. Private beneficiaries of education, in particular, should be expected to bear a larger share of the costs as higher levels are reached simply because their future incomes will benefit directly from the higher education they are receiving. Direct subsidies will need to be replaced increasingly with loan schemes for qualified students from poorer families.

Subsidies and family size

Subsidies that are intended to meet very specific individual or family needs may have unintended and adverse social effects, making for difficult policy choices. The effects of poor health care and malnutrition on the future productivity of children suggest that subsidizing better health care will benefit both the children and, in the longer term, society as a whole. But if subsidies for bearing and raising children stimulate parents to have larger families, the effect will be to raise the rate of population growth above the socially optimal rate of growth.

It can be argued that parents, on average, contemplating the full costs and expected benefits of having children will prefer the number of children that is both privately and socially optimal. If information and technologies for controlling family size are available to all parents, it can be assumed that the preferred family size would be realized in practice. If, however, the costs of bearing and raising children are heavily subsidized, the private perception of the net benefits of having another child will exceed the social net benefits which must take into account the full costs of producing larger families regardless of how those costs are shared. Hence, parents may choose to have larger families than social considerations would suggest.

This dilemma is not easily resolved. If subsidies to the young are in order, other means must be found to offset the built-in incentive to have larger families, if the socially optimum family size is an objective. Education is one such method; direct incentives, such as limited tax deductions and payments for vasectomies, are another; and quotas, with which China has experimented, are another. But determining the socially optimum family size is itself a difficult task. In particular, some estimates will always be needed of the present value of the future environmental costs stemming from a larger global population, the effects of these costs and overcrowding on the quality of human life, and the crowding-out effects on other species. The effects of future technological change on these costs must also be considered, but the hope, entertained by some, that such change can always fully compensate seems remote indeed.

The role of private facilities

One way of sharing the costs of education and health care is to encourage the provision of such services by the private sector. Private services will normally be provided only at full cost, but their availability reduces pressure on public facilities. Governments can subsidize services provided by the private sector to targeted groups if this approach is more cost-effective than relying on public facilities. Moreover, governments can stimulate self-help and other forms of charitable contributions by making them tax deductible.

Sustainable budgeting

Most governments in Africa have encountered great difficulties in controlling their budgets. Some of these difficulties reflect the misuse of borrowed funds and the consequent inability to manage debt service obligations, but some of the problems have arisen because of the volatility of foreign funding and the management problems this volatility has entailed. Poor planning and budgeting procedures have contributed to the mismatch between revenues and expenditures in many countries and, in particular, to continuing imbalances between development and recurrent expenditures.

Beyond project evaluation methodologies

Governments evaluate projects in much the same way as private corporations do. Projections of future revenues and expenditures are used to obtain a stream of net receipts whose discounted value can then be compared with the estimated cost of the project. For most government projects designed to produce essential public services, such as defence, internal security, education and health care, estimates of net benefits must be substituted for net receipts because the services being provided will either not be sold or will be sold at subsidized prices. It is probably precisely those services whose net benefits are most difficult to quantify that are the essential services that governments should provide.

But if expenditures on projects in primary education, basic health care, essential water supplies, and internal and external security cannot be seen to be easily recovered out of future net receipts derived from the operation of the projects, it becomes necessary to use alternative budgetary principles to construct government budgets. This is, of course, what governments do. They estimate future government revenues from all sources and seek to allocate them sensibly between development and recurrent expenditures.

Estimating future recurrent revenues

Leaving aside borrowing as a source of funds, the factors governments must consider in estimating future revenues are reasonably clear. The first requirement is to ensure that the revenues government collects and the real resources it diverts for its own use will be used by government in ways that yield at the margin higher returns than could be earned by them if left in the private sector. In this regard, government must be concerned with the disincentive effects of its taxation and subsidy policies, and seek to limit their distortionary impact on relative prices and the allocation of resources.

Governments must also be concerned with the effects of their revenue collection efforts on income distribution. The distribution of earned incomes, including wages, rents, dividends, interest and profits, is usually very unequal, reflecting differential advantages in access to material resources, education and talent. Providing basic needs and using progressive forms of taxation may reduce these income disparities, an effect that must be carefully considered in designing a tax system that is both effective and equitable.

Another factor affecting budgetary planning is the role governments must play in controlling recessions and inflation. While monetary policy plays a major role in stimulating or retarding private sector activity, fiscal policy must also play an active as well as a supporting role. The total demand for domestic goods and services emanates from both the public and private sectors. If total demand is excessive and inflation is threatening economic stability, fiscal policy can reduce demand by moderating government expenditures or raising tax collections in order to reduce private sector demand.

These many dimensions of fiscal policy make it a major instrument of a nation's development strategy. While the Ministry of Finance may be primarily concerned with revenues as a source of funds, the development impact of fiscal policy must engage the interest and attention of many other ministries, and indeed of Cabinet itself.

Because of these several considerations and the difficulties of deriving recurrent revenues by summing returns from development expenditures, projections of recurrent revenues are usually made on the basis of projections of gross domestic product, the revenue base. If development expenditures are allocated wisely and projects are efficiently implemented, they should be reflected in increases in GDP, but private sector investments are probably the major source of GDP growth. Hence, recurrent revenues of government may be substantially independent of the allocation of those revenues between development and recurrent expenditure. We make that assumption as we begin to examine how revenues should be allocated between development and recurrent costs in order to ensure that government budgets are sustainable in the long term.

Sustainable development shares in recurrent revenues

We assume initially no foreign grants, no foreign or domestic borrowing, no inflation and no extraordinary revenues from such things as asset sales. We consider initially two variables: r, the rate of growth of recurrent revenues, which is assumed to equal the rate of growth in GDP, and c, the ratio of the increase in recurrent expenditure required to operate, maintain and manage the projects financed by development expenditure. The ratio c is assumed to be constant over time, although it is an average of ratios that can differ widely from project to project. The question we now seek to answer is, 'What proportion of recurrent revenues can safely be allocated to development expenditure without jeopardizing the proper future maintenance and operation of government's development projects?'

Given values for r and c, it can be shown that in equilibrium the proportion of recurrent revenue allocated to development expenditure should equal $[r/(r+c)]$.[2] Table 10.1 indicates the sustainable share of revenues that can be devoted to development expenditure for a range of values for both r and c.

If an annual increase of 20 units is required in recurrent expenditure for each 100 units spent on development expenditure, and recurrent revenues are growing at 5.0 per cent per annum, 20.0 per cent of recurrent revenues can safely and sustainably be allocated to the development budget. If the development budget absorbs a larger share of recurrent revenues, development projects cannot be

Table 10.1 Sustainable shares of recurrent revenues allocable to development expenditure

c / r	0.01	0.05	0.10	0.15	0.20	0.25	0.30	0.35
0.01	0.500	0.167	0.091	0.063	0.048	0.038	0.032	0.028
0.02	0.667	0.286	0.167	0.118	0.091	0.074	0.063	0.054
0.03	0.750	0.375	0.231	0.167	0.130	0.107	0.091	0.079
0.04	0.800	0.444	0.286	0.211	0.167	0.138	0.118	0.103
0.05	0.833	0.500	0.333	0.250	0.200	0.167	0.143	0.125
0.06	0.857	0.545	0.375	0.286	0.231	0.194	0.167	0.146
0.07	0.875	0.583	0.412	0.318	0.259	0.219	0.189	0.167
0.08	0.889	0.615	0.444	0.348	0.286	0.242	0.211	0.186
0.09	0.900	0.643	0.474	0.375	0.310	0.265	0.231	0.205
0.10	0.909	0.667	0.500	0.400	0.333	0.286	0.250	0.222

adequately operated, maintained and managed. The budget is not sustainable. If the composition of development expenditure shifts toward projects having higher recurrent cost implications, the share of recurrent revenues that can be safely allocated to development must decline.

Managing supplementary revenues

Recurrent revenues can be supplemented by revenues from other sources, such as commercial borrowing, foreign aid, and asset sales. It is usual to reserve such sources of funds for development expenditure on the grounds that, properly invested, these should enhance the growth of the economy and, at a later date, recurrent revenues. In our scenario, such sources of funds, if expected to continue indefinitely, can be treated as a simple addition to recurrent revenues. Problems arise, however, if such sources of funds dry up at some point.

Infusions of funds that turn out to be temporary in nature enable governments to increase development expenditure and to finance the consequent increase in recurrent costs by diverting a larger share of recurrent revenues to that portion of the budget. When these special sources of funds diminish, however, the arithmetic says that the full brunt of the decline must be absorbed in the development budget. But reducing the development budget quickly is not easily done because of work in progress and other outstanding commitments. Hence, the recurrent budget is usually expected to share in the necessary reduction in total expenditure. The underfunding of required repair, maintenance and operating costs results in failed infrastructure and poorer quality of the services delivered. The budget process must seek to avoid these consequences if budgeting is to remain sustainable. Fluctuations in revenues from special sources must be reflected in similar fluctuations in development expenditures if essential commitments to the recurrent budget are to be honoured. Donors can assist with this task by modifying their aid commitments more slowly as the need to do so arises.

Financing local authority responsibilities

A related problem plaguing many African nations is the division of revenue and expenditure responsibilities between central and local governments. Devolution is currently given much support on the grounds that it makes government more responsible to the local people being served. But devolution without accountability may simply transfer waste and corruption from the centre to the local areas. Similarly, transferring responsibilities for such things as primary education, basic health care and local road maintenance to local authorities without giving them self-generated sources of revenues may simply lead to waste and continuing grants from the centre to finance growing local deficits. Grant formulas may need to be devised that give local authorities grant commitments that can be used at local levels as a basis for responsible planning and expenditure control.

Enhancing Africa's voice in global affairs

Many in Africa feel that structural adjustment has been imposed on them by external forces, and that its relatively narrow definition has limited the ability of many nations to define for themselves a broader and more equitable approach to economic reform. Beyond this, both politicians and the intellectual community in Africa feel that Africa's voice in global affairs has been muted in delivery and ignored in reception. There is clearly a need on the African side to develop a sounder basis for African positions on global matters and to cultivate a stronger and more influential delivery of the African message.

More effective research directed to accelerating development in Africa seems to be needed. Intellectual resources are relatively thin in Africa and the national demands on these resources are already stretching them to the limit. Some reorganization of those resources may be in order if some of the pressing needs for a more continental approach to development research are to be met. The research gaps that need to be addressed are (1) a greater use of comparative studies so that nations can benefit on a larger scale from the experiences of others, (2) more attention to sub-regional development considerations, and (3) a deeper and more comprehensive view of the development opportunities that lie ahead for the continent as a whole.

Comparative studies of such issues as population management, means for curbing corruption, decentralization, employment policies, different facets of economic reform, and privatization should be of direct benefit to those countries that participate in the studies and of indirect benefit to those to whom results and recommendations are disseminated. The network of national institutes developed with aid from the African Capacity Building Foundation is a nucleus through which comparative studies could be mounted.

Sub-regional studies may be more difficult to arrange. First, in many cases, such as studies of river basins and lake regions, there are no authorities to make policy decisions on the basis of research recommendations. Such recommendations would have to go to national authorities who may well be at a loss as to how to proceed. Second, requests for research on such issues are unlikely to emanate from national authorities, and if they are made they may very well be ignored. Third, the several organizations established to promote economic integration have not excited much confidence in either their sincerity or their ability to take binding decisions. Despite these difficulties, constructive research on sub-regional problems should contribute positively to improving economic co-operation efforts among affected nations in Africa.

Research on continental issues would feed directly into the construction of sounder African positions on such matters as international trade, the law of the seas, global warming, cross-border pollution, and the sharing of common resources. The lack of an African position on the formation of the World Trade Organization has made it abundantly clear that African views were neither well formulated nor effectively presented.

Identifying the need for research along the lines discussed above falls far short of recommending the institutional arrangements that might be needed to define more specifically the priority topics for research and the means by which such research might be managed and conducted. The objective seems to us worth pursuing.

African nations must also be concerned about their representation in organizations such as the World Bank, the International Monetary Fund, and the World Trade Organization. The first two are not only sources of finance. They also play leading roles in shaping public opinion and political positions on development matters affecting African nations. The WTO is the main forum for the discussion and resolution of issues affecting Africa's access to international markets. Improving Africa's representation in these bodies is an obvious way in which Africa's voice in global affairs can be strengthened. But an effective voice requires a sound message to deliver. Such a message depends on basic research and the co-ordination efforts of African institutions, such as the Organization of African Unity and the United Nations Economic Commission for Africa.

4. Conclusion

Pursuing economic reform in Africa along the lines discussed in this essay will not be an easy task. The two essential ingredients are a clear recognition that broad and substantive reform is necessary and the political will to design a consistent development path and to stay the course. There will be resistance from established elites with a vested interest in maintaining the status quo. Winning them over will be better than perpetuating their adversarial role.

There are, however, a number of factors that will contribute to the successful management of economic reform programmes. First, the intellectual resources available on the continent are light years ahead of the situation at independence. Harnessing these resources to produce policy-relevant research should assist governments to design effective and specific economic reform programmes. Implementing those programmes will also require talent and dedication. Skilled and committed manpower will need to be put in place, but the people are there.

Second, the labour force in Africa is now better trained and has embraced a more modern work ethic. Given opportunities to learn and gain experience, the people power in Africa can achieve improved productivity.

Third, many countries in Africa have already taken positive steps towards more sensible macro-economic policies and have moved forward with privatization and liberalization. Bringing budgets under firmer control still requires firmer resolution, but progress is being made.

Fourth, while infrastructure throughout Africa is in a bad state of repair, it can be rehabilitated. As governments relinquish more responsibilities to the private sector, they should be able to allocate more resources to that very substantial task, and should also be able to enlist greater participation by the private sector in providing and maintaining infrastructure services.

Finally, if many countries participate in successful economic reform programmes, the continent as a whole should grow more rapidly. There is little that is more stimulating to the growth of a national economy than to be located in a region that is taking off. Africa must strive to become such a region. Economic reform alone is not enough. Political leadership will be put to a stern test as it structures reform and exercises the political will to make it effective.

Notes

1 E. Edwards is Senior Policy Research Consultant with the Africa Office of the International Center for Economic Growth. W. Kinyua is General Manager of Ambank, Ltd. The views expressed in this essay, however, are solely those of the authors. They would like to acknowledge earlier discussions and correspondence with Philip Ndegwa, particularly on macro-economic policies, population management, sustainable budgeting, privatization and decentralizaion, and with Jay Salkin on the application of sustainable budgeting in Botswana. Helpful comments have also been received from Jean Edwards, Ryn Edwards, Akin Mabogunje, Courtney Nelson, and Frank Sutton.

2 In equilibrium, revenues and expenditures must grow at the same rate. Hence, $rR = rD + rC$, i.e., the increase in recurrent revenue must equal the increase in development expenditure plus the increase in recurrent expenditure. But we also know that the increase in recurrent expenditure, rC, must equal cD. Substituting cD for rC in the equation above and solving for D/R yields the formula given in the text.

11

Roads to Regionalism: Survival, Security and Efficiency

Reginald Herbold Green

> Is economic regionalism in Africa best analysed as a branch of applied international trade theory or as an extension of applied national development theory?
>
> Philip Ndegwa, 1985

1. Pan Africanism: Quicksilver constant

Pan Africanism, an approach that looks beyond national boundaries and seeks to identify common concerns and ways of acting to further them, has been an abiding strand in African discourse, mobilization, aspiration and – somewhat less frequently – performance for three-quarters of a century. There are three main themes within Pan Africanism: self-respect, self-determination and self-reliance. Despite the protean nature of Pan African thinking, writing, mobilizing and institutionalizing, these three objectives have remained constant.

Self-respect was, probably inevitably, the first theme to emerge among peoples colonized at home and discriminated against abroad. In its earliest stages, Pan Africanism was dominated by the people of the diaspora, who found it easier to organize, and for whom hurtful contact was more of a daily event than for people in much of colonial Africa.

Self-determination – a concept that initially encompassed participation in rule, then independence, and now also includes meaningful participation in the international system – has been seen as a condition necessary for self-respect. This has at times been a theme causing divisions within the Pan African movement: self-determination in North America and in Ghana could hardly be the same, and in polities such as South Africa distinctly different views emerged regarding whether a 'rainbow nation' was either possible or desirable.

Self-reliance did not normally mean autarky against but rather unity for, although the distinction has necessarily been blurred in the context of unity in the face of repressive (e.g., colonial) or aggressive (e.g., apartheid vis-à-vis Southern Africa) forces. The unity sought has ranged from the level of the community through national and sub-regional levels to the Sub-Saharan or continental African level. Increasingly, self-reliance has been perceived as being crucial to a form of self-determination consistent with self-respect and respect from others.

The enduring nature of the quest for regionalization in Sub-Saharan Africa (SSA) cannot be readily understood outside the prism of Pan Africanism. There is no real Asian or Middle Eastern (or Arab) or North American parallel, and the Pan Americanism of Bolivar and the late nineteenth-century Spanish American exile movements evaporated as a practical force within a decade or two of independence. The modern North American, Latin American, South-east Asian and – less clearly – Western European Regionalisms are much more driven by considerations of economic efficiency, although the origins of the post-World War II European Movement did include the same strands as Pan Africanism. That is perhaps not surprising, as this movement arose in a region devastated by repetitive wars, deeply shamed by its sudden relapse into poverty and external dependence and (not least because of the dire results of economic failure fuelled by economic efficiency-oriented nationalism in 1930s Germany and Italy) yearning for a more value-inspired set of goals than economic functionalism.

Without Pan Africanism, regionalism would have had far weaker political and popular roots in SSA. Common markets and joint railways have next to no 'political sex appeal' unless they are set within a broader and more humanly compelling frame. By the same token, without Pan Africanism some of the more foredoomed efforts to unite countries at one leap or to move to near instant creation of a common army would never have been contemplated, or these initiatives might have arisen later and more gradually out of a network of more functional initial relationships which would have given them greater chances of success.

2. Strands toward regionalism

Regionalism in Africa has had three key influences, however, only one of which is Pan Africanism. The other two are both external – one colonial and one post-colonial.

Because African colonies were usually small in terms of area and population as well as economically, colonial powers sought to build up sub-regional collaborative relationships. The most far-reaching were the Francophone Western and Equatorial African Federations which included a substantial merger of governance functions; the most economically significant were the Anglophone East and Central African Common Markets and associated institutions – although the latter was in a sense the result of dividing the previously unified territory of the British South Africa Company and adding the then Nyasaland labour reserve. South African attempts to achieve economic regionalism were somewhat different, based as they were on a sub-regional hegemonic thrust largely designed to strengthen South Africa's economic and political self determination vis-à-vis the UK, and lacking the underlying framework of common political suzerainty behind the British and French economic agreements.

It would be wrong to assume that the colonial regional arrangements were devoid of territorial tensions arising from perceived conflicts of interest. These were perhaps more easily resolved during the colonial period in the Francophone

Federations with their governor generals. In the Anglophone groupings, governors could, and frequently did, promote territorial interests almost as vehemently as their successor independent heads of state, although they could not use the ultimate threat to withdraw. Even in the Francophone case, the rapid withdrawal of the independent Côte d'Ivoire from most arrangements seen by it, in large part correctly, as overly favourable to Senegal and, less clearly, the attrition and collapse of the Mali Federation bear witness to the building of sub-surface tensions in the colonial period.

These colonial and South African arrangements or their ghosts have significantly influenced post-colonial regionalism, for better and for worse. In West Africa, the Anglophone groupings disintegrated soon after independence, but economic aspects of the Francophone alliances survived, and, because they had a functional reality, a history and external backing, they have been an impediment to creating and consolidating broader West Africa regionalism.[1] In Eastern and Southern Africa the impact has been more complex. The emotional and historic appeal of the East African idea, combined with trade and transport links, led first to radical reform of the old East African Common Market/Common Services Organization into an East African Community (EAC).[2] This subsequently fell victim to Idi Amin Dada's political regime and countries' pursuit of narrow self-interest. It was followed by a decade of repeated efforts to recreate a Kenya–Uganda–Tanzania unit.[3]

The problems of over-centralized administration in largely non-accountable hands and over-concentration of gains in the 'lead' economy in both EAC and Rhodesia/Nyasaland clearly influenced the patterns of decentralization and pervasive national involvement characteristic of SADCC/SADC.[4,5] The South African heritage's influence is clear. It encouraged the state bureaucracy and business to look toward the region and thus, perhaps ironically, complemented ANC's positive outlook arising from the days of its support by the Front Line States (of which SADCC was the *de facto* economic wing). To date this history has not resulted in a drive for hegemony by South Africa within SADC nor, therefore, to a reaction against it based on the highly unequal past South African Customs Union/Rand Monetary Union arrangements. It is fair to say that economic and political economic regionalism has been most operational (albeit often with limited success) in sub-regions with a colonial heritage of economic co-operation and common institutions, even if these have also had more problematic consequences. Mozambique, the apparent exception, is less an anomaly than it appears because of its economic history as 'a British colony under the Portuguese flag' and as a service auxiliary sector of the South African economy, although the dominant reason for the strength of its commitment to SADCC was rooted in the politics of survival.[6]

Thus the colonial inheritance contributed toward regionalism in Africa basically in a functional rather than a theoretical way. Economic analysis – beyond a rather vague attempt to identify sources of raw materials and markets and to limit urban subsidies – played little part in colonial administration or the intellectual rationalization of colonialism in Africa at least until its terminal years.[7]

The newer external strand contributing to African regionalism, emanating basic-ally from the perspectives of the EEC, as it then was, has a body of contextual theory, or at least ideology, that goes beyond functionalism. However, as adopted in Africa, post-colonial regionalism focused almost exclusively on the creation of common markets. The common industry thrust, itself in part a variant on the Iron and Steel Community predecessor to EEC, has waned with a near total record of practical lack of success. Various new sectors for regional initiatives, ranging from domestic enterprise involvement to ecology, have been added somewhat eclectic-ally from sources including the Andean Pact Treaty. But the result is rather like a Christmas tree with a common market trunk (except in PTA/COMESA and the surviving pre-independence Francophone groups, a near totally aspirational one), trimmed with a variety of other sectors as mid-air decorations (and these sectoral goals are usually no closer to being actually achieved than is a common market).

This focus on common markets in the narrow sense of elimination of fiscal – and less prominently currency – barriers to trade flows form the underlying intellectual basis of analysis behind most writing on the economics of African regionalism. Its base is the neo-classical argument that enlarging tariff-free areas is likely on balance to be a useful step toward global free trade because it reallocates resources to regionally more efficient industries, with regional trade-enhancing effects likely to outweigh trade diversion away from more efficient extra-regional sources. This argument is peculiarly inappropriate to Africa, at least in its original form, because structural change over time from new production, not reallocation within largely constant regional patterns over a brief period, was and is central to economic development. While many writers on African economic regionalism attempted to deal with this constraint, the focus on common marketing remained.

The notable exception to this characterization has been SADCC/SADC, which owes relatively little to borrowings from EEC, has had strong decentralized sectoral units from the start and has habitually viewed trade as a means to, and a con-sequence of economic regionalism rather that a primary end in itself. The reason for this may be that it has drawn very little on neo-classical trade theory and its conditional justification of regional common markets as way stations to global free trade. SADCC's goals, as the *de facto* economic arm of the Front Line States, did indeed include promoting unity for the sake of efficiency, but stressed even more survival in the face of apartheid South Africa's entrenched hegemony and aggress-ive onslaught on the region. As such, the dynamic political economic vision focused on production, transport, energy and knowledge to sustain survival polit-ically and militarily, and trade was seen as a means whose facilitation required positive (e.g., transport and production measures plus a habit of co-operation and exchange of knowledge) more than negative (tariff reduction) measures. This is a very different intellectual base than neo-classical trade theory and, ironically, one more in keeping with the initiation and evolution of EEC/EU.

Common Market centrism, combined with borrowings of form – if not neces-sarily substance – from the EEC/EU has created another problem. Common markets, for better or worse, limit state intervention to protect and to promote domestic sectors which are regionally weak, and also require de facto subsidization of sectors in other member states which are regionally strong but globally weak (because of high costs). That reality has a tendency to set the interests and requirements of the Common Market against those of member states, as perceived by the states.[8] From such a clash only one winner can emerge – a point graphically illustrated by two decades of failure to agree on initial tariff reductions in ECOWAS. Other sectors, including cost-reducing trade promotion via co-ordinated and improved transport and power sectors, offer more obvious net gains and, at least sometimes, create less conflict of interest. In the case of the EAC, the net gains were probably at least two thirds from joint services (ports, harbours, railways, posts and telecommunications and tax collection),[9] and it was these gains which held the community together over 1965–77 and whose erosion catalysed the community's collapse.

3. Politics and practice: regional rhetoric or regionalism?

It is indisputable that African regionalism is a field to which the comment 'When all is said and done more is said than done' applies. The rhetoric of regionalism is both less expensive and more politically profitable than the arduous, slow and setback-prone realities of building actual regionalism.

However, the fact that regionalist rhetoric, often reflecting the Pan African rather than the imported discourse, has remained pervasive, and that substantial resources have been put into trying to turn it into treaties, institutions and processes, is of itself significant. The Organization for African Unity (OAU), despite its deficiencies, has been influential, not least in averting substantial wars between members. The UN Economic Commission for Africa (ECA), at least in the past, was often the most influential of the UN's Regional Commissions within its own region. ECOWAS has – rather surprisingly given the abject failure of its customs duty reduction and clearing house efforts – remained of some significance and has begun to develop a regional security capacity. PTA/COMESA and SADCC/SADC are, in rather different ways, bodies with significance and at least some forward momentum.[10] South Africa has chosen to make sub-regional (and broader) African economic relationship development and conflict resolution its economic and international policy priorities, in the former case even at the expense of its relations with the EU.[11]

The repeated creation of new interstate bodies – frequently overlapping older ones – is a more problematic aspect of the Pan African dynamic toward regionalism. It is opposed by some analysts for two reasons: first, a minority argument would prefer a single stage advance to an all-encompassing continental economic (or economic and security) union, and a second, dominant argument perceives multiplicity of regional groupings as economically and politically inefficient.

The first objection to the multiplicity of regional bodies echoes the old Nkrumah–Nyerere division of the early 1960s. President Nkrumah believed that there was an urgent need to create common, continental economic and security institutions. He also contended that newly independent states with less vested national interests could make that leap soon after independence, but they could not necessarily do so later.

Mwalimu Nyerere did not necessarily disagree that rapid continentalization, including with regard to security forces, would be desirable. His objection concerned the means of implementing such an arrangement and was based on practicability. Facing the collapse of his efforts to secure the political and economic unification of East Africa (even at the expense of delaying Tanzanian independence), he did not believe that political unification was generally practicable for newly independent states. He also realized that in the absence of political union, military union was neither practicable nor desirable. Further, he saw a step-by-step approach that deepened existing sub-regional links and expanded core groupings (e.g., linking Kenya–Uganda–Tanzania to Zambia, Rwanda, Burundi, Ethiopia and Somalia in EAC seemed likely in 1969–71) as the only viable route toward economic integration which could lay the foundations for closer security and political co-operation and, less certainly, union.

The nature of the OAU and of subsequent practical focusing on sub-regional economic (and later security) co-ordination and integration demonstrate that Nyerere 'won' the debate or, more precisely, judged more accurately what was, and in the ensuing decades what would be, acceptable to many African states.

The argument that sees multiple regional groupings as inefficient has greater validity. Overlapping general purpose interstate bodies aspiring to economic union are a contradiction in terms, and, especially if more than one has some real vitality, can dissipate effort. However, the number of functioning, duplicative broad front bodies in SSA has not been as large as is often suggested. Many have retained a ghostly, inefficient profile long after their substantive death – e.g., the long-defunct Great Lakes Community (Rwanda–Burundi–Zaire) which may legally still exist but which has been non-operational for over a quarter of a century. Some other nominally broad front bodies, e.g., the Mano River Union of Liberia, Sierra Leone and later Guinea, never had any substantial resource allocations nor economic reality.

The two main cases of conflict, or less than beneficial competition, have been ECOWAS/UMOA and PTA (COMESA)/SADCC (SADC). In both instances there has been a case for a division of labour. The EEC for many years included a Benelux subgroup with substantially fuller integration than the community as a whole, and Belgium and Luxembourg operate a currency union. SADCC, because of its approach to trade as a consequence of, and a major validating means for, production, knowledge and security integration was quite prepared in principle to see PTA carry the ball on customs reduction and trade balance clearing arrangements. In the former case, Anglophone resentment at perceived French domination and Francophone suspicions of Nigerian motivations, and in the latter case rather clumsy statements and resultant personal and governmental animosities have prevented any such specialization and division of labour.

However, most interstate bodies, on examination, do not turn out to be broad front but are in fact highly specialized. Some focus on river basins – a few like those among Senegal, Mali and Mauritania with respect to the Senegal River Basin relatively effectively, and most, like the Kagera Basin Authority among Rwanda, Burundi, Tanzania and Uganda much less so. While it is true that SADC has chosen to group river basin concerns in one of its sectoral units, there is no overriding case for all communities to do likewise – the EU on the whole does not. Similar considerations apply to transport (e.g., the routes from Mombasa and Dar es Salaam to landlocked states and Zaire) and transport/production corridors (e.g., the Beira Corridor Authority and proposed Rand–Maputo Corridor). The East African examples are, nominally, integrated into COMESA, while the Southern African are formally independent of SADC but fall within its broad thematic approach and structures of co-ordination. Whether such bodies and smaller research and training ventures should be integrated into broad front communities is usually a marginal issue and one not closely related to their competence or cost efficiency (which are frequently low, but with a number of significant exceptions including the cases cited).

Regionalism has faced political problems for three reasons:

1   Conflicts of interest tend to be resolved in favour of immediate, pressing considerations.
2   Regionalism, whatever the rhetoric, has rarely been perceived as a short-term life or death or national/governmental survival issue.
3   External crises and external prescriptions for overcoming them have tended to be anti-regional in result, even if not necessarily in intent.

The most pressing problems usually receive attention first, especially under conditions of crisis management. Further, the degree to which a problem is perceived as pressing depends in part on there being an organized interest group (whether a large enterprise or a potential rioting mob) to make it so.

Regionalism rarely scores high on these scales. Domestic pressures usually far outweigh regional and, even when broadly popular, regionalism rarely has organized support groups either in politics, economics or even government structures. SADC's systematic attempts to build up regional and national enterprise links, achieve deeper and more frequent publicity than annual conference coverage, site sectoral units in each member state (within months of accession for Namibia, South Africa and Mauritius), involve large numbers of senior officials in sectoral meetings and workshops and encourage member states to create both overall and key ministry regional units demonstrates a clear concern with these issues, and, by the stark contrast to other groupings, how little they have been addressed.

SADCC until the 1990s demonstrates the second issue by being an exception. The hegemonic regionalism of South Africa, running consistently from Jan Smuts in the 1920s to J. B. Vorster in the 1970s, was seen as a threat to the self-determination and self-respect of independent Southern African states, especially as it had increasingly become a key instrument for the defence of apartheid and retaliation for even moderate moves to criticise or to disengage from South Africa. President Sir Seretse Khama of Botswana did see regional solidarity embedded in practical co-operation as vital to his country's freedom to develop on its own lines, and potentially crucial to the its survival.[12] That largely explains his and his successor's priority commitment to SADCC/SADC, even though, except in the long term, it could be at best of marginal positive economic significance to their country. The overriding concern with survival became more pronounced and general over 1981–90, when South Africa turned to a 'forward policy' of offensive action to make Southern Africa safe and profitable for apartheid.

External crises, like other pressing issues, tend to shorten the practicable forward perspective informing decisions and to focus attention on defending what exists. Neither shift is normally favourable to medium-term regional economic integration building. Again SADCC – whether by design, good fortune or both – was something of an exception. Southern Africa was in grave need of resources for transport and communications. SADCC therefore was directly relevant to problems which had to be faced immediately, offered at least some clear cost and technical input advantages with respect to them and was able to mobilise additional (at least for key transport projects) external resources that national ministries had failed to secure.

External advice, prescription and supporting finance in reaction to post-1979 economic crises has also been, on balance, anti-regionalist for several reasons:

1 Pressure to cut or to constrain expenditure tends to disfavour regionally oriented projects for the same reasons as do crises more generally.
2 The trend toward global free trade prescription and reaction to past, often highly inefficient, national protectionism has led to pressure to cut domestic tariffs radically, leaving much less margin for interim preferences than a more gradual, phased reduction of external tariffs subsequent to regional integration would have done.
3 Revenue concerns (while overridden by the trend toward global free ideology) have led to at least some proposals to raise preferential intraregional tariffs (especially in UMOA).
4 The World Bank and many bilaterals do not understand regionalism in any detail, while some African common market-focused regional bodies have few projects to put up for finance. This constraint applies least to multi-sectoral regional bodies planning and mobilizing in common but building and operating on a co-ordinated national basis – e.g., SADC and the Senegal Basin Authority.

4. Directions of discourse

The evolution of thought, discourse and, to a degree, action in political economic and broader integration has gone through three broad phases. The first, which took place over 1960–80, sought to Africanize and to develop the common market and an associated sector approach and was broadly within neo-classical theoretical constructs and EEC operational experience. The second, from 1980 to the early 1990s, shifted the focus to identification and action on regional concerns seen to be more effectively acted on in common. The third, from 1990, re-engages overtly with the security concerns inherent in early Pan African thought and implicit in SADCC's strategy (e.g., the economic and technical as well as military and strategic

'Defence of the Beira Corridor'[13] perceived by both Zimbabwe and Mozambique as essential to their national survival and by apartheid South Africa as key to breaking the hostile regional coalition confronting it). However, it re-engages on a broader front, introducing – however tentatively – minimum standards of acceptable governance and a deeper as well as a broader view of security, including household food security, ordinary person friendly law and order as well as macro military and political security (e.g., SADC with respect to the 1994–7 Interlake Conflict as it impacted on Tanzania, Angola and, less directly, Zambia).

The earliest major African-based academic literature on regional integration[14] stressed the importance of dynamic growth and development promoting reallocation and enhancement of new investment as being more crucial in African Common Market construction than static reallocation within a broadly unchanged regional economic structure envisaged in the neo-classical, industrialised economy model. It stressed – in a period when except in East Africa such sectors were in retreat – the importance of sectoral integration of transport and trade as integral to reducing regional production and trade costs. It advocated a Nyerere (rather than an Nkrumah) oriented approach – beginning with sub-regions and increasingly close economic co-operation and integration.

In the late 1960s the Common Market and Common Services of the East African Community had been plagued by the (probably accurate) belief in Uganda that it gained little if anything, and in Tanzania that it was a net loser under existing arrangements because of historical pre-independence support for 'settler' industry in Kenya and the over-centralization of all the Common Services at Kenyan-based headquarters.[15] The Phillip Commission road from East African Commission to Community therefore included a fixed period of infant industry arrangements, an East African Development Bank (EADB) with lending targets intended to address uneven manufacturing base sizes and a partial decentralization of Common Services combined with moving four headquarters out of Kenya to Tanzania and Uganda. These measures in fact worked relatively well until overtaken by the 1974 economic crisis and the political fallout of the Amin regime in Uganda. The EADB did find viable investments in Uganda and Tanzania, Tanzania's ratio of exports to Kenya to imports from Kenya did rise, services decentralisation did result in clear net gains to each state even if Kenya still had the largest absolute total (though less than before decentralization and relocation).

A series of negotiations geared toward bringing in up to five new members to the EAC was begun, but in the end (1977), the EAC collapsed. Economic crisis had distracted attention and led to cost overestimation (apparently especially by Kenya). Interference with interstate, intraservice flows had created both tensions and loss of efficiency. The corrosive impact of Amin – which for several reasons prevented the EAC's taking any new initiatives and reduced it to fire fighting – and the opposition of certain Kenya politicians who had never been pro-regional (basically because of their antipathy to Tanzania) interacted with the external crisis to bring EAC's demise when it should have been celebrating its tenth birthday.

The failure of the EAC led, in the 1980s, to doubts about the common market (as opposed to common interest) centred approach, because it had proven to be inadequate for mobilizing and sustaining a breadth and depth of political commitment to survive adverse times.[16] The Lagos Plan of Action for an African Common Market was as much a defence of African initiated strategic development agendas (in contrast to the earlier, more rigid, less African owned variants of structural adjustment programmes) and a symbol and reaffirmation of regionalism as it was as an endorsement of specific agenda items or the viability of a swift leap to a continental common market. By 1985, academic discourse had shifted to a 'common interests commonly perceived' approach as being more politically viable than an automatic focus on free trade.

The present stage of discourse and analysis begins in about 1990. It continues the emphasis on 'common interests commonly perceived' but extends the scope of common interests beyond the traditional boundaries of the economic. The single umbrella term for the new areas is 'security'. In that sense the evolution of regionalism has come full circle, round to Kwame Nkrumah, George Padmare, W. E. B. du Bois and the other early Pan Africanists and – as is less realized in Africa – to Jean Monnet and the 'European idea' of integration to avert tensions and to build structures undergirding peace. Security has, in present African regional discourse, been redefined as a spectrum and in more micro (or human) terms.

Food security is a key illustration, and its prominence flows in part from SADC's successful co-ordination of early warning systems, in-depth country profiles, international validation, donor mobilization and logistics to ensure that (except in the Angolan and Mozambican cases in which war impeded distribution) the great Southern African drought of 1991–2 and consequential great food scarcities of 1992–3 did not become the great death of 1992–3. Livelihood security – in this context a synonym for basic needs or absolute poverty reduction – is a somewhat vague addition (at least in terms of concrete regional action). The rationale is clearer: deep and widespread poverty is unacceptable in itself and leads to uncontainable cross border migration, gun running, smuggling and drug trafficking. Law and order for the ordinary person, including freedom from cross border criminal activity, implies a rather standard definition of security with respect to cross border crime, including drug and other smuggling and mass undocumented immigration. However, the discourse focuses on development and poverty reduction as means to reduce crime and economic refugee flows both to enhance household security and to reduce pressure on policy. Geopolitical and military security also came to be perceived as integral to regional community economic projects.

The renewed focus on security, its redefinition to begin at household level and to include causes (e.g., poverty leading to destabilising migration) and the – even if implicit and hard to pin down – inclusion of minimum standards of governance raised a series of organisational, procedural and substantive problems within SADC and, perhaps even more, with respect to the relationship between interstate regionalism and both national and regional civil society.

SADC's sectoral council on security, while in form a parallel structure reporting directly to the Heads of State, is in fact a fairly clear analogue to other sectoral Councils of Ministers backed by Committees of Officials. Its membership is at least at present rather traditional, comprising Foreign, Defence and Home Affairs (police and immigration). However, the concern with household security and basic causes mean that in practice other sectors – e.g., Food Security, Transport and Communications (with respect to access to food security) and the Corridor Authorities/Projects (to enhance employment and economic activity in ways establishing livelihood and residence) are within the overall security outlook. The means to achieving useful interaction and the division of labour are likely to be tentative and to focus at first on seeking functional means of operating together – a SADCC/SADC institutional hallmark that has variously (if not necessarily accurately) been characterized both as 'pragmatism' and 'institutional disorder'.[17]

The substantive problems turn on geopolitical diplomacy and the use of force if necessary to sustain security, and on means for holding countries accountable with respect to governance standards. The first major test with respect to the geopolitical front has been the Interlake Zone series of crises because of their financial cost to Tanzania (as attempted mediator and refugee host) and the real (even if only in deploying and putting troops on standby for precautionary reasons) destabilization and security present costs and future spillover risks to Angola and Zambia as well as to Tanzania. These factors explain in large measure why President Mandela, as the Chairman of SADC's security sector, has taken an increasingly active role in trying to resolve the Rwanda, Burundi and Zaire crises.

This sequence also illustrates the governance theme. The SADC states, whether acting formally as such or in *de facto* co-ordination, have not been neutral as to what outcomes in the Interlake zone and greater Zaire/Congo would address the basic causes of conflict. In Rwanda and Burundi an end to genocide and of ethnic group dominance plus a credible process toward reconciliation and rehabilitation have been the bottom line; in Zaire a speedy and as non-sanguinary as possible transition from the dying Mobuto regime to a more broadly based, Zairois (Congolese) friendly government are the essentials.

Zaire illustrates the governance issue in another sense. In its early days, SADCC was under pressure from some external co-operating partners to include Zaire in its membership. Its flat refusal was overtly a good governance based one. Zaire was perceived as a bad neighbour, a covert friend of South Africa, a personalized dictatorship. The 're-emergent Congo' (former Zaire) has recently joined SADC.

Governance standards have never been formally set by SADCC/SADC. Nor has the African Convention on Human and People's Rights been formally associated with community goals and standards. However, these standards have been real. One bottom line has been the unacceptability of military governance – almost used to exclude the first Lesotho military regime in the mid 1980s and actually used to exclude the attempted second military coup group a decade later. Personalized dictatorship of a repressive nature is also looked at askance (even if the definition is not precise enough to handle 'borderline' cases). The Leabua Jonathon and Hastings Banda regimes are cases in point – never formally excluded, certainly included in dialogue and in non-political area actions, but treated with a palpable reserve and excluded from the Front Line States (not that 'Hastings Bandastan', as some critics termed it, would have desired to join).

The rapid reversal of the 1993 'military coup with a royal facade' attempt in Lesotho led to undue optimism as to the potential for intergovernmental regional governance improvement. Lesotho is an island within the sea of South Africa, both literally and economically, and is also subject to non-violent sanctioning by South African civil society groups (not least trade unions). Further, the purported coup regime was never recognised by any SADC member state, so that legally action was in support of a member threatened by insurrection. That practical/legal combination is unlikely to be common.

The two main present problem cases (at least as perceived by political and civil society leaders in several SADC member states), Swaziland and Zambia, illustrate the difficulty of even *de facto* regional actions. The Swati state and royal government are in law and origins legitimate. The deadlock over how the constitution should evolve and how the transition from a near absolute ruling king to a constitutional, limited reigning monarchy should be achieved relate to real divisions in Swati society and are, in detail at least, inappropriate topics for outside prescription. But a descent into armed conflict in Swaziland is of legitimate regional concern (not least because key regional transport arteries transit the country, as do key river basins requiring user compacts and management co-ordination). None of the eleven other SADC members view absolute as opposed to constitutional monarchy as a viable governance form for the next millennium. South African trade unions are close allies of their Swati siblings, who lead the coalition for a multi-party parliamentary system with a constitutionally defined reigning (not ruling) monarch, and clearly will act on their own to impose rather severe 'civil society'-based sanctions if the present impasse continues. 'Quiet diplomacy' at multiple levels has been the answer to date – with unclear results, since the regime has not been denounced and Swaziland has not exploded, but a domestic resolution does not appeal to be in train as yet.

Zambia is even more problematic. In form its laws on eligibility for election are not grievously restrictive and at any rate not more so than these of, for instance, the USA. But they were in fact amended to ban the only serious opposition candidate for president and, *inter alia*, his party's prime ministerial candidate. As a result, eight parties (not only the one most directly affected) withdrew, and the surprisingly strong independent and minor party protest vote still left a *de facto* 'uncontestedly' re-elected president with an overwhelming parliamentary majority. Partly because of somewhat ill-chosen northern donor rhetoric and partly because many SADC state leaders are so closely linked to the banned candidate (former President Kenneth Kaunda) from FLS days, the issue has been very low key and – because Zambia borders the Interlake zone – has been put on the back burner until Rwanda, Zaire (Congo) and Burundi no longer pose security threats.

In neither the Swaziland nor the Zambia case could SADC conceivably act formally – no unanimous vote of ten states to suspend these two is conceivable (nor, for that matter, either prudent or even desirable). But clearly relations with other members and, even more, with their civil society groups are affected and discussions around SADC meetings plus co-ordinated mediation initiatives are inevitable. How these will take place is problematic, and how successful they will be is uncertain.

Both security and governance raise the issue of regional level state/civil society relations. Trade unions have been involved since the 1960s in intergovernmental groupings with respect to migrant labour (no less an issue since the demise of the apartheid state, even if the forms of the problems have changed) and also in alliances between South African and Lesothan and Swaziland trade unions on good governance themes. Good governance is of direct concern to the increasingly outspoken civil society groups (predominantly trade unions, religious groups, civic/community associations and women's groups with some support groups) and it is much easier for them both to develop personal level regional relationships and, in consequence of these relationships, to take critical stances in solidarity with cross border partners. In some ways this may be irritating to governments, but in others it can lay the groundwork for mediation and in extreme cases for governmental critical statements and/or sanctions.[18]

SADCC/SADC have a long history of outreach to actors beyond governments, but also one of groping to find mutually satisfactory productive relationships. In this they are rather like the EU and unlike most African regional groupings, which have made little effort to achieve ongoing dialogue beyond their own state members (or prospective members) except with external donors. Both NGO and Enterprise conferences – on the occasion of the annual SADCC/SADC meeting with external co-operating partners or free-standing – date back over a decade. So does a policy of conscious encouragement to, and desire to liaise with, national and, especially, regional groupings, particularly but not exclusively of enterprises and trade unions. But what relationship patterns would be desirable was, and is, unclear to all parties; none wished satellitism and each tended to confuse stating its own agenda with dialogue.

The increased emphasis on the security sector marked a renewed – and for that purpose at least more useful – outreach to civil society groups. A conference with majority participation by them was important in formulating the broader definition of security and strengthening (if not necessarily clarifying) the commitment to minimum standards of good governance.

This stylized, thematic representation of the flow of discourse dialogue and action with respect to economic regionalism and its partial return to broader Pan African themes is not complete because the Western African and continental dynamics have been somewhat separate. They have also been more prone to stagnation, although in the past few years may they have begun to re-emerge.

West Africa initially led both in Pan African and economic regional discourse and in the founding of the first broad front regional economic community, ECOWAS, a quarter century ago. The latter was to a large extent the achievement of Adebayo Adedeji, as scholar, public servant and minister. Unfortunately, sustained political will to overcome Francophone-Anglophone Africa divisions (or perhaps Paris–Lagos divisions) did not exist, at least after he was transferred to Addis Ababa as UNECA head. Further, the economic crises of 1980–1990s have hit West Africa harder, and subsequent recoveries have been weaker, than has been the case in Eastern and Southern Africa. Economic crises and structural adjustment programmes simply did not provide a viable political analogue in West Africa to South African aggression and Southern African liberation as a political driving force in SADCC. Further, Nigeria's collapsed external balance deprived ECOWAS and especially its homegrown solidarity fund, of the means to build up a broader West African benefit-based alliance to counter Paris–Abidjan–Dakar support for Francophone sub-regional systems.

At the continental level, UNECA continued to publicize and promote economic integration but with limited catalytic effect (with the exception of PTA/COMESA, which, unlike ECOWAS, has its preferential tariff, documentation, transit traffic and clearing systems up and running). In retrospect, UNECA's focus may have been too common marketist and functionalist and its relations with African states too headmasterish. PTA/SADCC differences did turn on such factors and on personalities, not on inherent antagonistic contradictions either in goals or actual areas of activity.

The Lagos Declaration and African Common Market Treaty of the 1980s and 1990s – formally OAU but in practice ECA initiated and guided – are more complex in symbolism, although both have, at least at first glance, remained dead letters. Lagos, as noted earlier, became a self-reliance/self-determination/self-respect symbol set up to counterbalance (or to oppose, depending on the use) externally designed structural adjustment programme (SAP) strategies. However, the Act of Lagos simply did not articulate a coherent strategy and its remarkably freestanding and detailed continental common market proposals were not immediately practicable nor, except for PTA and SADCC, were the sub-regional building blocks toward them.[19]

Partly as a result, ECA's initial alternatives to structural adjustment programmes – the African Priority Programme for Economic Rehabilitation (APPER and in a neutered unfunded form UNPPAERD)[20] – had very broad strategic goals at one level with a mélange of projects at a quite different one, but with little interactive articulation between them. The ensuing African Alternative to structural adjustment of the mid-1980s was far closer to being an African structural adjustment agenda with rather unclear differences on ways and means. More state intervention and less devaluation and a degree of autarky like Korea's 1990s 'austerity programme' against elite consumer imports, plus a remarkably unsaleable, however courageous, demand for good governance far more open and thorough than any external funders ever put up or backed were the semi-concealed major strategic priority differences. Neither had strong African political backing, both had substantial (if often less than public or overt) Northern opposition. The predictable result was a combination of mild praise, waspish criticism, grudging (or even condescending) endorsement and near total inaction.

By the early 1990s the continental arena had become near peripheral since the Abuja Treaty nominally following up on the Final Act of Lagos faced the realities of only two substantially functional subregional bodies (COMESA and SADC) in problematic relations with each other but equally sceptical of continental level progress before the millennium and fiercely guarding their own freedom of manoeuvre. The OAU did not in fact set up an economic analysis unit until well into the 1990s; UNECA drifted after Adedeji's retirement, the continuing economic weakness of almost all of its members plunged the African Development Bank into chaotic problems of rising arrears on hard loans (for which it lacked World Bank, IMF or even bilateral leverage to retrieve), falling resources for soft credits and few members for whom hard loans were a sensible prescription.

The middle of the 1990s may have seen a beginning of reunification of these strands with the main – and recently mainly Eastern and Southern African – dynamic. ECA remains weak but this reality is more clearly perceived by both staff and member states. Given that its acquired comparative advantage is in regionalism it may become more of a leading factor there; especially as the OAU now has an economic policy analysis unit with which to co-operate and via which to relate the political and security side of present explorations toward a more pro-active OAU role.[21] While to date not enunciating strategic thrusts, the ADB has begun to get on top of its managerial and financial problems and has secured funding to reopen its soft loan window.

ECOWAS has not disintegrated – a minimal but necessary achievement. Further it has, whatever the initial reasons,[22] taken action in support of 'good governance' in Liberia and Sierra Leone and shown rather considerable staying power and the capacity to prevent utter dissolution in Liberia.

While to date less evidently going beyond institutional rechristening and failed conferences, the old IGAD (against drought) of Kenya–Uganda–The Horn has (under the pressure of events in Somalia and the Sudan) refocused on regional peace and orderly (implying broad-based consent) governance.

These are as yet straws in the wind moving toward a recovery parallel to a still fragile Southern and Eastern African dynamic toward self-reliance, self-determination and self-respect using economic and security instruments. However, they too suggest a return toward the original Pan African vision of regionalism combined with more functionalist and technical instruments and – perhaps – suggest the present limits of the politically possible.

5. Regionalism renewed or revisited: glances ahead

Regionalism attracts more attention, both operational and intellectual, in SSA than it did a decade ago. The economic strands and the broader Pan African ones are substantially more interwoven than they were at previous high points of interest in, and efforts to build, regionalism. But three questions arise:

1 Is the late 1990s concern with both economic and security-based regionalism a sustainable dynamic or a cyclical rerun of mid-1960s fashions?

2 Is the apparent synthesis of pragmatic functionalism (partly drawn from colonial inter-territorial arrangements) and of broadly defined security (including food security) with common marketry and classic Pan Africanism actually a synthesis or clearer strategic prism or is it merely a conflated pastiche?

3 Is the shift of the cutting edge in discourse and decision-taking from West to East to Southern Africa a sign that regionalism is a passing enthusiasm following the retreating tide of empire, which then ebbs once reality impinges on new (or newly African-ruled) states within a decade or two?

It is possible to interpret the evidence more positively than these questions imply, however. Crises may force a return to – as opposed to a fleeing from – common approaches, as occurred in Southern Africa. SADC/SADCC really is not ECOWAS in its days of hope come again, nor is the mid 1990s discourse limited to the common market/functionalist economics and the then rather separate Pan African political prisms of the early 1960s. There are elements of progress as well as of cyclicality.

How far the 1980–96 trend will go, and in what directions, cannot easily be projected, in part because of the importance of external forces in Africa (including such things as weather, market prices and conflicts), and also in part because the impact of major structural political change in Southern African and the Horn and Central Africa is as yet undetermined – although the initial evidence from Southern African is positive with respect to both regionalism and good governance.

However, it is important to recognize that for most people in Africa, especially those living under conditions of crisis and of poverty, actions aimed at immediate results must have at least as much importance as the design of a road map to the medium- to long-term future. In that frame it may be useful to pose the basic questions the answers to which (in practice not on paper) will determine whether Pan African-informed regionalism as a dynamic can be a significant part of regaining development momentum, or whether it will remain an intriguing but isolated discourse punctuated by false dawns of apparent breakthroughs. Five of these questions are:

1 Can regionalism advance *security* and *good governance* both at the level of the cooking pot and basic service delivery as well as on the frontier and in the audited accounts?
2 Are *common interests* building outward from sub-national through national to regional and continental levels likely to be, and to be seen as being, a compelling organizing priority for national and enterprise political and economic strategies?
3 Can *states* be *active participants* in regionalism in a way that builds support for, not tensions between, regional and national interests?
4 How can a state framework for regionalism be an arena for active enterprise and civil society participation that will produce economic gains and political sustainability?
5 Do answers to the earlier questions offer indications on size, breadth of activities, sequences and timings of regional organizations, singly and collectively?

These questions are not likely have uniform answers: for one thing, what is possible or desirable in different sub-regions in Africa is unlikely to be uniform, and for another, the potential for (but by no means the certainty of) creative breakthroughs in the Central and/or Horn regions is real. The prospects for achieving progress and the particular forms it might take are as incalculable as those with respect to Southern Africa were in 1978. Nor, because they relate to and interact with processes, can answers now be more than tentative and temporally and contextually bound.

The first tentative conclusion is that to maintain a regional dynamic, continued success in SADC – and its ability to evolve working conceptualizations of structural co-operation for development, household security and macro security – is crucial. A second factor that would help to retain momentum would be for COMESA to be able to either regroup or redefine itself to go forward (with South Africa opting not to join, its take-over bid for SADC is effectively dead, a view underlined by Mauritius' subsequent and apparently consequential accession to SADC).

How to regroup is problematic. A Tanzania–Rwanda–Burundi–Kenya–Uganda and a Horn subgroup might make sense, assuming continued dual SADC/COMESA membership by Tanzania, although the Horn (Sudan–Ethiopia–Eritrea–Somaliland–Djibouti–Somalia) group, if modelled on SADC, might prefer not to have formal links with the East African group, and, if peace is achieved, Rwanda and Burundi as well as Zaire might become SADC members.

Breakthrough depends on what happens in the Horn, Central Africa and, above all, West Africa. In the Horn the key is achieving decent governance in Khartoum and a federal (not only North–South) settlement backed by consolidation in Somaliland and the emergence of at least a confederated coalition of domestic regions in Somalia.

Central Africa as a subregion beyond UDEAC has never functioned. With Rwanda and Burundi in COMESA (and perhaps SADC bound) and Congo (former Zaire) now (as it was not in the 1980s) welcomed into SADC for both economic and security reasons, no resurrection seems likely. The old UDEAC states (plus Equatorial Guinea) would then logically look to becoming the southern tier of a Novakchat–Brazzaville community. However, any such eventuality depends on resolution of ECOWAS' chronic political malaise and low to negligible substantive performance.

The West African trajectory over 1997–2007 is the most problematic. As long as the region, and especially Nigeria, is dominated by dictatorial military governments (even if nominally civilianized by controlled elections of equally nominally retired senior officers), prospects are poor. The same probably holds true unless resources – perhaps through a refloated Solidarity Fund – can make regionally oriented projects additional and therefore politically attractive. If somewhat more uniform genuinely civilian governance – and a majority of cases of passable governance including at least Nigeria and either Côte d'Ivoire or Senegal plus Ghana as a core – and clear gains from joint action were achieved, breakthroughs on the long-stalled trade preference and clearing fronts would be more likely. In that event both Anglophone and Francophone states could more readily accept the Francophone subgroupings as interim sub-units analogous to the early Benelux in the EEC.

This sketch draws attention to four factors:

1 The big battalions matter: South Africa's continued progress is vital to SADC and Angola's emergence from conflict would be extremely positive, as would that of Congo (ex-Zaire) and its accession. Similarly, Nigeria's un-happy record of poor governance and economic decline, so long as it continues, probably dooms ECOWAS to economic irrelevance and, with fitful, fleeting exceptions, to political and security impotence. *Per contra*, if the Sudan can achieve a dynamic analogous to Ethiopia's, the Horn is likely to become a focus for regionalism (whether within COMESA or sep-arately).

2 Regional contributions to macro-security matters for all aspects of regional-ism (not least because it often has great 'political sex appeal'). If Angola, Mozambique, Congo/Zaire, Rwanda, Burundi, Sierra Leone, Liberia, Sudan, Somaliland and Somali achieve decent governance, an end to conflict and stability, it will be in large part because of co-ordinated regional security action partly taken on the grounds of self-interest and partly on humanit-arian grounds. Indeed, in the Central African and Horn cases it is arguable that regional action will have been the dominant factor, as the net results of global interventions have clearly been negative. Again, it is noticeable that the probability of success is with, in descending order, SADC, the Horn and ECOWAS – with COMESA illustrating its rather simplistic avoidance of political economy by remaining aloof.

3 Human security issues – food, law and order, quality of governance – are, with the major exception of joint action taken in response to drought, harder to handle than macro security. Within SADC, the transitions to stable, modern, acceptable (to broad majorities) governance in Lesotho, Swaziland and Zambia are not subject to regional fiat (even ignoring veto powers) because each is a state with substantial legitimacy. But at least in the first two cases quiet (but well known) mediation, discourse and diplomacy have at the minimum averted violent conflict and perhaps begun cumulat-ive positive changes. Similarly, the attempt to understand migration issues and cross-regional drug and smuggling problems in terms of both insuffi-cient law enforcement capacity and in terms of deprivation can be product-ive economically and politically.

4 Economic gains require production to be sustained by trade, which in turn requires physical and institutional infrastructures. Internal armed conflict and degraded domestic governmental capacity are rarely consistent with building the needed infrastructure or increasing production. Regionalism can help limit erosion and/or begin clawback to the extent the sources of conflict are external and additional resource transfers (global and/or regional) can be mobilized – as in Mozambique – but situations involving the probability of future internal armed conflict or poor governance are likely to be less susceptible to regional remedies than they were in the 1980–92 aggressive apartheid era.

The more integral involvement of enterprises and enterprise associations as well as of civil society groups is important from three perspectives:

1 Most production is carried on by enterprises (including households), and without producer involvement both macro policy and specific infrastructure/service provision are likely to be less efficient than would otherwise be possible.
2 Human security (and causes of insecurity) is best known by affected people, and one of their channels to informing regional action is via civil society involvement in that action.
3 Enterprise and civil society groups' own links across borders are basic to creating a regional sense of common concerns beyond official and elite circles, to giving an indication of human security and household production priorities, to broadening and complementing official diplomatic initiatives with respect to governance quality and to creating a political constituency for regionalism that raises its benefit/cost ratio. The last is a necessity if competitive elections, influential national assemblies and resulting peaceful changes of government become increasingly common.

At the continental level, success will be marked not so much by achieving major advances (least of all toward an African Common Market by 2002), but rather by halting decline, building up a body of applied research and using it to support sub-regional and specialist initiatives. For ECA this is part of a much broader need to rebuild professionalism, innovativeness and morale and to do so in a way more responsive to its member states. For the OAU, with its new economic policy research unit, the need is to take a lead in rethinking dimensions of sub-regionalism as well as of security and governance and relating the two. The ADB's restoration of donor confidence – allowing reopening the soft credit tap suitable to most member needs – may afford an opportunity to seek to relate more effectively to co-ordinated project programmes.

Ministers of Agriculture, as well as the one sub-regional body with a significant agricultural knowledge focus (SADC), should accept responsibility for using the two main global/continental agricultural research centres' (ICIPE, Tropical Agriculture) results, and for proposing priorities for research and technical assistance to them. This should be backed up with at least symbolic funding increases to encourage renewed donor support.

As to the goal of achieving an African Common Market by 2002: there may be enough sub-regional groupings – e.g., Southern Africa (including Zaire), Eastern Africa plus Horn and/or (less probably) a revitalised ECOWAS–UDEAC – to begin building from that base. This will be especially true if SSA's overall economic trends encourage Mahgrebin States (notably Egypt) to invest the political capital necessary to clear potential WTO and EU barriers to SSA countries' entry – such barriers potentially affect South Africa, which it is clearly giving priority to overcoming or bypassing them. However, the devotion of energy toward creating sub-regional, let alone continental currencies remains a clear misallocation, except, perhaps, for very long time horizon conceptual academic research. There simply is not enough convergence of national economic structures, balance, trajectories or resilience to make that road passable, even were adequate reserves, institutional capacity and external credibility readily available or mobilizable – all highly unlikely in the near future.

Insufficient knowledge has been another factor detracting from regionalism in SSA, in two quite different ways. First, knowledge is as important to regional institutions as it is to enterprises and national governments. The production, assembly, analysis and application of information can be a strength of regional bodies (examples include the co-ordinated drought resistant crops work in SADC, pooled with other research and extension data at the Centre for Agricultural Research, and the co-ordinated national early warning system data, pooled and analysed by the Food Security Unit which then co-ordinated a prompt national and external response).

Second, knowledge of regionalism's history – from conceptualization to operation to results (positive through disastrous) – and of its potential trajectories is very feebly developed in SSA, especially outside Southern Africa. This gap is especially serious because the region is relatively unsuitable for even applied 'import substitution' let alone direct common market textbook adaptation. While the initiative of the University of Ghana to set up an institute linking all major African university foci on regionalism is desirable,[23] it can only be successful if there is more to link, and if the rather economistic nature of most regionalist proposals is broadened in the light both of historic Pan African goals and thinking and of a broader approach encompassing human and macro security together with political economy and trade facilitation.

The prospects are problematic but not unpromising. The period 1980–95 did see progress in regional thought and practice in Eastern and Southern Africa, and a reversal of that dynamic is unlikely. Potential breakthroughs in the Horn, and, less probably, West Africa by 2002 are not unlikely. The test is not whether everything sketched above is achieved fully throughout SSA or whether there are no setbacks. Rather it is whether Pan African Regionalism (via Sub-Regionalism) moves up the priority agendas of both citizens and politicians, whether the present operational dynamics continue, whether at least one additional sub-region begins to show signs of takeoff and whether the Pan African big three – ADB, ECA, OAU – begin to be part of the cutting edge and driving force toward the regionalist goals, rather than showing limited capacity to innovate and arguably being as much obstacle as means to strengthen individual state or institution initiatives. While deeply concerned as to how the balance would evolve, Dr Ndegwa believed it was possible for SSA to pass that test. He was in the forefront of those who believed in regionalism and the abiding themes of Pan Africanism – self-determination, dignity, self-development. Since the early 1960s, he and others kept faith and kept up efforts to bring about 'out of Africa...something new', despite the bitter experiences of the intervening decades. That continuing effort, by him and by others, is a reason to believe that more thoughtful, carefully worked out, structural and lasting breakthroughs were and are attainable.

Notes

1 This has led to a vicious circle. Half-hearted Francophone support has limited ECOWAS ability to generate benefits and, therefore, further reduced its appeal to Francophone states.

2 Philip Ndegwa was an advisor to the Kenya delegation (as was the present author briefly to the Ugandan and thereafter to the Tanzanian delegations) to the Phillip Commission, which was remarkably successful both in preserving net gains and in creating a potential dynamic which would make the division of gains and the Community institutions less Nairobi-centric. The post-1971 erosion of EAC related primarily to the political vacuum created by the Amin regime and to the economic crises of the 1970s, not to inherent weaknesses in the 1967 Treaty.

3 This despite evident problems of compatibility with SADC and COMESA, unless the unit were to be limited to a forum for dialogue (not least in respect to Uganda's access to the sea) plus a handful of specialized training and service units.

4 See glossary of acronyms, attached.

5 Tanzania, Malawi and Zambia, as well as Angola and Mozambique (as overseas provinces providing foreign exchange surpluses to Lisbon) had unsatisfactory experiences with past economic unions, and Lesotho, Swaziland and Botswana had similar reservations about their institutional economic linkages with South Africa. The cost of large secretariats was a factor, but a secondary one, and perhaps more with respect to senior personnel than to funding. The principles of demonstrating need before hiring and putting most profess-ionals as close to programmes as possible rapidly led to a substantial total of sectoral unit personnel but administered by host governments and reporting to sectoral subcommit-tees and commissions of national officials and ministers directly, not via the central Secretariat.

6 Mozambique for several years was very cautious about joining anything beyond the OAU and UN bodies. Its desire to join the Commonwealth only came to full fruition in 1997. Its supposed interest in CMEA was never as high as the Northwest feared, nor was it viewed by economic ministers and officials as a serious alternative medium-term, concessional funding route. As long as Mozambique was a tentative World Bank and IMF member and not an ACP state, SADCC was very important in helping mobilize joint finance just as the Front Line States (FLS) were crucial to co-ordinating joint defence, militarily and diplomatically. Angola was less integrally involved – oil reduced its eco-nomic dependence; its high tech war with South Africa required high tech suppliers and advisors; the Cold War entanglements of its struggle had an erosive effect on regional diplomatic initiatives on its behalf. Its previous links to the other eight SADCC states (or even to South Africa) had been relatively low and there was no comparable history of a pervasive British presence.

7 Colonial apologists did stress the value of colonies as markets and as sources but not, perhaps, very analytically, and, even in magisterial tomes like Lord Hailey's, not all that convincingly. France's African colonial empire in particular doubtless produced *gloire* but its primary economic role – even after the 1920s/1930s *mise en valeur* (growth of output) strategy – seemed to be to handle domestic transfer payments by providing open-air relief employment and markets to less competitive French professionals and enterprises. Belgium's colonial realm was run as a profit-making business, as it had been from its private enterprise founding by King Leopold, but was rarely analysed as such. The Gold Coast under Governor Guggisberg was an exception – a strategy of education, transport, export diversification and food security was articulated in a Seven Year Plan, but Guggisberg was an engineer and his approach attracted little emulation by admin-istrators in other colonies or analysis by academic economists.

8 The attempt to reconcile free trade and state intervention regarding production location in order to balance gains rarely worked well even if agreements were struck (as fre-quently happened in East Africa). Either the allocatee could not find an enterprise to

take up the slot and/or a non-allocatee state would go ahead in contradiction with what had been agreed.

9 The one attempted numerical study of the pre EAC Common Market and Common Services Organization (by the present author as an East African Institute of Social and Economic Research discussion paper) estimated about a mid-1960s 2.5 per cent net gain to regional product – 1.5 per cent from Railways-Ports-Post and Telecoms-Airlines and the balance about half and half Common Market and other joint services.

10 COMESA has tariff preferences, a functioning regional clearing mechanism, progress toward customs and transit documentation harmonization, and a modest trade/trade related financial institution. SADC has a series of effective sectoral/co-ordination/integration programmes (transport, communications, animal disease control, food security, energy in particular over 1980–1995); a growing range (e.g., river basin and water boundary, household to macro security) of key issues brought into common concerns/ common action fora and the accession of Namibia, South Africa and Mauritius.

11 EU pressure for a mutual free trade area with South Africa is clearly prejudicial not only to the South Africa–Botswana–Lesotho–Namibia–Swaziland customs union but also to existing preferential agreements with some other SADC member states (e.g., Zimbabwe) and future SADC external tariff/internal preference co-ordination. South Africa has bluntly rejected EU proposals to jettison these and forced serious – as yet unresolved – dialogue on the regional implications and concerns.

12 Botswana needed transport access, market access and diplomatic/military support to stand up to South Africa as actively as it wished or as publicly as it desired. Further, as a small (in population and defence terms), rich, landlocked state, it needed friends to survive and partners to diversify both production and market access (including but not only routes to the sea and global markets).

13 Because the Beira Corridor was vital to Zimbabwe, not only did Zimbabwe need to allocate armed forces to act with Mozambique in its military defence, but the two countries also to had to achieve a viable institutional vehicle for joint planning and financial mobilization to sustain the route's physical operationality once defended.

14 This included a volume by Philip Ndegwa on the then East African Common Market, a volume by Ann Seidman and the present author on the economics of Pan Africanism, and a conference synthesis volume by Dharam Ghai and the present author.

15 The empirical study cited earlier suggested a 6 per cent GDP gain for Kenya, less than 1 per cent (plus or minus) for Uganda, and in excess of a 3 per cent loss for Tanzania. Overcentralization of railways management and workshops offset the full cost operating losses of the Tanzania and Uganda sections so far as territorial GDP and external flows were concerned.

16 External trade is not normally seen by ordinary people as an end in itself. Jobs, factories, roads, schools are so seen. Export growth may have appeal, but mercantilist export and inward transfer payment maximization linked with import and outward transfer payment minimization is a strategy for eroding and destroying, not sustaining a Common Market/Common Services Organization.

17 SADC has never seen itself as short term or marginal in orientation. It has perceived successive, substantive, cumulative steps as the most practicable way toward structural change; assessment of results as a key input into next steps, and language both clear as to fundamentals while remaining stylistically accessible and acceptable to a broad range of domestic publics and of external co-operating partners as desirable policy and articulation tools. Similarly, while the Lusaka Declaration, Annual Programme and Administrative Arrangements Memorandum of 1980–90 did not constitute a normal treaty frame, they facilitated institutional evolution, encompassed main goals, programmes and procedures and, in practice, did not hamper co-operative action when states were agreed on it.

18 At least in Southern Africa this is not merely speculation. Initially Zimbabwe and later South Africa (backed firmly by Botswana, Namibia, Tanzania and Mozambique)

    spearheaded the drive for Commonwealth condemnation of and sanctions against Nigeria. And in the end only Gambia backed Nigeria and Sierra Leone abstained, thus Ghana, Malawi, Mauritius, Zambia, Kenya, Uganda, Lesotho and Swaziland joined in the attempt to exert pressure.

19 The sub-regional building block phase was in fact not in the initial draft. It was inserted on the initiative of the then SADCC nine, backed by the extra SADC PTA members.

20 APPER was a rehabilitation and recovery strategy based on bridging an external balance gap threatening fixed investment over a three year period. It assumed that early 1980s economic recovery globally and in SSA would build momentum, a projection backed by World Bank, IMF and OECD (but not UNCTAD) forecasts, but which was very much falsified by results. The country programmes were in fact not uniform. Some – e.g., Tanzania – were supplementary investment programmes beyond basic budget projections designed to restore annual growth to a 5 to 6 per cent trend, but most appeared to be total investment support requirements and/or somewhat unco-ordinated shopping lists.

21 In 1995 the unit held a workshop evaluating progress toward the African Common Market (ACM) envisaged by and mandated in the Abuja Treaty. Unfortunately its terms of reference were not well adapted to dialogue, suggesting the ACM, however key a medium-term working and current symbolic goal, was not an immediate operational one until COMESA and SADC were strengthened, ECOWAS revitalized, Horn and Central African regionalism reconceptualized and made real (requiring major political change, especially in Kinshasa and Khartoum as a precondition) and the ECA's intellectual and the ADB's analytical and financial leadership and catalytic roles revived.

22 The initial – largely Nigerian – force deployment to Liberia seemed to be an intervention by the Abuja military government on behalf of its 'colleague in arms' Sgt Samuel Doe. Whether valid or not, that perception did less than nothing to mobilize Francophone ECOWAS, or broadly based domestic Liberian, support.

23 The proposal, discourse related to it and possibilities of broadening it are included in the University of Ghana's conference volume to appear in 1997/98.

Initials and acronyms glossary

AAFSAP   African Alternative Framework for Structural Adjustment Programmes (1987). ECA alternative. More interventionist and far more good governance-oriented but broadly similar in terms of fiscal and other macro frames.

ACM   African Common Market, proposed by the OAU in 1980 Final Act of Lagos and embodied in 1990 Abuja Treaty. Currently stalled as 1990–95 sub-regional phase advanced only in overlapping SADC/COMESA sub-regions (Eastern and Southern).

ADB   African Development Bank. Continental regional bank but with majority Northern voting equity.

APPER   African Priority Programme for Economic Rehabilitation (Recovery). Launched by ECA in 1986 to seek to mobilize resources to reverse sustained decline following 1979–81 shocks. (See UNPAERD)

CEAC   Central African Economic Community, nominally former UDEAC (successor states to French Equatorial Africa and Cameroon) plus Equatorial Guinea and (then) Zaire.

CELA   Economic Commission for Latin America (Latin American parallel to ECA).

CFA   Communauté Financière Africaine [African Financial Community]. Francophone monetary groupings (West African, Equatorial African, Malagasy), linking CFA currencies to French franc (since 1994 at 100 to 1, previously 50 to 1) with limits on state central bank borrowing and with French Treasury currency and budget backing.

COMESA	[Economic] Community of Eastern and Southern Africa. Successor to PTA. Nominally Cape to Khartoum and Kinshasa to Port Louis but several states (notably South Africa) have not joined, others are nominal members only (Horn and Congo, ex-Zaire), while over half of members are also SADC member states.
EAC	East African Community (1967–77) of Kenya, Uganda, Tanzania.
EADB	East African (Kenya, Uganda, Tanzania subregional) Development Bank. Originally part of EAC family of institutions but survives as freestanding body.
ECA	Economic Commission for Africa. UN regional body controlled by Secretary General's office subject to member state councils and committees on policy, but not on budget or staff.
ECOWAS	Economic Community of West African States.
EEC	European Economic Community.
EU	European Union (successor to EEC).
FLS	Front Line States (in struggle to achieve end of apartheid): Tanzania, Zambia, Botswana, Mozambique, Angola, Zimbabwe, Namibia. Recast as security aspect of SADC in 1994–6.
IGAD	Rechristened IGADD, with 'Development' substituted for 'Drought/Desertification' and focus shifted to attempted mediation in Horn civil wars.
IGADD	Intergovernmental Group Against Drought and Desertification (Horn plus Kenya, Uganda).
IH	Interahamwe. Rwandan waHutu political civil society body committed to and practising genocide against waTutsi and moderate waHutu in 1994. Subsequently involved in then Zaire, Congo (Brazzaville), Burundi crises as mercenaries and in efforts to recapture Rwanda.
IMF	International Monetary Fund.
OAU	Organization of African Unity. African continental (although Morocco has withdrawn) state grouping. Founded early 1960s to avert territorial conflict among independent African states and to serve as continental spokesman for them on areas of common concern (especially decolonization, including ending apartheid state in South Africa).
PTA	Preferential Trade Area of Eastern and Southern Africa (1982–91, after which became COMESA). Proto-economic community parallel to ECOWAS and CEAC (and non-launched North African) in ECA four sub-continental zone scheme. Core Zimbabwe, Zambia, Kenya, Uganda, Tanzania, Mauritius, Rwanda, and Burundi.
SADC	Southern African Development Community, successor to SADCC by 1990–91 Treaty. SADCC plus South Africa, Mauritius, Congo (former Zaire) as of end of 1997.
SADCC	Southern African Development Coordination Conference (1980–90). Economic proto-community of nine independent Southern African states (Tanzania southward) plus, on independence, Namibia.
UDEAC	Economic and Customs Union of Central African (Cameroon, Central African Republic, Chad, Congo-Brazzaville, Equatorial Guinea, Gabon).
UMOA	L'Union Monetaire de l'ouest de l'Afrique. West African monetary and economic groupings.
UNECA	See ECA.
UNICEF	United Nations Children's Fund (originally United Nations International Children's Emergency Fund).
UNPAERD	United Nation's Programme for African Economic Recovery and Development. Revised (non-binding and in the event non-operational) form in which the UN General Assembly endorsed APPER (1986–91).

12
Africa in the Global Economy[1]
Gerald K. Helleiner

1. Introduction

Philip Ndegwa was always keenly aware that an important part of Africa's 'problem' has been its high incidence of civil strife and political instability, some of it undoubtedly rooted in economic and environmental pressures; indeed he was among the earliest post-independence analysts of the economic consequences of ethnicity. He was also a vigorous proponent of stronger domestic efforts, within Africa, for the promotion of equitable and sustainable development. Among his most important contributions, however, were those in the international arena. Perhaps the greatest loss from Philip's premature departure from the community of international policymakers and analysts will be the loss of his wise voice as Africa tries to address its future role in the 'globalizing' world economy.

Everyone is talking of 'globalization'. Some hail it; others fear it. In Africa, however, the question is more typically 'Why isn't there more of it?' Discussion of Sub-Saharan African prospects often features concern over its 'marginalization' in the global economy, as African shares of global trade and investment continue to decline. Even those African countries that are doing 'well' are typically falling behind relative to the rest of the world or at serious risk of doing so.

Recent trends in the direction of globalization seem impressive. Important features of the modern global economy – e.g., those associated with the informatics and transport/communications revolutions, and an unprecedented pace of technical change – are entirely new. It is important to recognize, however, that the most usual globalization ratios (trade to GDP, and net capital flows as a proportion of GDP) are not so different now from those at the turn of the twentieth century; they are only now climbing back from the troughs to which they plunged in the 1930s and 1940s (Pritchett, 1995). The current globalization is therefore, in some respects, less historically unique, particularly in Africa, than is sometimes suggested.

The global increase in trade – output ratios in the post-Second World War period is mainly the result of developments in manufacturing (WTO, 1995:19). In Africa, where manufacturing plays a relatively small role, there has not actually been much change in this ratio over the past two decades (although there was a modest rise in the export – GDP ratio from the mid-1980s onwards). Even this very recent increase in African trade 'openness' in some countries has generated trade ratios that are probably not so different from those in their (somewhat distant) colonial past. Similarly, African countries' marginal position in the global investment community is not a new problem; and it is not now, nor ever was, entirely their own 'fault'. Still, the new globalization raises important policy questions for today's African governments as they seek to navigate relatively uncharted, because more globalized, international waters.

African governments are today strongly urged by the international financial institutions to 'open' to external trade and capital and to 'integrate' with the global economy. The Managing Director of the International Monetary Fund puts it as follows (Camdessus, 1995):

Globalization offers considerable opportunities to accelerate economic progress throughout the world. At the same time, experience suggests that countries that are unable to adjust enough to integrate themselves into the mainstream of the global economy risk marginalization … the challenge for African countries is to pursue [a] … strategy that enhances the prospects of benefiting from globalization, while avoiding the risks.

In immediate and practical terms, what choices do the relatively small and weak African governments really have? Surely theirs is not a simple dichotomous choice – yes or no – as they contemplate their potential integration into the rapidly changing world economy. Nor is it easy to construct indicators that can unambiguously measure gradations of openness or policy towards it. Unidimensional measures of openness or openness policies are bound to oversimplify; and are not themselves always highly correlated one with another.

A significant feature of recent adjustment experience has been the long (and often unexpected) lag between policy changes and outcomes. Weak initial conditions in Sub-Saharan Africa have often been reflected in particularly low short- and medium-term supply elasticities in response to altered incentives, and sluggish or non-existent responses to improved policy environments on the part of private investors and savers. Extreme vulnerability to external shocks, notably in the terms of trade, exacerbates this problem. It is therefore likely to be extremely misleading, in the African context, to attribute recent weak economic performance purely to weak policies, whether those on openness or on anything else. Many analysts of African experience, hoping to prove the benefits of policy reforms, have learned this only recently and to their sorrow. World Bank analyses of recent African experience have been ambivalent about these problems. Some Bank analysts have taken full account of them (e.g., World Bank, 1995a and 1992; Easterly *et al.*, 1993). Others, however, have been more inclined to belabour African governments for their 'weak' policies and failure to do as well as better-performing parts of the developing world, notably East Asia (World Bank, 1994).

Overly simple association of outcomes with policies has infected recent Bank analysis of economic openness and developing country integration with the global economy. Having constructed a very crude index of global integration outcomes (based on trade and foreign direct investment shares of GDP, credit rating by external agencies, and the share of manufactures in exports), World Bank analysts have pronounced African integration to be weak and slow (1996b:25). Finding their index (and changes therein) not surprisingly correlated with growth, they blame the weak integrators for their own relative misfortune! Analysis of the link between policy and either integration or growth outcomes (pp. 27–9) is cursory, relying heavily upon the crude, though much-quoted (in Washington) earlier work by Sachs and Warner (1995).

This paper seeks to address important dimensions of Africa's economic relationships with the world, and to do so in the pragmatic and policy-oriented spirit that Philip Ndegwa brought to his analysis of these and other issues. On some external policy issues there is by now fairly general agreement. Where controls, administrative complexities and misaligned exchange rates create socially costly interferences in economic relationships between individual African countries and the rest of the world there should be no hesitation in unilateral African liberalization. International co-operation to achieve it is unnecessary; indeed negotiations over its details may even slow it down and, conceivably, may lessen the domestic sense of 'ownership' of the policy reforms. The continuing debate in Africa, as elsewhere, concerns other dimensions of external liberalization.

Should one simply liberalize *all* such international transactions – in both the current and the capital account – as quickly as possible and to the maximum possible degree? There exists a case for such an approach to trade and investment policy – what one might call the 'Washington approach' (although it is not fully practised in the US). It rests on the presumption that, while there may be theoretically sound grounds for governmental interventions in market processes, and there may even be some governments that have intervened with a degree of success, African governments that have tried to do so, for whatever purpose, have typically made a mess of it and are likely to continue to do so whenever they try. While markets cannot necessarily be trusted to get allocations developmentally 'right', African governments, it is argued in this approach, will almost invariably get it 'wrong'.

Alternatively, can one develop an approach that consciously seeks to make as many transactions/links with the rest of the world as possible directly *functional* to medium- to long-term development objectives, as perceived by the policy-makers? (See, for instance, Lipumba, 1994; Lall, 1995.) This is likely to involve selective and differential incentives and disincentives, and a more activist state. On the East Asian model, it could involve close co-operation between indigenous private firms and the state as both interact, in more co-ordinated fashion, with external actors – in pursuit of the buildup of indigenous technological capacity and development-supportive institutions. In this 'Tokyo approach', fewer private international transactions are likely to be internalized within foreign transnational corporations, and external capital inflows are likely to be more carefully controlled.

Section 2 of this paper considers trade policy. Section 3 addresses policy on capital flows. There follows a brief conclusion.

2. Trade and trade policies

Overall approaches and constraints

International trade played a major role in nineteenth- and twentieth-century African development, and it will continue to do so in the coming century. International exchange creates the opportunity for greater specialization, increased use of capacity and the import of productivity-increasing goods and services. Some speak of the economic development of low-income countries, particularly the smaller ones, as (actually or potentially) export-led. It would be more accurate to speak of such development as investment-led. Whatever its other requisites, sustainable African development will certainly require increased investment. The key question is where such investment is likely to be profitable. In small, poor countries, investment in production for export markets is an obvious area of greater potential than most. Yet dependence on exports has also created problems, particularly when, as in the past two decades, traditional exports have faced severe real price deterioration in world markets.

Rapid growth of the global economy and ready access to its markets are fundamental to Africa's export prospects and indeed, since African economies are so 'open' and 'dependent', to African development more generally. Neither rapid global growth nor market access can be assured. Trade and related policies must now be constructed in an international economic environment that is more hostile than before to many of Africa's traditional exports. Happily, there may be better prospects for non-traditional exports – if Africa can only shift quickly enough towards them. There is much that policies within Africa can do to raise the prospects of export success and there are important issues of development strategy and tactics in this regard that need to be addressed.

The market prospects for Sub-Saharan Africa's traditional primary product exports are not generally considered very attractive over the medium to long term. According to World Bank projections, real non-oil commodity prices will decline, on average, by about 2 per cent per year over the coming decade – 'metals and minerals by about 1 per cent, agricultural commodities by about 2.5 per cent, and beverages by 5 to 6 percent' (World Bank, 1995b:19). (Timber is the only commodity group projected to benefit from real price increases; and many fear the environmental consequences of rapid expansion in this sector.)

Africa lost market shares in global markets for many of its traditional commodities in the 1970s and 1980s. (Sub-Saharan Africa's share of world trade fell from about 3 per cent in the mid-1950s to only a little over 1 per cent in 1995.) With increased incentives and productivity increases, Africa could claw some of these losses back. Exchange rate and other domestic policies that discouraged agricultural production, whether for domestic or export markets, have been costly to many Sub-Saharan African countries' development. Fortunately, these costs are now more widely understood; and the important role of smallholder agriculture is generally recognized. But the prospects for expanded traditional export volume, while certainly not zero (as is sometimes suggested), are somewhat limited, particularly in the important case of tropical beverages, which make up over one-third of total exports in ten African countries (World Bank, 1995b:74), by low world price elasticities and the risks of rendering the already bleak price prospects even bleaker.

Economies that are small, poor and dependent upon primary exports are highly vulnerable to external influences and external shocks, particularly those from sharp changes in the terms of trade. Their structural rigidity (or, in Killick's (1995) terminology, 'inflexibility') and limited access to offsetting external credit result in particularly heavy costs from temporary adverse shocks which hit them, in any case, on average more severely. Good luck as well as good policy matters greatly to development performance (Easterly *et al.*, 1993).

Sub-Saharan African countries experienced enormous trade shocks in the 1980s – larger than those suffered in the 1930s – and the costs to their progress have been severe. African governments have not recently managed their commodity booms and busts well. In the absence of international reforms to stabilize commodity prices and/or primary exporters' import volumes (the prospects for such reforms at present look bleak), there must be increased attention to the management of shocks (both positive and negative) so as best to preserve prospects for longer-run development. The global economy seems likely to continue to be as turbulent as it was in the last two decades, possibly even more so. African governments must learn to live within a highly unstable world.

Steady deterioration in the terms of trade of the traditional export basket, such as was found in most Sub-Saharan African countries in the 1980s, *should* be met with a shift to new non-traditional activities, both exporting and efficiently import-substituting. Yet Sub-Saharan Africa has achieved remarkably little diversification of its traditional primary export base over the years despite an evidently increasing need for it. The share of manufactures in African exports actually fell from 1980 to 1990 – from 27 per cent to only 22 per cent (IMF, 1995:47).

Sub-Saharan Africa's endowments of relatively abundant natural resources and relatively scarce human skills appear to offer it little hope of developing significant manufacturing for export in the near future, except in some unskilled-labour-intensive primary processing activities. This familiar proposition has recently been buttressed by empirical research on the roots of comparative advantage in a world of mobile capital and immobile resources and labour of different skills (Wood, 1994; Wood and Berge, 1994). Investment in human capital has a very long gestation period so that even if Africa could accelerate it – and, under current constraints, it is unable to do so – it would be many decades before its relative factor endowments could significantly alter. Sub-Saharan Africa's (static) comparative advantage therefore lies unquestionably with primary production – agricultural and, where possible, mineral (and petroleum) production and related unskilled-labour-intensive activities; and this will continue to be so for decades to come.

But what does this imply for Africa's longer-run development and its future role in the global economy? Unskilled-labour-intensive activities can be a technological dead-end, unconducive to the productivity enhancement and indigenous learning upon which ongoing development is now generally believed to depend.

Analysts from Adam Smith to Grossman and Helpmann (1991) have called attention to the risks attendant upon specialization in activities with few 'dynamizing' possibilities. Import-substituting industrialization, which was so imperfectly implemented and has attracted so much opprobrium from trade economists, was motivated significantly by such theoretical (and practical) considerations. There is still an unfortunate vacuum in the theoretical and empirical literature concerning the appropriate government policy stance in circumstances where static comparative advantage clearly rests with primary activities, but the relevant activities may be weak in 'development' effects. Economists still know remarkably little about the potential dynamic properties of different economic activities, and different degrees and forms of specialization.

It can sensibly be argued that unless the purportedly dynamic (productivity-increasing) effects of alternative production patterns manifest themselves fairly quickly, the more immediate gains from 'proper' static allocation are likely to dominate them. Future gains, after all, have to be discounted at some (rough) social rate of interest; beyond fifteen years or so, future possible gains simply peter away. The social profitability of consciously directing resources away from the sectors in which there exists comparative advantage toward those with dynamic potential obviously hinges upon the static costs of this misallocation for the sake of possible productivity gains, the size and timing of any such productivity gains, and the appropriate rate of discount. Each is surrounded by controversy.

Despite confident assertions by advocates of liberal trade, there is still no conclusive evidence that liberal trade regimes are associated with greater productivity increases (Pack, 1992; Helleiner, 1994). But neither is there much evidence, one way or the other, that supportive government policies have such effects, or that some economic activities are more 'nutritious' in this respect (in terms of learning effects, positive productivity spillovers, linkages, etc.) than others. If such government policies can only be driven by 'hunches' as to future productivity effects, it may well be safer simply to avoid the imposition upon oneself of static welfare costs that are known to be greater than zero (even if their measured size is often small).

It can also be argued that productivity increases are associated less (or not at all) with production patterns than with inputs, notably inputs that can only be acquired via importing and that continue to generate productivity gains as global technical change continues (World Bank, 1991:88, 98). If that is the case, the focus should be on the acquisition of necessary foreign exchange – through exports and capital inflow, perhaps particularly through foreign direct investment which frequently can bring other key inputs along (without pocketing all the resulting rewards). The most important determinant of long-term productivity increase is then the capacity to import; and, to increase that, *any* form of export will do.

Leaving the precise nature of export specialization to the market, however, imparts a significant degree of randomness to the eventual export composition and overall product-mix in countries with comparative advantage in primary activities. Scale economies in processing, transport and marketing – even if such scale effects are weak in production – would generate locational decisions on the part of global investors, if they are left to make them alone, that concentrate investments and production in relatively few places rather than wherever the objective conditions would make them profitable (Krugman, 1989). Externalities may further encourage processes of concentration in the evolution of the 'geography' of international trade (Krugman, 1991). The literature on the locational decisions of transnational corporations (including analyses of the efficacy of investment incentives) is certainly relevant here; but has not been integrated very well with that on international trade.

In actual fact, trade typically *follows* developments in publicly provided infrastructure, other malleable endowments, and prior private investment decisions. To the degree that the latter private investments are influenced by governments at all, they are usually the product of other (non-trade) kinds of policies. Chile's dramatic success with the (non-traditional) export of fruits, wine, forest products and fish in the late 1980s and 1990s was the product not merely of the newly favourable real exchange rate but, more fundamentally, of specific public investments of decades earlier in agricultural and forestry education, research and development, and infrastructure, without which the eventual private response could not have occurred (Meller, 1995). Roads built primarily for military purposes have played an important role in agricultural development in Thailand. In the modern globalized economy, private international (direct) investment and international trade are, in large part, *jointly* determined in the evolution of 'international production': they are both part of the same process. They should be studied, as much as possible, in an integrated way. It follows that government policies affecting incentives should also be analysed in an integrated way – rather than through separate approaches to trade policy, industrial or agricultural policy, FDI policy, etc.

Sub-Saharan Africa's best strategic course will, for the present, certainly be to build upon its primary production base; in most cases, this means smallholder agriculture. Paradoxically, the greater is the growth in the agricultural sector, the better are the prospects for more-than-proportionate growth in manufacturing and relative growth in the size of the industrial sector. But this does *not* necessarily mean leaving everything to the market and having *zero* industrial or agricultural policies. Progress in agriculture and agriculture-related industry and in other activities, meeting the demands both of domestic and of export markets, can be assisted by conscious governmental encouragement.

Among the governmental policies that matter most in this respect are different kinds of support (including creation or support of relevant institutions) for research and development, training/education, and infrastructure as well as the more direct instruments of subsidies, tax concessions, preferential credit, government procurement policies and the like. Totally level playing fields (and national treatment for foreign firms) may not always be appropriate in circumstances where local capacity-building is of such dominant importance.

It is surely peculiar to argue, as some do, that governments cannot, do not, or should not influence private investment, production and employment decisions.

The building of appropriate capabilities and institutions, where action is much more difficult to quantify, may be as critical to success as incentive structures (which seem to have proven insufficient in recent African experience) (Lall, 1995; see also Lall, 1990, and, in Latin America, Bekerman and Sirlin, 1995). In this area, as in others, Africans could usefully draw on others' related experiences, particularly in low-income (or recently low-income) Asia. The advantage of the African latecomer lies not only in the possibility of technological catch-up but also in the possibility of learning from others' experiences with alternative patterns, processes of change, and policies.

African policy-makers will require more information and assistance in the development of their industrial, trade and investment policies – based on solid supportive research rather than presumptions and ideology. Such research and assistance is what they should be able to expect from the international community, rather than the policing of others' rules which run contrary to African interests and aspirations. Predictability and transparency are likely to help the weaker participants in the global economy. But total harmonization of their domestic policies with international 'standards' over which they have had little influence, and endless litigation as to their proper compliance with the rules, are *not*.

Trade liberalization

International liberalization

There is broad agreement that the short-term consequences of the Uruguay Round will be negative for most African countries – principally because of the reduction of previous preferences enjoyed under the Lomé Convention or the GSP and the increased import prices likely to be faced by food-importing countries in consequence of the agreements to reduce agricultural protection in the North. Africans are generally told that these losses are relatively small, that they are temporary and that their gains from trade are, in any case, determined more by their own trade policies than by external market barriers, with or without the Uruguay Round. (The results of these studies are summarized by Weston, 1995 and 1996.)

The fact remains, however, that despite all the enthusiasm about the great gains to the world from this landmark liberalizing agreement, there will also be clear immediate losers, that these losers are among the poorest countries in the world and that the prospect of longer-term gains for them is far from certain. In that same longer-term in which gains are expected to materialize for these countries, their use of the instruments of trade policy that others have used in their industrialization efforts will be more severely restricted by the new WTO rules (from which they receive some partial short-term exemptions) (Agosin *et al.*, 1995). In addition, low-income African countries, whose legal and administrative capacities are already stretched, are obliged by the rules of the new WTO to introduce (and enforce) a whole new battery of legal instruments relating to intellectual property and review their entire existing legal machinery as it relates to trade to ensure WTO-consistency; such efforts also involve costs. Under the terms of the Uruguay

Round, such losses and costs to low-income countries are to be compensated in various ways by the gaining countries (Weston, 1995, 1996). Unfortunately, the appropriate size and mode of such compensation and/or assistance was stated in distressingly vague terms in the agreement and there is, as yet, no sign of its delivery. On the contrary, aid to Africa continues to decline.

International market access will continue to be critically important to African countries as they seek to expand non-traditional exports. 'Process protectionism', in the form of litigation and threats to impose anti-dumping and countervailing duties against purported export subsidies or to block access on the basis of health, labour and other standards, poses a particular threat to them. Small and poor African exporters (especially those without links to powerful firms in the import-ing countries) cannot sustain the costs of endless defence in Northern courts. The promised longer-run gains from Northern trade liberalization are far from assured.

Trade liberalization within Africa

Of all the trade and exchange rate policy reforms that might be contemplated within Africa, changes in the import regime are probably the most controversial and difficult. Rodrik has noted that the 'political cost-benefit ratio' of trade liberal-ization is typically very high: five dollars of income being reshuffled for every dollar of efficiency gain (1992). In assessing the desirable and the possible in this realm it is important to take account of the fact that import tariffs (as well as licences, prohibitions, and controls) are typically the product of multiple object-ives. The need for government revenue is among the most obvious; in the short-run the alternatives to customs duties are fairly limited. No less important is the fact that import barriers are often the product of balance of payments pressures rather than import substitution objectives. It can therefore be quite misleading to introduce the question of import regime reforms purely in terms of the cost of 'protectionism' (as does, for instance, DeRosa (1992)). Where import barriers originated with fiscal or balance of payments difficulties they can only be assessed in the context of exchange rate and other macro-economic policies which are primarily directed, or could be directed, at fiscal and external balance objectives respectively. Once in place, however, interests in the continuation of such barriers may accumulate and strengthen, rendering it politically difficult to reduce them again (O'Connell, 1995).

African countries have gone some way towards liberalizing their own external trade regimes in recent years – removing controls and/or replacing them with tariffs and/or currency devaluation, simplifying customs duties and their admin-istration, etc. These liberalizations, usually undertaken in conjunction with increased external finance (although not in a period of buoyant exports), apart from their frequent raising of government revenues and the beneficial conse-quences of simplification, have typically increased the relative price of exportables vis-à-vis non-tradables; and this has been critically important to development prospects as far as incentives relate to them at all. Frequently, they have reduced anti-export bias within the tradables sector; and this too may often have been helpful.

Less evident is the role, positive or negative, of changes in the precise structure of incentives in the importables sector; pressure for these changes from external analysts and policy advisors has probably been greater than their productivity inherently warrants. Credibility and sustainability are, in any case, critically important. If key economic actors do not believe that the new incentive structures will be sustained, the effects of reforms can be worse than nothing.

The transition to a more liberalized trading environment may involve significant economic and political adjustment costs. The removal of disincentives and regulatory requirements for exporters are generally unlikely to pose serious immediate problems relative to the welcome they will certainly receive among export producers. Where inefficient state marketing boards or previously monopsonistic co-operatives are forced to shed workers in the face of fresh competition, however, there may be some transitional costs, and associated political difficulties. Political difficulties may also arise if the export trade looks like being taken over by private monopsonies or oligopsonies or, in some cases, politically even worse, by foreign or ethnic minority interests.

Heavier transitional costs are generally anticipated from reductions and liberalizations in import barriers. The average effective protection against imports, or even against manufactured imports, may not change much initially in an import liberalization that is preceded or accompanied, as it typically should be, by currency devaluation. Even a fully compensating devaluation, however, will leave significant changes in inter-industry incentives as the hills and valleys of the import barrier structure are smoothed en route to a simplified (more uniform) system; and, of course, there may be further such industry-level effects if there continue to be further moves toward lower and more uniform import tariffs. Some previously more protected industries and firms will thus always lose from liberalization. Whether they respond by 'exit' or by raising productivity, there is bound to be some loss of employment and incomes. Especially in low-income countries, where investment is low and response capacities are slower, one can expect that the losses will be felt more quickly and in greater concentration than the possible eventual gains from redeployment and increased efficiency in other (notably export) sectors. In poor countries, for the same reasons, these transitional costs are likely to last longer. Hence there is a strong case, on both economic and political grounds, for encouraging and liberalizing exports first – as Korea, among others, did – and leaving major import liberalizations for later, after exports have been set moving. These arguments are particularly strong when the government is simultaneously reducing its expenditures, privatizing its assets and otherwise rationalizing its activities – creating further short-term to medium-term labour market pressures.

'Opening' fully to external trade can also impact upon domestic income distribution. It is usually confidently asserted that in Sub-Saharan Africa, trade liberalization and the consequent expansion of trade will both reduce poverty and improve income distribution. This presumption is based on the further twin presumptions that agriculture will benefit relative to urban sectors and that export activities, not least in agriculture, are more labour-intensive than import-substituting ones. But many forms of export production are not so evidently labour-intensive, e.g., mining, estate agriculture, and some manufacturing; many non-tradeable activities, including some food production, are highly labour-intensive; and some very poor people are net consumers of tradeables, including urban groups that have newly been put out of their previous jobs. Moreover, the skill requirements of export production, and even their (particularly working) capital requirements, may be greater than many have assumed and greater than those of many alternative domestic activities. The distributional and poverty outcomes will depend significantly on the (eventual) nature of expanding exports. They also differ in the short-run from their longer-run outcomes; and the short-run effects are almost certainly worse.

The evidence at present available does not support the traditional optimistic presumptions concerning increased trade openness (Horton *et al.*, 1995). Governments would therefore be sensible to treat them with caution – and to prepare to deal with the frequently nastier consequences, for which there *is* some evidence.

3.   External capital

The current outlook for aggregate external net transfers to the poorest countries is quite bleak. Sub-Saharan Africa (SSA) has not as yet been fully integrated into the newly globalized markets for capital. African borrowers, whether sovereign or private, have been considered poor credit risks by bankers and bond markets; and the poor economic performance of most of Africa in the 1980s and 1990s and its enormous and still rising debt 'overhang' have, if anything, worsened external perceptions of creditworthiness. Half of the African countries rated by the *Institutional Investor* were given worse credit ratings in 1993–5 than in 1983–5 (World Bank, 1996b:69). Foreign direct investors have also been chary of further involvement in Africa, except in particularly favourable circumstances with very high rates of return (Bennell, 1995; UNCTAD, 1995). SSA received only 2 to 3 per cent of total FDI flows to developing countries in the mid-1990s (World Bank, 1997:29). More usually, SSA has been 'rationed out' of private credit and investment allocations.

Foreign direct investment

Africa needs to attract foreign private capital that is prepared to make a long-term investment in the development of productive facilities. In current circumstances this type of capital is unlikely to come to Africa unless it is permitted a significant degree of detailed control over its use, i.e., any such capital flow is likely to take the form of foreign direct investment, and then only when there is a minimal degree of governmental involvement in what precisely it does. Foreign direct investment in Africa has been stagnant in recent years. In 1995 it dropped by one-third (and was heavily concentrated in Nigeria and South Africa) (World Bank, 1996a).

In terms of the likely size of direct investment flows, the best short-term prospects are unquestionably in the mining and petroleum sectors where Africa has long been, in the truest sense of the word, 'underdeveloped'. Exploration and development expenditures in mining were only an estimated 4 per cent of the world's total in the 1980s (IFC, 1995:10), far less than Africa's likely share of exploitable mineral resources.

Tourism is another sector with under-exploited export potential, in which foreign direct investment could also be confidently expected to expand. Greater developmental spillovers might be expected, however, from foreign direct investments in manufacturing and agro-allied activities, particularly where it collaborates with indigenous enterprises, including those of small and medium size – both in rehabilitating and restructuring existing dilapidated assets (often previously publicly owned) and in new investments. Interesting innovations, for instance, have been undertaken in Kenya (and elsewhere) in contract farming (Glover and Kusterer, 1990). Unfortunately there is not at present much new foreign investment in these spheres in Sub-Saharan Africa. Foreign firms have been important players, however, in efforts to raise efficiency in these sectors and particularly in Africa's public sector enterprises. Management contracts (with private foreign companies) for the running of state-owned enterprises have been common in Africa and, with some exceptions, have been fairly successful – particularly when established and negotiated with the necessary care (World Bank, 1995c:134–5, 149–50) – although typically not in increasing indigenous capacity. To the extent that privatization of state assets gains greater momentum, over-coming continuing political resistance and the enormous difficulties of doing it honestly and efficiently, foreign investors may also come to play an important role in one-off increases in government revenues.

Differences in the details of the modes of foreign direct investment and the choice of different instruments of private (or public) technology transfer to Africa can have a profound impact upon the prospects for technological spillovers, indigenous capacity-building and longer-term productivity growth. It is now widely recognized that in terms of the longer-run purported objective of official technical assistance to Africa – 'achievement of greater self-reliance in the recipi-ent countries by building institutions and strengthening local capacities in national economic management' (UNDP, 1993:244) – the results have usually been abysmal. But it would be naive to expect that foreign investors or commer-cially-driven foreign suppliers or inputs or technology are likely to do much better. Like aid donors and their employees, they too are driven primarily by motives other than those of long-term building of local capacities and strong local institu-tions. They too push inappropriate packages, overuse the (demonstrably ineffect-ive) resident export counterpart model, are extremely reluctant to transfer or delegate real decision-making power to locals, and favour short-term payoffs over longer-term results. Nor is there yet much evidence to suggest that perform-ance significantly improves when foreign investors form joint ventures with local investors, whether private or public. Exhortation to improve their behaviour is no more likely to influence profit-oriented private firms than to influence aid donors, and quite probably less.

There is a major dilemma here. Commercially motivated foreign suppliers of capital and technology are unlikely to come to Africa unless they have a fairly free hand; yet that freedom of manoeuvre is unlikely to engender the kinds of change towards local capacity-building that Africans now more clearly seek. At the same time, the typical African state is too 'soft' and too fiscally constrained to be very effective about influencing these outcomes.

Exhortation directed at aid donors, foreign investors and suppliers (and, in some cases, even African governments) cannot do any harm. 'Codes of conduct' for foreign business and 'principles' for effective aid may at least serve to remind the key players of what social objectives are supposed to be, even if they are not always observed. More complete information on current practices and their effects may also help a little and, in any case, is an intellectually challenging area for research. However, for real innovation in external modes for the provision of technology so as to achieve effective transfer, capacity-building and long-term productivity growth in Africa, it is probably best to rely on institutions that have these as their express objectives while working with highly specialized knowledge and within the context of the private sector. The IFC and the African Development Bank have special responsibilities and opportunities in this sphere. So does the Commonwealth Development Corporation. Some bilateral donors have analogous institutions or programmes; and those that do not might acquire them.

Portfolio capital

Although direct investment, involving direct control over African enterprises, is the most likely form of foreign private capital flow to Africa in the immediate future, there have recently been some promising beginnings of broader and more flexible approaches from portfolio investors – in the form of new 'Africa funds' organized by institutional investors.

The fact that Africa remains, for the present, a relatively unattractive venue for the world's long-term investors does not free African governments from the need to develop suitable approaches to global financial markets or to consider the capital account effects of domestic fiscal and monetary policies. Orthodox policy recommendations have frequently been crude and undifferentiated: liberalize both the domestic financial market and the market for foreign exchange, including the capital account, at the same time as restoring or maintaining macroeconomic balance. Where financial institutions are fragile (or even already basically insolvent) and prudential supervision weak, as in Africa, this may not be a sensible course. Financial opening for countries of the Sub-Saharan African type may be hazardous and harmful. Top priority must be assigned instead to the strengthening of domestic financial systems.

One would not expect investors, either within Africa or internationally, to be highly responsive to African interest rate changes in normal circumstances. Other influences – relating to inflationary and exchange rate expectations, the credibility of government policies, 'confidence' and the like – certainly dominate portfolio decisions in a context in which African borrowers are seen as broadly uncreditworthy to begin with. Marginal interest rate changes will certainly be of small import to global investors. But sharp macro-economic restraint and financial liberalization can quickly produce *very* high real interest rates – rate changes that are far from marginal (with correspondingly dramatic effects for domestic balance sheets, especially in the financial sector, and for governmental debt service costs). To such interest rate changes – often coupled with a degree of increase in government credibility and investor confidence – some foreign lenders and investors *will* respond. Private capital may surge in – bringing what has been recently (and aptly) labelled 'Uganda disease' but has also been found in Ghana, Kenya, Zambia and Zimbabwe, among others. (In 1993–4, private capital inflows to Uganda reached an extraordinary 8 per cent of GDP!-Kasekende and Martin, 1995). Such surges are likely to be short-term in their nature; in Africa, most appear to be trade credits and investments in Treasury bills, though the data are so imperfect that it is usually difficult to tell what they are (Kasekende *et al.*, 1997).

The result of such inflows is real appreciation of the currency, and associated problems both for short-term macro-economic management and for longer-term development (particularly through the disincentives created for exports and import substitutes). Private capital flows in Africa have been shown to be statistically significantly related to international interest rate differentials (between African and global interest rates), just as they are in other places, at least over the ranges experienced in recent years (Asea and Reinhart, 1995; see also Kasekende *et al.*, 1997).

Advice to open up the capital account, such as has often flowed from the IMF, therefore needs to be carefully weighed against the counter-arguments. Marrying a very thin, immature and therefore volatile set of domestic financial markets to the notoriously volatile (and huge) global financial and exchange rate system may be foolhardy. At the least, policies must be tailored to the specifics of local conditions, as shown, for instance, in a recent comparison of Ugandan and Zambian policy reforms. Exchange controls were previously so ineffective in Uganda that their complete liberalization probably had very little practical effect. Where, however, they were still to some degree binding upon would-be capital exporters, as in Zambia in 1992–3, liberalization permitted significant substitution out of the local currency and thus losses in seigniorage for an already fiscally stressed Zambian government (Adam, 1995). There are thus powerful arguments for the use of capital controls, direct or indirect or both, over both inflows and outflows, as part of the armoury of African macro-economic and/or development (notably fiscal) policy instruments. At a minimum, they can 'buy time', like reserves, for the deployment of other more fundamental policy instruments.

It is well known that controls over the external capital account or cross-border payments taxes are difficult to police and that the new technologies in international financial markets have probably increased the difficulties. The efficacy of such controls or taxes also probably declines over time as market participants find new avenues for evasion. But it does *not* follow that they therefore cannot work *at all* and/or that they need to be eliminated and governments forever foresworn against their future use. When formal financial institutions are simple and few, there can be considerable macro-economic policy mileage in the deployment of both direct controls and indirect measures to discourage capital surges, such as, in the case of inflows, increased reserve requirements against foreign deposits or taxes on foreigners' interest earnings, or even on all transactions in foreign exchange. As Obstfeld has recently observed, 'A coherent case can be made for a Tobin tax in the context of stabilizing developing countries, which need to manage exchange rates and have relatively shallow financial markets, and where the cost of failed stabilization is extremely high' (1995:188; see also Dornbusch, 1997; Williamson, 1991 and 1993). Capital inflows are typically easier to manage than outflows since foreign owners of capital are more likely to employ formal channels so as to ensure legal title to their assets, and the monetary authorities are, in other respects as well, likely to be in a much more favourable bargaining position.

The efficacy of alternative instruments of control over (or other policy response to) unwelcome surges of capital, in or out, needs to be studied in the context of specific African situations. So do the consequences of total liberalization of capital controls and interactions with other domestic reforms, where these have been introduced. Again, there is much to be learned from the experiences of other countries.

Official development assistance

Official development assistance is relatively more important in Sub-Saharan Africa than in any other region. Africa's aid 'dependence' has been lamented for two decades or more. Cuts in official development assistance budgets seem likely to reduce grants and concessional lending to poor countries in more countries than not over the coming few years. (Were the debt-distressed poorest countries expected to fully service their debt, the outlook would be even worse.) Moreover, the potentially beneficial social and economic impact of much of the available external finance continues to be constrained by procurement restrictions, conditions that do not relate to developmental objectives, high transactions costs, and poor co-ordination among donors.

On the face of it, the aid relationship, as at present practised, is a wholly unsatisfactory basis for linking Africa with the world. Too much of it comes in forms and on terms that undermine, rather than support, long-run African development. Aid donors and international financial institutions (IFIs) have been driving far too much of Africa's recent policy change, with the inevitable result that there is insufficient indigenous 'ownership' of public programmes and consequent failure to realize 'societal learning...from societal mistakes' (Collier, 1991). It is unlikely that reforms that are pushed upon dubious aid recipients will stick. While this is now recognized in aid rhetoric, the practices are driven by bureaucratic incentives and other interests, and are slow to alter. In the meantime, African governments remain too weak to withstand current external governmental and IFI pressures, and, in many instances, the aid relationship has probably made them even weaker.

Aid would have to be massively transformed if it were to serve as a major instrument for mediating Africa's future relationships with the world. Since such a transformation is unlikely and since aid flows to Africa are, in any case, declining, it is probably best to assume that the role of aid in African development will be *much* less in 10 to 15 years than it now is (which is not to say that it cannot play some useful roles or that efforts to reform it should not continue).

In actual fact, African governments now frequently have little idea of the total size or nature of aid donors' activities in their own countries. Significant proportions of aid expenditures go directly to foreign or local personnel or suppliers, without making contact with the recipient government's budgetary, accounting or planning procedures at all. In this sense they are similar to purely private capital inflows. No doubt many of these direct expenditures by foreign governments do some good, if only by raising some local incomes. But such aid does not strengthen the already weak capacities of African governments to develop their own priorities for government expenditure. On the contrary, it probably weakens them by generating an unco-ordinated hodgepodge of public sector activities, bidding off some of the brightest and best employees from other public services, and reducing any local sense of ownership of development programmes. Worse still, these external flows are inherently unreliable. Such aid relationships do not therefore seem a very healthy long-run basis for linking Africa with the world economy in the interests of long-run and sustained African development.

Any consideration of the external resource requirements and possibilities for the achievement of development objectives in Africa must adopt a holistic approach. This involves projections of desired and reasonable rates of overall economic growth and human/social development, and the combination of investment, fiscal performance, exports and aggregate net transfers (public and private) from abroad that are necessary for the achievement of such targets. It is most practical to consider these matters primarily with reference to *particular countries* and their impact on patterns of investment and government expenditures in these countries. In the very large number of African cases where external debt is not being fully serviced, it is also necessary to consider and address the implications of accumulating arrears and the consequent rising stock of external debt.

A holistic approach to the external financial needs of individual poor countries requires the development of coherent positions within individual donor/creditor nations. It is futile to promote integrated and consistent international approaches to external assistance to poor countries if national donor country approaches are themselves working at cross-purposes. In particular, donor approaches, as manifest in the IMF and the Paris Club, frequently continue to reflect the relatively short-term financial concerns of treasuries and finance ministries with respect to appropriate debtor conduct and their own immediate national budget problems rather than declared longer-term and more global social and economic objectives such as are expressed in Ministries of Foreign Affairs, aid agencies, the UN, the multilateral development banks, and even the international (private) investor community.

Consideration of the possibilities for provision of increased external resources through new devices, including debt relief, requires analysis of whether individual 'improvements' are actually *additional* to the previous aggregate net transfer of resources (and whether they are likely to improve their quality). If, for instance, some grants or concessional loans are extended for the sole purpose of enabling recipients to service their external debt, debt relief could result in the cessation of other previous such assistance – with no practical effect for net transfers whatsoever. If, however, such grants and soft loans can be retained for developmental purposes at the same time that debt relief is offered – and that is the objective for which proponents of debt relief strive – the outcome would be entirely positive.

Reducing external debt service obligations in severely debt-distressed low-income countries can 'free' external resources for much more productive and socially-desirable purposes – provided that the donors/creditors are themselves prepared to use them in this way, rather than to permit them to cut back their overall programmes. Additionality they must therefore be part of all agreed official debt relief schemes that are undertaken for social and economic development, rather than accounting, objectives. Reducing the debt overhang can also, of course, reduce transactions costs (a terrible burden on policy-makers in African countries) and significantly reduce disincentives to private investors, both domestic and foreign. A dollar of reduced debt in these countries is therefore likely to be more valuable than an additional dollar of conventional aid. There is thus an overwhelming intellectual case for significant further reductions in the external debt of debt-distressed low-income countries in Africa and elsewhere, particularly if the resources thereby made available are truly additional.

4. Conclusions

Africa now has the potential to move more quickly towards sustainable development. Much of the continent is rich in natural resources. Its human capital has been immeasurably strengthened since political independence in the 1960s. After a period of macro-economic turbulence and setback, many African countries have stabilized their economies and restored appropriate exchange rates. Still lacking are the investments that are required to realize the rising potential and the confidence in the future upon which they depend. What most of Africa now needs, then, is more investment and more time. It is tragic that external flows of official assistance are now falling – at the very time when they could at last, if properly deployed, be most productive.[2]

The new globalization of the world economy creates both opportunities and risks for the peoples, firms and countries of Sub-Saharan Africa. They cannot realistically expect significant favourable changes in the way that the global economy is governed such as might increase these opportunities or decrease the risks. They must therefore try to find their own new way on the basis of their own public policy approaches to a primarily market-driven world economy. Africans' options as to how to link themselves to the world economy are best considered in terms of a variety of different dimensions of such possible links. Simple, generalized solutions are unlikely to be optimal.

It is clear that Sub-Saharan Africa must, for the present, build upon the base of its primary production, in which it has and will continue to have (static) comparative advantage. This does not imply, however, a totally laissez-faire approach to trade or sectoral policies. Lessons can and should be learned from others' experiences with the benefits and costs of alternative policies for diversification and further development.

In the capital account, direct foreign investment has performed weakly – not least in developing indigenous capacity. It can nevertheless play an expanded and improved role in Sub-Saharan African development. The return of African 'flight capital', both human and financial, can also play a greater role. Confidence and, in particular, the political, legal, and macro-economic stability that do so much to build it, are critically important if private investors, local or foreign, are to commit firmly to Africa.

Policy approaches to portfolio capital flows raise different issues. Complete international financial integration poses major potential risks and problems for African macro-economic managers; caution is therefore appropriate in this dimension of liberalization initiatives.

Official development assistance appears likely to decline. Much of it is – in its present forms in any case – of limited value to African development. Although major donor reforms are unlikely, greater African selectivity as to its makeup is possible and could be productive.

Policies for development in Africa can and should build upon the knowledge of others' experience. This knowledge must be fully internalized within Africa, however, if it is to serve its purpose; the relevant research and learning must be fully 'owned' by those who are involved in it and/or are to benefit from it. If it is to be fully credible within Africa it has to be free of others' 'priors' and agendas. Apart from that, research undertaken by the economists, other scientists, and policy-makers of the countries being studied is likely to be much more informed as to local realities. Research undertaken by Africans and African institutions is therefore likely to be far more cost-effective than that undertaken by aid agencies and international institutions. Exchanges of experience and joint research projects on developing countries' problems are best undertaken through direct interaction among the developing country participants, unmediated and unfiltered through the World Bank, IMF or donor agencies. There are potentially *very* high returns from rigorous empirical research at the country level together with direct and unmediated exchange of experience and research results. Sustained development in Africa can only occur if it builds firmly upon Africans' own knowledge, experience and aspirations. Indigenous capacity-building is essential for the development of appropriate relationships with the world. In the medium term this may imply some favouring of local firms and people.

African governments need not succumb to 'mindless globalization' via their total abandonment of any role in the mediation of national links to the world economy. Their economic policy-makers have important options as they address the future of Africa's relationships with the world.

Notes

1 This paper draws heavily, and with permission, on two earlier papers: 'Linking Africa with the world: a survey of options', in A. Oyejide, B. Ndulu and B. Greenaway (eds), *Regional*

Integration and Trade Liberalization in Sub-Saharan Africa, Volume 4: *Synthesis*, and 'Towards Autonomous Development in Africa: External Constraints and Prospects', in R. Culpeper and C. McAskie (eds), *Autonomous Development in Africa*.

2   None of this is to minimize the problems (noted in the opening paragraph of this paper) of war, ethnic rivalry and political disorder. They continue to disfigure many countries of Africa. (A recent cross-country econometric investigation of the roots of African economic growth over the past 30 years finds that a significant proportion of the differentiation between countries' experiences is associated with ethnic fragmentation and conflict. Easterly and Levine, 1996). I have chosen to emphasize the (more typical) recent experience of African countries that are not at present constrained by such factors.

References

Adam, C. (1995) 'Fiscal adjustment, financial liberalization, and the dynamics of inflation: some evidence from Zambia', *World Development*, 23(5):735–50.

Agosin, M., D. Tussie and G. Crespi (1995) 'Developing countries and the Uruguay Round: an evaluation and issues for the future', *International Monetary and Financial Issues for the 1990s: Research Papers for the Group of Twenty-Four*, Vol. VI. New York and Geneva: United Nations.

Asea, P. and C. Reinhart (1995) *Real Interest Rate Differentials and the Real Exchange Rate: Evidence from Four African Countries*. Nairobi: African Economic Research Consortium.

Bekerman, M. and P. Sirlin (1995) 'Trade policy and international linkages: a Latin American perspective', *CEPAL Review*, 55 (April).

Bennell, P. (1995) *British Manufacturing Investment in Sub-Saharan Africa: Corporate Response during Structural Adjustment*, IDS Working Paper 13. Sussex: Institute of Development Studies.

Camdessus, Michel (1995) 'Africa and the IMF: the challenges ahead', address at the Society for International Development, Washington, DC, 14 December 1995 (mimeo).

Collier, Paul (1991) 'Africa's external relations: 1960–1990', *African Affairs* (July): 90(360):339–56.

DeRosa, D. A. (1992) 'Protection and export performance in Sub-Saharan Africa', *Weltwirtschaftliches Archiv*, 128(1):88–124.

Dornbusch, R. (1997) 'Cross-border payments taxes and alternative capital account regimes', *International Monetary and Financial Issues for the 1990s*, Vol. VIII. New York and Geneva: United Nations.

Easterly, W. and R. Levine (1996) *Africa's Growth Tragedy: Policies and Ethnic Divisions*, Washington, DC: World Bank (mimeo).

Easterly, W., M. Kremer, L. Pritchett and L. Summers (1993) 'Good policy or good luck? Country growth performance and temporary shocks', *Journal of Monetary Economics*, 32: 459–83.

Glover, D. and K. Kusterer (1990) *Small Farmers, Big Business, Contract Farming and Rural Development*. London: Macmillan.

Grossman, G. and E. Helpmann (1991) *Innovation and Growth in the Global Economy*. Cambridge, Mass.: MIT Press.

Helleiner, G. K. (ed.) (1994) *Trade Policy and Industrialization in Turbulent Times*. London: Routledge.

Horton, S., R. Kanbur and D. Mazumdar (1995) 'Openness and inequality', paper presented to the International Economic Association World Congress, Tunis (mimeo).

IFC (International Finance Corporation) (1995) *IFC Review* (Fall).

IMF (1995) *World Economic Outlook* (October). Washington, DC: International Monetary Fund.

Kasekende, L. and M. Martin (1995) 'Macroeconomic policy research issues: the sequencing, consistency and credibility of structural adjustment in Africa', AERC Senior Policy Seminar (March), African Economic Research Consortium, Nairobi.

Kasekende, L., D. Kitabire and M. Martin (1997) 'Capital flows and macroeconomic policy in Sub-Saharan Africa', *International Monetary and Financial Issues for the 1990s*, Vol. VIII. New York and Geneva: United Nations.

Killick, T. (1995) 'Flexibility and economic progress', *World Development*, 23(5):721–34.

Krugman, P. (1989) 'New trade theory and the less developed countries', in G. Calvo, R. Findlay, P. Kouri and J. De Macedo (eds), *Debt, Stabilization and Development, Essays in Memory of Carlos Diaz-Alejandro*. London and Helsinki: Basil Blackwell/WIDER.

Krugman, P. (1991) *Geography and Trade*. Cambridge, Mass.: MIT Press.

Lall, S. (1990) *Building Industrial Competitiveness in Developing Countries*. Paris: OECD Development Centre.

Lall, S. (1995) 'Structural adjustment and African industry', *World Development*, 23(12).

Lipumba, Nguyuru (1994) *Africa beyond Adjustment*, Policy Essay 15. Washington, DC: Overseas Development Council.

Meller, P. (1995) 'Chilean export growth, 1970–90: an assessment', in G. K. Helleiner (ed.), *Manufacturing for Export in the Developing World: Problems and Possibilities*. London: Routledge.

Obstfeld, M. (1995) *International Currency Experience: New Lessons and Lessons Relearned*, Brookings Papers on Economic Activity, 1. Washington, DC: Brookings Institution.

O'Connell, S. (1995) *Macroeconomic Harmonisation, Trade Reform, and Regional Trade in Sub-Saharan Africa*. Nairobi: African Economic Research Consortium (mimeo).

Pack, H. (1992) 'Learning and productivity change in developing countries', in G. K. Helleiner (ed.), *Trade Policy, Industrialization and Development: New Perspectives*. Oxford: Clarendon Press, for WIDER.

Pritchett, L. (1995) *Capital Flows: Five Stylized Facts for the 1990s*. Washington, DC: World Bank (mimeo).

Rodrik, D. (1992) *The Rush to Free Trade in the Developing World: Why So Late? Why Now? Will It Last?* National Bureau of Economic Research Working Paper 3947 (January).

Sachs, J. and A. Warner (1995) *Economic Reform and the Process of Global Integration*, Brookings Papers on Economic Activity, 1. Washington, DC: Brookings Institution.

UNCTAD (1995) *Foreign Investment in Africa*. New York: United Nations.

UNDP (1993) *Rethinking Technical Co-operation: Reforms for Capacity-Building in Africa*. New York: United Nations.

Weston, A. (1995) 'The Uruguay Round: unravelling the implications for the least-developed and low-income countries', *International Monetary and Financial Issues for the 1990s*, Vol. VI. New York and Geneva: United Nations.

Weston, A. (1996) 'The Uruguay Round: costs and compensation for developing countries', *International Monetary and Financial Issues for the 1990s*, Vol. VII. New York and Geneva: United Nations.

Williamson, J. (1991) 'On liberalizing the capital account', in R. O'Brien (ed.), *Finance and the International Economy*, No. 5. London: Amex Bank.

Williamson, J. (1993) 'A cost-benefit analysis of capital account liberalization', in H. Reisen and B. Fischer (eds) *Financial Opening*. Paris: OECD.

Wood, A. (1994) *Skill, Land and Trade: A Simple Analytical Framework*, IDS Working Paper 1. Sussex: Institute of Development Studies.

Wood, A. and K. Berge (1994) 'Exporting Manufactures: Trade Policy or Human Resources?', IDS Working Paper 4. Sussex: Institute of Development Studies.

World Bank (1991) *World Development Report*. Washington, DC: World Bank.

World Bank (1992) *Adjustment Lending and Mobilization of Private and Public Resources for Growth*, Policy and Research Series, 22. Washington, DC: World Bank.

World Bank (1994) *Adjustment in Africa: Reforms, Results and the Road Ahead*. Oxford: Oxford University Press.

World Bank (1995a) *A Continent in Transition*. Washington, DC: World Bank.

World Bank (1995b) *Global Economic Prospects and the Developing Countries*. Washington, DC: World Bank.

World Bank (1995c) *Bureaucrats in Business: The Economics and Politics of Government Ownership*. Washington, DC: World Bank.

World Bank (1996a) *World Debt Tables*. Washington, DC: World Bank.

World Bank (1996b) *Global Economic Prospects and the Developing Countries*. Washington, DC: World Bank.

World Bank (1997) *Global Development Finance*, Vol. I. Washington, DC: World Bank.

WTO (1995) *International Trade, Trends and Statistics*. Geneva: World Trade Organization.

Philip Ndegwa: A Biographic Profile

Philip Ndegwa (*b.* 18 October 1936; *d.* 7 January 1996) was known by many, but few, if any, were fully acquainted with the many facets of this man of so many dimensions. His broad range of interests, his sharp intellect, courage, independence and his fierce adherence to principle characterized his life and have made his contributions to Kenyan and international society outstanding and long-lasting.

While Philip Ndegwa pursued many interests and took on many challenging, indeed formidable, tasks, in all of these endeavours he sought, consistently and forcefully, to promote human welfare and national unity.

Philip Ndegwa was a patriot who served Kenya and its first two presidents in many capacities through the years from 1965 until his death. That service began as a Senior Planning Officer in the newly created Ministry of Economic Planning and Development. Within a year, he was promoted to Chief Planning Officer and in 1967 was appointed Permanent Secretary in the same Ministry. During his tenure with the Ministry, he contributed to and directed the production of the nation's Development Plans and participated in the drafting of Sessional Paper No. 10 of 1965 entitled 'African Socialism and Its Application to Planning in Kenya', a highly regarded statement of national principles that continues to provide guidance to the government on many issues.

During 1969 and 1970, Philip Ndegwa served as Permanent Secretary in the Ministry of Agriculture, and then from October 1970 to 1974 as Permanent Secretary to the Treasury. In both of these roles, his leadership and direction contributed to the development of national agricultural, fiscal and monetary policies. His mark on these sectors continues to influence the course of their development.

While he was often frustrated in his search for constructive and progressive change, he never failed to pursue economic and social objectives that reflected his principles. His dedication to these principles was undoubtedly a factor in his appointment in 1978 as Economic Advisor to the newly elected President, His Excellency Daniel arap Moi.

Among Philip Ndegwa's most significant contributions to Kenya's national development strategies as he served in that capacity are the reports, prepared under his chairmanship, of the Parastatal Review Committee (1979), and the Working Party on Government Expenditure (1982). He also chaired the Presidential Committee on Employment (1990). All of these reports contain far-reaching, insightful and imaginative recommendations, and merit careful reading even today. They are an important part of Philip Ndegwa's legacy.

In 1979 he became Executive Chairman of Kenya Commercial Bank. In this capacity he guided the development of Kenya's largest bank, placing special emphasis on its social responsibility by introducing a loan programme intended to benefit the growing number of small entrepreneurs who were then emerging in Kenya. In 1982 he was appointed Governor of the Central Bank of Kenya, where he served with distinction for six years. Among his many accomplishments he enhanced the capability and integrity of the Bank, promoted measures to contain inflation, to boost export earnings and build up the country's foreign reserves, and to strengthen supervision of the banking industry.

His national activities continued until his death. At that time Philip Ndegwa was Chairman of Kenya Airways, the Kenya Revenue Authority and the Kirinyaga Kanu Branch.

Philip Ndegwa's vision, insights and concerns extended beyond national boundaries to all of Africa. He sought to encourage regional and continental co-operation as a means of promoting the growth of African nations, improved standards of living for all Africans, and a more prominent place for Africa in the world economy.

He pursued these interests in a variety of ways, including serving as a member of the Board of Governors of the Institute of Development Studies at the University of Sussex, as a Trustee of the International Food Policy Research Institute in Washington, DC, as a member of the Board of Directors of the European Centre of Development Policy Management in Maastricht, as a member of the North–South Roundtable, as a member of the United Nations Committee for Development Planning, as a member of the United Nations University Board, as a member of the Global Coalition for Africa's Eminent Persons Group, and as Chairman of the Society of International Development's Kenya Chapter.

His wider global interests were reflected in his decision in 1974 to be seconded from Kenya's Civil Service to join the United Nation's Environment Programme. He served four years with that organization, successively as Senior Economic Advisor to the Executive Director, Director of the Division of Economic and Social Programmes, and Deputy Assistant Executive Director of the Programme Bureau. Philip Ndegwa continued his association with UNEP by serving in an advisory capacity for many years. He continued to address environmental and developmental issues throughout his life.

Philip Ndegwa's work also included many varied and demanding personal business interests. In particular, as chairman of First Chartered Securities he was instrumental in guiding the development of that group of companies into one of Kenya's most successful corporations.

Philip Ndegwa's enormous appetite for work and scholarship is also reflected in his several publications. In addition to numerous papers and published articles, he wrote the following books: *Common Market and Development in East Africa* (1965, revised in 1968), *Africa's Development Crisis and Related International Issues* (1985), *The African Challenge – In Search of Appropriate Development Strategies* (1986), and *Africa to 2000 – Imperative Economic and Political Agenda* (with R. H. Green in 1994). He set great store by continued self-development, particularly through reading and writing, and succeeded in encouraging many others to do likewise.

It is intended that these essays written by distinguished persons – most of whom knew or worked with Philip Ndegwa during his rich and varied life – will contribute to the world's knowledge of development issues, particularly with respect to his beloved Africa.

1. Positions held

1963–4	Research Fellow and Lecturer in Economics, Makerere University College, Uganda
1965	Senior Planning Officer, Ministry of Economic Planning and Development, Kenya
1966–7	Chief Planning Officer, Ministry of Economic Planning and Development, Kenya
1967–9	Permanent Secretary, Ministry of Economic Planning and Development, Kenya
1969–70	Permanent Secretary, Ministry of Agriculture, Kenya
Oct. 1970–1974	Permanent Secretary, Ministry of Finance & Planning, Kenya
1974 (Oct.)	Senior Economic Advisor, United Nations Environment Programme
July 1975 to 1977	Director, Division of Economic & Social Programmes, UNEP
July 1976 to Sept. 1978.	Officer-in-Charge, Programme Bureau, UNEP
(July) 1977 to Sept. 1978	Deputy Assistant Executive Director, Programme Bureau, UNEP
Oct. 1978	Economic Adviser to H.E. The President of the Republic of Kenya
Dec. 1979	Chairman and Chief Executive, Kenya Commercial Bank Group
Dec. 1982 to Jan. 1988	Governor, Central Bank of Kenya
Until his death	Chairman, First Chartered Securities Limited

2. Other governmental responsibilities

1979	Chairman, Parastatal Review Committee
1982	Chairman, Working Party on Government Expenditure
1985–93	Chairman, Kenyatta University Council
April 1990 to Jan. 1991	Chairman, Presidential Committee on Employment
April 1991 to Sept. 1992	Executive Chairman, Kenya Airways
Sept. 1992 to 1996	Chairman, Kenya Airways
1994	Vice Chairman, National Investment Committee
June 1995	Chairman, Kenya Revenue Authority

3. Honorary international appointments and engagements

1967–91	Member of the Board of Governors, Institute of Development Studies, University of Sussex
1969–74	Member of the United Nations Committee for Development Planning
1979–96	Chairman, Society for International Development, Kenya Chapter
1982–8	Trustee, International Food Policy Research Institute, Washington, DC
1982	Member of the Commonwealth Secretariat Expert Group on Protectionism, which produced the report *Protectionism: Threat to International Order* (1982)
1987–90	Member of the Board of Directors, European Centre for Development Policy Management, Maastricht, Holland
1987–90	Member, North–South Roundtable
1987–8	Member of the UN Secretary-General's Advisory Group on Financial Flows for Africa
1989	Member of a study group of the World Institute for Development Economics Research (WIDER) of the United Nations University
1991–3	Member, Business Council for Sustainable Development.
1994–6	Member of World Institute for Development Economics Research (WIDER) of the United Nations University
1994–6	Member of Global Coalition for Africa Eminent Persons Group

4.   Academic achievements honours and awards

BSc Econ. University of London (University College of East Africa) 1962

Rockefeller Foundation Scholarship, Harvard University, USA

Doctor of Laws, University of York, Canada. June 1978

Doctor of Letters, Kenyatta University, Kenya. October 1995

National honours

Elder of the Order of the Burning Spear (EBS) 12 December 1984

Chief of the Order of the Burning Spear (CBS) 12 December 1986

5.   Writings

Books

The Common Market and Development in East Africa, East African Publishing House, 1965.

The Common Market and Development in East Africa, (new edition with three additional chapters), East African Publishing House, 1968.

Africa's Development Crisis and Related International Issues, Heinemann Educational Books, Nairobi 1985 (reprinted 1985 and 1988).

The African Challenge: In Search of Appropriate Development Strategies, Heinemann Kenya, Nairobi, 1986.

Africa to 2000 and Beyond: Imperative Political and Economic Agenda, East African Educational Publishers, Nairobi, 1994 (with R. H. Green).

(joint editor with L. P. Mureithi and R. H. Green), *Development Options for Africa in the 1980s and Beyond,* Oxford University Press, 1985, and *Management for Development,* Oxford University Press, 1987.

Articles

'Future trade, balance of payments and aid requirements in East Africa' (with B. van Arkadie), *East African Economics Review,* June 1965.

'Preferential trade arrangements among developing countries', *East African Economics Review,* December 1965.

'The strategy of Kenya's development plan 1966–1970', (with O. D. K. Norbye), in James2 R. Sheffield (ed.), *Education, Employment and Rural Development,* East African Publishing House, 1967.

'Requirements of more rapid growth in "Black Africa" during the next decade', prepared for Columbia University Development Conference (1970) and summarized in Barbara Ward (ed.), *The Widening Gap,* Columbia University Press, 1971.

'Identification of the least developed among developing countries', paper E/AC.54/L.57, prepared for the UN Committee for Development Planning, 1973.

'Employment in Africa: some critical issues' (with John P. Powelson), 1973. An introductory article to a book of the same title published by ILO, Geneva.

A review article on the World Bank Report entitled '*Accelerated development in Sub-Saharan Africa: an agenda for action*', 1983.

Report on Symposium on Development Options for Africa in the 1980s and beyond (with L. P. Mureithi and R. H. Green), 1983.

'Co-operation among Sub-Saharan African countries: an engine of growth?' *Journal of Development Planning,* 115, UN, 1985.

'Critical issues for Africa in the Eighties: external indebtedness' *Central Bank of Kenya Staff Papers,* 1(1), 1986.

'Africa and Uruguay Round multilateral trade negotiations' paper prepared for seminar on Expanding African Trade through GATT and Uruguay Round, Nairobi, October 1988.

'North–South Trade Policy Issues' in Khadija Haq (ed.), *Linking the World*, North–South Roundtable Islamabad, Pakistan, 1988.

'National policies for development in poor countries in the context of the prevailing international politico-economic environment', paper prepared for the OECD Development Centre Symposium on 'The Next Decade: Interdependence in a Multipolar and Two-track World Economy, February 1989, Paris.

'Africa and the world: Africa on its own', paper prepared for the 20th World Conference of the Society for International Development, 6–9 May 1991, Amsterdam.

Food and Freedom, paper for Society for International Development, Kenya Chapter, 1991.

'Africa and the World Bank', *Eastern Africa Economic Review*, 9(2), December 1993.

In addition a number of papers for conferences, some of which are included in books edited by conference organizers; and a number of official reports and papers prepared for the Kenya Government and UN organizations, especially the United Nations Environment Programme.

Index

DATE DUE

MAY 2002			
JAN 0 2 2007			
MAR 2008			

HIGHSMITH #45230

Printed
in USA